COMMUNISM IN SOUTH-EAST ASIA

Communism in South-east Asia

Justus M. van der Kroef

UNIVERSITY OF CALIFORNIA PRESS

Berkeley   Los Angeles

University of California Press
Berkeley and Los Angeles, California

Printed in Hong Kong

1 2 3 4 5 6 7 8 9

Library of Congress Cataloging in Publication Data

Van der Kroef, Justus Maria.
    Communism in South-east Asia.

    Includes index.
    1. Communism—Asia, Southeastern.   2. Communist parties—
Asia, Southeastern.   I. Title.
    HX395.8.A6V36 1980   335.43′0959   80-51244
    ISBN 0-520-04118-6

Contents

Preface

Compared to South-east Asia's other political and economic problems and developments, the rise, débâcles, resurgences, programmes and tactics of Communism and Communist parties in the region have suffered from a relative neglect. To be sure, the continuing conflict in Indochina first between the Communists and their opponents and now among Communist regimes themselves, has produced a spate of studies. But often these have focused only to a degree on the character of the Vietnamese Communist movement itself and more, say, on the balance between the two Vietnams or on the international implications of the US and allied involvement in the struggle in the region. Indonesian Communism similarly has been the subject of a number of studies in recent years. But the abortive 1965 coup in that country and the collapse of the Indonesian Communist Party have now tended to shift attention primarily to the Suharto regime's internal political and economic troubles or to its place in South-east Asia's post-Vietnam war regional security strategy. The Malayan jungle war between 1948 and 1960 during the so-called 'Emergency' has found its chroniclers but in Malaysian Communist developments since then scholarly interest has tended to wane. There are no full length or comprehensive up-to-date studies, certainly not in any Western languages, on the historical evolution and present state of Communism in Burma, Thailand or the Philippines. Yet all those are countries confronted by active Communist insurgent movements and active underground parties. Only an occasional essay in the past decade has focused on the more recent tribulations and tactics of Communist Parties in Peninsular Malaya and Sarawak. Particularly noteworthy is the dearth of comparative analytical approaches to South-east Asian Communism, e.g. of common themes in appeals to local classes and interest groups or in the use of common united front tactics. The last comprehensive volume which sought to describe the

Communist movement in the region as a whole, the trailblazing study of Brimmell, is now twenty years old.*

Communism in South-east Asia in this writer's impression tends to be a lot talked about, but notwithstanding the furore surrounding the Vietnam war and its once much discussed possible 'domino' effects on neighbouring states, and despite such dramatic events as the failed 1965 coup in Indonesia, or an occasional daring raid by Thai or west Malaysian Communists, it has actually tended to be only little analysed. Most frequently it is considered to be a part of a larger public policy problem of finding a viable domestic political format in a given South-east Asian nation. Or again it is seen as an extraneous oddity, some unassimilated feature of the national body politic the exact implications of which are only dealt with in passing. To study Communism in South-east Asia *per se* as if it had, just possibly, distinctive dynamics or objectives of its own, might even be considered suspect, though the central political reality of South-east Asia as a region today is that one segment of it is in fact Communist (if internally quarrelling) and the other part pursues relentlessly anti-Communist domestic policies. The reason for the suspicion, the present writer conjectures, may not be unrelated to certain attitudes in some academic and other intellectual circles in the West which regard preoccupation with Communism, even in a scholarly sense, as somehow reflecting an ideological bias on the part of the researcher. In short, the ghosts of the McCarthy era and of the Cold War even now tend to make the primary study of Communism somehow less respectable and attractive as a field also to younger scholars, notwithstanding its obvious importance.

The following pages are in no way intended to fill the relative lacunae in Communist studies on South-east Asia. This book is intended primarily as an introductory survey for the general reader, although it is hoped that here and there the specialist may also find matters of interest. Along with offering an historical introduction to party origins and developments in earlier decades of this century, the book also attempts to relate Communist tactics and appeals in individual South-east Asian countries to problems of the national political and economic environments in which they must operate. Some attempt is made to trace the paradoxes arising out of official domestic anti-Communist policies in the non-Communist segment of

* J. H. Brimmell, *Communism in South-east Asia: A Political Analysis* (London: Oxford University Press, 1959).

South-east Asia with the current attempts to reach a new *modus vivendi* with the Communist states of Indochina. Two chapters seek to approach, in a comparative way, the programmatic themes, social appeals and organisational structures of the Communist parties themselves. Communists in China even before the formation of the People's Republic there, as well as of course the USSR, historically have influenced South-east Asia's Communism, and in recent years, particularly since the end of the Vietnam war, both Moscow and Peking appear to have altered their perceptions of the policies pursued by governments in the region. A separate chapter seeks to analyse this Soviet-Chinese-South-east Asian interplay, also in light of the current conflict between Hanoi and its Cambodian opponents. Throughout these pages an effort is made to deal with Communist and non-Communist South-east Asia as separate entities, which are now compelled by circumstance to find means of responding to each other's needs and interests.

Many have assisted me with comments and advice during the preparation of this book. But I would especially wish to express my appreciation to the library staff of the University of Bridgeport for its ever friendly readiness to obtain needed reference materials. I am also particularly grateful to Mrs Judith Augusta for a conscientious and careful typing of a difficult manuscript.

This book is for J.O., *isteri setiawan.*

Bridgeport, Connecticut   Justus M. van der Kroef

1

Communism's rise in
South-east Asia

A. Historical origins

When, during the second decade of the present century, Communist organisations began to appear in that part of the littoral and archipelagic region of the Far East that today is called South-east Asia, they had to come to terms with varied and widespread sentiments and movements of nationalism that had already taken root there over a number of years. Both the concept of a distinctive South-east Asian region, comprising Thailand, Malaysia, Singapore, Indonesia, the Philippines and the Communist states of Vietnam, Laos and Cambodia, as well as the advent of nationalism in it, are linked to the historic impact of the West. Primarily since the sixteenth century, Western commercial contacts had gradually begun to evolve into patterns of colonial domination, from which only Thailand, of all the countries in the region, was to be formally exempt. Superimposed on or displacing indigenous South-east Asian cultures and political structures, that had been moulded in turn over the centuries by the religious, literary and feudal-bureaucratic heritage of neighbouring Hindu-Indian and Chinese civilisation, and still later by Islam, were the legal and administrative norms of the Western metropolitan powers – mainly England, the Netherlands, Spain, and France. The Western impact could be direct and incisive, touching religion, language, family values, law and organisation of the economy, as, for instance, in Spanish rule in Luzon. It could also proceed more gradually, making a virtue out of what came to be known as 'indirect rule' and which left the formal structure of the authority of the indigenous rulers and of their feudal vassals, as well as the religious and legal lore of the rural folk, relatively untouched. British control in Burma and Peninsular Malaya was of this kind. In either case, however, decades before the 1917 Russian Revolution and the Bolshevik seizure of power, the slowly widening impact of modern education and Western values through the matrices of colonial rule provided powerful nationalist impulses. Equally significant, however, especially in Indonesia and Malaya, was the influence around the turn of the century of Islamic modernism and reform movements, emanating from Cairo.

The emergence of new élites in the professions and commerce, and a resurgent political self-consciousness stirred by various international developments ranging from the 'Young Turk' movement in the dying decades of the Ottoman Empire, to Japan's victory in its war with Russia (1905), eventually found expression in a variety of nationalist organisations, or less structured movements. Some of these, like the so-called Katipunan (*Kataastaasan Kagalanggalang Katipunan ng Mga Anak Ng Bayan* – 'Highest and Most Respected Association of the Sons of the Nation') in the Philippines, founded in 1892, were essentially secular and dedicated to the attainment of independence from colonial rule by revolutionary means if necessary. Others like the *Budi Utomo* ('Noble Endeavour') in Indonesia, founded in 1908, reflected the interests of the Javanese aristocracy and concerned themselves primarily with educational development, social service, and the revival of 'native arts and sciences'. Yet others were impelled by the dominant religion in the country. Thus in the first two decades of the present century, Young Men's Buddhist Associations were organised in Burma, led by the Buddhist clergy. Interest in these associations soon shifted from promoting a religious and indigenous cultural revival, however, to problems of political independence. The *Kaum Muda* (literally 'Youthful People') in Malaya focused their interest on a modernisation of Islam, in harmony with Western science and principles of democratic and constitutional government and took their inspiration from the Malay language periodical *Al-Imam* ('The Leader') which began publishing in 1906. Still other Muslim groups, like the *Sarekat Islam* (Islamic Association) in Indonesia, founded in 1912, reflected the economic interests of Muslim merchants, landowners and petty industrialists and though at first proclaiming its loyalty to the Dutch colonial government, soon moved in a more radical direction.[1] In this mixture it would be difficult to find much similarity in the substance of national development or independence, let alone in the methods to be used in achieving them.

Perhaps not surprisingly, from the beginning, controversy and uncertainty characterised the attitudes of most Bolshevik leaders and their Asian friends toward these and later nationalist manifestations in South-east Asia and, for that matter, in other colonial areas. Optimistically, when writing in *Pravda* in June 1913, Lenin had noted the 'spread of the revolutionary democratic movement' in the 'Dutch Indies' (Indonesia), and the 'amazing speed with which parties and unions' were being founded there. In this connection, Lenin projected an alliance of the 'proletariat of the European countries' with the 'young democracy of Asia'.[2] But as to just who the adherents of this 'young democracy' in Asia were, and in what way, specifically, they might be mobilised as allies in the struggle against 'imperialism' which Lenin, it will be recalled, viewed as the terminal stage of capitalism, soon became a matter of some dispute. For Lenin, the 'bourgeoisie' of what he called 'advanced Asia' was democratic and 'still siding with the people against reaction', whereas in 'backward Europe', he wrote, the 'decay' of the 'entire' bourgeoisie was evident, leaving the proletariat as the 'sole advanced class'[3] there. The concept of collaboration with the bourgeoisie in the colonial independence struggle and in its 'democratic' movement, if temporary to be sure and requiring such execution as not to jeopardise the proletarian cause, was also endorsed by Lenin in his draft 'Theses on the National and Colonial Questions' presented to the Second Congress of the Communist International (Comintern) held in Moscow from 17 July to 7 August 1920. Lenin's views provoked dissent, however (notably from the Indian Communist delegate M. N. Roy), over the question of the reliability of those 'bourgeois democratic' movements in colonial areas which turned out to be not really 'revolutionary' after all, but merely reformist.[4] Admittedly Lenin's revised theses urged the Comintern only to endorse 'revolutionary movements of liberation', but even so among the 'Supplementary Theses' on the 'National and Colonial Questions' adopted by the 1920 Comintern Congress one reads, among others, that (a) for the overthrow of foreign capitalism, which is 'the first step toward revolution in the colonies', the co-operation of 'the bourgeois nationalist revolutionary elements is useful', and (b) that while the leadership of the revolution should be in the hands of the Communist Party, 'the revolution in the colonies is

not going to be a communist revolution in its first stages', but will go
through 'successive' periods of 'revolutionary experience'. Presumably this allowed a place for 'bourgeois' and 'democratic' elements,
and indeed for a preliminary 'bourgeois-democratic' phase in a
multi-stage revolutionary process.

   Among the other important 'Theses on the National and Colonial
Questions' adopted at the Second Comintern Congress which were to
be of particular significance for South-east Asia were the condemnation of the 'pan-Islamic' movement (described as an attempt by
Turkish 'imperialists' to strengthen their power) and of the 'reactionary medieval influences of the clergy', and the admonition to Communists to support 'the peasant movements in backward countries
against the landowners and all feudal survivals'. The need to give
these peasant movements a 'revolutionary character' was also stressed, along with a warning that it would be 'extremely erroneous in
many of the oriental countries' to attempt to solve 'the agrarian
problem' according to 'pure Communist principles'. Rather, according to these 'Theses', in the early stages of revolution, 'petty bourgeois
reform clauses' including 'division of land' would have to be adopted.
This did not mean, however, that revolutionary leadership would
have to be surrendered to the 'bourgeois democrats'; on the contrary.
Proletarian parties should continue vigorously to propagate the
'Soviet idea' and to organise 'peasants' and workers' Soviets as soon
as possible'.[5]

   All this was not merely idle theorising. For by the time that the
Second Congress of the Comintern convened, and even as Bolshevik
power was still struggling to consolidate itself in Russia, South-east
Asia already had its first formal Communist Party. On 23 May 1920,
the Communist Party of Indonesia (eventually called *Partai Komunis
Indonesia* – PKI) had come into existence at a meeting in Semarang,
Central Java, of a Marxist organisation, founded six years earlier, the
Indische Sociaal Democratische Vereeniging (Indian, that is, Indonesian,
Social Democratic Association). Initiatives for the founding of both
the latter organisation and of the PKI (which is, in fact, the oldest
Communist party in all Asia) had come from the redoubtable Dutch
Communist H. J. F. M. Sneevliet, who as a Comintern representative
under the name 'Maring' was also to play a role during the nineteen
twenties in the Chinese Communist revolution. The party's initial
programme was brief and poorly developed but by 1920 had become
more specific. Not only creation of 'Soviets' (from the factory to the

provincial level) was demanded but also universal free education, the eight-hour working day, and freedom of speech and political action. From the start, the PKI had particular difficulties in implementing some of the Comintern's 'Theses'. For example, in the previously named Sarekat Islam, which had grown rapidly and by 1920 had tens of thousands of followers throughout Indonesia, including younger intellectuals attracted to modern Muslim reform organisations, the Comintern's attack on 'pan-Islamic' movements had come to be interpreted as an attack on Islam itself.[6] A similar problem was eventually encountered in Malaya when such PKI (and Comintern) representatives as Tan Malaka began cautious attempts at proselytising there. The Comintern's criticism of 'reactionary medieval influences of the clergy' did the Communist cause no good either, nor could the rural Javanese bourgeoisie of Muslim landowners and small traders take much comfort from the Comintern's support of 'peasant movements' directed against them.

At the Fourth Comintern Congress held in Petrograd and Moscow (5 November to 5 December 1922), Tan Malaka raised the question of pan-Islamism again, declaring, in effect, that the pan-Islamic movement was a movement for national independence and hence wholly merited Communist support.[7] But the Fourth Comintern Congress's 'Theses on the Eastern Question' still viewed pan-Islamism as but a means by which the Great Powers would be able to exploit the masses, and asserted that as the 'national liberation movement' grew, pan-Islamic 'watchwords' would be replaced by 'concrete political demands'.[8] One should not exaggerate the Comintern's influence on the Indonesian Communists. But the Comintern leadership's apparent inability to perceive that pan-Islam's 'watchwords' were not mere slogans but also reflected something of the rising political self-consciousness and deep nationalist aspirations of the Muslim bourgeoisie, certainly was to contribute to the increasing polarisation between the PKI and the then most influential nationalist organisation in Indonesia, the Sarekat Islam. The polarisation seemed to diminish if not nullify the possibility of Communist participation in a bourgeois-democratic stage of political change.

Perhaps it would not have been possible, in any case, for the PKI to forge, however temporarily, a tactical alliance with the new Indonesian bourgeoisie in these formative years of nationalism and of prologue to the eventual Indonesian revolution. Even so, one might note that the Fourth Comintern Congress's sharp warning against the 'hybrid, imperfect and intermediate forms' of capitalism in the colonial countries, and against the obstacle presented to 'successful mass struggles there' by 'bourgeois democracy', seemed in marked contrast to the 1920 'Supplementary Theses' of the Second Comintern Congress urging Communist co-operation with the 'bourgeois nationalist revolutionary elements'. Even in supporting anti-imperialist 'national revolutionary movements', the Comintern advised in 1924 that a 'consistent revolutionary line' based on active mass support and on an 'unreserved break with all advocates of compromise with imperialism' was necessary. In Indonesia, despite the counsels of Tan Malaka, other PKI leaders were driving their young party into a sharp confrontation with virtually all other Indonesian groups, except those in the trade union movement in which the party had some influence.[9] Committing itself according to its 'action programme' in 1924 to developing factory and village Soviets could have little practical significance and meant, in effect, the PKI's increasing isolation because it had little consistent outreach among the peasantry, even as its doctrinaire hostility to the more dynamic indigenously Indonesian 'bourgeois nationalist' elements, if anything, deepened further. In 1925, in response to a new Comintern directive, to be noted presently, the PKI was to change its tactics and become more sympathetic toward all those regardless of class who had nationalist aspirations. But by that time the damage was done.

In retrospect, the Comintern's early tactical counsels, or at least the spirit of these counsels, to what its 1924 'Theses on the Eastern Question' – *pace* Lenin – now chose to call the 'backward East', contributed in the case of Indonesian Communists to that hothouse atmosphere of revolutionism which Lenin had already castigated as 'an infantile disorder' and which was to be a factor in the débâcle, in 1926, of the first of the PKI's three coup attempts in its history thus far. Whether Comintern leaders in the absence of frequent and regular contact with Communists *in situ*, particularly those in its Executive Committee (EKKI), had an altogether realistic perception of the social and political changes taking place in South-east Asia may well be doubted.

Moreover, not South-east Asia – and certainly not its individual countries – but China held the spotlight of their concern. It sometimes seemed as if South-east Asia was considered a mere appendage of China in Comintern strategic thinking and the early founding of the PKI owed more to Sneevliet's initiatives than to Comintern direction.

Chinese Communists figured prominently in developing the Communist movement in the region not least because it was believed that the communities of Overseas Chinese in the various South-east Asian countries (numbering in all an estimated 2.8 million by 1925) offered a useful recruiting ground. Thus in 1923, six cadres of the Chinese Communist Party, led by Lin Xue (Lin Hsueh), left Shanghai to begin their proselytising among the Thai Chinese, and in 1925, upon Tan Malaka's suggestion, the Chinese Communist Party in Guangzhou (Canton) sent its representative, one Fu Ta-ching to Singapore and Malaya to work among Chinese there and to maintain contact also with PKI representatives. The Lin Hsueh and Fu Ta-ching missions were to lay the basis for the subsequent founding of the Thai and Malayan Communist parties, respectively. The Comintern's Far Eastern Bureau in Shanghai meanwhile funnelled Chinese Communist organisers into the Malayan branches of the Kuomintang party. These branches were major Overseas Chinese support groups for the Kuomintang with adherents in the Singapore-Malayan area as well as in Indonesia. In an evident bid both to strengthen its hold on South-east Asia's Chinese and to provide co-ordination generally for the Communist movement in the Southeast Asian region, including Communist-led labour unions in Indonesia and Malaya, the Chinese Communist Party, in 1926, formed a 'South Seas Committee'. The latter group sought to maintain contact with 'national revolutionary' organisations in Indochina, Burma, Thailand, Malaya, and Indonesia. But within two years the disastrous PKI coup attempt in west Java and west Sumatra, as well as the break between the Kuomintang and the Communists in China, necessitated still closer direction. By early 1928, at the Comintern's urging, fresh Chinese Communist organisers had been sent to Malaya. These, building on local Communist-led trade unions and radical Chinese student groups in Malaya, but also charged with wider organisational concerns, began developing a more structured, intra-South-east Asian Communist regional grouping called the *Nanyang-kung-ch'an-tang* or 'South Seas Communist Party'.[10]

With the PKI lying shattered, all Communists and their sympathisers not only in Indonesia but also in Malaya and indeed as far away as Indochina, Burma, Thailand and the Philippines as well, were at least formally expected to adhere to this party and its predominantly Chinese Communist leadership. A degree of nationalist resentment of this regional and Chinese-dominated party struc-

ture would soon emerge among local Communists, the more so since
in the USSR itself a national line had triumphed with the supremacy
of Stalin. Within a few years separate Communist parties would be
established in Indochina, the Philippines, Thailand, and even in
Malaya itself. It seems well to stress however that revolutionary
Marxist and Leninist doctrine was traditionally ambivalent about the
place of nationalism and by implication of national Communist
parties; and furthermore that the idea of a regional intra-South-east
Asian Communist movement, or at least one that transcended political boundaries, was not wholly alien to the view of even non-Chinese
radical circles in the area. For example, in the aftermath of the failure
of the PKI coup of 1926, a number of prominent Indonesian Communists, among them Tan Malaka and Alimin, sought refuge and
began proselytising in Malaya, giving an impetus to radical leftist
Malay nationalism. A major tenet of the emergent Malay nationalist
left, evident, for instance, in the utterances of its principal spokesmen,
Ibrahim bin Yaacob and Ishak bin Haji Mohammad, was that
Malays and Indonesians belonged together in one powerful ethnic
Malay nation, a nation that would have done away both with the
power of the colonial imperialists and of traditional indigenous feudal
authority.[11] In the early 1960s, during Indonesia's so-called 'Confrontation' of the new Malaysian Federation, this idea was to have a new
vogue among Malay leftists who sought refuge in Indonesia and
retained close contacts with the PKI.

China was also the early matrix for the development of Vietnamese
Communism. As one leading Vietnamese Communist theoretician,
in describing the early career of his leader in the Vietnamese movement has put it, Guangzhou, in 1924–5, where he had gone in order to
be an interpreter for the Comintern's chief agent in China, Mikhail
Borodin, was the place that the thirty-four-year-old Nguyen Tat
Thanh, soon to be better known as Ho Chi Minh, 'got in touch with
Tam tam xa ("Organisation of People Upholding One and the Same
Ideal"), a revolutionary organisation of the Vietnamese in China' at
the time. This contact was to strengthen Ho's conviction that 'a
strong political party was needed which would organize the masses'.[12]
Ho's work with the *Tam tam xa* led directly to his founding in Canton
in 1925 of the 'Vietnam Revolutionary Youth League' (*Viet Nam
Thanh Nien Cach Mang Dong Chi Hoi*), usually called Thanh Nien, the
main matrix for the creation of several rival Indochinese Communist
parties four years later. Several hundred Thanh Nien activists even-

tually spread through Indochina, monitored by an informal Ho-supervised cadre and drawing on the ferment of a number of later strikes and demonstrations by nationalist student groups. However, many Thanh Nien supporters reflected particularist regional as well as middle class interests of bureaucratic and professional families, and because it was 'too bourgeois' Thanh Nien was refused membership by the Comintern. Then, too, nationalist organisations like the so-called Tan Viet (*Tan Viet Cach Menh* or 'New Vietnam Revolutionary Party'), established in 1926, and especially the VNQDD (*Viet Nam Quoc Dan Dang* or 'Vietnam Nationalist Party'), founded in 1927, offered a mildly Socialist but non-Leninist alternative to Ho's group of young revolutionaries. To be sure, some elements in the Tan Viet were drawn to radical Marxism and the Thanh Nien, but generally, any transcendent secular ideology, whether Communist or otherwise, would have had difficulty making headway in the severely fragmented and parochial Indochinese society of this time.[13]

After the Kuomintang's falling out with the Communists, Ho left China for Moscow, and thence went as Comintern agent in 1928 to Thailand where he assisted in the work of the 'Communist Youth of Siam' (CYS). The latter group, consisting mostly of several hundred young Thai Chinese with radical Marxist leanings, had been founded in 1927, and was in fact the most visible manifestation of the Communist Party of Siam which some Thai sources claim had been organised at about the same time as the CYS. Ho's function among others was to co-ordinate the CYS, the Chinese party's 'South Seas Committee' and later the 'South Seas Communist Party'. But events in his native Vietnam cut short his efforts. For one thing, the Thanh Nien, still the main organisational vehicle of Marxism-Leninism in Indochina, was by now badly riven by factional and regional disputes, eventually reflected in the emergence of three rival Communist parties in the course of 1929: the Indochinese Communist Party (formed by Thanh Nien cadres in Tonkin), the Annamese Communist Party (formed by the Thanh Nien Central Committee), and the Indochinese Communist League (organised by Ho's erstwhile Communist cadre core in the Thanh Nien). Another reason, and perhaps even more important in the long run, was the débâcle which by early 1930 had overtaken the VNQDD and with it the non-Communist nationalist movement in Indochina. Though drawing both worker and white-collar support in North Vietnam, the VNQDD lacked a mass base and its campaign of violent confrontation of French colonial authority was soon crushed and thirteen of its principal leaders were executed. The Thanh Nien, or rather its tripartite Communist organisational apparatus, had attempted to exploit the wave of protests, demonstrations, strikes and peasant insurrections which, also prompted by the effects of recent food shortages and crop failures, had erupted during the last stages of VNQDD agitation and in the aftermath of the execution of its leaders.[14]

Clearly an opportunity presented itself to provide new organisational coherence and unified direction to the gradually radicalising and emergent nationalist temper of Vietnam. On instructions from the Comintern, which on 27 October 1929 had sent a directive to the three rival Communist organisations in Vietnam declaring that their differences and divisions 'cannot be tolerated' and demanding that a single 'popular Communist party' having the 'class characteristics of the proletariat' be formed in Indochina, Ho Chi Minh had gone to Hong Kong in order to supervise a 'unification conference'.[15] Officially, on 3 February 1930, the three rival Indochinese Communist parties merged into a single Vietnam Communist Party (VCP) which, at the Comintern's urging, was to change its name to the Indochinese Communist Party (ICP). The VCP programme, influenced by a document referred to as 'Recommendations of Comrade Nguyen Ai Quoc', called for the completion of 'a bourgeois democratic revolution' in Indochina. This revolution would include 'a land revolution', the overthrow of the French colonial regime and of 'the feudalists', confiscation of all 'big enterprises' and 'all lands' of the French 'imperialists' and handing this property over to the 'worker-peasant-soldier government'.[16] In the aftermath of the VCP's founding, Vietnamese Communist sources today claim, popular opposition to the colonial authority intensified, including new strikes and peasant insurrections, also because of the worsening economic depression. Thus it is claimed that in 'several districts of Nghean and Hatinh provinces committees of poor peasants distributed land and set up a popular power'; these committees were the so-called 'Nghean Soviets'.[17]

The relative success of the Vietnamese Communists in capturing direction of the nationalist movement in their area was not paralleled elsewhere in South-east Asia, however. Indeed, in Indonesia, where organised Communism had had its earliest start in the region, the débâcle as a result of the abortive coup in 1926 seemed particularly serious, while in Malaya and the Philippines the movement appeared doomed to furtive trade union proselytising and precipitous and unproductive strike ventures. This was in a way surprising, perhaps, because the basis for a new and more promising strategy had seemed to have become available. For by the mid- and later nineteen twenties, the Comintern, in response at least in part to the urgings of Tan Malaka and its other agents in the region, had begun to adopt a more forthcoming and collaborationist posture toward the 'national democratic' movement in the colonial areas of the world, and, for the moment at least, seemed to be pushing more doctrinaire suspicions of the role of the bourgeoisie and demands for a speedy Sovietisation of the colonial revolutions into the background. For example, already at the Fifth Comintern Congress (17 June to 8 July 1924), where the report on the 'National and Colonial Question' was delivered by Dmitri Manuilsky, Stalin's spokesman, the new trend had become apparent. Manuilsky, after having taken note that the Comintern had 'allowed the Communists in Java' to participate actively in the local 'workers' peasants' party' there (presumably the PKI), went on to say that because of uncertainty and 'timidity' in Communist circles, induced by fear of 'class collaboration' and of the dangers of working with the 'petty bourgeoisie', the result had been that 'we lose control over the national liberation movement which passes into the hands of native nationalist elements'.[18] Such losses should not have occurred, Manuilsky seemed to imply. By April 1925, the Comintern's Executive Committee (EKKI) had drafted a new programme specifically for the PKI which demanded in effect the party's closer collaboration with the nationalist movement and the enunciation of broadly popular nationalist rather than 'proletarian' slogans. The justification for this, as EKKI viewed it, was that since an indigenously Indonesian bourgeoisie was virtually non-existent, the Indonesian nationalist movement would tend to be more inclined toward revolution than in other areas anyway.[19] Then, in May 1925, Stalin himself, in addressing students of the 'University of the Toilers of the East', criticised 'the Communists in Java', who, in allegedly overestimating the revolutionary potential of the 'liberation movement', and 'in an under-estimation of the role of an alliance between the working class and the revolutionary bourgeoisie against imperialism', had 'not long ago mistakenly put forward the slogan of Soviet power' in Indonesia.[20]

In Indonesia, meanwhile, the PKI leadership seemed uncertain and divided on the application of Moscow's new counsels. While, on the one hand, the party did begin to mitigate its attacks on nationalist rivals, and now even attempted to reach out for support in Islamic circles, on the other hand its labour and peasant agitation and strike campaigns suggested imminent confrontation.[21] Despite Tan Malaka's objections, other PKI leaders, persuaded by Alimin, committed the party to a coup.[22] On the evening of 12 November 1926, small uncoordinated groups of Communist-led dissidents fought with police in a number of West Java locations. In Batavia, the Netherlands East Indies' capital city, the telephone exchange was briefly occupied. But within hours most of the bands had been arrested or dispersed by police and security units, and preventive arrests elsewhere in Central and East Java further helped to nip the insurrection in the bud. On the west coast of Sumatra, a small PKI-led band unsuccessfully attempted to seize Sawah Lunto, the headquarters of the Ombilin coal fields, in the first days of January 1927. Here, too, leaders were quickly apprehended and followers dispersed. The speed and extent of arrests (eventually some 4 800 were sentenced) of coup participants were perhaps as significant in the whole affair as the lack of co-ordination among insurgent gangs and leaders, and a subsequent government analysis of those apprehended showed that the rebels had come from all social strata, the poor as well as the relatively well-to-do, and that few had had any clear understanding of their objectives. Vague religious and political utopian expectations, rather than specific economic grievances or a sense of 'class consciousness' had impelled their participation. In its own post-mortem, the Comintern's Executive Committee in November 1927, while noting that the party had 'made great efforts' to prepare itself, criticised the 'lack of serious political and organizational preparation' of 'the movement as a whole'. Subsequently, authoritative PKI historical accounts described the 1926–7 rebellion as the product essentially of 'left wing Communism' and of the desire of party leaders precipitously to 'solve all the problems' of the country in one stroke.[23]

The PKI disaster, however, did lead a number of fugitive Indonesian Communists to visit Malaya and the Philippines and to contribute to a quickening of the movement in those countries. Already in 1926 both a Communist-led 'South Seas General Labour Union' and a 'Communist Youth League' had been established in Singapore. These organisations, working eventually as fronts for and acting in concert with the previously mentioned 'South Seas Communist Party' founded shortly thereafter, provided proselytising and agitational impulses in and through sometimes violent strike activity (for example, in Singapore, in March 1928), and in the Chinese schools in Malaya and Singapore where both students and teachers tended to be easily stirred to militant anti-British demonstrations. But to the degree that agitation became more widespread, repressive measures also increased. Particularly, arrest and deportation of Communist labour leaders and teachers cut into the Malayan movement's effectiveness. Also, the then disorganised state of Indonesian Communism following the 1926–7 coup attempt and the organisational division in the ranks of Indochinese Communists already noted, prompted the Comintern to begin considering a reorganisation of its entire South-east Asian operations. The 'intra-regional' model of the 'South Seas Communist Party' no longer seemed adequate, while the party's China-focused origins had also produced some local nationalist resentments throughout the region, as we have seen. At the close of April 1930, the 'South Seas Communist Party' dissolved itself at a secret meeting in Singapore. But although the decision to establish a new group, the Communist Party of Malaya (CPM), as well as transform the 'South Seas General Labour Union' into a new body, the 'Malayan Federation of Labour', was made at this meeting (all in conformity with Comintern directives), actual implementation of this decision had to be postponed for almost a year because of the arrest of a score of prominent Communist and Comintern leaders in Malaya and Hong Kong.[24]

In the early thirties, however, as the worldwide economic depression began to make itself felt in Malaya's rubber and tin industries, CPM penetration of trade unions and Chinese schools accelerated again. Moreover, the re-activation of the Comintern's Far Eastern Bureau in Shanghai, in 1933, provided the CPM with new tactical guidelines, which were to bear fruit in the eruption of occasionally serious labour agitation. Toward the close of 1935, for example, a strike at the Batu Arang mine in Selangor state resulted in a complete takeover by the strikers who were led by the CPM. A briefly functioning 'Soviet' government was established by the workers at the mine, before hundreds of Malayan police and security forces stormed and retook control of it. The CPM's aggressiveness and organisational momentum reflected the leadership of Lai Tek, a Vietnamese Communist and one-time companion of Ho Chi Minh, who in 1939 was to become the MCP's secretary general.

Perhaps even more than in Malaya, trade unions formed the early matrix of organised Communism in the Philippines. Marxist ideas had gained some currency among Filipino intellectuals even before the outbreak of the Philippine Revolution of 1896. Also, and perhaps even more important for the development of a radical spirit, was the fact that there had been frequent peasant resistance movements – some with religious and millenarian overtones – throughout the Spanish colonial period, the dynamics of which continued into the twentieth century and the era of US control.[25] Crisanto Evangelista, 'the father of Philippine Communism', as early as 1906, formed a Marxist-oriented printers' union. In 1913, he became one of the leaders of the 'Philippine Workers' Congress' (*Congreso Obrero de Filipinas* – COF), which for many years was to remain the country's largest labour federation and initially did much to heighten worker radicalism in the post-World War I period. In 1924, Evangelista, having been unable to win nomination for a Manila municipal councillor's position on the slate of the Nacionalista Party, organised his own Workers' Party (*Partido Obrero*) whose programme was to become the basis six years later of the Philippine Communist Party. In 1924, also, a radical tenants' and farm workers' association was established which, by 1928, had become the 'National Union of Filipino Farmers' (*Kalipunang Pambansa ng mga Magbubukid sa Pilipinas* – KPMP) and which was later to merge both with the Philippine Communist Party and with the insurgent Huk guerrilla organisation during World War II.[26]

In all of these organisations, an anti-colonial (that is, anti-US) objective was tied to specific demands for the improvement of living conditions such as the eight-hour work day, free education, reduction in land rents, and so on. Class war rhetoric pervaded slogans and speakers' rhetoric. US Communists, like the labour leader William Janequette (an alias for Harrison George) and Earl Browder, at that time representative of the Comintern's China-based Pan Pacific Trade Union Secretariat (PPTUS), as well as such Asian Communist leaders as Tan Malaka, visited Manila and gave further impetus to the budding Philippine movement in the middle and later nineteen twenties, and in June 1927 the COF formally affiliated with the PPTUS.[27]

This affiliation, the increasing involvement of Evangelista in Comintern labour affairs, and the trickle of COF-affiliated trade union leaders who were beginning to find their way to the Comintern's Far Eastern Bureau in Han Kou (Hankow) and to Moscow's 'University of the Toilers of the East', alarmed non-Communist COF leaders. In

May 1928, taking advantage of Evangelista's temporary absence from the country, these leaders ousted him from his post as COF president. A year later, having been unsuccessful in regaining the leadership, Evangelista, KPMP leader Jacinto Manahan, and their associates formally broke with the COF. On 12 May 1929, within days of this break, according to Philippine party history, more than two dozen COF-affiliated trade unions held a conference in Manila which gave birth to a new Marxist labour federation, the 'Association of Workers' (literally 'Association of the Children of Sweat' – *Katipunan ng mga Anakpawis sa Pilipinas*, or KAP). The same conference directed a committee headed by Evangelista to write the constitution for a new workers' party. This committee, completing its work in July 1930, decided to adopt what it called the 'Marxist' programme of the earlier but now dissolved *Partido Obrero* (Workers' Party). Evangelista and the KAP Central Committee then agreed to proclaim the new party on 26 August 1930 (the date of the beginning of the Philippine Revolution). But although on that date the Communist Party of the Philippines (*Partido Komunista ng Pilipinas* or PKP) was, in fact, founded at a gathering of about sixty KAP and KPMP activists in Manila, it was decided to declare 7 November of that year, the anniversary of the Russian Revolution, the formal date of the party's establishment.

Describing the new party's tasks, one commentator in the Comintern's main news organ wrote that the just-founded PKP had to become as soon as possible 'a mass Party rooted in the factories, mills, docks, plantations and villages', and as well would have to develop further both the KAP and the KPMP as its organisational outreach among labour and the peasantry respectively.[28] Measured against these objectives the early PKP cannot be said to have been much of a success. On 9 and 10 May 1931 the PKP's First Congress took place, which, apart from electing Stalin and US Communist Party chairman William Foster as honorary members of the party Presidium, also adopted a manifesto. This document declared that in the present 'bourgeois democratic stage' of the Philippine Revolution, the party's objectives had to be the achievement of independence, the implementation of an 'agrarian revolution', and bringing about a 'radical improvement' in the workers' condition.[29] Despite their leadership experience in trade union and peasant organisations, PKP cadres seemed unwilling to invest time or effort in the building of a broader mass support structure for the party. In case after case, even as a number of serious strikes erupted, and even as in Tayug, Pangasinan, in January 1931, hundreds of peasants rose up against landowners and the Philippine constabulary, party leaders seemed unable to capitalise on, or give direction to, the unrest and the deepening popular misery following the international economic depression of· this period. In the words of one party historian, the later PKP secretary general José Lava, the PKP's campaigns at this time were 'guided more by determination and enthusiasm rather than solid Marxist knowledge'.[30]

As early as February 1931, having incautiously ignored official Philippine reaction to the public proclamation of the party the previous November, Evangelista, Manahan, and some other PKP leaders had been arrested on charges of sedition. Though shortly released on bail, they and other party cadres kept periodically being detained and released as they attempted to hold public meetings without official licence until, in mid-September 1931, the PKP and the KAP were formally declared by a Manila court to be illegal organisations. At the same time, twenty prominent party leaders, among them Evangelista and Manahan, were sentenced to eight years and one day of *destierro* or banishment to distant provinces on charges of sedition and illegal association. About a year later the Philippine Supreme Court upheld the decision. Going 'underground', the party during the thirties was nevertheless able to send younger activists to Moscow for training and to cultivate a number of fronts, also among Manila intellectuals. One of these fronts was the 'League for the Defence of Democracy', ostensibly a book review and political discussion club. Some of the labour unions affiliated with the proscribed KAP also offered an organisational haven for PKP activists. In particular, a number of unions among harbour workers and in the printing trades remained within the party's orbit.[31]

Despite its reverses, the PKP's theoretical approach and programme showed little change until the mid-thirties. Although one commentator on the party's activities in the Comintern's main news organ wrote that the PKP's call for 'immediate organisation of Soviets' in effect meant, given the party's lack of organisational contacts in rural and trade union circles, 'simply to play with the slogan of establishing Soviets',[32] official PKP theory held to an uncompromising revolutionary course. As late as April 1935, the PKP issued a fire-breathing manifesto which, among other things, called for total revolutionary struggle, rejected the notion that inde-

pendence could be won by 'peaceful "constitutional" methods', and
asserted that 'only through the Soviets' could the Filipino masses
solve their problems of 'national freedom, land, power, food, and the
eight hour working day'.[33] The manifesto was also a specific repudia-
tion of collaboration with other nationalist and parliamentary
Filipino parties and with the process of constitutional change toward
freedom under US tutelage. Within a few months, however, the
implementation of the decisions of the Comintern's historic Seventh
Congress, calling for a worldwide united front against Fascism, would
begin producing changes in the PKP's status and policies.

During the South-east Asian ferment of the twenties and thirties,
Communist activity and organisation in Thailand and Burma were
comparatively less significant. The Communist Youth of Siam (CYS)
and the Communist Party of Siam (CPS) remained initially under the
supervision of the 'South Seas Communist Party' (which, presumably, also spoke for Thai Communists) and it will be recalled that Ho
Chi Minh had been in Thailand in 1928 to assist in this supervisory
process. Though the CPS subsequently had more or less regular
contact with the Comintern's Far Eastern Bureau in China, it was the
Vietnam Communist Party (VCP) that had perhaps the strongest
influence on Thai Communism. This was to be the case also in
subsequent decades. Indeed, some VCP leaders, because of heavy
French security pressure in their own country, between 1931 and
1933 established a temporary party headquarters in north-east
Thailand.[34] Here they also drew support and protection from among
the Laotian and Vietnamese minorities in the area.

The revolution in Thailand on 24 June 1932, though it ended royal
absolutism, offered little opportunity to the CYS and CPS, mainly
because the chief reformers of the period such as Pridi Phanomyong
and other elements of his People's Party, followed an uncertain
course, which soon permitted conservative military and business
elements to win control.[35] The identification of Marxism and 'Communism' with the Chinese – seemingly easy to substantiate in view of
the virtually entirely Chinese membership of both CYS and CPS –
legitimised for the Thai public the deepseated anti-Chinese Thai bias
in national (and nationalist) terms. The 2000-member CYS, in
September 1932, had issued a manifesto denouncing 'feudalism' and
'imperialism'. The manifesto led the government of the conservative
premier Pya Manopakorn formally to outlaw Communism by the
following April, and thereby forced the few Thai trade unions with

Communist cadres officially to 'cleanse themselves'. It also set the
stage for the further growth of an official and pervasive anti-
Communism which has characterised public policy in the country
ever since. From the middle thirties onward, the Thai military,
directly or covertly, assumed increasing authority in virtually all
aspects of public life, and Communist underground activity became
more and more defensive. Such activity consisted mainly in the
issuance of inflammatory pamphlets and proselytising among hill
tribe and Vietnamese minority dissidents. Meanwhile, sources of
support primarily remained the Thai Chinese. The Thai government's seriously anti-Chinese discriminatory and repressive measures – among them encouragement of a *de facto* boycott of Thai
Chinese businesses and products, onerous taxes falling particularly
on Chinese, and new barriers to naturalisation[36] – helped to maintain
a seedbed of grievances, easily exploited by Communist proselytisers.

Organised Communism in South-east Asia bloomed last in Burma,
a region long considered by the British to be an appendage of their
Indian colonial empire, and only formally acquiring separate constitutional status in 1937. The Communist Party of Burma (CPB) was
not founded until 1943 by two young nationalists Soe Gyi and Than
Tun, both of them graduates in the famous class of 1937 of the
University of Rangoon, which provided a number of leaders for the
new Burma. In the early nineteen thirties, Soe, Than Tun, Aung San,
and others, were identified with a group of university students who
called themselves Thakins (literally 'masters', the Burmese variant of
sahib and the standard colonial mode of address for the British).
Drawing on early nationalist impulses generated in the nineteen
twenties by Buddhist clergy (*phongyi*) and the earlier mentioned
Young Men's Buddhist Association, some of the Thakins were an
important conduit for the introduction of Marxist ideas into the
Burmese independence movement. The Thakin outlook generally
tended to be syncretic, however, and Buddhist philosophy, historic
Liberal and secular perceptions, as well as Marxist tenets and
aspirations tended to be mixed in their political views and into the
Dohbama Asiayone ('We Burmans' Association), which they founded.
Marxist elements also entered into the budding Burmese labour
movement in this period, and the 1938–9 oil field workers' strike, in
which a number of radical Marxist Thakins played a prominent role,
was a pre-war high water mark for Burma in the kind of labour
agitation with anti-colonial, independence movement overtones that

had already been familiar to the rest of South-east Asia for a score or more years. In 1939, students and labour unions joined in founding a rapidly growing 'People's Revolutionary Party', essentially a Socialist group with critics as well as supporters of Stalin's policies.[37]

Diversity of views among the Thakins at first obstructed achievement of a sharp organisational focus. Some Marxist Thakins, notably Thein Pe who had studied in Calcutta, retained close connections with Indian Communism, while others like Than Tun had a more 'Titoist', that is, national (and nationalist) Communist orientation. Still others, again, saw no reason not to collaborate during World War II with the Japanese Occupation authorities in Burma, in view of Japanese promises of autonomy if not independence, while yet others from the start insisted on forming an anti-Japanese front. It was not until March 1944, however, that the leaders of the fledgling CPB and of the 'People's Revolutionary Party', which in September 1945 called itself the 'Socialist Party', along with some other groups such as the 'Fabian Party', agreed on launching an anti-Japanese resistance movement. From this, within a few months, there would develop the 'Anti-Fascist People's Freedom League' (AFPFL) with Than Tun as secretary general, and Bogyok Aung San, the Burma government's defence minister and military commander under the Japanese Occupation authority in Burma, and perhaps the country's most revered nationalist figure, as president. The forces of the AFPFL were subsequently to play a not insignificant role in the Allied forces campaign in Burma against the Japanese in the closing year of World War II. It was in its role as a political matrix uniting major leftist, including non-Communist, and more conservative Burmese nationalist figures in a common political cause, that the AFPFL was perhaps more important. However, unlike the case of the Huks in the Philippines, or the MPAJA (and its successor organisations) in Malaya, the Communists in Burma would not succeed in using the principal anti-Japanese guerrilla organisation for their own ends in the post-war era, as we shall see.[38]

First we must take note, however, of the major tactical impulse behind the formation of such groups as the Huks and the AFPFL during World War II, and of one of the principal turning points in the development of South-east Asian Communism and, indeed, of Communist movements elsewhere in the world.

From 25 July to 20 August 1935, the Seventh Comintern Congress met in Moscow, hearing the Bulgarian Communist Georgi Dimitroff

urge the formation of a 'broad people's anti-fascist front' including
organisations under 'bourgeois leadership' on the basis of an international proletarian united front, and adopting a resolution calling,
among other points, for 'joint action with the Social Democratic
Parties' and trade unions against the common Fascist danger.[39]
Implementation in the South-east Asian region of this resolution
would mean not only a more co-operative posture toward Socialist
and non-Marxist nationalist organisations, but also eventually a
comparative softening of Communist confrontation of those colonial
or 'imperialist' regimes whose home governments were or would in
time be aligning themselves against the Berlin-Rome-Tokyo Axis.

South-east Asian countries differed, however, as to the possibilities
of 'united front' action. In Indonesia, in the middle thirties, the PKI
had still not risen from its 1926–7 débâcle. The party was deeply
underground, scattered, with most of its cadres in detention or in
exile. The radical thrust in the country had been taken over by a
number of nationalist parties, at first the National Indonesian Party
(*Partai Nasional Indonesia* – PNI), founded in 1927, and later by such
groups as the Indonesian People's Organisation (*Gerakan Rakjat
Indonesia* – Gerindo), founded in 1937. One of Gerindo's leaders, Amir
Sjarifuddin, a future premier of the revolutionary Indonesian Republic, was to declare later that he had been a Communist since the
middle of the nineteen thirties; among Gerindo's members Sjarifuddin was not a unique case.

In response to the Comintern's new 'united front' directive, Communists in Gerindo and other nationalist groups did in the later
thirties join in various federative nationalist organisations. But their
demands, even when raised in a joint anti-Fascist context, met with
little sympathy from the Dutch colonial authority. In any case, the
nationalist federations were too tenuous and the role of the Communists in them too circumspect to have been able to mobilise an effective
'broad, people's' anti-Japanese resistance movement as occurred
elsewhere in the region. When, moreover, Dutch colonial authority in
Indonesia as of 1942 was wiped away by the invading Japanese
Occupation government, a number of prominent Indonesian
nationalists, among them PNI leader Sukarno, collaborated with
the Japanese, presumably in the hope of eventually furthering
Indonesia's independence.[40]

Scattered anti-Japanese resistance in Indonesia during World War
II, according to later PKI history, included a number of small and in

some cases little more than paper Communist groups. Among these was the 'Movement for Indonesian Freedom' (*Gerakan Indonesia Merdeka* – Gerindom), led by the later PKI chairman, D. N. Aidit. But popular resistance tended to confine itself to an occasional easily quelled outburst, and at no time did a 'people's army' of any size take the field against the Japanese.[41] Upon the Japanese surrender, therefore, the PKI could make little if any claim to leadership, even as the independent Indonesian Republic which had been proclaimed on 17 August 1945 began structuring its government and political system. The party was formally permitted to re-establish itself (21 October 1945). But it would take some months before it had been sufficiently reorganised to begin to play a role in the affairs of the fledgling republic, embroiled almost at once in a life and death struggle to preserve its freedom against the returning Dutch authority.

In Thailand during the war, Communists on the whole tended to be equally ineffective. By the end of December 1941, the Thai government to all intents and purposes had acquiesced in Japan's domination of its own territory and the conquest of much of neighbouring South-east Asia, and it had begun a passive collaboration, even to the point of issuing a *pro forma* declaration of war on the Allies. Pridi Phanomyong, perhaps the best known leftist (though not formally Communist) politician of the period, alternatingly resisted and worked with vacillating wartime Thai government policies. But he did give impetus to a small, poorly organised, US-supported, anti-Japanese Thai resistance movement, including some guerrilla groups, and in which some CPS and CYS members participated. Chinese and Chinese Thai, however, continued to dominate the party and, on 1 December 1942, a group of Chinese Communist and CPS activists met, reportedly in a hamlet north-east of Bangkok, for what was later termed in party histories the founding 'First Congress' of the CPS. On 8 December 1942, a party policy statement was issued which, according to party history today, urged 'holding high the banner of the national and democratic revolution' in Thailand.[42] An 'Executive Committee' (that is, Politburo) of the party was also formed at the Congress, but it was shortly divided into two sections, one of which was to concentrate on work with Chinese Thai, the other on non-Chinese Thai.

Small and ineffective as the CPS was then (total active membership was perhaps no more than 3000, including its CYS satellite), this ethnic division remained operationally necessary even in the im-

mediate post-war period when a new Thai government, having
repudiated wartime collaboration with the Japanese, now sought a
rapprochement with the victorious Allies. In October 1946, probably
in an effort to win favour with the USSR, which otherwise might have
blocked Thai entry into the United Nations, the 1933 measure
outlawing Communism in Thailand was repealed, and the movement
could once more operate openly. By the end of 1946, according to
Thai government sources, two Communist organisations had in fact
appeared.[43] First there was the original CPS which since the 1942
'First Congress' had called itself the Communist Party of Thailand
(CPT), and which had both a few ethnic Thai and Chinese Thai
members. It had its own front and satellite groups among the trade
unions and youth (the CYS). Secondly there was the smaller, more
covert, Chinese Communist Party of Thailand (CCPT), which
though it maintained liaison with the CPT seemed to be functioning
primarily as the Thai branch of the Chinese Communist Party and as
one of a number of voices for the Chinese Thai community. The CPT
though recognising 'minority rights' repudiated ethnicity, insisting in
its programme on the need for joint action by all those working for a
'democratic' Thailand, and on support for the common political
rights of all citizens regardless of social status or origin. Though CPT
cadres attempted to give new impetus to the trade union movement,
especially in Bangkok, the party also in this field found it difficult to
shake off its particular ethnic identification. Even among Thai liberals, anxious to promote modern constitutional government in their
country, the CPT continued to be essentially appreciated as a rather
narrow pro-Chinese political lobby. CPT publications of this period,
by their emphasis on recognition of the business and political rights of
Chinese in Thailand, and on the need for the Thai government and
people to develop good relations with China, tended to foster this
impression further.[44] There is little or no evidence for current CPT
claims that during the first post-war years the party was particularly
successful in mobilising a discontented peasantry and in forging a
'worker-peasant alliance'. CPT proselytising in fact was little involved in the generally low-key instances of rural discontent becoming evident in the long neglected north-east, for example.

Compared to Indonesia and Thailand, the contrast in the extent of
Communist militancy in the rest of South-east Asia, especially in the
Philippines, Malaya and Indochina, during the war and immediate
post-war years, was quite sharp. Beginning in 1936, in furtherance of

the Comintern's new 'united front' line, the Communist Party USA sent its emissary Sol Auerbach (travelling as 'James S. Allen') repeatedly to the Philippines. Auerbach tried not only to win the release of Evangelista and other incarcerated PKP leaders but, more importantly, also attempted to weld together a 'Social Democratic' and eventually nationalist alliance against Fascism.

Auerbach found favourable circumstances. Philippines Commonwealth President Manuel Quezon had long been concerned with 'Social Justice' for the masses. He was also interested in uniting as broad a spectrum of domestic opinion as possible in order to impress US politicians with advancing the cause of the Philippines' complete independence. Whatever the reason, Quezon acceded to Auerbach's requests to set the imprisoned Communist leaders free. Eventually Quezon, at the end of 1938, even permitted released PKP leaders to resume open political activity. The PKP itself, however, remained formally proscribed. Partly to overcome the liability of the party's continuing ban, and also hoping to create an acceptable leftist political core around which Philippine anti-Fascist sentiment could be rallied, Auerbach succeeded, in October 1938, in bringing about a merger between the PKP and the Socialist Party of the Philippines (SPP). The latter group, founded in 1933, had close ties with a major peasant and tenant workers' association (*Aguman Ding Maldang Talapagobra*) and, though not a PKP front, had served as an organisational haven for some underground cadres. Now called the 'Communist Party of the Philippines' (Merger of the Socialist and Communist Parties), and still acknowledging Marx, Engels, Lenin and Stalin as 'the greatest teachers of mankind', the PKP entered into the parliamentary political sphere. Seeking unity with others in a 'Popular Front' directed against Japanese and other Axis powers, the party even before the Japanese invasion of the country also urged on a suspicious Philippine government the formation of an 'Anti-Japanese United Front' of volunteer citizen fighters.

Because of their incautious movements, principal PKP leaders, among them Crisanto Evangelista, were arrested by the Japanese when the latter occupied Manila in January 1942. But the following month a conference of remaining party and some other resistance leaders headed by Vicente Lava met at Cabiao in Nueva Ecija province and reached agreement on formation of a broad-based national resistance front. Regional front and local committee offices throughout the country, most run by cadres, were established and expected to co-ordinate resistance activities. This network, much of it on paper, along with the March 1942 formation of the Huk resistance army, provided the structure of an extensive underground party-dominated counter-government. The Communist counter-government nominally also had at its disposal numerous BUDC (Barrio United Defence Corps) units, composed of from five to a dozen persons in the villages, which 'carried out recruiting, intelligence collection, supply, and civil justice' often under the party's aegis.[45] There were, to be sure, a number of independent guerrilla and resistance groups, including some of the US military and even one composed of Filipino Chinese, avowedly sympathetic to Chiang Kai-shek.[46] But by far the most important force, numbering some 10 000 by March 1943, was composed of the PKP-created *Hukbo ng Bayan Laban sa Hapon* ('People's Army Against Japan') or Hukbalahap or Huks for short.

Officially formed on 29 March 1942, at the same Cabiao Nueva Ecija site where the preceding month party leaders had established their national resistance front, the Huks were headed by Luis Taruc as commander-in-chief and at least at the higher command level were supervised by special PKP military cadres. Whether Taruc is or ever was a Communist or PKP member is a matter of controversy. In a discussion with this author in 1966, Taruc, then in detention at Camp Crame, near Manila, denied he had ever been a Communist, insisting that his political views were inspired rather by the social justice tenets of Christianity.[47] Other Huks have maintained a similar position. One might also note that not just the Japanese but also some Luzon landlords who had long been targets of peasant anger, fell victim to Huk reprisals.[48] Veterans of Mao Ze Dong's (Mao Tse-tung's) 'Eighth Route Army' participated in the direction of some of the Huk training. Such training generally tended to be quite haphazard, however. Chinese disdain for alleged Huk 'amateurishness' later led some 1 000 Filipino Chinese, most but by no means all Communist-oriented, to form their own so-called '48th Detachment' of the Huk army. This detachment, known as the 'Wachi', operated independently in the Manila and Bulacan areas.[49]

Chinese disdain of Huk 'amateurishness', particularly of the latter's proclivity for sudden but poorly organised raids, was not unfounded, and on 5 March 1943 a Japanese force succeeded in all but destroying a poorly guarded Huk headquarters in the Cabiao forest of Nueva Ecija. This débâcle first led to a more cautious 'retreat for defence' policy, yet a number of Huk guerrilla units and their village supporters aggressively and incautiously continued to engage the Japanese Occupation forces in combat. As the resistance movement continued, the question increasingly arose as to the extent to which the PKP cadre core actually was able to co-ordinate not only the Huks but also other front organisations, regional committees and BUDC activities.[50] In September 1944, Vicente Lava was ousted as party secretary general, and eventually, after a three-man interregnum period, replaced by Pedro Castro. With the collapse of the Japanese Occupation authority, the party attempted at first to maintain its united front policy. It developed new workers' and peasants' organisations and, on 15 July 1945, participated, despite misgivings of some party leaders, in the formation of a 'Democratic Alliance', composed among others of Huk and other resistance veterans, the Civil Liberties Union, trade and peasants' unions. In the 1946 general elections, six DA congressional candidates, among them Luis Taruc and the later PKP secretary general, Jesus Lava, were elected. But charging electoral fraud, their political opponents in the Liberal Party-dominated Philippine Congress denied them their seats. As tensions between Huks and the government of President Manuel Roxas and that of his successor Elpidio Quirino heightened, the PKP repeatedly changed leadership, eventually abandoning a policy of limited parliamentary and constitutional struggle in favour of hardline, armed confrontation. In May 1948, with the accession of Mariano P. Balgos as party secretary general, the militant faction in the PKP led by José Lava, now the real leader of the party, triumphed.[51]

Luis Taruc who had originally accepted the government's amnesty offer, also changed his mind, declaring in a widely circulated address on 31 July 1948 at Cabanatuan, Nueva Ecija, that 'our movement' had hoped to engage in 'accepted legal parliamentary methods', but that the 'feudal caciques [landlords], backed by American monopolists using Roxas and the Liberal Party did not permit us to achieve our objectives through such methods of struggle'.[52] Many Huks, particularly in Central Luzon, refused Quirino's amnesty offer on condition that they surrendered their weapons by 15 August 1948. Instead, they flocked to PKP military cadres and began preparing themselves for all-out renewed combat. Fortified by the Soviet Union's new hard line of anti-Western confrontation also articulated at recent Communist-led youth conferences in Calcutta, the PKP, under José Lava, reorganised the Huks for 'people's war'.

On 7 November 1948, the Huks were renamed the *Hukbong Mapag-*

palaya ng Bayan (usually abbreviated to HMB) or 'People's Liberation
Army', and the intermittent pattern of Huk ambushes and raids, as
well as periodic brief occupations of whole villages and even towns,
became regular and extensive. In what José Lava now referred to as
the Philippines' 'revolutionary situation', the PKP announced as its
objective the establishment in the Philippines of a 'New Democracy',
a concept similar to Mao Ze Dong's and envisaging a regime in which
'all members of the nation', workers and peasants, as well as the
middle class, would elect representatives 'of their own group' in order
to 'look after their own welfare'.[53] Huk training centres meanwhile
gave new recruits a smattering of Marxism-Leninism.[54] But it was the
long historic tradition of unassuaged peasant grievances in Luzon
that provided the HMB with followers and with its driving force.[55] By
the middle of 1950, the HMB had some 23 000 armed followers, with a
back-up force of sympathisers and unarmed cadres of perhaps three
times that number.

With the appointment in September 1950 of Ramon Magsaysay as
defence minister and a new, US-supported counter-insurgency programme, combining effective psychological warfare and a resettlement
and land distribution scheme (Economic Development Corps) for
surrendered Huks, the tide began to turn.[56] As early as October 1950,
José Lava and top PKP Politburo figures had fallen into government
hands, but it was not until May 1954, that Huk 'Supremo' Luis Taruc
himself surrendered. In the following years the scattered, demoral-
ised HMB gradually began to devolve into mere localised banditry
and criminal racketeering. To this brigandage some Huk 'commanders' occasionally sought to impart a vague ideological aura of
populist 'social justice' as they exacted rough, Robin Hood style
retribution from rapacious landlords. The Philippine military and
constabulary meanwhile began to find it useful to sound the alarm
over the persistent Huk problem, usually at times when the Philippine Congress would be considering the Defence Department's
budget.

For all its not insignificant strength in numbers, the sympathies of
Pampanga tenants and of Manila workers and *lumpen* intellectuals,
the HMB never managed to develop the degree of disciplined and
co-ordinated leadership nor the organisational outreach among the
peasantry as well as dissident, middle class groups which would have
been needed to overthrow the Philippine government. Scattershot
localised guerrilla raids as in the days of the Japanese Occupation

could be no substitute for evolving tactically concentrated 'people's war' style battles. The dispersed, insular nature of the Philippine national territory would have made organisational unity difficult in any case. Also, the lack of a developed mass base of HMB or PKP supporters in Manila and other cities prevented the insurgents from mounting the kind of headline-grabbing, confidence-eroding confrontations in the major centres of public authority that could have swung significant segments of both domestic and foreign opinion against the government. Finally, the US, determined not to let the recent 'fall of China' have a domino effect in Asia, provided the extensive financial, advisory and logistical support to the Quirino and Magsaysay regimes without which the anti-HMB campaign, during the critical period of the early nineteen fifties, almost certainly would have floundered.

The case of the Philippines was not the only failure of post-war Communist insurgency in South-east Asia. Malaya provided another example. After the Seventh Comintern Congress's new united front policy was announced the CPM gradually began to moderate its strike agitation, in favour of uniting the Chinese in a broad-based anti-Japanese alliance. This effort culminated in the formation of the 'Overseas Chinese anti-Japanese National Salvation Association' in December 1941. CPM labour agitation and the campaign against the British were briefly resumed, in accordance with the policy demands of the Non-Aggression Pact between Germany and the USSR. But soon the CPM committed itself again to a united front policy, opting for collaboration with the British against the expected Japanese onslaught. In December 1941, a number of Malayan Chinese Communists briefly underwent training in a British guerrilla training school in Singapore. These Chinese subsequently moved into Malaya and became the cadre core for an anti-Japanese guerrilla force. As the Japanese Occupation of Malaya and Singapore solidified, the guerrilla nucleus had no difficulty winning recruits primarily from the Malayan Chinese community. By March 1942, the CPM's Central Committee had formally organised the separate guerrilla units into the Malayan People's Anti-Japanese Army (MPAJA).

The MPAJA reached a peak strength at the end of the war of about 7 000 armed men and women. They were backed by a civilian volunteer group, the Malayan People's Anti-Japanese Union (MPAJU), which served as a conduit of intelligence and supplies, and as a recruiting arm. Though claiming to draw support from ethnic

Malays and the Indian community in Malaya and Singapore, the
MPAJU was predominantly a Chinese organisation, however.[57] How
effectively the MPAJA used Allied arms and supplies which began to
flow to it by 1943, and the extent to which the MPAJA in fact
damaged the Japanese Occupation authority, are matters of controversy. But there is little doubt that in the MPAJA's camps and
routine activities no opportunity was missed to provide ideological
training: 'Almost daily classes in political indoctrination were conducted; the clenched fist salute, the "International" and the "Red
Flag Song", and all the other formal trappings of Communism had to
be accepted by all.'[58] The CPM's 1943 programme not only demanded the defeat and expulsion of the Japanese from Malaya, but
also the establishment of a 'democratic' Malayan Republic (which,
because of subsequent developments, it might be noted here then also
meant inclusion of Singapore), with due recognition of the rights of
different ethnic groups, including rights to free schooling in various
languages. The programme also called for an alliance with the USSR
and China in a common struggle for the 'independence of the
oppressed nations of the East'.[59]

The Japanese surrender on 14 August 1945 left a relative power
vacuum which the MPAJA did not seek to fill. The Communist
Party's secretary general Lai Tek wavered, perhaps because of
rumours of an impending occupation of Malaya by Chiang Kai-
shek's forces, and because of significant anticipated opposition from
other Malayan quarters to a Communist power seizure.[60] While some
5 000 MPAJA members permitted themselves to be formally de-
mobilised and handed in their weapons under the aegis of the
returning British colonial authority, hundreds of other cadres did not.
As the party quickly re-established its influence in segments of the
post-war Malayan labour movement (notably the Pan-Malayan
Federation of Trade Unions), it could also begin to capitalise on the
disquiet over various British proposals for constitutional reform
leading to independence for Malaya in a planned Federation of
Malay States that excluded Singapore. Opposition to the citizenship
provisions of the Federation concept was particularly strong in the
Chinese community because of alleged discrimination in these provisions against Chinese residents of Malaya. The planned preservation
in the Federation concept of the traditional Malay structures of
power, particularly of the Malay rulers, further deepened Chinese
suspicions and antagonisms which the CPM and its satellite groups

were quick to exploit. Meanwhile, militants in the CPM, led by Chen Ping (Chin Peng), a wartime MPAJA commander who had been decorated by the British for his services, pressed for a more aggressive confrontation, and when, in March 1947, Lai Tek was found to have disappeared with a sizeable sum of party money, Chin Peng became secretary general.[61]

Within a year, Stalin's new post-war hard-line policy of confrontation of the West had been interpreted for, and articulated to, Communists and their allies in South-east Asia, among them a CPM delegation which attended the February 1948 'South-east Asian Youth Conference', sponsored by the Moscow-directed World Federation of Democratic Youth, in Calcutta. There continues to be controversy as to whether the Calcutta Youth Conference was a direct causal factor of the Communist insurrections which subsequently intensified or erupted in Malaya, Indonesia, the Philippines and Burma. But certainly the militancy of the conference speeches, and the adoption of the major conference resolution demanding the seizure of power 'by the peasants and workers by any means' provided potent impulses to Communist parties in the region to adopt tactics of violent confrontation against any government, colonial or independent, they did not control. At a CPM Central Committee meeting in March 1948, Chin Peng was officially confirmed as secretary general and a 'mass struggle' programme against British imperialism in Malaya was announced.

Thus there began the period in Malayan history known as the 'Emergency' (1948–60).[62] Within months, assassinations of anti-Communist Malayan Chinese, violent strikes and sabotage erupted as the MPAJA, first calling itself the Malayan People's Anti-British Army, and then from February 1949 the Malayan Races Liberation Army (MRLA), took the field. The latter name was adopted in an effort to convey a broad, inter-ethnic image for the insurgent force, but as in the case of the MPAJA, Chinese continued to dominate the MRLA and the CPM. The Malayan Communists, following Maoist military doctrine, hoped to establish 'liberated' areas after an initial campaign of what may perhaps be called economic terrorism (destroying rubber estates and tin mines, killing their managers, and attacking lines of communication).[63]

But while the CPM showed a readiness to alternate guerrilla violence with renewed united front tactics (for instance, in 1951 and 1955), significant mass support, despite proselytising efforts through a volunteer 'Min Yuen' (People's Movement), never developed. After some initial tactical failures, British and Malayan government counter-insurgency policies began to have effect. The CPM's 'liberated' zones never materialised. Carefully supervised 'New Villages' were created by the government as resettlement sites for the rural Chinese population suspected of aiding the insurgents. Earlier in the Emergency, 'pure self preservation' dictated a 'principle of "sealed lips"' on the part of villagers and estate workers, surrounded by the insurgents' network.[64] But, with the gradual improvement of public information, security and intelligence services, and the increasing development of an inter-racial Malayan nationalism, capped by the British promise (and achievement) of Malaya's independence on 31 August 1957, the psychological tide, no less than the military-political one, turned decisively against Chin Peng, terrorism and the CPM. Refusing government offers of surrender accompanied by promises that there would be no prosecution of Emergency-related violations of law, the dwindling CPM-MRLA, still under Chin Peng's direction, retreated to the southern Thai border area. Here, during the early sixties, the Communists regrouped. They established new jungle camps for their 'regiments' and Min Yuen support groups among Chinese on both sides of the frontier, including in the 'New Villages' founded during the Emergency, and began penetrating with new united front tactics into the developing patterns of national Malayan politics.

The third instance of wartime guerrilla Communism in South-east Asia failing to capture the post-war national government occurred in Burma. The AFPFL initially had brought together much of the leftist and nationalist leadership among the Burmese, including the CPB, it will be recalled. But the attempts of Than Tun's nascent Communist Party of Burma to dominate the AFPFL were resented by others in the coalition, notably by Socialist Party leaders. Within months of the Japanese surrender the Socialist Party, the CPB, and various non-Marxist peasant and trade union organisations began jockeying for power, as meanwhile the initial British plan for the further constitutional development of Burma provoked sharp reaction in a broad range of Burmese opinion. In February 1946, Thakin Soe (Soe Gyi), one of the original CPB founders, broke with his colleague Than Tun over the question of the policy to be adopted toward the British constitutional scheme, and shortly thereafter formed his own Communist faction. All-out revolutionary war against the British and

Burmese 'feudalists' and the creation essentially of a Leninist Burmese Republic, were the aims of Soe's faction. In subsequent years
Soe's faction retained the name of, and generally remained known
formally as, the CPB. But it also came to be identified as the 'Red
Flag' Communist Party of Burma. Than Tun's Communist faction
was now called the 'Burma Communist Party' or 'White Flags' and
initially sought to maintain co-operation with the government. The
'Red Flag' CPB embarked on a campaign of violence first against the
residual British colonial authority and its Burmese allies and, after 4
January 1948, when the Union of Burma formally acquired its
independence from Britain, against the independent Burmese government of premier U Nu and all his subsequent successors.[65]

Meanwhile, Than Tun's persisting attempts to dominate the
AFPFL and win power for himself and his party in the future Burmese
government further polarised his opponents. When it became apparent that he had failed in securing a post, Than Tun became ever more
critical of the AFPFL and, at the end of March 1948, began urging a
'people's rising' against the U Nu government and the destruction of
the 'fascist' AFPFL coalition. It might be noted that a month before,
in February 1948, Than Tun had attended the previously mentioned
South-east Asian Democratic Youth Conference in Calcutta, and had
also participated in the Second Congress of the Indian Communist
Party held in the same city and at the same time. It is likely that the
atmosphere of the Calcutta Youth Congress, as well as the influence
on him of Indian Communist Party advisers, predisposed Than Tun
to adoption of a policy of violent confrontation for his party upon his
return to Burma. In any case, after Than Tun's break with the
AFPFL, his 'White Flag' Communist Party mustered a significant
guerrilla force. The 'White Flags' thus became one of several different
insurgent groups operating against the U Nu government (others
were the 'Red Flags', Karen and Mon ethnic nationalists, and
elements of a militia force, the *Pyithu Yebaw Ahphwe* or 'People's
Volunteer Organisation' controlled by rural political leaders opposed
to U Nu) and in subsequent years occasionally joined in common
anti-government strikes with them.[66] Yet the Union government did
not collapse, and by 1954 the Burmese armed forces were not only
steadily expanding government authority into the interior, but were
also forcing both 'White' and 'Red Flag' Communist units to retreat.
Radical Marxists, some of whom may well have had a foot in the
camp of either of Burma's Communist parties, briefly reasserted their

influence in national politics and parliament during the nineteen fifties through their Burma Workers' and Peasants' Party (BWPP) and its allies in the National Unity Front (NUF). But by the close of the decade, BWPP and NUF factional disputes (some favouring a national, 'Titoist' line, others having either a pro-Chinese or pro-Soviet orientation), as well as loss of electoral support, had robbed the Communists and their ideological allies on the Burmese party scene of much of their strength, even though the badly riven AFPFL government increasingly seemed unable to hold the country together. By the late fifties some 9 000 'White' and 'Red Flag' insurgents had surrendered and been granted amnesty.[67]

Like the PKP-Huks, and the CPM-MRLA, Burmese Communism entered the nineteen sixties at a low ebb. Yet new organisational and tactical impulses would shortly lift all these movements again to political prominence. In assessing their chances for a resurgence, leaders of these failed guerrilla Communist movements in South-east Asia could take heart perhaps from the experience both of the Communists in Indonesia, and above all from those in Vietnam. The Indonesian case is unique for its time in the history of South-east Asian Communism. This is not so much because of the absence in Indonesia of a significant Communist-directed or -influenced anti-Japanese guerrilla resistance movement, usable in an immediate post-war setting of 'people's war'. For in Thailand, too, such a movement, though perhaps relatively more developed than in Indonesia, had little significance. It is rather because of the speed with which the Indonesian party was able to recover from a disastrous coup attempt, subsequently expand to its largest extent in its history, and then in 1965 plunge again into disaster after involvement in yet another coup venture – all in less than two decades.

For months after Indonesians, on 17 August 1945, had proclaimed an independent republic, thus launching a four-year period of revolutionary resistance against the returning Dutch colonial authority, the Indonesian Communist Party (PKI) had floundered organisationally and tactically. It had promoted agrarian 'sovietisation' schemes which brought it into conflict with other parties and interest groups in the fledgling republic. It had also lent itself to the schemes of Tan Malaka who, though no longer Moscow's friend, was attempting to rally a broad-based, leftist nationalist 'fighting force' not only against the Dutch but also to seize control of the republic's government from its president, Sukarno. Even though Malaka's venture failed, the PKI, under new leaders and having organised its own labour following and armed volunteer groups, was able during 1946–7 to become an increasingly important factor in the republic's domestic politics. It began to play a major role in the republic's embryo-parliament through its participation, along with fellow-travelling Socialist and Labour Parties and radical youth groups, in a united front organisation, the so-called *Sajap Kiri* (Left Wing). Indeed, in the latter half of 1947, during the cabinet of premier Amir Sjarifuddin, who later admitted to having been a Communist since the thirties, PKI influence reached a new high, but also aroused partisan opposition. This opposition eventually culminated in early 1948 not only in the fall of the Sjarifuddin cabinet but also in the break-up of the united front and a split among the Socialists.[68]

The polarisation between a new leftist, PKI-dominated united front, the 'Democratic People's Front' (*Front Demokrasi Rakjat –* FDR), and most of the rest of the political parties and the republic's cabinet led by premier Mohammad Hatta, a veteran and revered nationalist figure, set the stage for clashes between pro- and anti-PKI military units, acts of terrorism such as kidnappings, and other what party history would later call 'provocations'.[69] In August 1948, the veteran PKI leader Muso returned to Indonesia from Moscow and the party subsequently adopted a resolution 'The New Road for Indonesia' (*Djalan Baru Untuk Indonesia*). This resolution urged formation of a broad-based national front in the development of a two-stage revolutionary process in Indonesia, now described as being in its first 'bourgeois democratic stage', as well as total confrontation of the 'imperialists'. Whether it was because of the 'provocations', the effect of this 'New Road' resolution or the influence of the South-east Asia Democratic Youth Conference in Calcutta (at which a PKI delegation had been in attendance) a few months earlier, or a combination of all of these, is not clear. But, on 18 September 1948, a number of second echelon PKI leaders acting without formal authorisation of top party leaders, along with a few local military commanders, seized control of the east Java city of Madiun in an evident attempt at a coup d'état. Loyal Indonesian Republic army units crushed the uprising, however, and principal PKI leaders like Alimin and Muso, who almost certainly had been taken by surprise by the Madiun events, were either arrested or killed.

Though not formally banned, the PKI entered the era of Indonesia's national independence at the close of 1949 (when the Dutch

finally accepted Indonesian sovereignty over their erstwhile East
Indies colonial empire) under the stigma of having stabbed the
Indonesian Republic in the back even as it was struggling for its
independence. However, in January 1951, a group of younger party
leaders, most notable of whom was the Sumatran Dipa Nusantara
Aidit, assumed control of the PKI Politburo. There now began a
remarkable tactical realignment and organisational reconstruction of
the party, including development of labour, peasants, youth, women,
veterans and other front groups, a more careful recruiting and cadre
training, and a close identification with President Sukarno in the
latter's power struggle with the army. Formally denying that it was a
party of 'coup-ists', the PKI under Aidit participated in elections and
parliamentary life and adopted a national ideological orientation. It
also attempted to maintain an independent position in the developing
Moscow-Beijing (Peking) dispute though it endorsed Indonesia's
ever closer diplomatic partnership with People's China in the early
sixties. By 1964 the party claimed more than two million members
and 'aspirant' members, with a following of additional tens of
thousands in front organisations.[70]

Yet, probably precisely because it had become the largest party in
Indonesia by 1964, organisational and tactical problems mounted at
the same time that the PKI's political struggle with a number of
anti-Communist army generals and political groups intensified. The
exact sequence of events leading to the formation of what in Indonesia
today is called *Gestapu* (from *Gerakan September Tiga Puluh* or 'Thirty
September Movement') remains unclear and controversial. But it
would appear that in the course of 1965 a number of party leaders,
among them Aidit, along with dissident army and air force officers,
began plotting to seize the government. There is no certainty, however, on many aspects of Gestapu, such as the foreknowledge and
encouragement of, and perhaps even the initiative of, Sukarno in the
plot, or the question of whether the plotters were attempting to
forestall a pre-emptive coup by army generals.[71] Reportedly the
People's Republic of China covertly supplied weapons to the plotters,
and Japanese Communists who visited Beijing in the spring of 1966
'returned with the conviction that the PKI had planned the coup at
the suggestion of the Chinese party', and, indeed, that 'the Gestapu
was generated by the PKI against the army as a dimension of China's
strategy against American imperialism in Asia'.[72]

On the night of 30 September 1965, in Djakarta and in sections of central Java, PKI leaders and members of its youth and women's fronts, as well as units of the Indonesian army and air force, attempted to seize power. Prominent among the military plotters was Lieutenant-Colonel Untung, commander of a battalion of the presidential guard. Six top army generals were killed by coup assassination squads. But army units, under the leadership of General Suharto, commander of the Army Strategic Reserve, quickly quelled the coup attempt in the capital, although sporadic fighting continued for several weeks in central Java where armed Communist bands operated. In the aftermath of the coup tens of thousands, and perhaps hundreds of thousands, of PKI and front organisation members, sympathisers and, it is to be feared, innocents, were massacred (the total number has never been accurately established) by Muslim youth gangs, army and police units. Also during the anti-Communist holocaust, additional hundreds of thousands were arrested on grounds of coup involvement and/or Communist sympathies. After three years, some 150 000 Gestapu or suspected Communist prisoners remained (some estimates go higher), and new arrests continued long after the coup. PKI chairman Aidit was killed by the army, while other prominent party leaders were either executed or sentenced to long prison terms after trials, or else held in indefinite detention.

By March 1966, Suharto had assumed *de facto* authority from Sukarno as the nation's chief executive, and the PKI, despite Sukarno's efforts to preserve its legitimacy, had been formally banned. Driven deeply underground, PKI remnants in central and east Java in 1966, 1967, and 1968, attempted to develop an underground guerrilla and terrorist movement, the 'Indonesian People's Liberation Army Command' (*Lasjkar Pembebasan Rakjat Indonesia* – LPRI).[73] In Blitar, east Java, in early 1968, former PKI editor Oloan Hutapea even briefly proclaimed a 'Revolutionary Indonesian Republic'. But this resistance also was quickly broken by the army. Only in West Kalimantan (Borneo) along the Indonesian border with the Malaysian state of Sarawak have a handful of PKI insurgents remained active, making common cause with the guerrillas of the Communist 'North Kalimantan People's Guerrilla Force' (NKPGF) operating across the frontier. As for the third time the PKI's fortunes nosedived in the aftermath of an abortive coup, the exiled and underground party remnant was further weakened by a split into pro-Soviet and pro-Chinese factions, each denouncing the other, and each developing their own explanation as to why the Gestapu disaster had overtaken the PKI. With their own spokesmen and media, these factions began outlining their own respective programmes for the future (see chapter 3, below). In Indonesia itself, meanwhile, the Gestapu incident, and what officially and frequently came to be called the 'latent' PKI underground threat, served to structure the security policies of the regime of President Suharto and the regime's avowed commitment to nip all manifestations of real or alleged subversion in the bud, in order to ensure national economic development.

B. The Communist victory in Indochina

To offset all those post-war failures, however, Communism in South-east Asia can point to its eventual formidable triumph in Indochina. Shortly after its birth in Hong Kong in 1930, the Vietnam Communist Party (VCP) had changed its name to the Indochinese Communist Party (ICP) at the Comintern's request, in order, presumably, to demonstrate that it also spoke for the Laotian and Cambodian, as well as the Vietnamese, revolutionary movement. The ICP plunged into strikes and peasant agitation – for example, in Nghean and Hatinh provinces. But, as in the case of the brief nationalist rising engineered by the non-Communist Viet Nam Quoc Dan Dang (VNQDD), in Hanoi, Yen Bay, and elsewhere, a few months earlier, the French colonial authority quickly quelled the unrest and all but destroyed the Communist organisation. Ho Chi Minh fled to Hong Kong where he was arrested and incarcerated, subsequently leaving for Moscow. Though he returned as a Comintern representative to China in 1938, Ho was not to surface again as a leader of Vietnamese Communists until May 1941, when, appearing in Jiangxi (Chingsi), in southern China's Guangxi (Kwangsi) province, near the Vietnamese border, he there organised the first congress of the *Viet Nam Doc Lap Dong Minh* or 'Vietnamese Independence League'. This League, commonly known as the Vietminh Front, came into being after French officials in Indochina, in compliance with the policies of Vichy France, had already begun active collaboration with the Japanese.[74]

Meant as a broad-based anti-Japanese resistance movement similar to those that were to emerge in the Philippines and Malaya, the Vietminh Front was however at all times under tight ICP control. According to Vietnamese Communist history today, the Vietminh developed 'revolutionary bases', launched guerrilla warfare, and indeed, 'in many regions, committees of the Viet Minh Front functioned in the place of enemy village administration'.[75] There was, not surprisingly, continuous wartime rivalry and conflict between the Vietminh and non-Communist Vietnamese nationalist groups, some of the latter supported by the Nationalist Chinese government. The Vietminh undoubtedly had the superior discipline and organisation. When in March 1945, with Gaullist resistance growing among French officials in Indochina, the Japanese abruptly arrested these officials and took over daily government from them, there was effective Vietminh resistance, made possible in part because of supplies of Allied weapons. In the face of the March 1945 Japanese takeover, the ICP issued tactical instructions emphasising that while conditions were 'not yet ripe' for a general uprising, circumstances favouring an insurrection were rapidly 'maturing'. The party and its allies were urged to concentrate on defeating the Japanese first and welcome and work with the liberating Allies, but 'in any case our guerrillas must always keep the initiative in the operations'.[76]

In the closing months of the war, and in the early post-war period, Vietminh determination backed by its guerrillas, and relatively secure in its rural liberated areas, was more than a match for a divided and often discredited political opposition that included among others the Japanese-encouraged regime of Bao Dai, the Annamese emperor, in Annam and Tonkin, Kuomintang-supported Vietnamese nationalists, and later Vietnamese collaborators with the returning French authority in Cochin China. On 16 August 1945, as Vietminh flags were flying over Hanoi, a Vietminh-sponsored congress sought to rally disparate nationalist factions, and established a 'People's Liberation Committee' under Ho Chi Minh's leadership. Meanwhile, ICP assassination squads had mounted an accelerating liquidation campaign and began purging 'counter-revolutionaries' and other opponents.[77] On 2 September 1945, Ho Chi Minh, a week after Bao Dai's abdication, at a mass rally in Hanoi's Ba Dinh Square, read the independence declaration of the 'Democratic Republic of Vietnam' (DRV). This declaration begins with a quotation from the American Declaration of Independence ('All men are created equal'), reflecting Ho's tactic of trying to win further US support for his venture, just as he had been able to secure assistance from the American Office of Strategic Services (OSS) during the war.[78] Asserting that 'the whole Vietnamese people' were determined to fight to 'the bitter end' against returning French colonialism, the declaration which Ho read said that the victorious Allies, which 'at Teheran and San Francisco have acknowledged the principles of self determination and equality of nations', would not refuse to recognise Vietnam's independence.

But just what kind of independence Vietnam would have quickly became a matter of violent contention in subsequent months as the DRV, its rivals and allies in the rest of Vietnam, including French-controlled Cochin China, and the Kuomintang Chinese government jockeyed for influence and power in the country. Having formally dissolved the ICP in November 1945 (the party became instead the 'Association for the Study of Marxism') in a bid to minimise the outward Communist appearance of their Vietnam revolution, Ho and his party associates nevertheless dominated the political process of the new DRV government. Ho himself in a conversation with a US official as late as September 1946 denied that he was a Communist.[79] In March 1946, Ho's initial acceptance of France's recognition of a Vietnamese 'free state' inside an Indochinese federation led to sharp partisan differences in Vietnam, the more so as French officials in Indochina soon showed little inclination to give substance to the 'free state' concept or to Vietnamese nationalist aspirations generally, except on their terms. Fighting between French and Vietminh forces intensified after a French naval attack on Haiphong (23 November 1946). Eventually abandoning further attempts to co-opt the DRV, the French by 1949 had proceeded with the creation of a new state and a single government, embracing all of Vietnam and headed by Bao Dai. A degree of Commonwealth style freedom was granted to this Vietnam state, as well as to Cambodia and Laos, within a French union. For many Vietnamese nationalists a Bao Dai-governed Vietnam offered the less desirable perspective on their political future, whatever their qualms about Ho's DRV regime.

Ho, meanwhile, asserted his DRV government's exclusive sovereignty over all of Vietnam. As major foreign powers now began lining up to grant diplomatic recognition and technical and military aid to the two rival Indochinese regimes, the stage was set for a long-term military and political confrontation. As far as the Vietnamese Communists were concerned, the military dimension of this confrontation was best summarised by the DRV's chief strategist as follows:[80]

Guerrilla war is the war of the broad masses of an economically backward country standing up against a powerfully equipped and well trained army of aggression. Is the enemy strong? One avoids him. Is he weak? One attacks him. To his modern armament one opposes a boundless heroism to vanquish either by harassing or by annihilating the enemy according to circumstances . . . no fixed line of demarcation, the front being wherever the enemy is found.

Stressing 'initiative, suppleness, rapidity, surprise, suddenness in attack and retreat', the thrust of this DRV strategy, militarily no less than in terms of its desired political and psychological impact on the enemy, was to 'exhaust little by little by small victories the enemy forces', as each 'inhabitant' of Vietnam was turned into a 'soldier', each 'village' into a 'fortress', and each 'Party cell' or village 'administrative committee' into a 'staff' on the side of the DRV's forces.[81]

As for Vietnamese Communist political strategy, the long-term confrontation demanded reassertion of clear leadership by an élite 'vanguard' party, backed, in turn, by a broad united front of all those throughout Vietnam opposed to French rule (or, eventually, opposed to any regime other than a Communist one). In March 1951, the *Lao Dong* (Workers' Party) became that vanguard, fulfilling the role of the still officially dormant ICP. The new united front in turn was provided by the *Hoi Lien Hiep Quoc Dan Viet Nam*, commonly called the Lien Viet, which Ho Chi Minh and the ICP had organised five years previously for this purpose, but which had remained relatively ineffective amidst the bickering among various Vietnamese groups over French policy aims. Now the Vietminh was formally fused with the Lien Viet and the new organisation became an instrument of Vietnamese Communist social mobilisation and ideological indoctrination. In September 1955, the Lien Viet, in turn, was changed into yet another front organisation, called *Mat Tran To Quoc Viet Nam*, or 'Vietnam Fatherland Front', and composed of various workers', peasants', women's, youth, and other special interest groups. Like its Lien Viet predecessor, the Lao Dong party dominated the Fatherland Front as well. Though based in the North, the Fatherland Front was also expected to serve those in South Vietnam who were for 'fatherland', and 'for peace and democracy'.[82] Ideological premises of these front organisations remained much the same over the years. Truong Chinh, the ICP's Mao-lining theoretician, already in 1947 had described the development of a national front based on a 'worker peasant alliance' operating under 'the leadership of the working class' as 'our home policy'.[83] In its struggle for control of South Vietnam, the DRV military perception also stressed the 'revolutionary force' provided by the 'ten million strong' reservoir of peasantry, along with the 'working class', as well as the revolutionary potential among 'oppressed and exploited' South Vietnamese petty bourgeoisie, national bourgeoisie (which 'to some degree evinces an anti-imperialist and anti-feudal spirit'), the ethnic and religious minorities (among whom a 'progressive tendency' was said to be gaining ground), and even among the ranks of the 'puppet army'.[84]

There is a question as to the extent to which the Vietnamese Communists even then saw themselves as struggling for the revolutionary 'liberation' of Laos and Cambodia as well as of Vietnam. A secret Lao Dong directive in November 1951 refers to an eventual unification of the revolutionary parties of Laos, Cambodia and Vietnam, implying also an eventual political merger of all of Indochina.[85] Certainly over the years, Vietnamese Communist and Hanoi's dominance of the Laotian Communist movement became only too apparent. On the other hand, there has long been Cambodian Communist resentment of Vietnamese Communist pressures and of the DRV, and later after the 1975–6 final conquest and unification of South Vietnam with North Vietnam there were frequent Cambodian clashes with the armed forces of the new unified Socialist Republic of Vietnam (SRV). Even so, at the time that SRV forces penetrated Cambodian border territory in January 1977, Hanoi felt it necessary to deny that it wished to establish an 'Indochinese Federation' as the Phnom Penh regime had charged.[86] The vision of a Communist Indochina in which at the least Laos, Cambodia and Vietnam, even if separate states, would be co-operating closely with each other may be fairly attributed to Ho and the Vietnamese Communists as of the earliest years of their movement.

By the early nineteen fifties, as Bao Dai's regime atrophied along with domestic French willingness to support it, in the intensifying struggle against the DRV, the political tide turned steadily in favour of the Vietminh. Even as peace negotiations at an international conference in Geneva were taking place, more than 15 000 French troops bottled up in the fortress of Dien Bien Phu surrendered to besieging DRV forces, a victory which its chief strategist described in

Maoist strategic terms as allegedly proving the frequently 'decisive' significance of 'a solid rear' in the pursuit of victory in revolutionary war.[87] The 1954 Geneva accords, involving a ceasefire between French and DRV forces, and an unsigned declaration accepted but not signed by the conference participants, envisaged elections in a Vietnam divided by the seventeenth parallel, the northern part governed by the DRV, the southern by the government of Bao Dai. The elections would be a prelude to unification, and belligerent forces would regroup in the North and South respectively.

In South Vietnam, premier Ngo Dinh Diem, backed by the US, which had been playing an increasingly important role in the support of the anti-Communist cause in Vietnam even before the Geneva accords, established his authority over dissident religious and political sects, and also secured much of the South Vietnamese armed forces' support. By October 1955, after a referendum had deposed Bao Dai as head of state, a new Republic of Vietnam was proclaimed with Ngo Dinh Diem as president. Though the DRV insisted that nationwide elections be held in conformity with the 1954 Geneva agreements, Diem refused. Diem pointed out that the South Vietnamese government at the time of the Geneva conference had already objected to the ceasefire and to the seventeenth parallel partition and he emphasised further that, given the authoritarian nature of the DRV regime in North Vietnam, 'free general elections by secret ballot' would be impossible. Although some 80 000 Vietminh did move northwards, Diem's government also noted (as did the US State Department) that the DRV left a covert cadre structure, with concealed arms caches in place in the South.[88]

By 1960, the Diem regime, despite its authoritarian features and periodic opposition conspiracies, seemed well established, at least for the moment. DRV prospects of unifying Vietnam under its aegis at any time soon seemed to be receding. The Communist answer to the problem was to intensify the insurgency in the South, in the context of a broad-based political movement for national 'salvation'. In September 1960, the Third Congress of the Lao Dong party was held in Hanoi. Party secretary Le Duan's statement to the Congress that 'the immediate task of the revolution in the South' was, among others, 'to achieve national reunification' after winning 'national independence', as well as the remarks and exhortations of other speakers on the state of the 'liberation' movement in South Vietnam, foreshadowed the formation three months later in South Vietnam of the *Mat Tran Dan Toc Giai Phong Mien Nam Viet Nam* or 'National Front for the Liberation of South Vietnam' (commonly abbreviated as NLF).[89] Over the next decade, as Communist forces (including the NLF and collectively referred to as 'Viet Cong' by their opponents) grew and widened the scope of their operations, the aims of the NLF (as defined, for example, by its August 1967 'extraordinary congress') carefully continued to avoid formal Marxist-Leninist terminology. Instead the NLF favoured broadly formulated objectives, couched in mildly 'progressive' sounding phrases calculated to be attractive to those in South Vietnam and abroad stirred by the general nationalist appeal of the DRV's struggle – for instance, the call for unity of 'all patriotic and progressive' elements struggling against the 'US imperialists and their lackeys', and for the establishment of a 'national union democratic government' in South Vietnam that would proceed with 'the peaceful reunification of the Fatherland'.[90]

Meanwhile, confronted by the divisive and eroding effects of protracted insurgency on South Vietnam's soil, and suspicious of US policies, Diem's autocratic regime seemed to rely increasingly heavily on some of his immediate family members. A serious religious-political crisis with the Vietnamese Buddhist leadership, aggravated by the Diem regime's heavy-handed repression of Buddhist protest, provided vocal critics of Diem's regime in the US with new ammunition. The devastating psychological effect abroad of public self-immolations by Buddhist monks set the stage for the fateful US policy decision that the Diem government had to go. The possibility and extent of Communist organisational impulses behind, and exploitation of, the Buddhist crisis (including the Communist antecedents of some anti-Diem Buddhist activists like Tich Tri Quang, who earlier had been a member of the Vietminh), and, indeed, the degree of artful and propagandistic contrivance of the Buddhist protest campaign against Diem, including the self-immolations (suspicion of the existence of such contrivance is aroused by the findings of a United Nations fact-finding mission which investigated the Buddhist problem in South Vietnam in October 1963), remain matters of controversy.[91]

There is, however, little doubt that the overthrow of Diem by a military junta on 1 November 1963 and his subsequent assassination marked a major turning point in the Vietnam conflict. President Lyndon Johnson was later to blame the Kennedy administration's role in the overthrow of Diem for having caused the ensuing chaos in

Vietnam and for the need of a sharply escalated US troop commitment to that country.[92] Political instability, military rivalries, a continuing campaign of Buddhist grievances all enhanced South Vietnam's vulnerability, as meanwhile Communist infiltration of manpower and weapons steadily accelerated and the scope and frequency of armed clashes increased along with stepped-up Communist attempts at establishing political control in rural 'liberated zones' in the South. According to a US State Department report in February 1965, during 1959–60, Hanoi had sent at least 1 800 men, and probably many more, into the South while, during the first eight months of 1964, the rate had been stepped up to at least 4 400. These were conservative estimates, however, and the State Department calculated in its February 1965 report that since 1959, in fact, 'nearly 20,000' Communist 'officers, soldiers and technicians are known to have entered South Vietnam under orders from Hanoi'. An additional 17 000 were estimated to have been sent South as well during the preceding six years. Northerners increasingly predominated among the infiltrators, according to this State Department report. Of the 4 400 who entered during 1964, for example, three-quarters were natives of North Vietnam.[93]

From 1964 on, the frequency of infiltration of battalion and regiment size units from the DRV sharply increased, while the network of 'irregular' Communist support groups also widened. US forces also poured into Vietnam (by early 1967, American military in the country numbered nearly 400 000, along with 44 000 South Koreans, 4 000 Australians, and smaller contingents of New Zealand, Philippine and Thai units). The conflict involved more and more, larger set-piece type battles with Communist forces that had grown to some 120 000 North Vietnamese and Southern Viet Cong 'regulars' backed by an additional 150 000 militia style 'irregulars', and additional tens of thousands of 'civilian' party cadres and logistical support forces and 'liberated zone' units.[94] The real battlefield, however, was the arena of US domestic public and political opinion, just as in the early fifties it had been the arena of French public opinion. By the spring of 1968, Hanoi's victory on this American battlefield had become a virtual certainty following the Communists' so-called Tet (the Vietnamese New Year) offensive late in January 1968. Militarily, this offensive could hardly be termed a triumph for the DRV and NLF. On the psychological and propaganda fronts, however, it was a spectacular success for the Communists, with President Lyndon

Johnson deciding not to seek another term and American opinion turning sharply against further US involvement in the Vietnam war.

Impelled by American war weariness, pressures to reach a negotiated settlement at the on-again off-again peace discussions in Paris now steadily mounted. Yet strategically the Communist position, weakened by the economic devastation of long years of war, could not be said to be a superior one. A new North Vietnamese offensive, begun at the close of March 1972, had been blunted by the South Vietnamese and by effective US air strikes. Moreover, the heavily US-backed South Vietnamese government of President Nguyen Van Thieu had the gravest misgivings about a future settlement in light of the demands of the Hanoi-directed 'People's Revolutionary Government' (PRG) for South Vietnam, created by the 'South Vietnam Central Office' of the DRV's Lao Dong party toward the close of 1968, as the organisational crystallisation of the NLF strivings and of Hanoi's long-term aim for the South, short of unification. US pressure on Thieu prevailed, however. The Paris peace agreement, signed by the DRV, PRG, US and Thieu's Republic of Vietnam on 27 January 1973, was in retrospect principally important for the provision that US and all other foreign forces would withdraw from Vietnam within 60 days.[95] Such provisions as dealt with ceasefire, with the prohibition against the introduction of any foreign military force into South Vietnam, or with the procedures of establishing South Vietnamese 'self determination' were either ignored or never implemented to any significant degree. Both sides broke the ceasefire and both sides sought to gain as much territory as possible. The provision prohibiting (as US state secretary Henry Kissinger understood it) the use of Laos and Cambodia for purposes of infiltration into Vietnam, and indeed the requirement that foreign troops (including the DRV's and its South Vietnamese allies) be withdrawn from Laos and Cambodia altogether, met with even wider justifiable scepticism, particularly in non-Communist South-east Asia. Under the heading 'We've Gone Through This Before', one leading Bangkok daily, for example, commented editorially:[96]

> Somebody must have astounding faith in the Communists to think first that North Vietnam will withdraw its forces from Laos and Cambodia, and second that they will not introduce war materiel into these two countries.

Even in Viet Nam the Communist intentions are clearly suspect. No less a person than North Viet Namese Prime Minister Pham Van Dong has said, hailing the agreement, 'We shall carry forward this struggle . . . in order to complete the revolutionary cause of the Vietnamese people. We shall continue to carry high the banner of peace, friendship and democracy so as to march ahead in the cause of liberation of South Vietnam and reunification of the homeland.'

The key phrase is 'liberation of South Vietnam', and it purports to show that the Paris Agreement has in no whit changed the intentions of the Communists. The evangelism has not died and clearly it encompasses Laos and Cambodia.

In a retrospective analysis of the two years between the signing of the Paris agreement and the entry into Saigon by the Communists, an unsigned DRV publication declared that the 'signing of the Agreement had breathed new vigor into the national struggle waged both by the forces rallied behind the banner of the NLF and the PRG', as North Vietnam in the meantime 'was more than ever the great rear base of the liberation struggle' in the South.[97] Still, in the initial months after the signing of the Paris agreement, DRV and NLF leaders proceeded cautiously, and a policy resolution adopted in October 1973 by the Lao Dong Central Committee warned Communist troops and party cadres not to expect an ultimate victory before 1979 at the earliest.[98] The DRV Generals Giap and Dung, reflecting later on their final 1975 offensive against Saigon, might write that in the aftermath of Paris 'our Party emphasized the continuous need to maintain the viewpoint on revolutionary violence' and resolved further 'to use revolutionary war'.[99] Yet there were 'doves' in the Lao Dong leadership and there was a good deal of circumspection in Hanoi's calculations during the early post-Paris agreement months. In this period, the Communist policy of 'strategic raids' was primarily being implemented against roads, airbases, storage facilities and other infrastructural elements of the South Vietnamese economy and logistical posture, as the Thieu regime, meanwhile struggling against the corruption, venality and incompetence of its own bureaucrats and military commanders, confronted a larger Communist force than at any time during the previous decade (estimates of total Communist troop strengths by the autumn of 1974 ranged from 285 000 to 387 000).[100]

The adverse effects of Communist 'strategic raids' on the South Vietnamese economy were aggravated by an eroding South Vietnamese morale following US troop withdrawals, the implications of the Watergate scandal and by various indications of an almost desperate desire in the US to extricate itself from any further involvement in Vietnam. By October 1974, in response to a new Lao Dong party Politburo directive, it was decided that a new and somewhat more aggressive DRV military policy could and should be implemented. Beginning in mid-December 1974, the North Vietnamese winter-spring campaign met with such success that by the end of the first week in January 1975, a still bolder North Vietnamese military strategy was promulgated by Lao Dong leaders, including a prospect for the possible 'liberation' of South Vietnam that same year.[101] The resistance put up by the Thieu regime soon turned into an ignominious rout. By 30 April 1975, North Vietnamese units had all but secured their hold on Saigon, soon to be renamed Ho Chi Minh City.

Thousands of South Vietnamese had attempted to flee their country in the last few weeks and days of the Thieu regime, and in subsequent months and years they continued to try to escape. Meanwhile, many of their less fortunate compatriots, particularly those who had held office in the South Vietnamese government and who were now deemed to be in need of 're-education', vanished into camps. At the end of 1976, as many as 200 000 and probably more were held in such re-education camps for 'remoulding' purposes. (According to official Vietnamese sources, however, the figure was only 50 000, or about five per cent of those who had been compelled to register after the end of the Thieu era.)[102] Instances of sporadic anti-Communist guerrilla resistance in the Central Highlands and in parts of the Mekong Delta region have been reported periodically. The resistance is led by a movement called *Phuc Quoc* (National Restoration Front), largely composed of former officers and men of the South Vietnamese armed forces as well as probably dissident Meo and other tribals.[103] There is, however, no indication that this resistance constitutes much of a threat to the new regime.

Carefully controlled elections for a new National Assembly to represent both North and South Vietnam were held on 25 April 1976, but they were hardly the kind of free, competitive elections for South Vietnam that had been envisaged by the Paris agreements of 1973. Predictably, on 2 July 1976, the newly elected National Assembly of Vietnam endorsed the merger of North and South Vietnam into a single state under the leadership of the 'advanced' Socialist government of the DRV. The newly united nation was henceforth known as the Socialist Republic of Vietnam. The Lao Dong party, current organisational vehicle for a Communist movement which, since 1930, it will be recalled, had been adept in changing its name as the tactical circumstances demanded it, held its Fourth Congress in December 1976, and altered its name once more, now calling itself the 'Vietnam Communist Party' (VCP). The change, as party secretary Le Duan put it, was in keeping with the new phase of 'socialist transformation' that now lay before the new, unified Vietnamese nation.[104]

And so today, Vietnam once again has a formal Communist party, even as its uneasy neighbours in South-east Asia, themselves confronted by a range of Communist guerrilla insurgencies and terrorism, have begun wondering what impact the emergence of the SRV (with its total armed forces of 700 000, the SRV has one of the largest military establishments in Asia) would have on them. In Malaysia, for example, there was officially voiced concern that the Communist successes in Indochina had 'given new impetus' to the Communist struggle in Malaysia, and that arms from the Vietnam war zone would be flowing to Malaysia's Communist insurgents.[105]

How justified such concerns actually turned out to be, and what Hanoi's relations with the rest of South-east Asia have been since the formal establishment of the SRV will be dealt with elsewhere in this book (see chapters 2 and 6). Now, however, it needs to be noted that the ultimate Communist triumph in Vietnam was accompanied by parallel victories for the Communists in Laos and Cambodia. This is not surprising, perhaps, because historically and tactically Communism in Laos in particular has always been strongly influenced if not in fact dominated by Vietnamese Communism.[106] It may be recalled that, at the Comintern's insistence, the name of the Vietnam Communist Party, founded in 1930 under Ho Chi Minh's aegis, had been changed to Indochinese Communist Party (ICP), in order to emphasise that Laotian and Cambodian as well as Vietnamese revolutionary interests were represented by a single party. Not until after World War II, and as the Vietminh's struggle against the French rapidly deepened, was an effort made to develop a more or less distinctive Laotian Communist movement, if always under Hanoi's direction, to be sure. In February 1951, at the time that Vietnamese Communists formed the Lao Dong party as a vehicle for their aspirations, it was also announced that a Viet-Lao-Cambodian (Khmer) 'alliance' had been established, suggesting that the three peoples of Indochina should be conceived of as separate, if allied, entities in the developing revolutionary struggle. This 'alliance', at least conceptually, marked the beginnings of more or less distinctive Laotian and Cambodian (Khmer) Communist movements. But it was not until 22 March 1955 that the Laotian Communist party, called the People's Party of Laos (*Phak Pasason Lao* – PPL) was officially organised, although some years before that a Lao Dong section for and of Laotian Communists with its own cells and covert infrastructure was probably already in existence.

Functioning covertly and in fact little known, the PPL has operated primarily through the 'Lao Patriotic Front' (*Neo Lao Hak Sat* – NLHS), the military arm of the Laotian Communist movement, and itself the product of a post-war Communist organisational evolution in the country. That evolution may be said to have begun with the close of the Japanese Occupation of most of Laos during World War II, and the subsequent failure of the attempt by a small group of Laotian nationalists in the so-called *Lao Issara* (Free Laos) organisation to give substance to their proclamation of Laos' independence even as French authority was preparing to re-establish its control. The failure to attain independence accentuated the split in the ranks of exiled Laotian independence leaders, one group of which, led by Prince Souphanouvong, believed that Vietminh assistance was essential to attain national independence. Resistance to this position by other Lao Issara leaders, among them Souphanouvong's half brother, Souvanna Phouma, eventually led to Souphanouvong's expulsion from the Lao Issara in May 1949. As the Lao Issara shortly thereafter made its peace with the re-established French colonial authority in Laos, Souphanouvong sought closer ties with the Vietnamese Communists. On 13 August 1950, while visiting Ho Chi Minh at his mountain redoubt of Tuyen Quang in North Vietnam, Souphanouvong proclaimed the Pathet Lao ('State of Laos') with Souphanouvong himself as premier.[107]

At once a rival 'government', competing with the then still French-protected Laotian monarchy, as well as a revolutionary movement in its own right, the Pathet Lao developed a number of 'action front' organisations, such as the *Neo Lao Issara* (Free Lao Front), founded in November 1950, which eventually crystallised in the earlier-mentioned Lao Patriotic Front (*Neo Lao Hak Sat* – NLHS). The NLHS held its first National Congress in January 1956. With the PPL as its deeply covert mentor, the NLHS sought to give the impression of being a broad-based 'progressive' nationalist movement, acting at the same time as an 'open' political party, a mass organisation with its own propaganda and agitational machinery and as the *de facto* administrative arm of the Pathet Lao 'counter-government' in those areas of Laos – Khang Khay and Samneua, for example – under its control. Vietnamese-assisted armed Neo Lao Issara and NLHS units had intermittently battled Royal Laotian Government forces, but it was not until 1965 that the NLHS formally developed a 'Lao People's Liberation Army', whose operations were principally directed (apart from North Vietnamese advisers in the field) by a central agency near Hanoi, usually known as 'Group 959'.[108]

Its combined political-military role, and DRV 'rear base', to all intents and purposes, made the PPL-NLHS an unbeatable force on the fluid Laotian political scene. Alternately participating in or openly opposing the Vientiane regime, sometimes joining in a dubious coalition with anti-Communists and 'neutralists' (as, for instance, in June 1962) because of the advantages to be had from an internationally agreed to 'neutrality' of Laos and then again militarily clashing with the Laotian royal government – amidst all these changes there was never any question of the ultimate objective of the PPL-NLHS 'Liberation Army' complex. In the hazy confusion of undefined spheres of political authority in Laos, the Hanoi-dominated small PPL (whose total membership in 1972 was said to be only around 4 000) manipulated NLHS and Lao People's Liberation forces according to a carefully calculated strategy. This strategy demanded that the struggle in Laos be kept within such bounds as to avoid a provocation that would force big power, particularly US, intervention. The strategy also required keeping the illusion alive of the possibility of yet another more permanent coalition, of Communists and their opponents in Laos, predicated on an internationally recognised Austrian style 'neutrality'. Such neutrality was also deemed desirable by Communist strategists in order to protect the DRV on its western flank and in order to facilitate the transit of necessary logistical support to the Viet Cong, as well as at the same time prevent US intervention. Thus there was created for Laos the image of a small country in which public authority was officially fragmented and practically stalemated between Communist, non-Communist and 'neutralist' forces, an image that seemed to be no threat and in any case of little significance compared to the struggle in

Vietnam itself. This impression both Hanoi and the Laotian Communists sought to maintain until North Vietnam's victory was complete by the middle of 1975.

As early as 1972 in the context of the Vietnamese peace discussions
in Paris, the royal Lao government of Souvanna Phouma and the
Pathet Lao had begun discussions to end the perennial fighting. The
January 1973 Paris agreements provided (article 20) that the
sovereignty and territorial integrity of Laos, already affirmed by the
1962 international conference on Laos held in Geneva, would be
'strictly' respected, along with Laotian 'neutrality'. Thus Laos' political image was reaffirmed. Yet hard on the heels of the 1973 Paris
agreement the major political factions, including the Pathet Lao,
struck a new political accord in Vientiane (21 February 1973) that, in
effect, gave the Communists full opportunity to pursue their aims
politically as well as militarily. The veteran Laotian Communist
Kaysone Phomvihan, today secretary general of the 'People's Revolutionary Party of Laos' (the renamed PPL), was subsequently to
declare that the Vientiane agreements marked 'the last stage' in Laos'
revolutionary struggle. But Kaysone Phomvihan, mindful that Vietnam remained the principal theatre of conflict, declared that it was
not until 'the final struggle of the army and peoples of South Vietnam'
and of Cambodia's 'liberation war' that 'adequate objective and
subjective conditions for a general armed rising' were deemed to exist
in Laos, and hence the PPL could take 'the necessary measures'.[109] As
a Soviet commentator was to put it: 'The victory of the Vietnamese
people and the total collapse of imperialism's policy in Indochina
made further democratic development [in Laos] possible.'[110]

The 'Provisional Government of National Unity', the product of
the 1972 Souvanna Phouma-Pathet Lao peace talks, and the last
manifestation of the illusion of a political standoff in Laos between
Communist and non-Communist forces disintegrated. On 2 December 1975, the 'Lao People's Democratic Republic' was proclaimed
in Vientiane by a new 'National Congress of Delegates of the People'.
The same Congress also appointed Souphanouvong president of the
new republic, as well as naming a Council of Ministers, with Kaysone
Phomvihan as premier. Also established was a forty-five-member
'Supreme People's Council', whose 'Standing Committee' (also
headed by Souphanouvong) is the principal, day-to-day legislative
body. Months before the 'Lao People's Democratic Republic' was
proclaimed, however, there had begun an exodus of thousands of

refugees – eventually totalling at least some 200 000 (out of a total population of about three million) comprising, as one commentator has put it, the best trained and élite elements in 'government, culture and finance', as well as 'little people'.[111] Moreover, more than 37 000 were herded into some thirty-five camps, where reportedly conditions have been such as to produce a very high death rate.[112]

Though in the early months of 1976 the fiction was kept alive of a government coalition of Communists and non-Communists, by the end of that year little substance remained of the coalition concept, and a number of 'neutralist' and leftist sympathisers had also disappeared into the camps for 're-education'. Meanwhile, Hanoi's influence, both on the 'People's Revolutionary Party of Laos' and on the new Lao government, has continued to be decisive: it is difficult to think of any significant Laotian policy position since 'liberation' that does not bear a Vietnamese imprint. At least 10 000 Vietnamese troops remain on Laotian soil. However, rumours of plots against Kaysone Phomvihan and other prominent party figures circulated widely throughout 1976–7. And in the Xieng Khouang region north-east of Vientiane, intermittent resistance, particularly by Meo tribesmen, against the Laotian Communist regime and its Vietnamese allies has also continued.[113]

Compared to Laos, Vietnamese influences, though significant, have been relatively weaker in Cambodia. Some Cambodian Communists formed an informal section of the Vietnamese Indochinese Communist Party during the nineteen thirties. Toward the close of the Japanese Occupation a 'Free Cambodia' (*Khmer Issarak*) movement developed, in which both Vietnamese and Cambodian Communists, as well as non-Communist Cambodians, participated. Indeed, in March 1945, the Japanese encouraged Khmer Issarak leader Son Ngoc Thanh, a Cambodian of Vietnamese ancestry, to proclaim an independent republic, as a counter-government to the regime backed by returning French authority. As fighting between French and Vietminh intensified in Vietnam, Communists in the Khmer Issarak with Vietminh assistance (and close Vietminh supervision!) organised their own party. This organisation, the 'Revolutionary Khmer People's Party', was formally established in 1951. A resistance movement sparked by the party was led by Son Ngoc Thanh, who, at this time, maintained close contact with the Vietminh leadership. However, Son Ngoc Thanh was not a Communist, and today Cambodian Communists do not regard the Revolutionary

Khmer People's Party as the beginning of their organisation. According to party history today, the 'Communist Party of Kampuchea' or CPK was founded in secrecy and under 'great difficulties' in Phnom Penh at a 'national congress' on 28 September 1960. (It is said that the CPK congress, in fact, was held in a room at the Phnom Penh railway station.) In 1955, however, the Revolutionary Khmer People's Party had also been responsible for the formation of a new front, the 'People's Party' (*Pracheachon*), because the Revolutionary Khmer People's Party had obviously become a wholly Vietminh-dominated organisation. The 'People's Party', however, soon acquired the same Vietnamese aura as its predecessor, and the secrecy surrounding the birth and activities of the CPK may have been due to concern on the part of Cambodian Communists that their movement would remain but an appendage of the Vietminh. There eventually appears to have been little love lost between Son Ngoc Thanh's followers and the Vietminh, not least because of Cambodian resentment of Vietnamese attempts to dominate the Khmer Issarak and Cambodian Communist movement. Their marriage was one of convenience. Shortly Thanh's attempts for the second time to seize power failed, primarily because of the skilful combination of military and political tactics and the appeal of the remarkable blend of populist nationalism and Khmer royal traditionalism developed by Cambodia's ruler, Norodom Sihanouk. It was under Sihanouk that independence was won from the French in November 1953. By developing his own political party, the 'People's Socialist Community' (*Sangkum Reastr Niyum*, commonly called the Sangkum), committed to a 'true socialist and egalitarian democracy', as well as to Khmer patriotic and cultural values, Sihanouk eventually was able even to draw leading leftist nationalists in the Khmer Issarak remnant to his side, overwhelmingly defeating Son Ngoc Thanh's Democratic Party and the Communist opposition in a general election in September 1955.[114]

Initially able – often with remarkable dexterity – to balance variously conflicting Soviet, Chinese, US and Vietnamese interests, Sihanouk developed a significant personal power base through the Sangkum and its youth group, the 'Royal Khmer Socialist Youth', despite frequent changes in the cabinet, claims of anti-government plots and the threats of armed revolts, and the diplomatic rupture of relations with South Vietnam and the US. By the middle sixties, however, Sihanouk's accommodating posture toward the Vietnamese Communists (the National Liberation Front of South Vietnam was recognised in 1967) only seemed to have led to a more and more blatant use of Cambodian territory by Hanoi and the Viet Cong, in violation of the 1954 Geneva accords, in which the Vietminh had agreed to withdraw from Cambodian soil. The Sangkum leadership became increasingly split between leftist and rightist factions. Although an armed rising in April 1967 in Batambang province, led by Sangkum leftists (among them Khieu Sampan, who was to surface nine years later as chairman of the State Presidium of the new Communist government of Democratic Cambodia), was eventually contained, by the early months of 1968, a Communist guerrilla insurgency by what Sihanouk and then everyone was commonly calling the 'Khmer Viet Minh' and later the 'Khmer Rouge' (Red Khmer) was rapidly spreading in other areas.

Leftist Sangkum politicians and young intellectuals, veterans of the Khmer Issarak and of the 'Revolutionary Khmer People's Party' and cadres of the 'Communist Party of Kampuchea' were making common cause with each other, and in the process receiving assistance from the Viet Cong in South Vietnam and from the DRV. Though increasingly singling out the Khmer Rouge in his verbal attacks, Sihanouk, in the course of 1967–9, typically tried to be evenhanded in his denunciations of various opposition groups. Thus he also attacked what he called the 'pro-US-Khmers', presumably a reference to the so-called Khmer Serei guerrillas whose organisation, led by Sihanouk's old rival Son Ngoc Thanh, was being supported by pro-Western circles in Bangkok and Saigon. But Khmer Serei depredations were relative pinpricks, according to Sihanouk, who claimed that treasonous Khmer Rouge and their 'Red Viet Minh Vietnamese masters' had come 'to enslave our Battambang Province for many a long year', and that 'in the Ratanakiri region the Vietcong and Vietminh have occupied one third of the province'.[115] During 1967 and 1968, it also became apparent that, possibly inspired by the 'Cultural Revolution' in China, Chinese merchants in Phnom Penh, via Chinese merchant vessels calling at Sihanoukville harbour, were supplying the Khmer Rouge, both those that were operating independently, as well as those teamed with the Viet Cong in Cambodia; the Chinese embassy in Phnom Penh, according to Sihanouk, appeared to be engaged as well in stirring up 'Maoist Cambodians'.[116]

But domestic Cambodian problems also provided a fertile ground for the proselytising efforts of the Khmer Rouge and their Vietnamese allies. Periodic food shortages sharpened the widespread criticism of the floundering Cambodian economy. Tax gouging of the peasantry, and harsh repression by Sihanouk's government of the resulting peasant revolt, was a major factor in the 1967 Batambang rising, and had been easily exploited by the Khmer Rouge. Tribal groups throughout South-east Asia have historically been at odds with their central governments. Laotian hill people from the Halang and Jarai tribes, roaming in north-eastern Cambodia's Ratanakiri province, were no exception, and Vietnamese Communists actively recruited among them. Some 1 200 of these tribal folk, collectively referred to as Khmer Loeu, functioned as *de facto* auxiliaries of the Khmer Rouge and Viet Cong.[117]

During 1970, at a time when the Khmer Rouge numbered perhaps 3 000, their ranks were significantly augmented by some 1 500 to 2 000 men who, as young boys in 1954, at the time of the Geneva agreements, had been taken to North Vietnam (Hanoi's explanation at the time was that they were orphans of Vietminh guerrilla fighters) and who now were returning to Cambodia as highly trained Communist organisers.[118] Meanwhile, other young Cambodians were undergoing training in Hanoi. By this time, however, the Sihanouk era had ended and Cambodia, like Laos well before it, had become irreversibly another theatre of the Vietnam war. Sihanouk's threats and entreaties to Hanoi had produced no diminution of the North Vietnamese and Viet Cong military presence in Cambodia (numbering some 42 000 troops by early 1970), nor a halt to Khmer Rouge hostilities, even though as late as February 1970, Lao Dong party leader Le Duan had reaffirmed that DRV policy was to respect Cambodia's sovereignty and territorial integrity.[119] In reality, as has been suggested, 'the North Vietnamese appear to have despised Sihanouk', and apparently believed that he had lost touch with the Cambodian élite, including the intellectual left, and that he would sooner or later be overthrown with an eventually resulting gain for the Communist revolutionary movement.[120]

As increasingly violent anti-Vietnamese riots erupted in various parts of Cambodia, and popular dissatisfaction with the Sihanouk regime mounted, Sihanouk himself was in France where he had gone in January 1970, ostensibly for medical reasons. On 18–19 March 1970, Cambodia's National Assembly accused the still absent Sihanouk of dictatorship, corruption and supplying the Viet Cong and deposed him as head of state, granting emergency powers to prime minister Lon Nol.[121] On 9 October 1970, after expressions of popular support from various factions and former dissidents during the preceding months, a new Khmer Republic was proclaimed, officially ending the centuries-long monarchy. But soon further leadership squabbles and disputes with the National Assembly weakened the new regime even as Lon Nol, in March 1972, declared himself both premier and president.[122] Already by December 1970, a visiting US congressional staff mission to Cambodia reported Phnom Penh to have become practically isolated from the rest of the country, as all but one of the major roads out of the capital had been interdicted by Viet Cong and North Vietnamese forces; northern and north-eastern parts of the country were said to be under North Vietnamese, Khmer Rouge or Viet Cong control.[123] Steady Communist pressure on the Lon Nol government was being maintained, as the DRV even brought in units from its divisions stationed in Laos.[124]

The deposed Sihanouk meanwhile still clung to power, now turning to the Communists for aid. As early as June 1965, Sihanouk had predicted that in the event of a Communist victory in Cambodia, 'I myself and the Sangkum that I have created would inevitably disappear from the scene.' And shortly before his overthrow, he warned that a united Vietnam would mean that Cambodia would be reduced along with Laos to mere 'Asian Czechoslovakias'.[125] But from Beijing, where he had found sanctuary, Sihanouk now announced the formation of a new united 'national liberation' front and army in which the Khmer Rouge were partners. For the Khmer Rouge, Sihanouk's Beijing-backed front probably was perceived as a way of balancing the heavy Vietnamese influence in the Cambodian Communist movement. On 5 May 1970, the *Front Uni National de Kampuchea* (FUNK) was proclaimed in Beijing. The Front's programme had something for everybody and used the kind of left-progressive nationalist terminology, free from formal Marxist jargon, appropriate to Communist tactics of national liberation evident elsewhere in Asia. It spoke of uniting all Cambodians against the 'American imperialists', of the overthrow of the Lon Nol 'dictatorship', and of the creation of a 'Neutral, Democratic and Prosperous Cambodia'. The latter would give political freedoms to Cambodians (freedom of the press, speech, opinion, association, residence, and elections, and the safeguarding of the 'inviolability' of persons and property), as well as guarantee the rights of landownership to peasants, encourage trade unions, help the 'national bourgeoisie', and meet the interests of school and university students. As to foreign policy, the FUNK promised to 'make con-

certed efforts', together with Laos and Vietnam, to make 'Indo-
China' into a genuine zone of 'independence, peace and progress'.
FUNK also expressed full support for the 'independence and freedom
struggles' of the 'peoples of Asia, Africa and Latin America'.[126]

Along with FUNK a 'Royal Government of National Union of
Cambodia' (*Gouvernement Royal d'Union Nationale de Kampuchea* –
GRUNK) was proclaimed, and Sihanouk was described both as
Cambodia's head of state and as chairman of FUNK. But such a
prominent CPK figure as Khieu Sampan (who would emerge in 1976
as State Presidium chairman, that is, president of the Communist
state of 'Democratic Kampuchea') was GRUNK's national defence
minister, and it was perhaps particularly noteworthy that GRUNK
spokesmen felt free to criticise the USSR for pursuing its 'own
interests' behind 'the backs' of the 'Indochinese peoples'.[127] To what
extent Khieu Sampan and other members of the so-called *Angka Leou*
('Organisation on High'), the rumoured leadership of the still deeply
covert CPK, were using both Sihanouk and FUNK, with Beijing's
encouragement, can only be surmised. As Lon Nol's regime, all but
confined to an increasingly isolated Phnom Penh, sank deeper into
bureaucratic inefficiency and corruption it became apparent that the
final Communist takeover was but a matter of time, despite outside
military efforts to save it, such as the US-South Vietnamese 'surgical'
incursion into Cambodia in April 1970. The provision in the January
1973 Paris peace agreement that the neutrality of Cambodia would be
respected, and that foreign powers would withdraw their forces from
Cambodian territory, had as little practical significance as the identi-
cal provision in the Paris agreement with respect to Laos. On 17 April
1975, only two weeks before the North Vietnamese secured their hold
on Saigon, and after Lon Nol had flown into exile, Khmer Rouge
forces seized Phnom Penh.

However, within months the long smouldering resentment of
Cambodian Communists over the historic attempts of the Vietnamese to dominate their movement and over their continuing military
presence on Cambodian soil, had erupted in bloody Cambodian-
North Vietnamese clashes over control of disputed border areas in
Cambodia's north-eastern provinces and small strategic islands in
the Gulf of Siam. The tension continued with little abatement over the
next months as both the new Cambodian regime and the SRV
government accused each other of border violations and committing
atrocities. Meanwhile the Angka Leou emerged from the shadows,

although it was not until 27 September 1977 that CPK secretary
general Pol Pot, at a 'mass meeting' in Phnom Penh celebrating the
party's seventeenth anniversary, announced that the CPK had 'decided to proclaim openly and officially the existence of the Cambodian Communist Party to both the national and international
public'.[128] No explanation was given as to why the party had not
publicly proclaimed its existence before.

By the time Pol Pot made this announcement, however, the new
government of 'Democratic Kampuchea' had been organised, with
Pol Pot himself as prime minister, and with a 250-member People's
Representative Assembly reportedly elected on 20 March 1976.
International controversy soon engulfed the new regime as numerous
refugees from Cambodia (totalling some 15 000 in Thailand, and
about 60 000 in Vietnam by the end of 1977) reported on the extensive
horrors of the forced migration of tens of thousands of urban inhabitants driven at gunpoint into the countryside in order to perform
agricultural and construction work, on the toll in human lives exacted
by executions and purges, and by malaria, exhaustion and inadequate medical services, and on the depredations of undisciplined
youthful liberation army soldiers.[129] 'Democratic Kampuchea's' determination to impose ruthlessly a new, severe, national morality of
public service, and to stamp out all vestiges of the old regime ('most
dreaded' in Cambodia was, reportedly, to be charged by the new
regime's minions with being 'old dandruff'),[130] seemed to render
Sihanouk as superfluous as FUNK and its promises of political
freedoms and economic betterment.

The degree to which the Angka Leou was motivated by a desire to
push back Cambodia's national frontiers with Thailand and the
SRV, so as to restore perhaps something of the territory of the old
Khmer empire, is a matter of speculation, but by the middle of 1976
Cambodia appeared embroiled in continuous border conflicts with all
her neighbours. The pattern of frontier clashes reached something of
a culmination in December 1977 when SRV forces, in response to
allegedly repeated Cambodian encroachments, began moving in
force into Cambodia's Suay Rieng and Kam Pot provinces. Phnom
Penh subsequently accused the 'annexationist Vietnamese' with
attempting to 'force Cambodia into an Indochinese federation' under
Hanoi's control, while Vietnamese media charged that 'Democratic
Cambodia has continuously violated our country's sovereignty and
territorial integrity since 1975'.[131] Whether the Angka Leou was fully

in command of its own limited manpower and state apparatus became increasingly a question when, despite efforts by Thai and Cambodian diplomats to improve relations between their two countries, new Cambodian raids into Thai border territory were reported late in January 1978.[132]

People's China, which since 1975 had supplied the Pol Pot-Khieu Sampan regime with foodstuffs and arms, and which could not but have been pleased at the disdainful Communist Cambodian attitude toward Soviet diplomats in Phnom Penh, had by early January 1978 evidently become somewhat embarrassed by its Cambodian protégé. This embarrassment, however, assumed new policy dimensions when Vietnamese forces invading Cambodia, after having captured Phnom Penh from the fleeing Pol Pot regime, proclaimed a new 'Kampuchean People's Revolutionary Council Government' on 8 January 1979. On 16 February 1979 People's Chinese forces invaded the SRV for the purpose of administering a 'lesson' to Hanoi. Although the Chinese withdrew after about four weeks' occupation of the northern Vietnamese border zone, SRV forces remained in Cambodia, where Pol Pot's government continued to put up a decreasingly effective guerrilla resistance. By the beginning of 1979 it appeared that Hanoi, through a network of 'friendship' treaties and agreements with and between allied regimes in Laos and Cambodia had, in *de facto* fashion, achieved an Indochinese federation, with far-reaching implications for the balance of power in the South-east Asian region.

C.   A summing up: some characteristics of the Communist evolution

While putting in the foreground the danger of generalising about any feature in the experience of the nine nations that today constitute what is commonly called 'South-east Asia', one might nevertheless suggest what seem to be some common aspects of the historical development of the Communist movement in the region.

If by Communism is meant the Marxist-Leninist ideology and its organisational correlates, then one should note first of all that the introduction of Communism into the individual South-east Asian countries was heavily dependent on foreigners, that is, non-native inhabitants either of a particular country of South-east Asia or indeed of the region as a whole. This stands in relative contrast to the growth of non-Communist nationalist organisations or movements in the area, which historically preceded them. Thus, the impulse to the development of the oldest Communist party in South-east Asia, the one in Indonesia, came from Dutch Marxists in the colonial Netherlands East Indies service, while US Communists, active in the China-based Secretariat of the Comintern's Pan Pacific Trade Union, gave significant impetus to the development of Philippine Communism, and Philippine Communism's merger in 1938 with the Socialist Party of the Philippines. It was at the behest of the Moscow-based Comintern that Communist parties in South-east Asia were made or unmade, or changed their policies. The establishment of the Communist Party of Malaya in April 1930, and the concomitant dissolution of the 'South Seas Communist Party', as well as the formation of the Vietnam Communist Party (later the Indochinese Communist Party) in February 1930, and the corollary merger with it of three smaller Vietnamese Communist parties, all occurred by direction of the Comintern.

Anti-Fascist united front building, clearly in obedience to the 1935 Seventh Comintern Congress policy, varied from the formation in December 1941 of the 'Overseas Chinese anti-Japanese National Salvation Army' in Malaya, to Ho Chi Minh's organisation in May 1941 of the Vietminh. It is apparent that implementation of the Comintern's anti-Fascist united front policy did not proceed without some resistance on the part of prominent South-east Asian Communists – for instance, Ho Chi Minh, Crisanto Evangelista and some of the leaders of the PKP. Compliance with Comintern objectives often meant a sharp break with previous party tactics and a number of important Communist figures in the South-east Asian area – like Tan Malaka, for example – eventually lost their readiness to comply with every zig and zag in Moscow's policies.

In some South-east Asian countries, the origin of the local Communist party lay in the work of non-native Asian inhabitants. Communism in Thailand, for example, began when agents of the Communist Party of China were sent to recruit among Thailand's Chinese minority during the nineteen twenties. Moreover, a distinctive 'Chinese Communist Party of Thailand' continued to function late into the nineteen forties, and probably even later, side by side with the regular Communist Party of Thailand. In the latter, Thai Chinese also were prominent. During the Japanese Occupation period of the Philippines in World War II, it will be recalled, Communist-oriented Chinese Filipinos, augmented by supporters from the Chinese mainland, preferred to operate in their own 'Wachi' unit of the Hukbalahap guerrilla resistance organisation. Then there is the matter of strong Vietnamese influence in, if not control over, most of the historic development of the Communist movement in Laos and Cambodia. This Vietnamese dominance, certainly in the case of the Cambodian Communists tolerated without much enthusiasm, may well have been a factor in shaping the structure of the Communist movement in Laos and Cambodia, for example in terms of the extreme secrecy of operations of the PPL and the CPK. The widening armed clashes between Cambodians and Vietnamese since the consolidation of the Communist regimes in both their countries cannot be divorced from this Vietnamese dominance of Cambodian Communism and the resentment it created.

The initially important role of Chinese agents, both of the Comintern and of the Chinese Communist Party, in the development of Communism in Malaya and Singapore was to be sure since the early thirties balanced, if not overshadowed, by the rise of younger, Chinese Malayans who were far more oriented toward the national political future of the Peninsula than the early organisers and leaders of the 'South Seas Communist Party'. Yet in Thailand, no less than in Malaya, the Chinese aspect of local Communism inevitably has been drawn into the sensitive and complex area of inter-racial or inter-ethnic relations within these countries. In the process, stereotypes and cat gories of political discourse and thought tended to emerge or to be accentuated which local Communist organisations would find difficult to overcome. Thus, opposition to Communism among ethnic Malays in Malaya who are generally Muslims has not just stemmed, for example, from the Comintern's early ambiguities toward the Islamic reveil in the Middle East and South Asia in general, and pan-Islamic movements in particular, or from reports on the problems of Muslim groups in the USSR today. Rather, this opposition is also rooted in the circumstance that for many years such Communists as Malays were likely to meet or hear about would almost invariably be Chinese. And, therefore, the nature of the MCP's programme and appeals could never be quite divorced for many ethnic Malays from the larger problem as to whether Malays would be economically and then politically submerged by the Chinese in their own country.

Loyalty to king and Buddhism marks the true Thai, or so the

national stereotype has it. The Chinese Thai, if Communist, tends by definition to put himself outside this hallowed ideological category, even if native born and generally quite assimilated. In recent years, the rebellious ethnic Thai student or opposition party leader confronting the Bangkok political-military establishment, may soon find himself identified with what may be viewed as alien, or in any case 'un-Thai' Chinese, or (in view of Hanoi's assistance to Thai Communist insurgents) Vietnamese, modes of thought. Probably everywhere Communists have had to face the problem of the 'foreignness' of their ideology and movement. In South-east Asia this problem has been accentuated by old and far-reaching racial and ethnic stereotypes.

Having said this, one must hasten to add that heavy foreign dependence is, however, most characteristic of the early stages of South-east Asian Communism. With the passage of years, local parties develop home-grown leaderships, seek to cultivate national constituencies, and take pride in identifying themselves in terms of national (and nationalist) objectives, as well as in terms of Marxist-Leninist ones. The success of the Indochinese Communist Party, the Vietminh, and the Lao Dong in Vietnam, or the initial appeal of José Sison's Communist Party of the Philippines (Marxist-Leninist) to students, intellectuals, and younger clergy cannot be explained without reference to deeply felt nationalist aspirations. And while critics referring to the alien origins of local Communist parties may persist in characterising them as a-national or anti-national, such descriptions do little to explain the extent to which Communist parties nevertheless have been able to become rallying points for frustrated nationalism.

Apart from this, of course, one should acknowledge a particular party's identification with nationalism and national symbols as sometimes having been dictated also by tactical necessity. Under D. N. Aidit, the Indonesian Communist Party formally identified itself not only with the official national ideology (the so-called *Pantjasila* or 'Five Pillars' of the Indonesian state: namely, belief in God, nationalism, democracy, social justice, and humanism) as all Indonesian parties and groups were and are required to do, but also with the acronym-laden semi-official political theorising of then President Sukarno. Indeed, Aidit, in his own voluminous writings, showed himself remarkably adept in harmonising his party's programme with the theories of Sukarno,[133] with whom the party for tactical reasons had to all intents and purposes developed a politically symbiotic relationship. Aidit's theoretical stock in trade was his party's 'national' orientation, its equality with, and independence from, all other Communist parties in the world arena (with due expressions of respect, to be sure, for the historic 'vanguard' role of the USSR, and for the 'inspiration' afforded by Mao's China), and therefore its right to be one of the legitimate institutions of the Indonesian nation state.

There is little question that Communist parties in South-east Asia had their most successful periods, in the sense of being politically most influential, or having their largest following, or, again, being able to seize and maintain government power, when, rightly or wrongly, their nationalist purpose or character was most widely perceived and accepted. It is for this reason, for example, that the MPAJA period during the Japanese Occupation of Malaya in World War II was the highpoint in Malayan Communism, a highpoint which it has thus far not been able to exceed. It is also why the Communist Party of Thailand (CPT) today appears to be entering the era of its greatest growth. Not just the significant Vietnamese and Laotian assistance in training of cadres and supply of weapons to the CPT is the cause of this growth, although it is a significant factor. Rather it is the circumstance that growing numbers of young, educated Thai have been swept up in what might be called a subculture of protest that makes heavy use of unassuaged nationalist sentiments. Angered by the apparent inability of various Thai regimes in the past five years to assert the nation's independence from post-Vietnam US security strategy in Asia, or to undertake desired reforms in and modernisation of the national economy and its corruption-ridden political-military correlates, Thai students and youths, after each bloody demonstration or clash with Bangkok police and troops, have flocked to the burgeoning ranks of the Thai Communist guerrillas or underground. The students' stay with the Communists may not be long, and conciliatory government policies are enticing many of the would-be guerrillas to return to their families. The point is, however, that the CPT continues to be perceived as the only realistic opposition movement and political alternative in a coup-ridden political environment in which, moreover, prevailing élites are viewed as mere appendages of the security and/or business interests of foreign powers.

But an effective nationalist appeal is not enough. The Communist record in South-east Asia in articulating policy positions other than in the nationalist category has been less successful, sometimes not just because of the issue but also because of organisational weakness. Comintern hostility in the early twenties to 'bourgeois' pan-Islamism was needlessly doctrinaire and abrasive, alienating, especially in Malaya and Indonesia, potential allies in the highly important Muslim modernist intellectual, trade union and small business circles. Though in the later nineteen fifties the CPM as well as the PKI secured much publicised support from a few Muslim intellectuals and even kiajihs (Muslim religious scholars), party front-building efforts in terms of outreach to middle class and entrepreneurial interests continued to be circumscribed (though not by any means wholly a failure) because of Islamic hostility, no matter how often Indonesian party chairman D. N. Aidit proclaimed that the PKI was not 'anti-religious', that it favoured 'belief in God' (as called for by Indonesia's official national ideology, the previously named Pantjasila), and so on.

On the other hand, categorical programme demands for improvements in, and, generally, concern with, the living and working conditions of the developing industrial proletariat, and with the problems of rural tenants, and of the landless labour force, have long encouraged organisational support for South-east Asian Communist parties, even in times of stress. In June 1948, for example, at the start of Malaya's Emergency period of conflict with the Communist insurgents, and after two years of intensive proselytising by non-Communist trade union organisers, 129 of Malaya's 302 trade unions, and 82 000 trade union members out of a total of about 150 000 were still controlled by the Communist Party of Malaya.[134] Luzon's tenancy problem during the earliest years of the PKP's existence would have provided that party with a large reservoir of potential recruits, responsive to the Communists' rent reduction and 'land to the tillers' policy, if the party had had the leadership and organisational expertise to exploit it. Between 1918 and 1938, for example, as the total Philippine population grew from ten to sixteen million, the number of owner-operated farms in the country declined from 1.52 million to 805 000, while the number of tenant-operated farms grew from 435 000 to 575 000 (exclusive of 255 000 part owners whose position was comparable to that of the tenants); by 1939, the total number of agricultural workers had grown to almost 3.5 million.[135]

And yet, even if the PKP, as, in fact, Comintern circles charged it should do,[136] had spent more time in developing a peasant following – what then? Historically, no Communist party in South-east Asia has been able to acquire significant political strength, let alone eventually seize power, on the basis of its trade union support alone or even in combination with a peasant following. Not only is mobilisation of various other, particularly middle class, strata essential as well, but also and above all the development of an effective organisational weapon. Again and again this has been South-east Asian Communism's fatal weakness. Mere party and front membership size can be misleading. By the close of 1964, the Indonesian party had a huge and varied front and interest group support complex, numbering in the millions, and ranging from students to peasants, and from industrial workers to fellow-travelling business entrepreneurs and even military, as well as various civil servants', women's, artists', veterans', and other 'functional' group supporters. But the swift, house-of-cards-like collapse of the PKI in the aftermath of the abortive 30 September 1965 coup attempt showed the front complex and the party to have been poorly co-ordinated to a fatal extent, unable to react swiftly to crisis, or to develop either significant political or armed resistance to its own post-coup decimation. Neither nationalist élan nor a range of carefully phrased programme appeals to different social classes thus can have much effect without the careful building of party and united front organisation and discipline.

Recourse to arms has sometimes been explicitly disavowed by Communist leaders in South-east Asia – for example, in the early nineteen sixties PKI chairman D. N. Aidit was wont to stress that his party was not one of 'coup-ists'. But throughout the region Communist parties have from time to time resorted to open force, as the use of both 'legal' (parliamentary) as well as 'illegal' (violent) means in achieving power is inherent in Leninism. There is no South-east Asian country whose history is without Communist violence, either in the form of brief clashes – for instance, during strikes or demonstrations, prolonged guerrilla war, or coup attempts. The Maoist principles that political power flows from the barrel of a gun, and that the revolutionary countryside must encircle and seize the cities is, today, explicitly endorsed and practised by Communist guerrilla 'liberation' forces throughout South-east Asia, from eastern Burma to the Philippines in their running clashes with government troops.

In this pattern of Communist violence, the value of the Maoist military concept of the 'protected rear base' has now been historically demonstrated. By comparison, outbursts of Communist-led violence in the thirties, and/or efforts to set up 'Soviets', for example, in Vietnam's Nghean and Hatinh provinces, or the brief 'Soviet' regime at the Batu Arang mine in Selanggor, in 1935, or attempted coups (like the ones in Indonesia in 1926–7, 1948 and 1965) obviously lacked the logistical and organisational backing needed to prevail. Apart from their radicalising effects on their participants, one can only guess as to the value that party leaders believed such violent confrontations would have. But the Communist victory in Indochina has decisively shown the tactical military value for South-east Asia of the Maoist concept of the 'protected rear base', and since the early nineteen sixties the enduring strength of the Communist insurgent movement in two other South-east Asian countries has confirmed the value of the concept also. Communist 'liberation' forces gradually growing in number today operate in North-eastern Thailand, with Vietnamese-controlled Laos and, beyond, with Vietnam itself, as their securely protected rear, whence they obtain trained cadres and weapons. Meanwhile in Burma, in the eastern half of Shan state, between the Salween River and the Burmese border with People's China, several thousand guerrillas of the 'White Flag' Burma Communist Party (BCP) are active today, led by China-trained cadres and supplied with Chinese-made weapons. The BCP guerrillas move about several hundreds of square miles of territory that is intermittently under government and BCP control. Periodic gestures of conciliation over the years between the Burmese and People's Chinese governments, as well as new anti-insurgency campaigns launched by Burmese security forces, have not altered the continuing strategic advantage afforded the BCP by their protected rear base in China's Yunan province across the border.

The Communist historical record in South-east Asia shows that the difficulty of organising a Communist revolution in areas which, unlike China, for example, had not previously first experienced a modernising, nationalist revolution, was at first, with a few exceptions like Tan Malaka, only imperfectly understood among the movement's regional leaders. A major reason perhaps is that the first generation of South-east Asian Communist leaders so often had come to their convictions in a hothouse intellectual atmosphere of future élite aspirations, uncontaminated by much, if any, organisational or work experience of some duration. Nor were these young Thakins, so impatient to seize the levers of government, in the main, the sons of workers and peasants. Ho Chi Minh's antecedents lie in the Confucian traditions of Annamese families of scholars and officials. Such early proletarian experiences as Ho had (for example, his 1907 journey from Saigon as a fifteen-year-old galley boy aboard a French ship and later as cook's assistant in London) in a long and eventful life were generally brief and far less decisive for his outlook than his experiences as a journalist and his rapid rise and popularity in the ranks of the Socialist Party in France. Darsono and Semaun, the earliest leaders of the PKI, came from the lower Javanese nobility, Tan Malaka's father was a village chief of the Menangkabau, in west Sumatra, D. N. Aidit's father a forestry official in the Dutch colonial service. Compared to fellow Indonesians of their day, all had above average schooling. Tan Malaka studied in Holland. Than Tun was the son of a timber merchant and landowner and, though later on, sometimes poor, he like most other early Burmese Communists and nationalists was a product of Rangoon University.[137] Perhaps Crisanto Evangelista, the first secretary general of the Philippine Communist Party, by virtue of his trade as a printer, could make genuine pretensions to proletarian status. Until one remembers that historically the printing trade in the Philippines was closely linked to nationalist intellectual circles: prominent Philippine writers and reformers were their own printers.[138] Then there is the unique case of the Philippine party's fraternal triumvirate, that of the three Lava brothers, scions of an old family of landowning gentry and merchants, educated as physicians, and all destined to hold such leading posts as PKP secretary general or Politburo member.

The reason for raising the question of family antecedents is that, from a Marxist-Leninist point of view, social class and family background have always been important indices of leadership reliability. Moreover, once established, Communist parties in South-east Asia would take class background into account as they considered applicants for party membership. Thus, according to the 1962 version of the constitution of the Indonesian Communist Party (similar clauses appear in the constitutional versions of the nineteen fifties), 'workers, agricultural workers, poor peasants or urban poor people' could become members of the party on recommendation of two party members and, after having been a 'candidate' member for at least six months. (Local party branch and section committee approval, of course, was also needed.) 'Intellectuals', however, or professionals, or 'middle peasants', who wished to become PKI party members had to meet more difficult requirements. Their period of candidacy was at least one year, and the party members who recommended them had to have been party members themselves for at least one year without interruption. Applicants whose 'social position' was even higher than the preceding confronted a two-year candidacy period, and the two party members who recommended them had to have been party members themselves for at least three years continuously.[139]

Even though after this establishment the parties' proletarian and peasant ranks grew, as party proselytisers and programmes deliberately reached out to these social strata, the historically uneven expansion of Communism in South-east Asia, and the different levels and rate of industrial development in the countries of the region, have not made the growth of the movement's proletarian and peasant base a uniform process. As early as the nineteen twenties, industrial trade unionism was providing a significant source of supporters for Communist recruiters in Indonesia, Malaysia, Singapore, and the Philippines. However, such a source was much smaller elsewhere in the area, for instance, in Burma, at the time. And, when one considers the antecedents of those leaders of the late-blooming Cambodian Communist movement who today direct the affairs of 'Democratic Kampuchea', one has a sense of *déjà vu*, as if the era of the twenties is coming to life again. The fifty-year-old Pol Pot (real name: Saloth Sar), the new Communist Cambodian state's premier, and concurrently secretary general of the mystery-shrouded Communist Party of Kampuchea (CPK), comes from a family of officials and well-to-do landowners of Kompong Thom province in Cambodia. He graduated from Phnom Penh's technical secondary school and thence was able to go to Paris, at the age of twenty-one, to study at the prestigious Ecole Française de Radio-Electricité. In Paris, Pol Pot was to meet such future CPK colleagues as Ieng Sary (now deputy prime minister for foreign affairs of 'Democratic Kampuchea'), who had been born of middle class Cambodian parents in South Vietnam's Vinh Binh province, and who later studied at the Lycée Sisowath in Phnom Penh before going on to Paris in 1950 to attend the Institut d'Etudes Politiques. In Paris, Ieng Sary, Pol Pot and other Cambodian students fell into a pattern which already a generation ago had characterised South-east Asia's future nationalist and Communist leaders, when as students from the colonial areas they had come to study in the metropolitan country: they founded or joined political study clubs (in the case of Pol Pot and Ieng Sary these were pro-Vietminh, Marxist-oriented clubs).[140]

Tan Malaka, José Lava and Pol Pot all exemplify the Leninist concept, of which Lenin himself, in view of his own family background in the Tsarist Russian middle class, was the prototype: that is, that membership in the Communist 'vanguard' depends less on social antecedents and more on ideological commitment. Education, formal or informal, usually obtained at some secondary, and often at a tertiary level, but also in the student bistros in a South-east Asian capital or in Amsterdam, Paris or London – this, not class, family background, or working experience, has been the original matrix of later Communist loyalties for many party adherents and guerrilla fighters in South-east Asia.

The development of post-World War II guerrilla Communism in Sarawak, for example, structured in recent decades by such organisations as the Sarawak 'Advanced Youths Association' and by the insurgents of the 'North Kalimantan Communist Party', cannot be separated from the educational atmosphere of the private Chinese schools in the state. Attended by Sarawak-born Chinese youths from predominantly merchant, planter and white collar worker families, these schools primarily, despite progressively more strict government supervision over their curricula, have been, as one official analysis has put it, 'soft targets' for the Sarawak Communist organisation 'in which to spread their ideology'.[141] This ideology, conveyed by the teachers in these Chinese schools, was a mixture of wounded Chinese ethnic and cultural pride and Marxist and Maoist political tenets, accentuated further by Sarawak's and indeed by Malaysia's racial problems.[142]

In Sarawak, the guerrilla rank and file over the years has consisted of several hundred (at the moment less than two hundred) young Chinese men and women, usually from middle class families, all products of Chinese schools and politically recruited while still in their middle or late teens. In many ways they are comparable to the Manila students and young intellectuals who in 1969 flocked to José Sison's new Maoist Communist Party of the Philippines (Marxist-Leninist), in order to form much of the cadre core of Sison's 'New People's Army', or to the Bangkok students who since the early seventies have joined the insurgents of the Communist Party of Thailand. Young students, rather than peasants or tenants, industrial workers or disgruntled entrepreneurs, independent professionals or civil servants, in the last decade or so have provided most of such vitality as South-east Asian Communist movements outside Indochina continue to demonstrate. Ironically, other students, at the same time, have been in the forefront of anti-Communist activity.

To the contemporary political environment in the South-east Asian region in which these Communist movements must operate, to the obstacles which some parts of that environment pose today to their possible expansion, as well as to the new responsibilities facing Communism in Indochina as a result of its triumph there, we now turn our attention.

2

The contemporary political environment

A. The non-Communist countries

Communism, as doctrine and programme of political action, polarises South-east Asia today. In the larger part of the region, Communist parties are either banned and/or government forces carry on running small-scale clashes with local Communist insurgents. In the Indochinese states, however, Communist governments now prevail, although, particularly in Laos and in the Socialist Republic of Vietnam (SRV), guerrilla dissidents of various political persuasions also battle government security forces. The uneasy relationship between the Communist and non-Communist segments of South-east Asia has been further complicated since 1973 by the border clashes and political conflict between Kampuchea (the Democratic Republic of Cambodia) and the SRV resulting in a rival 'People's Republic of Kampuchea', backed by Hanoi, being installed in Phnom Penh in January 1979.

With the exception of Burma (where the Burma Socialist Programme Party or BSPP is the only nationally recognised political party), all the countries of the non-Communist segment of South-east Asia have formal multi-party systems, functioning in competitive general elections. Sometimes the parties involved are few. For example, in Indonesia only three parties participated in the May 1977 parliamentary elections. Sometimes there are many: in Thailand forty-two political groups took part in the January 1975 general elections. In the Philippines the suspension of partisan political

70

activity following the September 1972 martial law declaration by
President Ferdinand Marcos was modified in connection with the
April 1978 elections for a new interim national legislature (*Batasang
Pambansa*). In consequence, the pro-Marcos party, called the 'Movement for a New Society' (*Kilusan Bagong Lipunan* or KBL), soon found
itself confronted at the polls by the opposition 'People's Force' (*Laka
ng Bayan*) and by other opposition candidates, including some with
ties to the old and presently dormant Liberal Party in the Philippines.

Communist parties in the non-Communist area of South-east Asia
are barred from all such partisan parliamentary processes and cannot
participate in elections, except perhaps through front organisations.
Allegations that an opposition party is in fact a Communist front have
been heard relatively rarely in the region in recent years, however.
The reason is that determination by the government that an organisation is, in fact, a Communist front will tend automatically to mandate
its demise considering prevailing security regulations. There are
exceptions. In the first few months and years after the founding (26
July 1961) of the 'Socialist Front' (*Barisan Sosialis*) in Singapore,
spokesmen of the ruling People's Action Party (PAP) like premier Lee
Kuan Yew were wont to characterise the Barisan as a front and as
having been infiltrated by the Communist Party of Malaya.[1] Such
allegations, despite periodic arrests of prominent Barisan personages
over the years, Barisan spokesmen have repeatedly denied. More
recently the PAP during Singapore's parliamentary elections has
focused on the alleged underground CPM threat without referring to
a front organisational vehicle. Thus, in the PAP's successful parliamentary elections campaign in December 1976, for example, Singapore's foreign minister, S. Rajaratnam, a PAP mainstay, asserted
that the 'real opposition' in Singapore was the banned CPM 'which
the PAP has been fighting without stop for years' and which, he said
without further elaboration, 'nearly entered this election but did
not'.[2]

Denial of political existence and activity to Communists is part of a
pattern of both formal and informal (that is, assumed and judicially
untested) legal controls by the government executive that varies from
country to country in the region. A few examples must suffice. In
Indonesia, on 12 March 1966, General Suharto, acting on behalf of
the then still President Sukarno, formally declared dissolved and
banned the Indonesian Communist Party (PKI). On 31 March 1966,
Suharto ordered all Indonesian government departments 'imme-

diately to intensify' the 'cleansing of personnel from elements of the
PKI'.[3] Suharto acted on the basis of powers conferred on him by
President Sukarno on 11 March 1966, which mandated Suharto to
'take all steps' necessary to guarantee domestic security and tranquillity. (Sukarno, widely suspected of having had foreknowledge of the
30 September 1965 coup attempt, had become the target of growing
student agitation.) The government personnel 'cleansing' order accelerated a process of arrests of tens of thousands of suspected
Communists or sympathisers that was to become increasingly controversial over the years. On 5 July 1966, Indonesia's People's
Consultative Assembly (*Madjelis Permusjawaratan Rakjat* – MPR), the
country's highest policy-making body, issued its decision outlawing
Marxist-Leninist doctrine in the country, except for purposes of
academic study.[4]

All these decisions, taken at the height of popular anti-coup
reactions, have never been repealed. Together with the special powers given local military commanders in Indonesia on the basis of
earlier 'state of war and siege' proclamations dating from the period of
the regional rebellions of the nineteen fifties, the post-1965 anti-
Communist decrees have provided virtually unlimited scope to the
Indonesian government, and especially its military, in combating
what is perceived to be subversion. Although in the second half of
1977 and in the early months of 1978, student and organised Muslim
political opposition to the Suharto regime was particularly prominent, the MPR at its March 1978 meeting reaffirmed with only slight
modification the special security powers granted Suharto on 11
March 1966, by Sukarno. To this reaffirmation the MPR added its
rationale that these powers were still needed in Indonesia in order to
'prevent a recurrence of the Communist coup [of 1965] and other
subversive threats'.[5]

Other South-east Asian governments have comparable powers. In
the Philippines, for example, the so-called Anti-Subversion Law
(Republic Act 1700) duly enacted by Congress and president on 17
June 1957, declares the Philippine Communist Party (PKP) to be
illegal, and membership in it a felony. Not only has this measure
never been repealed but also Philippine President Ferdinand Marcos'
promulgation of his Proclamation no. 1081 on 22 September 1972,
placing the country under martial law, has buttressed the government's posture against domestic Communism. The constitutionality
of Proclamation no. 1081 has been upheld by the Philippine Supreme

Court, and it is to be emphasised that at the time the proclamation was announced, Marcos in justification referred not only to a condition of 'lawlessness and criminality' in the country but also to the alleged threat of subversion coming from the 'New People's Army' (NPA), the guerrilla force of the Maoist-oriented Communist Party of the Philippines (Marxist-Leninist).[6]

To name a final example, in Malaysia, where the Communist Party has been illegal since 1948 and the onset of the Emergency, the arrest and investigatory provisions of the Emergency Regulation Ordinance of 1948, designed to combat the Malayan Communist insurgency, were subsequently continued in Malaysia's Internal Security Acts of 1960 and 1970. Moreover, Malaysia's 1976 Constitutional (Amendment) Act specifically sets aside such constitutional guarantees as the right of *habeas corpus* and legal counsel for those arrested 'under any law relating to the security' of the Malaysian Federation.[7] Also in Malaysia itself the controversy over the so-called Essential (Security Cases) Regulations of 1975, providing for certain other special procedures in security cases (for example, defendants in security cases will be presumed guilty until proven innocent, evidence can be given even if accused and defence counsel are absent, and there will be no jury trial in security cases) has deepened, as the Malaysian Bar Council has advised its members against assuming the defence in such cases even though by the end of 1977 some forty persons remained condemned to death under internal security convictions.[8]

Before briefly considering the present political context of individual South-east Asian countries in which Communist movements operate, it seems well to stress that the extensive Communist control and security apparatus, sometimes organised in special government 'Commands' (Thailand's 'Internal Security Command' and Indonesia's *Kopkamtib* or 'Preservation of Order and Security Command', for example) serves to reinforce the semi-authoritarian character of regimes committed to rapid economic development. In the interest of that economic growth, preservation of domestic security is seen as imperative, so as to ensure the continuing flow of foreign investment capital and trade. The whole range of political and security controls, from martial law to counter-insurgency programmes, is designed to reflect this public policy emphasis on domestic stability. Too rambunctiously dissident students and intellectuals, a too freewheeling press, or mystics appealing to ancient messianic traditions in criticising their governments are as much the objects of

these controls as are the Communists. Thus existing manifestations of
guerrilla insurgency or other Communist activity, though in some
instances as in Thailand increasing in relative severity in recent years,
afford just the degree of legitimisation for the operations of the
security apparatus which South-east Asian governments believe they
need to carry on their development programme.

Even in those regions of South-east Asia where organised insurgency is non-existent or minimal in scope, regimes appear to have a
stake in keeping the alleged Communist threat alive in the public
mind, and indeed, in exaggerating that threat on occasion, so as to
ensure the continuance of a controlled political environment thought
to be required for economic expansion. In Singapore's December
1976 election campaign, when, as indicated, some leaders of the
ruling PAP referred to the Communists as the 'real opposition', other
PAP spokesmen, like premier Lee Kuan Yew, emphasised corollary
economic themes in their speeches. As Lee put it, whether people in
Singapore 'have jobs or not depends on the political stability in
Singapore', particularly on whether people and government can
'convince industrialists to set up in Singapore factories with high skill
content', and Lee also warned Singaporeans not to break up what
they had built 'in terms of stability, security and confidence', since
'once the country goes down it cannot come up'.[9] In Indonesia,
meanwhile, warnings to dissenters to be careful in their expressions of
political opposition to the government, lest the 'latent' danger posed
by the Communists and by the possibility of their 'come-back' be
aggravated, are common. But it is to be noted also that the much
prized national efforts at *pembangunan* (development) are viewed from
time to time by Indonesian officials as being threatened by various
economic conspiracies and sabotage by the Communist underground, including smuggling, disrupting supplies of goods, driving
up local prices, and other 'attacks in the economic field'.[10]

Considering then what one might perhaps call the political and
juridical need among governments in the non-Communist segment of
South-east Asia for a certain level of real or exaggerated Communist
activity within their borders, a need dictated by the desire to maintain
the system of political and security controls believed indispensable to
planned economic growth, one would be tempted to describe these
government relationships as symbiotic.

This is not to say, however, that some regimes would not wish for a
more manageable level of Communist opposition. In two countries of

the non-Communist South-east Asian orbit, namely Burma and Thailand, that level has reached the point that portions of the national territory, without properly being considered as Communist 'liberated zones', nevertheless are not under effective or continuous government control. In the Wa states area of Burma's eastern border zone, near the frontier of People's China, and around the towns of Kengtung and Mongyang, some 10 000 'White Flag' Burma Communist Party insurgents are in intermittent *de facto* control of several hundreds of square miles of Shan state territory.

The 'White Flag' force is but one of several dissident and/or ethnic secessionist factions, among them Shans, Karens, Kachins, Mons, Arakanese and others. The organisational structures of some of these groups seem in practice to have all but displaced those of the central Burma government. In Shan state, for example, a 20 000-man 'Shan Liberation Army' and local village militias guard 'liberated' zones of a functioning Shan counter-government, with its own officials, customs bureaux controlling merchant traffic, Shan language schools, and so on, while in the Kayah state some 150 000 Karens are continuing their twenty-five-year-long independence struggle.[11] The Rangoon government, though claiming periodic success against various, including 'White Flag' Communist, insurgents, somehow is never able to destroy their resistance once and for all. Still, it is not enough to hold with one knowledgeable US political observer recently that 'perhaps only 40 per cent of the land area of Burma is under firm government control week after week',[12] for even though creaking and seemingly splintering somehow the Union of Burma has now lasted for more than three decades.

During most of the first fourteen years of Burma's national existence (1948–62) its then prevailing constitutional parliamentary government was dominated by the AFPFL and later by its chief reform faction (the 'clean AFPFL') which emerged victorious in three national elections (in 1951–2, 1956, and 1960). The drain of seemingly endless confrontations by ethnic dissidents, by remnants of China's Nationalist military forces, and by Communist rebels, as much as the bitterly polarised political atmosphere in which the only significant opposition to the AFPFL government seemed to come from pro-Soviet and other Marxists in the BWPP and its allies in the anti-AFPFL 'National Unity Front', all did little to help shape a common and durable working format of government. Already in 1958 premier U Nu, unable to hold his AFPFL organisation together any longer, had turned to the commander of the Burmese army, General Ne Win, to assume national leadership with parliament's approval. Upon U Nu's return to power in April 1960, after the election victory of his 'Clean AFPFL', serious secessionist dangers among Kachins and Shans arose once more, however, and on 2 March 1962, Ne Win and his military 'Revolutionary Council' seized power, dismissing parliament and cabinet.[13]

Over the years the Ne Win regime has sought to streamline and provide greater co-ordination to the Union government. Also, on the basis of its broadly phrased political creed, 'The Burmese Way to Socialism', it has attempted to adjust Marxism to indigenous Burmese and Buddhist ideological values, and, as it criticises 'democracy' as unsuitable, has also tried to develop, mainly through authoritarian bureaucratic and juridical controls and through the pervasive voice of its own (and the only permitted) political party, the Burma Socialist Programme Party, a greater sense of national unity and dedication.[14] The rigidities of doctrinaire Socialist planning, total operational controls by state corporations and severe curtailment of foreign cultural influences by 1970 had created a dangerously stagnating economy that was at the same time a black market operator's dream. The regime also managed to continue to alienate Rangoon's restive university students and intellectuals, and eventually elements of the Buddhist clerical and military establishments as well.

Already in 1965 Ne Win himself had dubbed his nation's economy to be a 'mess', and Burma, which in the years before World War II had exported some 3.1 million tons of rice, by 1967–8 was exporting only 350 000 tons; meanwhile food prices increased by more than 76 per cent in the period from 1964 to 1972.[15] In June 1975, an editorial in Rangoon's leading daily delicately complained that most of the nation's intellectuals were still adopting a 'neutral attitude towards the social revolution', though presumably being in sympathy with it, and that it was therefore 'necessary to train and breed the new intelligentsia imbued with socialist ideology' in Burma.[16] If the Ne Win regime and the BSSP view themselves as the articulators of that socialist ideology, one can only note that as of the anti-Ne Win riots by, and army massacre of, Rangoon University students on 6 July 1962, at the start of the present regime, through such latter day high points of anti-government opposition as the 7 June 1975 Rangoon student demonstrations protesting unemployment, food shortages, spiralling prices, and the country's 'unconstitutional rule' generally,

Burma's young intellectuals appear to see no virtue in the government, its creed and its policies.[17] As in Thailand after the 6 October 1976 military overthrow of the Seni Pramoj government, when eventually some 2 000 Bangkok student dissidents joined the Thai Communist insurgents, so, in the aftermath of the 1975 Rangoon demonstration, Burmese student dissidents fled to various illegal opposition groups. Some went to the Shan state headquarters of the largely underground non-Communist but bitterly anti-Ne Win 'People's Progressive Party' (PPP). Others reportedly joined the BCP. And still others began working toward a coalition of opposition groups among restive urban workers, Buddhist clergy, and dissident military, including the PPP's leader General Bo Let Ya. The advantage to Burma's Communists of such a climate of opposition need hardly be emphasised. But as we shall see, it is another matter as to whether the BCP or the small, currently more quiescent 'Red Flag' Communist Party of Burma is in a position to make effective use of this environment.

Periodic efforts at revitalising the regime and the Burmese economy have a way of coming to nought. The serious mid-1975 anti-Ne Win demonstrations, for example, came only a year after seemingly promising new political changes. A new constitution had been promulgated on 3 January 1974, after it was officially reported that more than 90 per cent of the nation's 14.6 million eligible voters had approved it, and the first general elections in fourteen years had been held between 27 January and 10 February 1974. The new constitution proclaiming Burma a 'Socialist Republic' affirms the pre-eminence of the BSSP, however, as well as the 'Burmese Way to Socialism' in developing the economy. Only BSSP candidates and a few 'independents' could run for the 451-member national parliament, the *Pyithu Hluttaw* or 'People's Assembly'. The promise of greater autonomy through regional elections in the ethnic minority states has turned out to mean little, since Ne Win and his military associates, directly or indirectly, continue to dominate the four principal national executive councils of government.[18]

In March 1976 defence minister General Tin Oo was dismissed and subsequently sentenced to a seven-year prison term, ostensibly on charges of corruption which, however, are widely discounted. Rather, it is believed, Ne Win wanted the popular Tin Oo out of the way. On 20 July 1976, it was announced in Rangoon that fourteen Burmese army captains and majors had been arrested for having

allegedly attempted to assassinate Ne Win, General San Yu, his
highly unpopular closest associate, and Colonel Tin Oo, head of
national intelligence (no relation to the imprisoned former defence
minister). The conspirators reportedly had considerable support
among the lower ranking officers, and saw themselves in a classic
'Young Turk' role opposing a corrupt and stagnating government.
Some were said to be supporters of former defence minister Tin Oo.
In the face of such serious army opposition, the Ne Win government
seemed at first to be accelerating its hithertofore hesitant pace
towards opening something of the country to Western development
assistance via an international consortium. Contracts with the World
Bank for help were renewed. In March 1976 a confidential report on
the Burmese economy by the World Bank noted that over the past
decade Burma's real gross domestic product had grown only at an
annual rate of 2.3 per cent, because of 'neglect of agriculture, forestry,
mining and transport', that the production of paddy (rice) had
'remained virtually stagnant in the face of rapid population growth',
and that the 'purchasing power of exports is less than half of what it
was ten years ago'.[19] The stultifying controls on the Burmese economy
continue to encourage smuggling and black marketeering on a large
scale. The following, typical item from the Burmese press is
suggestive:[20]

> Four motor schooners laden with more than one million kyats
> worth of contraband were seized by three Naval boats at sea off
> West Mergui yesterday.... The Navy seized 12,628 pounds of
> rubber, 500 viss of *ngapi*, cashew nuts, chilli bags and other marine
> products worth more than one million kyats from the three vessels.
> A total of 24,000 kyats (in cash) and 181 Thai bhats were also
> seized. The smugglers and the contraband were handed over to the
> Special Investigation Department today.

The 1977 Third BSSP Congress acknowledged 'failure' in past
economic planning, and there is some evidence that new efforts are
being made, after the revamping of the Council of Ministers, to
attract development loans and other assistance from an international
consortium, the so-called 'Burma Aid Group', in which Japan,
assisted by the World Bank, the US, and major Commonwealth and
West European powers, has taken major initiatives. A spread of some
$100 million in loans and assistance grants, from sources ranging

from the Asian Development and World Banks to the OPEC Special Fund and UNICEF, are being made available for such projects as improvements in tin and tungsten production, harbour facilities, rural drinking water supplies, copper mining smelting, and so on.[21] It is generally conceded, however, that it will be some time before these and similar modest inputs will significantly affect the economy, and above all the general living conditions of the average Burman. Moreover, other recent on the spot foreign assessments have noted that little or 'nothing remains' of the development impulses coming from the World Bank and other sources: Western and Japanese offshore oil prospectors in Burma stopped their activities by the close of 1977, not just because only natural gas deposits had been found thus far, 'but also because of the endless frustration of being caught in the miasma of the self-sabotaging Burmese bureaucracy'.[22]

As Beijing-supported BCP forces periodically intensify their operations, apparently unaffected by a new relative cordiality in Sino-Burmese relations following Ne Win's late September 1977 visit to Beijing (indeed, in early April 1978, BCP forces, launching one of their biggest military drives in years captured, and then only after heavy fighting were driven from, Kunlong near the Chinese border), so too does the pattern of ethnic secessionism persist. In fact, the thriving Burmese black market economy is heavily supplied by ethnic secessionists. For example, the 'Karen National Liberation Army' is actively engaged in smuggling large quantities of consumer goods and manufactures via Thailand into Burma; just as the BCP not only permits the illegal production of opium in the areas under its control, but also organises its transport and marketing, preventing rivalries among distributors.[23]

Socio-political centrifugalism, including Communist rebellion, thus can prey on and aggravate the weaknesses of Burma's political economy. Meanwhile the Ne Win regime's equally doctrinaire adherence to preserving a national cultural purity continues to arouse anger among the nation's intelligentsia, eager to open more windows on the world. In May 1977 it was announced that the Home and Religious Affairs Ministry, through its central registration board for printers and publishers, would be 'privately screening' all books and other printed materials before granting permission for publication. A government-controlled newspaper's editorial justified the measure because some publications allegedly had been found to 'centre on decadent themes'.[24] It is noteworthy, perhaps, that the BCP's clandestine radio transmitter, 'Voice of the People of Burma', since 1977 has paid special attention to the Burmese studentry's and intelligentsia's frustrations, and to the inadequacies of the educational system and its failure to encourage more vocational preparation.[25]

It must be emphasised, however, that the armed ideological and ethnic dissent in Burma, as in Thailand, while seriously debilitating national authority and development policies, is unable to provide a likely alternative to the present central government. Such dissent is internally too divided and too varied for that. Thus the Union of Burma can limp along, with an at best sluggish economy and with all manner of dissidents in the interior of the country. But in the absence of a new coup, or short of a centrally imposed change of regime and policy, Burma seems unlikely to be taken over by any of its insurgent factions, whether Shan or 'White Flag' Communists.

Comparatively, Thailand today is in a stronger position. Popular adhesion to the Thai monarchy, to Buddhism as a national religion, and the relatively greater racial and cultural homogeneity of the population[26] (disregarding for the moment restive minority elements such as the 50 000 Meo and other so-called 'hill tribes' in the north, or the nearly one million Thai Muslims, mostly Thai of Malayan origin, in the south) provide the kind of powerful centripetal forces that Burma lacks. But, as in the case of Burma, Thailand too is confronted with a Communist insurgent movement, grown from an estimated 1 700 hard-core guerrillas in 1967,[27] to the developed 8 000-man, Vietnam- and Laos-supplied 'Thai People's Liberation Armed Forces' (TPLAF) of today. In the north-eastern Thai provinces areas such as Nakhon Phanom and Ubon Ratchathani, as well as increasingly in the Cambodian frontier areas (for example, Thailand's Sisaket province), Thai Communist guerrilla forces claim (and Thai government spokesmen sometimes concede) to have established their 'liberated zones'.

And as in Burma, so too in Thailand insurgency feeds on domestic instability, particularly on the country's proclivity in the past few years to lurch seemingly from military-dominated regimes to parliamentary governments with ministerial responsibility. In the immediate post-World War II period (1945–9), the military authoritarianism of the kind that had become increasingly dominant after Marshal Phibun Songkhram had become prime minister in 1939, seemed at first likely to go into an eclipse. But already by 1947, Phibun, in the wake of yet another military coup, had returned to power. A 1949 counter-coup on behalf of Pridi Phanomyong, one of the principal figures in the 1932 revolution that had established modern constitutional practices in Thailand, failed. For the next eight years, Phibun style 'controlled democracy' sharply polarised political life, the chief political opposition focusing on a mildly Marxist 'Socialist Front' coalition, led by some of the exiled Pridi's former associates.[28]

The Front's modest electoral successes in 1957, which aroused fear in conservative quarters as much as Phibun's inability to placate army dissatisfaction, set the stage for the 1958 coup d'état of Field Marshal Sarit Thanarat. Upon Sarit's death in 1963, his confidant Marshal Thanom Kittikachorn succeeded him as prime minister. By December 1972, notwithstanding rising opposition from students, labour, and some parliamentarians, the constitution of 1968 had been set aside, the parliament that had been elected in 1969 had been prorogued, and a new 'temporary' constitution had been promulgated. The latter endowed Thanom as premier with special powers if national security demanded, and a new appointive national legislature convened in which the armed forces and police held nearly two-thirds of the seats. Opposition continued to simmer, especially from students, and there were, for example, demonstrations in 1971 against alleged Japanese dominance of the Thai economy.[29]

Military-dominated regimes have a way of cultivating the seeds of their own destruction. The Thanom variant has been a significant if not necessarily unique political variant in South-east Asia. There is, for example, the assistance the Thanom regime gave to the rapid growth in the number of students – the ultimate source of the regime's downfall. In the decade and a half of Sarit's and Thanom's rule (1958–73), one notes not only the significant growth of new universities (Chiang Mai University in northern Thailand was established in 1964, Songkla Nakarin in southern Thailand was founded in 1967, a new College of Education in Pra Nakorn was started in 1969), but in fact rapid growth in school enrolments at all levels. Secondary school enrolment during the 1960–70 decade, for example, rose by 95 per cent from 302 655 to 590 307.[30] Thailand's close ties in the same period to US strategic interests dictated expansion of the domestic road network. This in turn provided significantly new impulses in population mobility, and investment, as well as acceleration in the monetisation of the rural economy.[31] During two five-year national development plans, ending in 1971, the rate of growth of gross domestic product had averaged 11.8 per cent, and in the decade from 1960 to 1970 Thailand's population grew by more than 7.89 million people, or 30.1 per cent, to a total of more than 34.8 million.[32]

The imbalances in, and strains on, any political system caused by such expansion, especially in terms of the expectations of the young (already in 1971 a Ford Foundation study noted the problem of 'educationally qualified people' exceeding 'the number of jobs in which they can use their abilities'),[33] were not moderated but rather aggravated by the relative benevolence of Thai style military-dominated rule. The degree of political suppression, whether in partisan activity or in the political press, seemed just mild enough to encourage a persistent undertone and brief periodic outbursts of dissent, without wholly stifling them. In 1972–3, the present author, in conversation with high-ranking Thai military and police officials regarding the nature of political and especially of student dissent in the country, invariably encountered an avuncular, almost proud, reaction to what appeared to be viewed as expected antics of idealistic youth. Moreover, there appeared to be some official belief that expressions of such dissent clearly gave the lie to opposition charges of dictatorial wilfulness on the part of the government.

On the other hand, even considering the pattern of economic growth in the Sarit-Thanom era, there is a question as to how much the Thai mass benefited. There were and remain wide differences in rural income, in urban as compared to rural income, and in regional income. For example, the country's central region has the highest per capita income, more than 50 per cent above the national average, while in the north-east, where Communist insurgency has become a fixture, there is the lowest per capita income, about half the national average.[34] Serious inequalities in land distribution have continued to persist. According to one Thai survey the bottom 10 per cent of Thai farms, by size, account for only 1 per cent of the total land area, while the top 10 per cent hold 34 per cent of all land; the bottom 60 per cent, in fact, hold 25 per cent of all land, and the upper 5 per cent hold 21 per cent of all land.[35] Changes in regime in Thailand tend to focus on the capital, usually reflecting the turbulence at the apex of the élite. Yet, after fifteen years, a change from military rule probably was welcomed by many.

The fall of the Thanom Kittikachorn government on 14 October 1973 came after his regime had already lost much credibility two years previously in a budget struggle with the previous parliament, and student criticism, increasingly spearheaded since 1970 by the National Student Centre of Thailand (NSCT), a federation of activist organisations, had become ever bolder.[36]

The arrest, on 6 October 1973, of students disseminating pamphlets demanding a new constitution was shortly followed by government statements that those detained were seeking to 'overthrow the government' and that 'Communist documents' had been found in their homes. Some military media, such as the 'Armoured Division's Radio', added fuel to the flames of political controversy by inflammatory news reports. In ensuing days, violent clashes of police and military with thousands of students demanding the release of those arrested, and the refusal of the Thai army commander-in-chief, General Krit Siwara, to deploy his forces against the students, convinced Thanom that he could no longer control events and led him to hand in his resignation.

For the next three years Thailand returned to another brief interlude of parliamentary democracy, interspersed by more press freedom, general elections, and constitutional changes – and, also, characterised by a deepening political polarisation in which each side manipulated students and other interest groups. Military-backed conservative organisations like *Nawapon* ('New Force'), active in the smaller towns, and the 'Red Gaurs', an organisation of student activists from the vocational institutions, both of which allegedly received direction and assistance from the government's chief counter-insurgency and domestic security agency, the Internal Security Operations Command (ISOC), and other Thai military, began confronting the NSCT and other groups such as the Federation of Independent Students of Thailand (FIST).[37] The latter two sought to mobilise villagers and labour unions on behalf of a vaguely formulated 'power to the people' programme of Socialism and reform, but organisational inexperience and excess zeal quickly doomed their ventures.

Meanwhile an intensifying parliamentary and electoral struggle (in the 26 January 1975 and 4 April 1976 general elections more than forty political parties participated), marred by political assassinations (for instance, on 28 February 1976, Socialist Party of Thailand secretary general Boonsanong Punyodyana was murdered) and voting frauds, and aggravated by declining foreign investors' and business confidence, suggested that it would be some time before the new Thai polity acquired a stable format.[38] The governments of the

Pramoj brothers, Kukrit and Seni, each of whom successively was to hold the premiership in this three-year interregnum of parliamentary democracy, were both to become the targets of mounting public concern over threats to national security, over political demonstrations and violence, and over waning foreign economic interest in Thailand.

On 6 October 1976, the Thai military once more re-established their government authority, after a bloody confrontation between student demonstrators at Bangkok's Thamassat University and police.[39] Student violence which had ended Thanom's military-dominated regime now became the occasion for the reimposition of military rule under Admiral Sa-ngad Chalawyoo and a 'National Administrative Reform Council' (NARC). There are grounds for believing that the conflict and fighting at Thamassat, which precipitated NARC's power seizure, had intensified as a result of provocations by 'Red Gaur' and other anti-Seni Pramoj government elements. The NARC-backed regime of the new premier, Thanin Kraivichien, was itself to last only a little more than a year, however. A bloodless coup on 20 October 1977, staged by Admiral Sa-ngad Chalawyoo and his associates in the armed forces, overthrew Thanin. Yet another 'Revolutionary Council' of state leadership was announced, but its members were virtually the same as those of the NARC which it replaced. General Kriangsak Chamanand subsequently became premier. The conservative policies of the brief Thanin Kraivichien era seemed like another sharp lurch, this time in the direction opposite to the more liberal approach pursued by the Pramoj governments.[40] Thanin's Victorian moralising and the sharply anti-Communist emphasis in many of his policy announcements appeared unlikely to moderate political passions and to many even seemed prone to play into the hands of the Communists.[41] The military became particularly alarmed over rapidly deteriorating relations between Bangkok and its Communist Indochinese neighbours at the very time that US policy under President Jimmy Carter seemed intent on de-emphasising the US commitment to the region and simultaneously on improving relations between the Communist and non-Communist segments of South-east Asia.

Thanin's removal and Kriangsak's ascendancy to the premiership were followed by determined Thai efforts to better relations with Laos and the SRV, as well as with Cambodia. This was despite continuing Thai-Cambodian border clashes and Thai charges of abduction of border villagers and other acts of terrorism by Cambodian-protected

Thai Communist insurgents, the so-called 'Siam organisation'.[42] Following the overthrow of the Seni Pramoj government on 6 October 1976, 'several hundred students', according to Thai government sources, as well as a number of Socialist Party of Thailand leaders, joined the TPLAF and some subsequently left for Laos and the SRV, whence, after training, they infiltrated back into Thailand.[43] However, after Thanin's overthrow, and after promises of lenient treatment, the Kriangsak Chamanand government claimed that many students began returning to their homes and families.

Yet the 6 October 1976 events and the Thanin era undoubtedly helped to radicalise Thai opinion. On 1 April 1977, for example, in a broadcast over the TPLAF's 'Voice of the People of Thailand', one former Chulalangkorn University student activist declared, referring to the Thai monarchy, that unlike the Thai nation as such and the Buddhist religion, the monarchy had become 'obsolete', so that if it were destroyed there would not be any adverse effects. Such dismissals of one of Thailand's most hallowed institutions would have been inconceivable a few years ago. It remains to be seen if the government can reconcile the restive students. The Kriangsak regime, as one former NSCT student leader put it to the author, may speak more softly than its predecessor, 'but the same old military crowd is still in charge'. It was noted that although according to Kriangsak elections are to be held in the near future, the premier's extraordinary powers to take whatever steps necessary to ensure national security are guaranteed by the present interim constitution, promulgated by premier Kriangsak on 9 November 1977 (the eleventh constitution in Thailand, one might add, since the revolution of 1932).[44]

There remain other domestic dissidents, like the secessionist Thai Muslims, organised in such groups as the Pattani United Liberation Organisation, four of whose members acknowledged responsibility for the bomb explosion at Tambon Sateng, in the province of Yala, on 22 September 1977, at which the visiting King and Queen of Thailand were not harmed but scores of bystanders were wounded. The worsening Thai-Cambodian border problem aggravates the nation's continuing confrontation of Communist insurgency. At the close of January 1978, the Kriangsak government declared that thirty-eight provinces of the country were now considered to be 'Communist infiltrated', even as Thai military sources, at about the same time, were claiming that lack of support and defections were decimating the ranks of the Thai Communist Party.[45]

Thailand and Burma, perhaps the least stable regimes in South-east Asia today, both seemingly farthest removed from finding a generally acceptable domestic political format, thus also appear to be those parts of the region where armed Communist insurgency is most intractable and entrenched. The entrenched strength of the Communist insurgents seems to be as much a causative factor and at the same time a result of the prevailing domestic instability, however. Efforts at improving diplomatic relations with the foreign countries harbouring support bases for these insurgent forces (in the case of Thailand, Laos, the SRV and Cambodia, in the case of Burma, People's China) seem to be of little avail. The experience of the Thanom regime in Thailand may also provide a warning for two other present South-east Asian governments, namely those of Ferdinand Marcos of the Philippines and of Suharto in Indonesia. These latter two regimes have both been formally shaped, in their present forms, by an avowed and continuing domestic anti-Communist commitment. Like the Thanom regime at one time they have both appeared to be relatively durable. But, again like the Thanom government, they also seem gradually to be losing a public consensus of support for their policy premises under a steady drumfire of eruptions of opposition.

The 22 September 1972 martial law proclamation in the Philippines by President Marcos ended more than a quarter century of perhaps the most freewheeling, competitive party and political system in post-war South-east Asia. But it had also become a system that produced growing public dissatisfaction over the extensive corruption and inefficiencies in virtually all public services, and generally by graft, influence peddling and nepotism in seemingly all phases of public life. Following the confidence-restoring administration of President Ramon Magsaysay (1953–7), the former defence minister, during which the Huk threat ebbed, in part because of an initially vigorous land reform programme, the administrations of Presidents Carlos Garcia (1957–61) and Diosdado Macapagal (1961–5) witnessed increasing public weariness with the congressional power plays of the two major parties, the Nacionalistas and the Liberals. Meanwhile, the politically protected polarisations of wealth, and the antiquated and inept tax system, appeared to make Philippine democracy the privileged playground of the wealthy few. One study by the Philippine Congressional Planning Office indicated that in 1965 about 50 per cent of all families earned less than 1 500 pesos (then about US$230) a year, while only 2.6 per cent earned 10 000 pesos or $1 600, or more, and the 'top 5% of income earners earned more than those in the bottom 60% '. A belief that the rich in such areas as the sugar industry and in the import sector were able to maintain themselves because of the specially advantageous status of post-war US financial interests in the country and the Philippines' foreign policy and military dependence on the US, further tended to sharpen the public discontent.[46]

Thus what was nominally a democratic system, but one dominated by an oligarchy of a dozen or so powerful families controlling public affairs and the economy, came to be viewed in many quarters, but notably among the young, in intellectual, labour and in some of the more outspoken clerical circles, as essentially unresponsive to the pressing need for accelerated economic development and social change. To a number of observers, Philippine political life seemed wholly preoccupied with 'the endless pursuit of influence and security through the exploitation of patronage, relationships of personal fealty and volatile alliances with equals who provided transient security in a shifting political battleground'.[47]

The PKP had been outlawed in 1957 (Republic Act 1 700) and the Huks had become increasingly discredited, sinking into fiefdoms of organised crime and banditry, though making occasional gestures, pronouncements on the need for justice and reform for the tenant farmer. As a result, some left-leaning, strongly nationalist Filipino youth, intellectuals, and trade unionists increasingly tended to turn in the nineteen sixties to a variety of Communist-infiltrated political, cultural and economic organisations and interest groups. These ranged from the 'National Youth' (*Kabataang Makabayan* – KM) and the 'Free Peasants' Union' (*Malayan Samahang Magsasaka* – *Masaka*) both founded in 1964, to the Socialist Party of the Philippines (successor to the pre-World War II group of the same name) and the 'Movement for the Advancement of Nationalism' (MAN), both established in 1967. José Maria Sison, the former University of the Philippines instructor, who was later to become the founder and chief leader of the 'Maoist' wing of the Philippines Communist Party and its 'New People's Army', was the founder of KM, while Masaka had been established by Felixberto Olalia, one-time chairman of the PKP's principal farmers' organisation. Olalia also helped reorganise the post-war 'Socialist Party of the Philippines'. Sison, again, was MAN's first secretary general, but this organisation initially attracted prominent non-Communist Philippine political figures and intellectuals.[48]

The overlapping memberships, as well as the number of these and similar left nationalist groups, facilitated both a radicalisation and a Communist-influenced united-front-building process. The same process, however, tended to draw the contrasts between the old PKP (most of whose principal leaders were in detention anyway), and the young impatient radicals around Sison, some of whom had surreptitiously travelled to Beijing, in ever starker colours. 'Maoism was militancy; it was "revolution now". Sison and his kind would have none of the flaccid "awaitism" of the older generation,' as Lachica has put it.[49]

From 26 December 1968 to 7 January 1969, probably near Capas, in Southern Tarlac province, Luzon, Sison and several scores of his Beijing-sympathising young friends, augmented by some of the more ideologically inclined young Huks, held a 'Congress of Reestablishment of the Communist Party of the Philippines', which created a new Communist Party, the 'Communist Party of the Philippines (Marxist-Leninist)' or 'Communist Party of the Philippines (Mao Ze Dong Thought)', usually designated as CPP(M-L). At the new party's initiative on 29 March 1969, at a 'Conference of Red Commanders and Soldiers of the People', probably also held near Capas, a new military force, the New People's Army (NPA) was established. The NPA dedicated itself to Mao style revolutionary 'people's war' tactics. The NPA not only drew on the ranks of CPP(M-L) activists but also on some younger Huks who, in the later nineteen sixties, had joined the 'New People's Democratic Force' (*Fuerza Demokratika Ding Memalan*) of Huk commanders Pedro Taruc and Faustino del Mundo ('Commander Sumulong').[50] By mid-October 1970 Sumulong had been captured and Taruc had been killed, and next to Sison the NPA's chief leader became one of Sumulong's protégés, Bernabe Buscayno ('Commander Dante'). A Philippine army lieutenant, Victor Corpus, defected to the NPA in 1970 and soon also assumed an NPA leadership role.

The organs of the decimated old PKP might stigmatise the CPP(M-L) for its alleged 'cowboy ideology', which the PKP said had turned 'the gun into a fetish'.[51] But there is little question that as the Philippine crisis of confidence in the workings of the nation's constitutional, political and party system deepened, Sison and Dante acquired a Guevarist appeal among the young. 'Dante for President!' anti-Marcos students reportedly shouted as they attempted to storm the presidential palace Malacanang in Manila, on the night of 30 January 1970, in one of the country's worst political riots.[52] According to Philippine constabulary sources, NPA guerrilla clashes rapidly increased in the first three years after the NPA's founding, with indications that 'urban guerrilla warfare' in the streets of the capital was in the offing.[53] Other observers, familiar with the Philippine constabulary's 'budget Huks' tactic (at the time of annual congressional hearings on the national defence budget, Philippine security services officials seemed wont to stress the dangers of insurgency in the country), were sceptical about such alleged 'Red scare' tactics.

By September 1972, Philippine President Ferdinand Marcos, first elected to office in 1965 (and re-elected in 1969), had seemed to become enmeshed in a rapidly worsening power struggle with his Liberal Party opponents. A Constitutional Convention which had been meeting in Quezon City was riven by pro- and anti-Marcos factions. The latter were determined to prevent a new legal formula from being adopted whereby the president, who could not succeed himself under the terms of the existing fundamental law, yet would find a way somehow to stay in power. A grenade explosion at a Liberal Party rally at the Plaza Miranda in Manila on 21 August 1971, in which several prominent Liberal Party figures were injured, was but an element in a pattern of heightening tensions and seemingly worsening political violence in which Marcos charged his Liberal Party opponents, among them his chief rival, Senator Benigno Aquino, with allying themselves with the NPA.

Marcos' repeated raising of the Communist spectre, whether or not justified by NPA activity, and by the extent of unrest and violence in the country, deepened his credibility problem in many quarters: 'Since the government cannot seem to stop the rising price of bread,' columnist Ernesto Granada wrote in the 28 June 1972 *Manila Chronicle*, 'it is apparently trying to offer us circuses as diversion. And these in the form of endless warnings about the rise of subversion in all areas of the country, starting with Isabela to Mindanao.' On 22 September 1972, shortly after defence secretary Juan Ponce Enrile's car was shot at as he was returning from his Manila office, and after another aggressive KM-led mass demonstration in Manila, Marcos proclaimed martial law. Both houses of the Philippine Congress were suspended and activities by political parties ceased. Controls were imposed on all media, and a number of dailies ceased publication. Within a few weeks, according to the government itself, nearly 30 000 persons were arrested, among them prominent political figures (like Aquino), journalists and editors, as well as local political bosses and racketeers with private bodyguards and 'armies', ordinary criminal elements, and those whose only crime was that local constabulary or security officials might deem them politically suspect. Most of these were subsequently set free; by May 1975 about 6 000 remained in detention, but new arrests continued. Well founded allegations of torture and inhuman treatment of many prisoners arrested after the martial law proclamation injured Marcos' 'New Society' era from the start, although upon discovery of some instances of such mistreatment, Marcos ordered appropriate disciplinary action against the officials involved.[54]

A flood of presidential measures, ranging from stepped-up attempts to curb criminality, particularly unauthorised use of firearms, and improvements in various public services, to land reform and a redefinition of the role of foreign investment capital began to cascade down on the Philippine public. Meanwhile, a good deal less came to be heard in official pronouncements about the depredations of the NPA (the immediate cause offered by Marcos, it will be recalled, for his promulgation of Proclamation no. 1081 establishing martial law). By 1974 knowledgeable Filipinos, including some in basic sympathy with Marcos, were virtually unanimous in their retrospective opinions expressed to this author that the NPA threat of, and the alleged danger of, Communist subversion generally had been exaggerated by Marcos in order to justify his martial law regime. Already three days after the martial law declaration, C. T. Villareal, the speaker of the Philippine House of Representatives, reportedly charged during a Tokyo visit that Marcos had decided on martial law long before he announced it, and that martial law imposition had in fact 'been studied for a long time'.[55]

Buttressed, however, by a Philippine Supreme Court decision upholding the legitimacy of the martial law declaration and by five Gaullist style popular referenda held since September 1972 on issues ranging from an endorsement for Marcos to govern indefinitely, to appointment of provincial officials and the grant of autonomy for the country's restive southern provinces,[56] Marcos' 'New Society' regime appeared to provide (as in the case of Lee Kuan Yew's Singapore and Suharto's Indonesia) a policy matrix of security and order for accelerated economic growth. This growth seemed to depend particularly on the investment confidence of the multinational corporations, and the benefits flowing from it presumably would also be for the mass of Filipinos. However, the eruption of anti-Marcos dissent on 7 April

1978, when the first parliamentary elections since martial law took place (involved were 165 elected seats of the 200 seats in the new 'interim' *Batasang Pambansa* or National Assembly), suggested that at least in Manila there was significant, if minority, opposition to the Marcos regime. This appeared to be the case notwithstanding the resounding electoral victory of Marcos' party, the 'Movement for the New Society' (*Kilusang Bagong Lipunan* or KBL) over its chief opponent, the *Laka ng Bayan* ('People's Force') party with which the jailed Aquino was identified. Anti-Marcos demonstrations and marches in Manila, well founded charges of government rigging of the ballot count and inevitably some 600 new arrests of protesters, all suggested that whatever its other achievements the Marcos regime had failed to reconcile, or at least moderate, some of the same sources of Manila-based dissent – such as students, clergy, and trade unionists – that essentially had already confronted the president before his promulgation of Proclamation no. 1081. At the same time, it seems well to emphasise, the 7 April 1978 elections, despite instances of fraud, do indicate that on the whole the Marcos regime remains the favourite of the majority of the Filipino electorate. Anti-Marcos candidates could and did win (for instance, in the Central Visayas), and the high-handed election conduct of the regime should not obscure the fact that, by and large, Marcos enjoys dominant electoral support. Civil servants, the military, business circles, and rural people all strongly supported Marcos in the 1977 elections.[57]

Total economic growth in the Philippines meanwhile has been 'respectable by world standards', according to one analysis, with average annual rates of real growth climbing to over 6 per cent in the past decade (fluctuating between 4.5 per cent in 1972 and 9.8 per cent in 1974).[58] In the Marcos era foreign investor confidence has returned. Between 1955 and 1970 there was actually a net outflow of direct foreign investment from the Philippines (US $1.4 billion inflow versus $1.78 billion outflow), partly because of concern over the country's domestic political stability. Today, hundreds of thousands of dollars from Japanese, US, West European, and Commonwealth sources are being invested, and by March 1975 forty-eight multinational corporations had opened their doors in Manila.[59]

On the other hand, there has been a question as to whether the mass of Filipinos has significantly benefited from this investment expansion and growth; moreover, as in the case of Suharto's Indonesia, there is evidence of serious malversations, and corruption among business figures allied to the prevailing regime. The index of real wages of skilled workers in the Philippines (1972 is 100) dropped from 95.4 in 1973 to 71.2 in 1976, according to Central Bank of the Philippines statistics, and for unskilled workers in the same period the drop was from 92.9 to 72.2. Restrictions on the right to strike, as in Singapore and Indonesia, have had a depressing effect on workers' living standards. In 1977 the top 20 per cent of the nation's income earners received 53 per cent of total national income, while the bottom 40 per cent received only 14.7 per cent. Controversy swirls around the land reform programme. Implementation of the original programme, under which some 1.5 million hectares under rice and corn cultivation were to have been transferred to tenants by those landlords who held more than seven hectares, has slowed because of bureaucratic tangles. By July 1976 only about 26 000 tenants (a mere 6 per cent of the total number originally envisaged) had actually stopped paying rentals to their landlords and had begun paying amortisation payments to the Land Bank – the important phase marking the implementation of the basic land reform process.[60]

On the other hand, one hastens to add that there is no doubt of the priority concern of land reform in Marcos' official political strategy. Also, in the 'New Society' era this historically often hapless reform effort in the Philippines has probably gone further than at any other time since the days of Magsaysay.

Close friends and political allies of Marcos' and his wife's families are reported to have particularly benefited in recent years from the 'New Society' through acquisition of various profitable business ventures. In July 1975 Marcos is said to have issued a secret presidential decree which imposed heavy duties on imports of materials used by a foreign-owned company producing cigarette filters, while retaining a much lower duty on such imported materials to be used by a filter-producing company owned by Herminio Disini, a Marcos friend and in-law. The discriminatory high import duty on the foreign company forced it to close, leaving Disini with a profitable monopoly. By early January 1978 a new scandal had erupted involving the Herdis group, a Philippine conglomerate of thirty-five companies, of which Disini is executive officer. A US corporation, Westinghouse Electric Company, reportedly paid Herdis millions of dollars as commission for 'assistance' received in obtaining from the government a contract to build the Philippines' first nuclear power plant.[61] Westinghouse denied that it made illegal payments, and it is unlikely that because of the Marcos' government's investigation of the affair, the contract with Westinghouse will be cancelled. Still, the incident, along with such other allegations as that the Philippine government's National Grains Authority in recent years derived some $100 million in profits by keeping the prices of wheat imported from the US artificially high, has provided new ammunition to those who see the Marcos regime as essentially a military-backed preserve for a few favoured Philippine big business interests allied with the president's family and with foreign corporations, as 'Juan de la Cruz' (the nickname for the Philippine man in the street) meanwhile remains as miserable as he was before.

Such characterisations lack balance. But other nagging national problems erode Marcos' leadership credibility. There is no indication, for example, that after six years of armed confrontation, interspersed with periodic peace negotiations and shortlived truces, the government is any nearer to ending the resistance of the 'Moro National Liberation Front' (MNFL) on Mindanao and adjacent islands. Though the MNLF is riven by factional and leadership disputes, it continues to receive covert assistance from the government of President Mu'ammad al-Qadhafi of Libya. In April 1978 the MNLF insurgents were still estimated as comprising a 20 000-man force. By early 1977, according to Philippine government sources, the insurgency had cost the lives of some 10 000 civilians and 4 000 military, and more than half a million Filipinos had been rendered homeless or had become refugees because of the internecine struggle.[62]

The concept of an autonomous regional government for thirteen southern provinces, originally proclaimed by Marcos on 26 March 1977, was stillborn. The MNLF and its supporters, drawn from among the nearly two million Muslim population of the several ethno-linguistic groups which, though characterised by significant cultural and economic differences, yet tend to be lumped together as the *bangsa Moro* (Moro people), seem essentially to desire a degree of regional 'autonomy' that would, in all but name, be independence. The long history of religio-political conflict between the southern Filipino Muslims and their Christian neighbours, a conflict dating from Spanish colonial times and recently sharpened by Christian-Muslim disputes over land ownership and tenure, has made for an almost ineradicable sense of Filipino Muslim estrangement from Manila ways and from the developing national Filipino polity.[63] The

Muslim sense of being discriminated against by his government is augmented by a feeling of necessary communal exclusivity dictated by his faith, even though one notes the participation of a number of prominent Filipino Muslims in the nation's political, economic and educational life.

Meanwhile the CPP(M-L) and NPA, in a 1977 policy statement, assured the MNLF of 'unswerving support' in its struggle for 'national self determination', and in recent years NPA combat and support forces, according to sources friendly to the NPA, may have grown to some 6 000 or more in Mindanao. Such estimates are likely to be too high, yet there has undoubtedly been evidence of NPA expansion in the southern islands since 1972. Prominent MNLF leaders such as Nuraladji Misuari have been identified with the *Kabataang Makabayan* in the nineteen sixties, and Philippine government spokesmen have claimed that there is NPA-MNLF collaboration today. Evidence for the latter, however, is limited and controversial. The MNLF leadership, of whatever faction, appears to remain sceptical that NPA support for Moro 'national self determination' necessarily encompasses the right to formal secession from the Philippine Republic.[64]

To be sure, the 'New Society' can hardly be blamed for the origins of the intractable Moro conflict. Still, the fact remains that the Marcos regime, presumably committed to priority development of Filipino national pride and unity, has yet to find a solution to the conflict. The southern Philippine rebellion today continues to be perhaps one of the most extensive, and certainly the most violent, of the various minority resistance movements in South-east Asia today.

Compared to the Philippines under Marcos, Suharto's Indonesia shows important similarities, but also contrasts. Between Indonesia's 2 May 1977 general elections and Suharto's formal re-election as president by the People's Consultative Congress (*Madjelis Permusjawaratan Rakjat* – MPR) on 22 March 1978, opposition to the post-Sukarno *Orde Baru* ('New Order', also referred to as *Orba*) came alive as never before – just as in the Philippines the 7 April 1978 elections for an interim National Assembly marked a new high of anti-Marcos public sentiment. As in the Philippines, so the Indonesian opposition appeared to be concentrated in the capital and some other major cities, involving particularly, though by no means exclusively, students and leaders of religious groups (Roman Catholics in the Philippines, Muslims in Indonesia). A notable

difference, however, is that the upsurge of student-Muslim opposition
to the Suharto regime also brought to light various degrees of
sympathy for such opposition among prominent Indonesian army
generals. Some of these, like former Djakarta governor Ali Sadikin
and former ASEAN secretary general H. R. Dharsono, held high civil
government posts; others, like former defence minister A. H. Nasution, are influential in some Muslim political circles long at odds with
Suharto's regime. In the Philippines, in contrast, nothing like this is
evident. Marcos, among whose first acts after proclaiming martial
law in September 1972 was to increase military pay and who, since
martial law, has expanded the Philippines military's size from 50 000
troops to more than three times that number, continues to enjoy the
support of senior commanders.

Since Suharto, in the aftermath of the abortive 1965 coup, was
gradually legitimised by the MPR in his executive powers, while
Sukarno, discredited by allegedly passive complicity in the coup,
formally remained president until Suharto's naming to the post by the
MPRS in 1968, economic and political stabilisation and *pembangunan*
(development) have been Indonesia's main policy priorities. As the
Suharto regime entered its second decade, these priorities have
remained the same. Late in March 1978, within days of his re-election
as president, and as he announced his new cabinet, Suharto declared
for example that continued implementation of the present (second)
national five-year development plan, and the drafting of the next
five-year development plan, were the first two principal tasks of his
cabinet. As for ultimate objectives of the cabinet, he said further these
included: to enhance 'social justice' by a wider distribution of the
'results of development', to foster a 'high economic development
rate', and to maintain 'national stability'. 'Clean' government, national unity, commitment to general elections and implementation of
a 'free and active foreign policy' that would strengthen 'national
resilience' – these were the remaining four of the seven announced
goals of the new 'Development Cabinet'.[65]

There is little doubt that also thanks to the $9 billion in credit and
development assistance provided since 1967 by a consortium of major
industrial nations and banking institutions (IGGI or the Inter-
Governmental Group on Indonesia), stabilisation and development
have been achieved in significant measure. There has been a halt to
the careening economic chaos of the later Sukarno years when the
Djakarta cost of living index (1958 is 100) leaped from 239 in March

1961 to 96 030 in April 1966,[66] when all principal exports and foreign exchange earners, with the exception of petroleum products, seemed to be stagnating or declining, and when much of the nation's communications and transportation infrastructure seemed to be degenerating toward total collapse. Sukarno, as one observer has noted, 'despised the systematic study of economics and proved slow to master the subject even under the pitiless tutelage of experience'.[67] In the Suharto era, economists and 'technocrats' have played a much larger role in the shaping of the political economy than ever before.

Also because of sensitivity to the political niceties in the industrial democracies on whose capital investment, aid and trade Indonesia so heavily depends, the Suharto regime, during the past decade, has attempted to project as much of the imagery of a constitutional democracy as its concerns with domestic stability and security will allow. General elections for parliament (*Dewan Perwakilan Rakjat* – DPR) and for provincial and local councils were held in 1971 and 1977 (respectively Indonesia's second and third national elections ever, the first having been held in 1955).[68] A multi-party system, including opposition parties, a varied press and an expanding educational system, providing a national literacy rate of about sixty per cent all do exist. But pervasive security regulations largely applied by the military, whose participation in all branches and levels of government, and in the administration of state enterprises, is seen as constitutionally proper, severely curtails freedom of political activity and expression.

Since 1971, nine major parties, most of them in existence since the Sukarno era, have merged through government pressure into two, the Muslim Unity Development Party (*Partai Persatuan Pembangunan* – PPP) and the Democratic Indonesia Party (*Partai Demokrasi Indonesia* – PDI). The third remaining party is the Suharto government's party, the organisation of so-called 'functional groups' called *Golkar* (from *Golongan Karya* or 'working associations'), technically an organisation of different interest groups ranging from business, professional and civil service groups, to farmers, women, students and others. Carefully mobilised through the pressures of the military and the civil bureaucracy, Golkar swept to victory in both the 1971 and 1977 elections, winning approximately 63 per cent and 62 per cent of the popular votes, respectively, and with it most of the 360 elected DPR seats (another 100 seats are reserved for the military and other functional groups, also mostly Golkar-oriented).

However, charges of intimidation of voters by Golkar-minded public officials, of arbitrary arrest of opposition party (particularly PPP) proselytisers, and of fraud favouring Golkar and the government in the counting of ballots during the 1971 and 1977 elections, have been made both by Indonesian and outside observers and appear to be well substantiated. Criticism of Golkar and the Suharto government, as Admiral Sudomo, staff chief of the country's principal internal security and counter-insurgency agency, the 'Preservation of Order and Security Command' (*Komando Pemulihan Keamanan dan Ketertiban – Kopkamtib*), put it in a warning on 13 August 1976, has to occur in a 'constructive' and 'fair and good' manner. He earlier said 'repressive' measures might be needed to combat 'distorted' political reporting.[69] Suspension for various durations of the publication of newspapers for printing reports displeasing to the government was common before, and has occurred frequently since, Sudomo's warning.

Sudomo's warning also appears to have been addressed to the more militant and politically self-conscious segment of the Indonesian Muslim community, now represented by the PPP, many of whose adherents have long felt slighted by the place accorded Islam and Islamic law in the Indonesian constitution and public policies of Suharto's officially quasi-secular and technocratic 'New Order'. The significant strength of the PPP was demonstrated in the 1977 parliamentary elections, when Golkar, though winning 62 per cent of the popular vote (its spokesmen had counted on 65 per cent to 70 per cent) lost four seats, winning a total of 232, and the PPP gained five seats, obtaining a total of 99 (the remaining party, the PDI, won 29 seats, one seat less than in the previous DPR). Allegations that the Suharto regime and especially its military officialdom have little regard for what Indonesian critics of the regime also call 'the rule of law', have focused on arbitrary arrests, extortions and illegal 'special levies' by local military on vendors and transportation, and above all on the so-called *tapol* question.

The latter refers to the mounting international dispute surrounding the Suharto regime's policies toward the *tahanan politik* (political prisoners), commonly referred to as *tapol*. Some 580 000 persons were arrested in the aftermath of the 1965 coup on grounds of suspected complicity and/or Communist party membership or sympathies. Most of these prisoners were eventually released, but an estimated 35 000 still remained in detention by the beginning of 1976. Controversy over the legitimacy of the grounds for their arrest, the slowness in adjudicating their cases, and the alleged brutality in their treatment have all made the *tapol* over the years an increasing source of embarrassment to the Suharto regime.[70] It is intended, however, that by 1979 all *tapol* will have been released.

But the impression of a repressive regime, insensitive moreover to international protestations, has been further accentuated by the Indonesian invasion of formerly Portuguese East Timor on 7 December 1975, and by the eventual absorption of that territory as Indonesia's twenty-seventh province on 17 July 1976. Despite resolutions in 1975 and 1976 by the United Nations' Security Council that Indonesia should withdraw her forces from East Timor and respect the territory's right to self-determination, the annexation of East Timor continued.[71] By the end of 1978, guerrilla resistance to the Indonesian takeover by the leftist (and according to some official Indonesian sources Communist-oriented) 'East Timor Independent Revolutionary Front' (*Frente Revolucionaria de Timor Leste*) or Fretilin, had been reduced to spasmodic guerrilla raids of a few hundred poorly equipped insurgents in the inaccessible interior of East Timor. Most of the East Timorese population appeared with varying degrees of enthusiasm to have acquiesced in their new Indonesian citizenship.

Unlike Bùrma and the Philippines where resistance of ethnic and religious minorities is of considerable scale and, as we have seen, provides a not insignificant tactical opportunity to local Communist insurgent movements, such resistance in Indonesia is much less so. There are occasional reports of a shadowy 'Free Acheh' movement which seeks independence for the province of Acheh, at the tip of Sumatra, and in the South Moluccan islands there is a small remnant of resistance by the 'Republic of the South Moluccas' movement whose most vocal and active adherents are mainly in exile in the Netherlands. More important has been the secret, militantly Muslim *Komando Jihad* ('Holy War Command'), several hundreds of whose followers in the course of 1977, according to the government, waged a campaign of terror and intimidation in a number of areas in western Indonesia, particularly in north and central Sumatra. The *Komando Jihad*, which denounced the 'infidel' Suharto regime, appears to have been a successor to the *Darul Islam* movement in west Java and its allies in the nineteen forties and fifties. Darul Islam insurgents also sought the establishment of a formal Islamic state in Indonesia.

Perhaps the most serious ethnic secessionist movement confronting the Indonesian government today is the so-called *Papua Merdeka* ('Free Papua') organisation in the Indonesian province of Irian Jaya (West New Guinea). The two thousand or so guerrillas and other activists of this group (backed by additional hundreds both in West New Guinea and among West New Guinea Papuan exiles in adjacent, independent Papua-New Guinea) seek the independence of their West New Guinea territory and some of them, perhaps, also a merger with Papua-New Guinea. In 1977, a change in the leadership of the Papuan insurgent movement in Irian Jaya occurred which has accentuated a new anti-Western and 'Socialist' orientation.[72] This inevitably will provide a new ideological dimension to the Papuan independence struggle of significance to local and neighbouring Communist parties which have thus far remained relatively aloof from the Papua Merdeka cause.

Suharto's *Orba* suffers from the same liabilities, at least in some of the international perception of it, which afflict Marcos' regime in the Philippines and Lee Kuan Yew's in Singapore: its authoritarian features are seen to detract seriously from the undoubted economic growth and stabilisation which these regimes have fostered. In the case of Indonesia, moreover, as in that of the Philippines, legitimate questions can be raised as to whether the mass of the population has necessarily benefited in equitable measure from the huge inputs of foreign credits and development investments, and whether the corruption and collusion in the military-business élite, allied with foreign trade and financial interests, are not too high a price to pay for Indonesian style *pembangunan* (development).

To be sure, there have been steady increases in Indonesia's production of such food crops as rice (from 10.6 million tons in 1969 to 15.7 million tons in 1976), and in principal foreign exchange earners as petroleum (186 million barrels in 1967 to 550.3 million in 1976), while both volume and value of such important exports as rubber, though fluctuating, generally have continued to grow. Rubber exports increased in recent years, for example, from 788.300 tons in 1975 to 811.500 tons in 1976, with a growth in value from $358.2 million to $531.8 million in the same period.[73] Near national self-sufficiency is being attained in production or manufacture of cement, paper, fertiliser and textiles, as the industrial and communications-transportation infrastructure is steadily widening. The inflationary rate continues on the whole to decline (20 per cent in 1975, 12 per cent in 1976, and, in August 1977, 9.7 per cent)[74] and though it remains high, it is nowhere near the catastrophic rate of the last Sukarno years.

On the other hand, relentless population pressure continues to erode gains in growth, and according to calculations by Professor Sumitro Djojohadikusumu, a noted Indonesian economist and one-time state minister for research, unless in the next decades there is a marked expansion in the labour-absorptive capacity of the Indonesian economy, 8.3 million Indonesians, or 13.4 per cent of the projected total 1985 work force (estimated at 62 million, as compared to 48 million in 1975), will be unemployed.[75] Indonesia's per capita income, as Sumitro has pointed out, is significantly lower than that of many developing countries, including its neighbours in the Southeast Asian region: $109 in 1970, $143 in 1975, and a hoped for $245 in 1985. This should be compared with a regional high of about $2 500 for Singapore in 1975. The poorest 40 per cent of the Indonesian population now accounts for only 15 per cent of gross domestic product. Surveys of land tenure, especially in west and central Java, indicated serious concentrations of large ownership in the hands of a few, with 30 per cent or more of rural households in some areas not holding land at all. A pervasive rural proletarisation and rootlessness will have increasingly more serious political and social consequences.

Meanwhile, the managerial deficiencies in the operations of Indonesia's huge oil conglomerate, Pertamina, which were revealed in the course of 1975–6, drew international headlines. Pertamina's indebtedness, eventually calculated at over $10 billion, compelled the Suharto government to draw heavily on its own foreign reserves, and for a while shocked foreign confidence. International investors' interest in, and development assistance to, Indonesia have aggravated already existing and pervasive patterns of bribery, graft and influence peddling:[76]

> Generals with outstretched palms often turn up when businesses become profitable. Payoffs for visas, telephones and various permits and clearances are endemic, and under the table costs, for example, can run up the price of a jar of peanut butter on an oil rig in the Java sea to between $6–$8. Low level government employees who were happy with a Pepsi a decade ago now want hard cash.

One hastens to add that, spearheaded by Admiral Sudomo's *Kopkamtib*, a major effort to combat graft, theft and other malversations, for example, in the operations of state enterprises and in halting 'special levies' on goods in transit, have been made. In the course of 1977–8, there were scores of arrests of civil employees and disciplinary measures against lower-ranking military. Still, most Indonesians are sceptical that the 'Third Development Cabinet' can basically reform the style of the nation's political economy. Worse, perhaps, whether justifiably or not, the taint of business corruption has also come to be associated in popular Indonesian perceptions with members of President Suharto's immediate family.

The 15 January 1974 riots in Djakarta, though ostensibly touched off by the visit of Japan's premier Kakuei Tanaka, actually were caused by a widening dissatisfaction with a confluence of economic developments and security policies that were seen as somehow typical of *Orba*. These included the allegedly nefariously exploitative role of foreign, particularly Japanese, capital and business interests in the national economy, the collusion with those interests of Chinese entrepreneurs in Indonesia, who in turn act as powerbrokers and fronts (*tjukong*) for the business interests of Indonesian military, the special political powers of some presidential assistants or so-called *Aspri* (since dismissed), and, above all, the inability of critical segments of the Indonesian electorate, particularly in the cities, to hold the national leadership and, especially, its élite military apex, accountable for their actions.[77] The main elements of this opposition have persisted, in one form or another, and have remained basic to the anti-Suharto movement of 1977–8, as well.

The absence of a defined and generally accepted mechanism of permitted political opposition appears to cause the dissent to flare up again and again. As we shall see, in Indonesia, as in Thailand and the Philippines, it is this reservoir of unstructured dissent that affords underground Communist proselytisers, parties and/or insurgent movements with some of their best opportunities for united front building and recruitment. It is then not just a question of the uncertain benefits for the mass of the population of the politically authoritarian economic development policies of the Indonesian, Filipino, Burmese or Thai regimes that can provide a seedbed for Communist and other radical appeals.

The case of Singapore in particular suggests that this may not be so. Separated from Peninsular Malaya as a colony in 1946, Singapore's further constitutional development was initially slow, although the first election for the Legislative Council was held in 1948 and political parties developed rapidly. Since the 1959 elections the Singapore government and legislature have been dominated by the People's Action Party (PAP), nominally democratic Socialist but strongly anti-Communist in character. Opposition to 'merger', that is, unity with Peninsular Malaya and the Borneo territories of Sabah and Sarawak, crystallised in the formation, on 13 August 1961, of the *Barisan Sosialis* (Socialist Front) by dissident PAP leftists. Not just the Barisan's ideological opposition to the formation of Malaysia, but its perceptions of the role of foreign capital in Singapore and of the policies of People's China, seemed to suggest an affinity with the MCP. To most observers the Barisan was, in fact, a Communist front. By 1965, two years after it had joined the Malaysian Federation, Singapore seceded, becoming an independent republic within the Commonwealth and following ever since, like its neighbours, a determined domestic anti-Communist policy.

Under PAP and Lee Kuan Yew the economic growth of the Singapore Republic has been the envy of her neighbours. Singapore's leap in per capita income from about US$1 000 to over US$2 500 in the past twelve years, her steady growth in national output running between 7 per cent and 8 per cent per annum in recent years, a minimal unemployment rate (which fell to 3.9 per cent in February 1978), a rise in the consumer price index (about 151 in 1977 as compared to 100 base in 1972) which is more than matched by productivity gains (the manufacturing production index alone was about 168 in 1975, as compared to the 100 base in 1970), and more social services such as hospital beds, doctors and clinics per thousand head of population than anywhere else in the region – all these make the island republic virtually a 'developed nation' exception to its 'undeveloped' region.[78] Population increase is low and stable (running between 1.8 and 1.6 per cent per annum over the past decade), and in fact is the lowest in the region, while the 22.2 per cent per year real growth rate in Singapore's gross national product between 1960 and 1973 was one of the highest, if not the highest, in the world.[79]

Yet despite (and perhaps because of) the ruthless efficiency of the Lee Kuan Yew government and the ability of his long-ruling People's Action Party to win parliamentary election after election over nearly two decades, the fact remains that a significant, non-Communist opposition, though intimidated, and except at election times quiescent, persists. This is less an index to the Lee regime's respect for democratic rights and more a result of the tenacity of the dissent itself. Over the years at least one in every four Singapore voters has demonstrated through the ballot box that he has no use for a regime whose often spectacular economic achievement has been accompanied by a stultification of political and much of intellectual life – and that in a region which because of its entrepôt commercial interests is among the most cosmopolitan in Asia.

The pattern of Singapore political life is perhaps well illustrated by the December 1976 parliamentary elections. In addition to PAP there were five small opposition parties in the running. Four of these, including the Barisan Sosialis, the Singapore Malays National Organisation, the United Front Party and the Singapore Justice Party, formed a 'Joint Opposition Council'. The fifth and perhaps most important opposition group, the Workers' Party, agreed with the other opposition elements not to enter the same constituencies and so weaken the anti-PAP position. The Barisan Sosialis' Communist antecedents are well known, though the degree of present MCP influence in the party, if any, and given the Singapore government's surveillance powers, is more difficult to establish. In no way, however, could the other opposition parties be considered as Communist-controlled or -influenced. Yet, in his 1976 campaign addresses, premier Lee Kuan Yew dismissed the opposition coalition candidates as merely voicing 'what the Malayan Communist Party believes are the popular things', and Lee's colleague, foreign minister S. Rajaratnam, echoed such sentiments, for instance by saying that the 'real' opposition in Singapore was the 'banned Communist Party of Malaya' which the PAP had been battling for years.

This emphasis on the Communist danger, along with warnings to the electorate not to erode foreign investors' confidence in Singapore's steady economic achievements, have not just been the formulas for PAP's continuing success at the polls, but they also constitute the *leitmotiv* of most of the Lee Kuan Yew government's major policies over the years. In the 1976 elections the PAP won 72.4 per cent of the votes and all 53 contested seats; even though more than a quarter of the electorate supported the opposition, the latter won not a single parliamentary seat under Singapore's present electoral system. Predictably, in the aftermath of the 1976 elections two United Front party candidates were convicted of having slandered Lee in suits brought by the premier, and a similar action against the Workers' Party secretary general and main opposition figure, J. B. Jeyaretnam, is, like such actions brought by Lee in the wake of previous electoral campaigns, also likely to be successful.[80]

Concepts of slander may differ, but the question arises, considering

recent Singapore practices, whether any criticism of a government
figure could not qualify. Given the prevailing political climate in
Singapore there is, moreover, no doubt that such libel suits have had a
further and seriously inhibiting effect on the development of competitive partisan politics.

All this is not to say that the Communist underground in Singapore
is inactive. It is to say, however, that official revelations of that
underground's activity require more evidence than government circles have been wont to supply. As Singapore's leading daily, usually
and without hesitation supportive of the Lee Kuan Yew government
has put it, 'it is incumbent on the authorities' not only to stop
subversion, 'but also to make proper and credible explanations to the
people at the right time'.[81] In the course of 1974, caches of allegedly
Communist propaganda materials and weapons were reportedly
discovered and, on 19 and 20 June 1974, booby-trapped banners
urging aid to the 'Liberation Army' and other endorsements of the
MCP's 'Malayan National Liberation Army' were strung in public
places in the city. Earlier, on 18 June 1974, some thirty persons,
including a few prominent figures associated with the Barisan
Sosialis, were arrested on grounds of being members of the CPM.
Shortly afterwards tensions between the Lee government and student
organisations, both at the University of Singapore and at the Singapore Polytechnic Institute, rose to new heights as the students
protested the 'repeated violations of basic democratic principles' in
connection with the arrests. In subsequent months, the Singapore
government took action against continuing student protests, and
foreign minister S. Rajaratnam, in December 1974, warned of the
danger of 'non-Communist' but 'New Left' subversion in the state.
He also criticised foreign news reports alleging repressive
conditions.[82] While some observers were ready to concede the possibility of a new upsurge of covert Communist activity in Singapore
during the preceding months, hard evidence of Barisan-, student-, or
'New Left'-centred subversion was, unfortunately, not forthcoming.

On 30 May 1976, the PAP formally resigned from the London-
headquartered Socialist International (SI), on the grounds, as premier Lee Kuan Yew put it, that the organisation had 'wittingly or
unwittingly become vehicle to further the Communist cause in Singapore'. There had been sharp criticism in SI-member circles of the Lee
government's domestic security policies during previous years, and
particularly of the recurrent arrests and prolonged detention of some

political prisoners. According to premier Lee Kuan Yew himself, in a London press interview in May 1977, sixty-one persons were being held at the time (some for as long as ten years or more) 'without trial under the Internal Security Act'. But the number of prisoners may well be higher, and while some prisoners and former prisoners have formally 'confessed' to various Communist activities or sympathies, other evidence to substantiate such alleged activities has not been offered and there has been concern that the confessions resulted from heavy pressure by Singapore's Internal Security Department and that they have been conditions for the release of some prisoners.[83]

The Singapore government's anti-Communist policy, however, appears to be but one aspect of a broader, 'nation building' effort, aimed at riveting the loyalties of the republic's citizenry to the state, not just through a ceaseless raising of the spectre of subversion, but also through maximising economic development and through education, national military service, and anti-drug abuse and other national campaigns.[84] In connection with this the PAP has become a principal channel of status advancement for young, and generally highly education-minded, Singaporeans, thus creating a co-optative élite recruitment process for 'technocrats' trained for and committed to the Lee Kuan Yew regime's priorities of maximum stability, efficiency and steady economic growth.[85] Political opposition in Singapore, whether Communist or non-Communist, is apt to be neither healthy nor financially profitable. Yet while successive graduating classes of Singapore's secondary and tertiary educational institutions know this message, the undercurrent of dissent persists.

In part, perhaps, because the dominance of one racial group is not so clearly established as in Singapore, and the intractable practical necessity for ethnic Malays and other *bumiputras* (indigenous inhabitants) in Malaysia to come to terms with the economic power of the Chinese in the country has made for a seemingly more multilithic political party system, in practice the pattern of one-party dominance prevails, even if that party is a multi-racial coalition. From 1957, when Malaya won its national independence, through 1963, when Singapore and the Borneo states of Sabah and Sarawak joined with Malaya in the formation of the Malaysian Federation, and until 1974, that one dominant party was the Alliance Party. In 1974 the *Barisan Nasional* (National Front), a still more widely based coalition, including parties from the Borneo states, replaced the Alliance, and the co-optative process of leadership recruitment in Malaysia, compar-

able to that of Singapore's PAP and Indonesia's Golkar seemed to
have become even more firmly established.

The heart of the Barisan Nasional, however, remains the old
Alliance pattern of organisations, dominated in turn by the pragmatic
political conservatism and moderate Malay sense of ethnicity of the
United Malays National Organisation (UMNO).[86] It has been, and
will be for some time to come, the essence of the Malaysian polity that
UMNO-approved leaders head the Malaysian government, just as,
in rotation, one of the nine rulers of the Malayan Peninsula's dynastic
states be Malaysia's *Yang di-Pertuan Agong* or sovereign head of state.
By the same token, an ethnic Chinese or Indian premier of Malaysia
(even if he were a mainstay of UMNO's long-time partners, the
Malaysian Chinese Association – MCA or the Malaysian Indian
Congress – MIC) would be as unlikely as a Sultan of Brunei
becoming Malaysia's *Yang di-Pertuan Agong*. Among the reasons for
Brunei's refusal to join Malaysia in 1963, reportedly, was the fact that
Brunei's rulers would not have had constitutional equality, in terms
of assuming the head of state position, with Peninsular Malaya's
dynastic rulers.

Between 1963 and 1965, Singapore premier Lee Kuan Yew's call
for a 'Malaysian Malaysia' (political and constitutional equality
between ethnic Malays, Chinese and other Malaysians) sharply
accentuated old racial animosities and, in some Malay quarters, did
so in terms of the spectre of Communist subversion.[87] Singapore's
1965 secession from Malaysia did not assuage Malay fears of a
resurgent 'Chinese Left', however. In the nineteen sixties such predominantly Chinese parties as the Democratic Action Party (DAP) and
the so-called 'Gerakan' (the Malaysian People's Movement or
Gerakan Rakyat Malaysia) appeared quite interested in equality between Malaysia's racial communities and even their mildly socialistic
programmes seemed to confirm stereotyped Malay perceptions. Yet
in the early nineteen seventies, practical political considerations
could triumph. The Gerakan and such other smaller Chinese parties
as the People's Progressive Party (PPP) formed local political or
electoral coalitions with the Alliance Party, and in 1974 joined the
Barisan Nasional. Another intermittent political enemy of the Alliance, the conservative Muslim, strongly Malay-oriented Pan-
Malayan Islamic Party (PMIP) has on occasion been able to ally
itself with UMNO and the Barisan. The PMIP since 1971 is usually
called Partai Islam (Islamic Party of the Malayan Peninsula or *Partai
Islam Se Tanah Malaya* – PAS).[88]

In 1974, another predominantly Chinese party, the Sarawak United People's Party (SUPP), joined the old Alliance core in the new Barisan Nasional that swept the parliamentary and state assembly elections of that year. SUPP's entry into the Barisan Nasional was the more remarkable because during most of the sixties it had primarily been the vehicle of opposition to the idea of Malaysia and the Alliance regime among the 320 000 or so Chinese of Sarawak (about a third of the state's total population, and its largest ethnic group). To the Alliance and its supporters in this period, SUPP was a Borneo variation of the feared 'Chinese Left' in Malaya. SUPP followers were widely thought to be members also of the proscribed Sarawak Communist Organisation (SCO), a conglomeration of Chinese youth, labour, and farmers' organisations which, during the days of Indonesia's anti-Malaysia 'Confrontation', developed a still continuing guerrilla resistance movement.[89]

The SUPP entry into the Barisan, like that of the Gerakan and PPP, suggested that ideological polarisation ('left' versus 'non-left') in terms of traditional communal cleavages need not be a fixture of Malaysian politics. Still, that combined polarisation and cleavage remains a basic element of Malaysian politics and the long history of the conservative MCA's partnership with UMNO sometimes seems to do little to offset it. That element is confirmed by the ongoing insurgency, assassinations and other terrorism carried out by the predominantly Chinese CPM and its factional offshoots along the Thai-Malaysian border and in Malaysian towns. It also seems confirmed for some Malays by the durability, despite reverses, of the 'North Kalimantan Communist Party' (NKCP), the SCO's new organisational matrix.

There is yet another reason. On 13 May 1969, in and around Kuala Lumpur, a frightful racial riot erupted in the wake of the general elections held in the country three days previously. The Alliance Party had again emerged victoriously but DAP and the Gerakan showed significant electoral gains. There had been inter-racial killing during this 1969 election campaign and, on 9 May, during a funeral procession in Kuala Lumpur of a slain campaign worker for the small, predominantly Chinese, Labour Party of Malaya (widely believed to be a front for the CPM), banners with sayings and pictures of Mao Ze Dong had been borne along. Post-election processions, rumours and mutually provocative behaviour by political partisans in the Malaysian capital soon led to new violent clashes. When the violence was over, 196 had been killed (all but fifty-three of them Chinese), according to official data. More reliable unofficial estimates put the number slain at closer to one thousand.[90]

In the riots' aftermath, a national emergency was proclaimed and parliamentary government suspended (it was reinstituted in February 1971) as a 'National Operations Council' temporarily assumed direction of the government.[91] In an effort to restore racial harmony new policies were implemented, ranging from a proscription of publication or dissemination of news or reports that might exacerbate racial tensions to the promotion of a new national concept of Malaysian identity, along guidelines established by a 'National Consultative Council' of prominent personages from all racial communities. The *Rukunegara* (national doctrines) first announced in August 1970 established common national objectives and principles as a kind of nation building 'civil religion'.[92] On the basis of such principles as belief in God and support for king, country and constitution, Malaysians are to practise inter-racial harmony, democracy, and participate in a fair sharing of national wealth in a just society. In July 1971, a 'New Economic Policy' was inaugurated by the Malaysian government within the context of its 'Second Malaysia Plan' (1971–5) and it committed the government to a more diversified and rewarding participation of ethnic Malays in the national Malaysian economy. This new Malay participation was quantified in a popular if not exactly accurate slogan that by 1990 thirty per cent of the nation's wealth should be in Malay hands.[93] New assistance was to be given to Malays in industry and commerce. To Chinese and other observers, however, the 'New Economic Policy' meant UMNO's and the Alliance government's capitulation to the more militant 'or chauvinistic' (that is, anti-Chinese) Malay critics of the government, long disturbed over Chinese economic dominance and over the seemingly worsening living conditions for certain Malay groups, particularly rubber smallholders.

Thus the 'New Economic Policy', presumably considered officially as a means of abating the tensions that had exploded in the May 1969 riots, tended to be seen by Chinese as further discrimination against them. The Third Malaysia Plan (1976–1980), in turn, sought to meet this Chinese criticism by emphasising the need to improve the economic and social conditions of all Malaysians, 'regardless of race'.[94] At the same time the major role of foreign (for example British) capital and corporate interests in the Malaysian economy has called for change.

These various nuances in national planning also suggest something of the diversifying communal character of the Malaysian economy. On the one hand, racially based economic disparities broadly persist. Though Malays form some 48 per cent of the nation's total population of 12 million (the Chinese and Indians 35 per cent and 9 per cent respectively, with the remainder composed of smaller groups such as Borneo Dayaks and others), their share in the nation's wealth, however one cares to measure it, is proportionally a good deal less. Probably less than 2 per cent of the corporate sector of the Malaysian economy is owned by Malays (as compared to 1 per cent for Indians, 22 per cent for Chinese and 61 per cent for foreigners) and household income per month has been estimated at M\$387 for Chinese, M\$310 for Indians and only M\$179 for Malays. Even in agriculture, still the main general employment category of Malays, the Malay share of ownership in rubber production is only one-third of 1 per cent (as compared to 1.3 per cent for Indians, 13.2 per cent for Chinese, and 77.7 per cent for foreigners). In all other forms of agriculture the Malay share again is only 3.6 per cent (one-fifth of 1 per cent for the Indians, 9.2 per cent for the Chinese, and 66.8 per cent for foreigners).[95]

On the other hand the 'New Economic Policy' did give impetus to the emergence of new Malayan commercial and industrial entre-preneurs and today generally sharp class demarcations based on wealth are becoming more and more apparent in the Malay commun-ity. There is now a slowly growing but distinctive Malay 'middle class' of some 50 000 or more, at an intermediate income level but with modern consumer aspirations, and usually affiliated with gov-ernment services, the professions and the larger, internationally oriented corporate enterprises. A much larger, poor lower class, comprising among others the 67 per cent of the Malay community who live in rural areas and who 'grow rice or tap rubber for either low prices or low wages', and a small, extremely wealthy, Malay élite, with top political and/or aristocratic family connections, are at the other ends of this developing Malay class structure.[96]

Social strata in the Chinese community are also becoming more marked, and there are some indications that class identification is transcending racial lines. There are at least some 300 000 Chinese farmers, mostly rubber smallholders, who are confronted by the same pressures of fluctuating prices for their cash crops and by inflation as the Malay peasantry. Additionally, there are some 800 000 poor

Chinese in the 400 or so 'New Villages' to which they were forcibly relocated by the government during the Emergency of the nineteen fifties. Because of their serious neglect by the government in the past decade and because of problems in securing land titles from suspicious Malaysian state governments these 'New Village' Chinese have become as promising a recruiting ground for CPM proselytisers as younger, better educated but unemployed or underemployed Chinese youths in the towns.[97]

Youthful joblessness, notwithstanding impressive overall growth in Malaysia's gross domestic product (from $13.8 billion in 1973 to an estimated $18.4 billion in 1977) and in rates of increase of total employment (3 per cent per annum during the 1957–67 decade), was already a problem a decade ago (running nearly 18 per cent on an average for those in the 15 to 24 age group) even as formal education expanded rapidly.[98] Although overall unemployment dropped from 7.4 per cent in 1970 to about 6.8 per cent in 1977, still, because of the 'huge backlog of unemployed' (in 1975 that backlog was 297 000, in a labour force of 4.2 million), and the estimated entry of 748 000 new entrants into the job market during the period of the Third Malaysian Plan (1976–80), the 'government faces a tremendous task of employment creation for the next five years'.[99] Difficulties are apt to be especially severe for those under 25 years of age. As one authoritative analysis has put it: 'One might say that unemployment is at the moment a particularly pressing problem of the urban young and inexperienced who have received a fair share of school education.'[100] This problem, it should be stressed, cuts across racial communities. It has been noted, for example, that 'not all Chinese youths are from rich business families', and that those Chinese youths those parents are petty traders are now discovering that, because of the system of licences and quotas favouring the Malays in small trade, the 'traditional scope of commerce' for young Chinese now 'is also dwindling'.[101] Meanwhile, educational opportunities too are narrowing for Chinese youths in Malaysia because of preferred consideration of Malay applicants. Of the more than 5 900 first-year students accepted in 1977 at Malaysia's five universities, 74.9 per cent were Malays, 19.9 per cent Chinese, 4.5 per cent Indians, and the remainder from other races.[102] These proportions are hardly in keeping with the overall racial composition of the Malaysian population.

Important efforts to resettle landless peasants on cleared land and provide them with adequate housing have been made by the Malaysian government under the auspices of such agencies as the

Federal Land Development Authority (FELDA). By 1974, after nearly a decade and a half of operations, FELDA had developed more than 627 000 acres for agricultural use, and more than 42 000 families had been settled on cleared land. However, problems of peasant indebtedness and of limitations on diversification of agricultural production, according to critics of FELDA, have prevented a significant containment of what in many areas must be perceived as a steady 'immiseration' of the growing rural population, with all its politically destabilising consequences.[103] Malaysia's prosperity, built on exports of rubber, tin, palmoil, lumber and petroleum, has a fragile base, and fluctuations in world prices can hit the small Malayan or Chinese producer and worker harder than the foreign conglomerates. In November 1974, in and near the town of Baling, in the northern part of the state of Kedah, and in such neighbouring communities as Selema, Sik and Changloon, Malay rubber smallholders, badly squeezed by falling latex prices and skyrocketing inflation joined with local agricultural workers and other food and cash crop farmers in protest demonstrations and in a 'hunger march' of some 12 000 persons which eventually had to be dispersed by police using tear gas.

Land reform to be sure is a reality in western Malaysia. But in circumstances where a minimum of six acres is required, according to official Malaysian sources, for a modest agricultural income, a polarisation of holdings is taking place in Peninsular Malaya, in which, according to official data, in the year 1974–5, for example, 48 per cent of smallholders had less than five acres of land each, while the top 12 per cent had holdings from ten acres on up, to as high as ninety-nine acres each.[104] There is a steady rural proletarisation in Malaysia. And coupled to the smallholder's problems, whether Malay or Chinese, this has given new appeal to the CPM's agrarian reform programme. CPM pronouncements, moreover, now continuously refer to the 1974 Baling protests as a turning point in the life of the Malaysian peasantry.

It is apparent that a commonalty of economic problems and interests is beginning to fuse the same but once separated social strata of Malays and Chinese. Such a process is of critical long-term significance to the Communist movement in Malaysia. Hard-pressed Chinese and Malay rubber tappers and rice farmers are finding a measure of kindred concerns, just as members of the developing, modern middle class of Malays, enjoying a significantly improved standard of living today, 'tend to identify themselves with the better-off Chinese'.[105] This new inter-racial dynamic can hardly be said to dominate the Malaysian political economy, however.

Meanwhile the Malaysian government, in a manner comparable to regimes in neighbouring Singapore, the Philippines or Indonesia, seems quick to attach the label 'Communist' to any manifestation of opposition. This tendency has the effect of polarising those caught in the above mentioned changes in the class structure of the country. UMNO's and the Alliance Party's 'grand old man', former premier Tunku Abdul Rahman, in his published analysis of the 13 May 1969 Kuala Lumpur riots, charged that Communists had been financing the opposition parties in the 1969 election, including the conservative Muslim PMIP. Rahman said that 'It was the Communists whose influence was at work behind the scenes urging on various other Opposition parties' speakers to harp on people's frustrations and place the blame on the Alliance Government.'[106] More than eight years later, the UMNO's and the government's perception of the opposition was still the same, even after former opposition parties had been welcomed into the Barisan Nasional coalition. Thus, in commenting on the bitter inter-party dispute within the Barisan coalition in the state of Kelantan, in October and November 1977, involving UMNO and the PAS (formerly PMIP), which had led to public demonstrations and the proclamation of emergency powers by the Federal Malaysian government, the Malaysian home affairs minister sounded a familiar theme. He warned that 'Communist terrorist elements' could 'take advantage' of the political dissension in Kelantan and that the 'infiltration of people and arms' from the Communist guerrilla strongholds across the Thai border could not be ruled out.[107]

It would be easier to dismiss all such pronouncements as mere political rhetoric, were it not for the new security measures under the 1976 Constitutional (Amendment) Act, which, as indicated earlier, deny fundamental constitutional rights, including *habeas corpus* and access to legal counsel, to those held under any of Malaysia's security laws or to those subject to prevailing measures on preventive detention and restricted residence or movement. Moreover, 'several hundred men and women are still in detention, untried, for political reasons', among them, for instance, a number of leaders and members of the Labour Party of Malaya (suspected of being a CPM front), and some of these have been held for a decade or more.[108]

The danger of Communist subversion is seen by the government as coming from unexpected sources. On 22 June 1976, for example, two prominent Malay intellectual figures, Abdul Samad Ismail, managing editor of the nation's premier daily, *The New Straits Times*, and

Samani bin Mohammed Amin, news editor of the Malay daily *Berita Harian*, were arrested on charges of having propagated Communism through their papers. Abdul Samad Ismail subsequently confessed publicly to having joined the CPM in 1949, and admitted having used a 'sophisticated and subtle approach' in influencing younger UMNO leaders to adopt his views.[109] On 3 November 1976 there followed the arrests of other political figures, among them the former deputy minister for science and technology, Datuk Abdullah Ahmad, and the former deputy labour minister, Tengku Abdullah Majid, because of alleged CPM connections. As evidence of all these charges has not been published, and no public trials have been held, scepticism surrounds the veracity of the confessions by Samad and others now being held because of supposed CPM ties.

The official Malaysian perception of all this is essentially that of *raison d'état*. For one thing, public disclosure of evidence in security cases may obviously not be in the interests of Malaysia's national security, particularly in light of the fact that the government is confronted by a persistent, armed insurgency. For another, there is no doubt of the legitimacy of the *process* by which the 1976 Constitutional (Amendment) Act on security policy was enacted into law, although the most serious questions about the substance and application of the Act have been raised in legal circles. No major court test involving the Act has thus far occurred.

Beyond these issues, of course, is the question of the future viability of the Malaysian state, considered in light of its history of racial tensions and pervasive communal problems. To maintain domestic stability and ensure national survival, the present sweep of security policy, as a democratically elected Malaysian parliament has clearly indicated, is considered justified. And yet, in non-Communist Malaysian opposition circles, such as the DAP, and in some quarters supporting the Barisan Nasional government too, the same question is asked which one can also hear today among the student critics of the Suharto regime in Indonesia, or among the anti-Marcos *Laka ng Bayan* (People's Force) in the Philippines: national security yes, but at what price?

B. Indochina

Between 14 and 20 December 1976, the Fourth Congress of the Lao Dong (Workers') party was held in Hanoi, attended by 1 008 dele-

gates from the now unified Socialist Republic of Vietnam (SRV). The
SRV itself had been formally created on 2 July 1976, when the
Vietnamese National Assembly in Hanoi endorsed the merger of
North and South Vietnam under North Vietnam's leadership. Additionally, there were present at the Fourth Lao Dong Congress delegates from some two dozen ruling and non-ruling Communist parties
from around the world, in keeping with the general self-
congratulatory character of the proceedings. The Fourth Congress
enlarged the party's Central Committee and Politburo. But the same
wartime, aging leadership, consisting of such veteran Vietnamese
Communists as Pham Van Dong (SRV premier), Le Duan (party
general secretary), and Vo Nguyen Giap (titular defence minister),
have remained firmly in control. As the aftermath of the death of Ho
Chi Minh in September 1969 already indicated, spectacular purges
and falls from power are not in the Vietnamese Communist style. In
the context of the Fourth Congress amended party by-laws also
changed the name of the party from Lao Dong party to Vietnam
Communist Party (VCP), and standardised membership procedures
and party organisation throughout the new unified SRV. According
to Politburo member and party organisation specialist Le Duc Tho,
official party membership at the close of 1976 was over 1.5 million, or
about 3.13 per cent of the total SRV population. Following the Fourth
Congress also special emphasis was placed on party youth work (the
party's youth organisation is now called the Ho Chi Minh Communist Youth Group), and on reform of party cadres, particularly those
in the South, many of whom were said to have succumbed to
opportunities to enrich themselves in the immediate aftermath of the
Communist occupation of Saigon (now Ho Chi Minh City), in April
1975.[110]

At the Fourth Congress the party's Politburo announced it was
proceeding with the complete 'socialist industrialisation' of the unified Vietnam state. The Second Five-Year Plan (1976–80), as
revised, outlines broad development policy objectives, including: (1)
maximising food production; (2) industrialisation, especially development of heavy industry; (3) relocation of labour, particularly in
the South, envisaging the movement of some 7.5 million South
Vietnamese and about 500 000 North Vietnamese to rural areas; (4)
creation of large combined agricultural-industrial production com-
plexes or 'agro-factories' with the necessary labour force to man them;
(5) and improvement of infrastructural (for example, communica-

tion), planning, and managerial systems, with some allowance for pragmatic, efficiency-oriented (that is, less ideological) production methods, and for local direction. As in the realignment of the educational, military, judicial, or other public institutions and establishments, SRV development policy has meant not just the development of a new national public administrative system for the entire country, but more particularly also the imposition of North Vietnam's will on the 'liberated' South. In the latter process, 'social' control, exercised by Northern party cadres and Northern public officials whose roles are sometimes indistinguishable from those of traditional colonial bureaucrats, has been the decisive element.[111]

The 'New Economic Zones' (*vung kinh te moi*), though part of a national SRV development effort, are meant also, and, perhaps primarily, as matrices of a 'transforming' re-educational experience and ideological indoctrination for tens of thousands of South Vietnamese. In the New Economic Zone, where large-scale land reclamation or development forms the basis for new food production and planned industrial projects, desired compliance with the new Communist work ethic is the obvious index to political loyalty. There are also an estimated 50 000 and perhaps as many as 200 000 inmates of some fifty special 're-education camps'.[112] These inmates particularly include former civil and military officials of the pre-'liberation' regime in the South, as well as the professionally trained and those with managerial and executive backgrounds. Conditions in the re-education camps reportedly vary, but in some they appear to be quite poor, and deaths from disease, and malnutrition, as well as executions of alleged recalcitrants have been common. It is noteworthy that prominent figures of Hanoi's erstwhile front groups or of the Hanoi-sponsored 'Provisional Revolutionary Government' (PRG) of South Vietnam, have been excluded from membership in the new Central Committee of the VCP. For example, Nguyen Huu Tho, the former president of the National Liberation Front of South Vietnam, Huynh Tat Phat, former president of the 'Provisional Revolutionary Government' (PRG) of South Vietnam, and Madame Nguyen Thi Binh, the PRG's 'foreign minister' and perhaps most publicised spokesperson at the Paris peace conference, were so excluded. But they have not sunk into obscurity. For example, Madame Binh became the SRV's education minister, and Nguyen Huu Tho an SRV vice president.[113]

Even as the SRV in the course of 1976–8 began contending with sharp declines in food production, caused as much by management confusion in the agricultural collectivisation schemes in the South as by various natural disasters, implementation intensified of the VCP's blueprint for the revolutionary transformation of South Vietnamese society. By the year 2000, when the country's population is expected to be around 100 million, most Vietnamese, it is expected, will be living in large 'agricultural production units' or 'agro-farms' of from fifty to one hundred thousand people, organised around some 500 district towns.[114] The relocation programme, apart from opening up farmland and facilitating more effective control over malcontents, reportedly will also aid in promoting national defence as settlements are established along the Cambodian frontier.[115] The New Economic Zones, meanwhile, having fulfilled their transitional role as land development, land reclamation and light industrial projects and as carefully supervised and policed 're-education' matrices for relocated Southern Vietnamese, will, presumably, disappear and be subsumed by the agro-farm structure.

A careful balance between agricultural production and urban-industrial production is envisaged, in accordance with the guidelines of a threefold revolutionary process. These 'three revolutions', as the closing resolution adopted by the Fourth National Trade Union Congress held in Hanoi in May 1978 put it, involve fundamental changes in 'the relations of production, in science and technology, and in ideology and culture'. Encompassed in this multiple revolutionary process is a national effort to 'strengthen the *socialist relations of production in the North* and *complete socialist transformation in the South*' [italics supplied], initiate 'emulation drives for productive labour' in order to build socialism 'with industry and thrift', and so that agriculture and industrialisation can be developed according to the Second Five-Year Plan.[116] The distinction drawn in VCP policy between North and South (where, unlike the North, the Socialist transformation remains to be 'completed') appears to have been reinforced by this revolutionary prospectus.

The SRV government seems quite prepared to deal with possible adverse social and political reactions to its 'transformation' measures, especially those in the South. An example is the campaign, which began in March 1978, to abolish in effect the middle class of entrepreneurs and traders in the country. As formulated by SRV premier Pham Van Dong, this campaign meant that:[117]

On the basis of developing the socialist trading network, the state, serving as an efficient rear service organization in production and as an excellent housekeeper for all the people, will encourage and help the majority of the innumerable small traders to switch to production. A number of people engaged in small scale service industries and small traders will be assigned to the trading network to serve socialism.

And Vu Dinh Lieu, 'chairman of the people's committee' (that is, mayor) of Ho Chi Minh City (formerly Saigon) at the same time explained that 'everyone must work in order for us to achieve self sufficiency', and so, at present, 'workers, peasants, white collar workers and even soldiers are carrying out production work'. Hence the 'switch' of 'bourgeois tradesmen' to 'production' (by which presumably is meant primarily agricultural and industrial employment) should be considered as being in accordance with the SRV's new 'strategic slogan' which is: 'Everything for production, everything for socialism, everything for the people's happiness.'[118] An editorial in Hanoi's principal daily, *Nhan Dan* (10 April 1978), described the petty urban bourgeoisie, like the landlord class, as being 'linked with the system of private ownership' and, therefore, 'historically' doomed to extinction. As the process of 'switching' the 'bourgeois tradesmen' to 'production' in effect meant forcible expropriation of private shops and other enterprises and 'relocation' of their former owners and employees, the stream of refugees from the SRV came to be swelled by tens of thousands of members of Vietnam's erstwhile 1.2 milllion ethnic Chinese minority. Abolition of small private enterprises particularly affected these Chinese residents and the expropriation process itself afforded opportunity to Vietnamese to express historic anti-Chinese sentiments. Some 90 000 Chinese residents of Vietnam, alleging inhuman treatment by Vietnamese, had fled across the border into People's China by the end of May 1978. Relations between Beijing and Hanoi, already strained because of China's cautious support and sympathy for Cambodia in its continuing border conflict with the SRV, deteriorated even more.[119]

Not just Chinese, but other inhabitants of Vietnam as well were overtaken by the sudden sweep of 'de-bourgeoisisation' of the SRV's economy. By April 1978 the rate of those escaping from the country – particularly in small boats – had reached a new high: in Malaysia some 2 300 refugee Vietnamese 'boat people' had landed in April 1978 alone, bringing the total to more than 8 800 Vietnamese in refugee camps in that country.[120] In Thailand, by that time, there were at least 180 000 Indochinese refugees (mostly Laotians and Vietnamese, but also at least 15 000 Cambodian refugees) and the hard-pressed Thai government, anxious to improve relations with the SRV, was reaching the limit of its willingness to accommodate still more escapees.

The plight of the refugees has clouded the SRV's international relations, as has to a much more limited degree scattered but continuing anti-Communist resistance in Vietnam itself. Their experiences in 'relocation' in the New Economic Zones, and having to deal with ubiquitous North Vietnamese cadres and officials who rarely conceal their disdain and distrust of South Vietnamese, have given many Southerners second thoughts about 'liberation'. Whether many of them still regard 'liberation' as one Da Nang resident did, who according to Hanoi's account 'for thirty years' had been 'dreaming of this moment. It's the happiest day of my life,'[121] may well be doubted. A guerrilla resistance by groups of former South Vietnamese military and their various covert and cautious sympathisers, together loosely structured in what is termed the *Phuc Quoc* ('national restoration') movement, is fed by the SRV's inability, thus far, to reconcile to itself prominent Roman Catholic and, particularly, Buddhist elements in the South. In November 1977, Thich Man Giac, a member of the central executive council of the United Buddhist Church in Vietnam, an organisation which in the nineteen sixties had been prominent in opposing the American-backed South Vietnamese government, arrived in Paris. He had been smuggled out of the country, in order, reportedly, to begin a worldwide tour calling attention to the religious persecution in Vietnam since the advent there of Communist power.[122] Instances of Vietnamese Buddhist monks setting fire to themselves in protest against the Communist regime have also been reported.[123] But unlike similar acts of Buddhist self-immolation in 1963 (when they were directed against the anti-Communist regime of President Ngo Dinh Diem of South Vietnam), the recent Buddhist suicides have not attracted much international attention nor stimulated organised protest.

Domestic resistance also continues to confront the new Lao People's Democratic Republic today. At least 30 000 Vietnamese troops were still stationed in the country in early 1978. The guerrilla forces operating against the Laos government now headed by Souphanouvong (as president of the Standing Committee of the

Supreme People's Council, that is, president of the republic), and
Kaysone Phomvihan (prime minister, and secretary general of the
Phak Pasason Pativat Lao or Lao People's Revolutionary Party, usually
designated as PPPL), appear to consist first of all of former Laotian
regular and irregular military, including defectors from the Communist regime, who are opposed to Laos having become a satrapy of
Hanoi.[124] Savannakhet, near Thailand's border, is one major centre of
the present anti-government resistance which, reportedly, receives
covert assistance from Thai military circles. There is also continuing
resistance by Meo tribesmen in the northern mountain areas, particularly in the region of the Plain of Jars.

However, official pronouncements of the PPPL-dominated Laotian government have since 1976 given the impression that the
Laotian people are united and are energetically setting about
'coordinating' the 'national revolutionary task' with 'democracy' and
with the interests 'of the three Indochinese countries' and 'world
peace'. A 'national congress of people's representatives' convened in
Vientiane on 1 December 1975 under the auspices of the PPPL acting
through its principal front, the previously named *New Lao Hak Sat* or
Lao Patriotic Front. The Congress formally abolished the monarchy
in Laos and established a 'people's democratic republic'. At the
Congress Kaysone Phomvihan's proposal that Souphanouvong be
proclaimed president of the new 'Lao People's Democratic Republic'
was also adopted and subsequently a new cabinet with Kaysone
Phomvihan as premier was announced. All earlier 'transitional'
governing mechanisms, that had afforded increasing political accom-
modation to the Communist Pathet Lao forces and to the PPPL in
previous years, such as the 'Provisional Government of National
Union', established on 4 April 1974 in order to maintain a precarious
balance between Communist and non-Communist forces in the
country, were declared to have been abolished.[125]

National development in the Lao People's Democratic Republic
has been seriously slowed, not just because of the domestic resistance,
but also by the persisting exodus of most trained and skilled Laotians
(as well as many illiterates and unskilled) who have poured into
Thailand and other neighbouring countries. Authoritative estimates
have put the total number of refugees from Laos following the
consolidation of Communist power in 1975 at from 100 000 to
200 000, out of a total population of about 3.1 million.[126] The flight of
merchants and tradesmen further aggravated the serious effects of

unrealistic controls over the movement of foodstuffs imposed by the victorious Pathet Lao forces. As prices rose, harsh attempts to combat inflation aroused popular resentment:[127]

> One attempt to get to grips with the inflationary spiral was to send troops to the market to arrest any seller who raised the price of red chili peppers above a stipulated maximum. When several old women were seized for the offence, the wrath of the market place fell upon the Pathet Lao. Why had they chosen only chilis? Why should chili sellers not be permitted to follow initiated increases by others? And why had the soldiers not grabbed Chinese and Vietnamese storekeepers accused by the Lao of pushing up prices? The Administration backed down in the face of this homespun protest. . . .

An intermittent Thai blockade of trade with Laos, as well as a serious mid-1977 drought, added further strains to the economy and at least 200 000 tons of rice imports were estimated as being required for the 1977–8 year alone. (The US, which had suspended aid to Laos since 1975, supplied 10 000 tons in 1978 on 'humanitarian grounds'.) But in a country such as Laos in which per capita income in 1977 was only $90, where there are fewer than one hundred physicians, and other public health facilities have been described as 'almost non-existent' (despite assistance by Soviet, Cuban, French and SRV medical teams), where even the rudimentary infrastructure and data for long-range planning are lacking, some achievements, for example in educational development (widening literacy, the opening of a new agricultural school in Xieng Khouang province in 1976; as meanwhile some 2 500 students study in Communist bloc countries), nevertheless can be noted. Meanwhile a whole range of nations, from the Netherlands to India, have been making aid commitments. However, heavy agricultural taxation (as high as thirty per cent of production of rice) has aroused the bitter opposition of the peasantry. Wisely, in view of farmer discontent, efforts at collectivisation have been limited to formation of labour exchange teams for joint planting, harvesting and other co-operative ventures.[128]

Kaysone Phomvihan, in an address on 2 March 1978 to a joint session of the Supreme People's Council and Council of Ministers, declared that the nation's efforts in 1978 would be directed toward producing about one million tons of unhusked rice and starchy crops, an increase of about 150 000 tons as compared to the previous year. It seems unlikely that this target will be reached, however, and the state of Lao food production today may, perhaps, be gleaned from Kaysone's statement that in areas where the 1977 harvest had not been good 'it is necessary to encourage the people to support each other with food supplies in order to insure success in this year's farming season'.[129] The present regime, though it has attempted to give its programmes some perspective, announced in December 1976 that it would be unable to adopt a four- or five-year development plan for the time being, but in fact would have to review and implement its various programmes on an annual basis..

The uncertainty of Laos' long-term relations with its neighbours, including those in the rest of Indochina, also affects planned economic development. The thousands of Vietnamese military in the country help to stabilise the Souphanouvong-Kaysone regime, and they also aid in the building of a new road system connecting Laos and the SRV and in the construction of an oil pipeline into Laos from Central Vietnam and an underground fuel storage facility.[130] But although Kaysone Phomvihan, on various occasions, has emphasised the 'solid and longstanding alliance' between his country and the 'two fraternal peoples of Indochina', and although Vientiane and Hanoi in 1977 signed a treaty of friendship that also regularised their mutual frontiers, it is clear that many Laotians take a different view from the present government when it comes to extolling Lao-Vietnamese relations as the 'vital factor' that guarantees 'normality in this region'.[131] Opposition to the heavy dependence on the SRV of the present Souphanouvong-Kaysone regime may be gauged not only from the numbers of former Pathet Lao who have now joined the resistance movement in the country, as noted earlier. It can also be seen from the estimated 40 000 to 60 000 persons who have left the country, among them not just one-time prominent officials of the pre-Souphanouvong-Kaysone government, but also French university-trained technicians and administrative personnel 'generally known for their leftist ideas'.[132] Early in December 1977 a combined force of Lao and Vietnamese military reportedly completed operations against Meo hill tribe rebels in north-east Laos, having killed some 1 300 Meos.[133] But Meo resistance has continued, as has the haemorrhaging of Laos' most skilled and ablest inhabitants, so that, in a vicious circle, the country's dependence on the SRV and its forces also continues, fomenting new Laotian resentments and resistance.

Of the three new Communist regimes in Indochina, however, that of Cambodia has, perhaps, attracted the greatest measure of international concern. Following the demise of the Lon Nol government and the Communist capture of Phnom Penh on 17 April 1975, a 'national congress' of the 'National United Front' of Cambodia was held in the capital at the close of the same year. On 5 January 1976, a new constitution was formally promulgated under which the Royal Government of National Union of Kampuchea (usually designated by its French acronym GRUNK) ended and the country henceforth became known officially as 'Democratic Kampuchea'. According to this new constitution, Cambodia is 'an independent, united, neutral, peace-loving, non-aligned and sovereign democratic country – a state of workers, peasants, and of other workers'.

An ad hoc pragmatism in the further development of governmental institutions is acknowledged, however. In conversations with a team of Yugoslav journalists, who visited Cambodia in April 1978, Pol Pot (formerly known as Saloth Sar), general secretary of the Cambodian Communist Party (KCP) and concurrently the country's premier, reportedly said, 'We have no model, the people will decide on every stage of the revolution,' and 'We do not want to copy anyone.' As Pol Pot explained further:

> There are no schools, faculties or universities in the classical sense, or as existed in our country before the liberation, because we want to put an end once and for all to all remnants of the past. There is no money and no commerce because the state cares for the needs of all its citizens. We had no money or commerce in the liberated territory either. The population from the towns has been moved out. This was the way it had to be. In the towns there were some 3 million citizens and peasants looking for shelter from the war devastation. We were not able to find enough food for them and were informed about imperialist plans to organize guerillas and counter revolution in the towns.[134]

Whatever the justification for the forcible relocation of the population from Cambodia's towns to the countryside, it appears to have been accompanied by systematic efforts to destroy the human infrastructure of the old regime. Tens of thousands of military officers, civil officials, intellectuals and professionals, and others of some prominence in the days before 'Democratic Kampuchea' and their families reportedly were killed, often in mass executions. Together with those who perished during forced marches into the countryside, or who died of hunger and malnutrition in 1975–6, the total number of victims of Cambodia's Communist revolution since April 1975 must be put at 800 000 at least, and probably at more than one million.[135] As the total population is about 7.4 million, the Cambodian holocaust approximates that of the Chinese and Soviet revolutionary purges. There is little question that the deaths of thousands of intellectuals, and of officials of the former regime and of their families, occurred as a matter of deliberate policy.

The fear and suspicion engendered by the violence eventually appeared to infect even the top cadre structure itself. In April 1978, a few days before the regime's third anniversary celebration of Phnom Penh's 'liberation', the national Kampuchea radio warned that there could be no compromise with 'the enemy'. 'Without a clear line' between us and 'other people', the 'enemy's view and ideology' would 'creep' into one's mind 'little by little', and 'it is possible' that 'several of our comrades' already had fallen 'into this trap'.[136] Although, on the surface, the control over the KCP exercised by such party leaders as secretary general Pol Pot, Ieng Sary (deputy premier for foreign affairs) and Khieu Sampan (state presidium chairman, that is, president of Democratic Kampuchea) seemed solid, in fact in August 1977 dissent within the cadre core and higher echelons of the party leadership flared into open rebellion. Revolts, extensive arrests and executions of military and party cadres were reported in the Undon Meechai and Siem Reap areas in western Cambodia. Reportedly, several hundreds of party cadres trained in, and suspected of undue sympathy for, Vietnam, were among those executed. Subsequently, the Chinese and North Korean media congratulated Pol Pot and the Cambodian people on having 'wiped out' an allegedly 'counter-revolutionary group of spies' in their midst. But just who the culprits were has remained a matter of speculation.[137] The intense secrecy surrounding the workings of the revolutionary cadre core or Angka Leou ('Organisation on High'), a group which on 27 September 1977 was formally acknowledged by Pol Pot to be one and the same as the KCP, adds to the aura of terror that pervades so much of Cambodian life today.

Strongly stressing to their people the virtues of economic self-reliance and of a highly puritanical code of hard work, denial of all pleasures, and sacrifice for a higher cause, Cambodia's leaders sought to implement an ad hoc programme of total social and economic change, in which the individual is part of a larger work co-operative or 'people's association', linked with other such units in common, mainly agricultural, production efforts, under the watchful eye of the military and party cadres.[138] Communal kitchens fed these production units. Families sometimes laboured together in one unit but they could also be broken up. A military style routine, requiring work that began before dawn and continued by torchlight well into the night, and which only occasionally was broken up by political lectures and discussions, now pervaded almost every Cambodian's life. Basic education was provided to young children and necessity increasingly dictated use of manpower in the maintenance of other public services, but major towns largely remained deserted.

As a result of the Vietnamese invasion at the close of 1977, some of the 'people's associations' were turned into 'self-defence' units as well. Official media claimed that the co-operatives were expanding in size; for example, in March 1978, fifty per cent of the co-operatives were said to comprise from 700 to 1 000 families, with the remainder ranging from 100 to 700 families. This 'improved collective system' was said to be the 'greatest factor in defense and continuation of the socialist revolution and in all areas of construction' and, indeed, had become 'the foremost strategic factor in national defense'.[139] How long the nearly exclusive stress on self-contained agricultural production could have lasted, however, not only considering its human toll but also the cost in neglect of other basic infrastructural needs, would seem to be in doubt.

A glimpse of Cambodian conditions was provided by the previously mentioned Yugoslav team of journalists whose extensive report was published in mid-April 1978. Among the team's observations were the following:[140]

(1) 'We became convinced there was definitely no longer any hunger in Cambodia because silos in many places were too full to take the entire rice harvests; there were whole mountains of sacks of rice outside the silos.' Fruit and fish, as well as rice are 'abundant'. There are 'no shops, coffee houses, post offices or a developed state administration', except for the co-operatives, and 'the state is the chief buyer and distributor' of all goods, including food. In commenting on these observations of the Yugoslav reporters, one should question, on the basis of Cambodian refugee reports, whether in fact food is all that plentiful and, certainly, whether the distribution of it is very effective,

since malnutrition and shortages are said to continue to exact their toll in human lives.

(2) Agricultural work projects are to be seen everywhere. Mobile brigades go from 'one construction site to another', building dams and artificial lakes. Members of such brigades and those of other co-operatives must do their work on rations of 'between 900 grams and 1 kilogram of rice a day', eating in common canteens that hold as many as 1 000 families, and receiving one suit of clothes a year. Suggestions 'can be made by the workers' to the committees which manage these labour units.

(3) In Phnom Penh 'all the buildings are empty. Shops, hotels, kiosks and gasoline pumps are closed. Road signs are painted over so that the rare foreign guests cannot orient themselves.' Sometimes an 'occasional minibus with Chinese or North Korean experts, of which there are, it is reported, about 3 000 at the moment in Cambodia', and trucks of the mobile brigades, are to be seen. In the absence of imports, the kitchen equipment, refrigerators, boilers and other equipment and appliances are being taken from empty apartments and houses in Phnom Penh by the authorities and put in 'working order'.

(4) 'We saw super-modern medical equipment in Phnom Penh hospitals and foreign diplomats told us they have no complaints to make.' Cambodian officials claim a '95 per cent success rate in combating malaria'. Again, in commenting on these particular observations of the Yugoslav reporters, one should question, on the basis of refugee reports, whether the excellence of medical facilities and public health services is necessarily available to the masses labouring in work units in the countryside and where, reportedly, little medical service is available.

(5) 'No one mentions or asks for aid from outside. Everything is done with spades and pickaxes and manual irrigation pumps. Kilometres of dikes are built with earth carried in baskets.' The only mechanised equipment consists of a few dump trucks and dredgers dating from the days of the previous regime. The main slogan of the KCP is 'Building and development with our own resources'. And yet: 'Some ten years will clearly be needed for Cambodia's rehabilitation to build accommodations for displaced persons and former town dwellers.' One 'has the impression' that the ruins left by war in the country 'will not begin to be cleared up immediately', as the first priority is given to increasing agricultural production. An 'incomprehensible radical-

ism' pervades implementation of this economic priority. For example, Phnom Penh steel safes lie unopened in buildings and 'our hosts told us that no one had tried to find out what they contained because of the principle that the new society should be built with newly acquired resources.'

These eccentricities and the other excesses of the new 'Democratic Kampuchea' would probably have moderated with the passage of time. The internecine conflict between Cambodians and Vietnamese which climaxed in the SRV's 60 000-man invasion of Cambodia in December 1977 after continuous border clashes, on the one hand, caused both Phnom Penh and Hanoi to assume a more forthcoming posture toward their non-Communist neighbours, and, on the other, to begin reassessing some of their domestic policy priorities. By May 1978, Singapore and Cambodia had agreed to revive their trade which had been ruptured when the Khmer Rouge occupied Phnom Penh in April 1975. Telecommunication contacts between Singapore and Cambodia were re-established as well, and the new rapprochement seemed likely to be a harbinger of similar new Cambodian trade contacts with other nations in the South-east Asian region.[141] People's China, herself currently in a less intensely ideological and more pragmatic phase of post-Mao national development, and even prepared to discuss (for cautionary purposes?) the extremism of her own 'Great Proletarian Cultural Revolution' and of 'The Gang of Four' was known to be exerting her quiet leverage on the Pol Pot regime in order to bring Cambodia out of her relative isolation. Increased Cambodian contacts with moderate Communist regimes such as Rumania, which also began in mid-1978, also pointed in the same direction. But the Vietnamese invasion in force by the close of 1978, the fall of the Pol Pot regime, and its replacement on 8 January 1979 by a new Hanoi-backed government seemed to have brought a more despotic phase of Cambodian Communism to an end.

C. Summary: South-east Asian political patterns today

Communist and non- (or indeed anti-) Communist South-east Asia are today in important political respects, remarkably congruent. Both, for example, are essentially committed to what may be called a 'devil theory' in their national development, and (to carry the simile still further), their political theologies both utilise their 'devils' in apparently symbiotic positions in relation to the 'saviour' roles played by national leaders and ideologies. For the non- or anti-Communist South-east Asian world the 'devil' of course is 'Communism' or sometimes a more broadly encompassing 'subversion', which may include religious (for instance Islamic) resistance and/or quasi-secessionist movements which Communists are said to exploit. In turn, in the Communist regimes of Indochina official demonologies are, perhaps, more complex, having to account not only for the continuing 'imperialist' danger coming from the US and her allies, but, as in Cambodia, also for the allegedly nefarious schemes of Hanoi and its attempts to swallow Democratic Kampuchea in an SRV-dominated 'Indochinese Federation'. The threat of the Soviets' 'social imperialism' must also be reckoned with, at least from the point of view of the deposed Pol Pot regime. People's China, in turn, since her 16 February 1979 invasion of Vietnam, is accused by Hanoi and its Vientiane and Phnom Penh satellite regimes of a 'hegemon-ism' of her own. The Chinese, faced with the difficult problem of retaining a measure of influence in the Indochina area, have also begun to encourage a 'Socialist Party' in Laos, as they covertly attempt meanwhile to supply Pol Pot's guerrilla forces. The Sino-Soviet dispute thus has deeply penetrated into Indochina's political constellation, with the result that Hanoi's non-Communist neigh-bours in the region are increasingly pressed to retain both their neutrality and their own security interests.

Since 1967, and the gradually increasing co-operation among most non-Communist South-east Asian countries (with the notable excep-tion of Burma) in the Association of South-east Asian Nations (ASEAN), there has been increasing emphasis on the importance of 'resilience'. As a security concept, both national and regional 'resili-ence' among the ASEAN members requires a mobilisation of human and other resources in order to withstand any untoward political and economic pressures coming from outside the region, and in order to deal with the threat of domestic subversion.[142] Such mobilisation, in turn, focuses on the need for rapid, but planned and orderly, national economic development and modernisation, a process that is fed in the ASEAN community to a large degree by the Western and Japanese money markets and by the multinational corporations. To ensure the continuing flow of this foreign investment capital, a stable domestic national leadership, capable of keeping the confidence of foreign business circles, is deemed essential. This in turn is believed to require maintenance of a strong security posture and a vocal domestic anti-Communism.

The latter need not be *pro forma* or merely ritualistic: the Communist insurgent problem in Thailand and Malaysia is real enough. In the Philippines such a problem at the moment is much less so, while in Indonesia it is virtually non-existent and even officially admitted to be merely 'latent'. Yet, real or not, the threat or its potential must as a matter of policy remain in the public mind, or so it is officially believed. Sceptics may well query if in Indonesia, for example, and even in Malaysia, the periodic official harping on the Communist or sometimes other allegedly subversive threats to the nation primarily serves as a means by which to justify extensive security powers of the state, required, it is thought, in order to guarantee the desired *pembangunan* (development). Hence this *pembangunan* seems almost to *depend* on the existence of a perceived threat of Communist or other subversion.

And, in turn, the Communist organisations and guerrilla 'armies' fighting in Malaysia, the Philippines and Thailand may perceive obvious tactical advantages for themselves in a political environment where extensive government security powers (exemplified by the arrest and detention practices of *Kopkamtib*, the 'Preservation of Order and Security Command' in Indonesia, or by the 'Essential-Security Cases-Regulations' of 1975 in Malaysia, noted at the beginning of this chapter) prevail. For these security powers inevitably arouse fear and resentment, even among those who otherwise would support existing regimes, but who yet desire a more democratic and less security-obsessed political environment. In other words, for South-east Asia's Communists, operating in a non-Communist South-east Asian country, the security policy of the regime in that country, though not intended to do so, can have a desirable polarising effect and thus can be very useful in building a front movement in Communist tactical terms in order to help overthrow that regime.

It is in this sense that anti-Communism and Communism in South-east Asia today establish curious interdependencies and symbiotic relationships, making their respective 'national salvation' (development) strategies dependent on the existence of 'devils' ('Communism', 'subversion', 'imperialism', and so on) and on the need to defeat them. Neither in Communist nor in non-Communist South-east Asia has the question really been faced as to whether the desired

economic national development and related organised population
effort can occur without recourse to an officially sanctioned political-
ideological demonology.

There are other parallels. Communist South-east Asia's political
processes are often perceived in authoritarian terms, appropriate to
what is, after all, a functioning Marxist-Leninist polity. But outside
the Communist orbit, other South-east Asians perceive their own
national political cultures frequently as equally permeated by authoritarian constructs and attitudes. Identification with a strong,
cunning or wise leader, the personality rather than issue-oriented
nature of prevailing Filipino conceptions of admired leadership, the
utilisation of modern political power and technology in order to
facilitate traditional élite dominance – all these have been perceived
as characteristic of Philippine political life.[143] Philippine President
Ferdinand Marcos' use of traditional paternalistic Filipino leadership
patterns (to the president, 'various government officials are his eyes
and ears, his arms and fingers. He is also the father and the rest of the
people are his children,' as one Filipino political scientist has
written)[144] is paralleled by similar practices in bureaucratic-political
relations and in other walks of life elsewhere in non-Communist
South-east Asia. *Bapakisme*, Indonesians call it – from *bapak* or father.

Such paternalistic, patron-client practices enhance the authority of
the central government and its office bearers, and undoubtedly
encourage the dominance of a prevailing government party, whether
it is the Golkar in Indonesia, the Barisan Nasional coalition in
Malaysia, or the *Kilusang Bagong Lipunan* ('Movement for the New
Society') in the Philippines. In terms of providing functional leadership in the interests of a concerted national development effort such
single government parties in non-Communist South-east Asia surely
bear a close resemblance to the one-party rule of Indochina's Communist states today, although the extent to which relatively open and
competitive elections involving a number of opposition parties exist in
the region's non-Communist states, makes for a critically important
difference between them and Indochina's Communist regimes.

Yet with the authoritarian and paternalistic motifs so strong in
non-Communist South-east Asian polities, there is a pervasive problem of determining the legally permitted scope of political criticism.
Despite freedom of partisan operations at election time, the opponents of the People's Action Party in Singapore cannot really feel free
verbally to attack the Lee Kuan Yew government. There is also the

related problem of acquiring the skills of meaningful constitutional opposition. Thus, in Thailand, student critics believe that it was their political militancy that deterred the Thai military from intervening in parliamentary government. What they overlooked was that their very militancy raised further doubts among the public and in various political circles, not just in those conservative ones allied with the Thai military, as to whether the fragile structure of parliamentary democracy in Thailand could or, indeed, should survive.[145]

Thai student 'overreaction' illustrates the inability of most non-Communist South-east Asian states today, with the exception perhaps of Malaysia, to develop broadly acceptable and respected ground rules for political opposition. This lack tends to predispose toward wide (if not wild) swings of the political pendulum, so that, as in Thailand, student opponents of authoritarian regimes (like that of Premier Thanin Kraivichien in 1976–7) see no recourse but to join the Communist insurgents, or else, as in Indonesia in 1978, to submit – 'until the next time'. The tendency, particularly evident in Indonesia, to imply that critics of a prevailing regime, including those who may be opposing the re-election of a governing chief executive, are somehow dangerous and disloyal tends to aggravate the problem. When, in January 1978, opposition to the re-election of President Suharto among Djakarta student groups reached a new crescendo, *Kopkamtib* chief Admiral Sudomo typically explained that recent arrests of some seventy students had taken place 'within the framework of ferreting out subversive elements who are believed to have taken advantage of the students'.[146] Equally typically, evidence for such allegedly 'subversive' influence was never provided to the public.

The stress on maximising national development and modernisation in both the Communist and non-Communist segments of South-east Asia has not safeguarded either segment from the evils of heavily bureaucratised, centralised governments. A common theme of student dissent from Bangkok to Djakarta is that the nationally planned and directed development effort, so heavily dependent on foreign capital and investment confidence, has benefited the mass of inhabitants only to a minimal degree, and that corruption and mismanagement among top officials and military, who are said to be in league with foreign capital, seriously invalidate the claim that tight domestic political controls must be kept so that rapid economic growth may continue. The bribes and pay-offs made to high-ranking Indonesian military and civilian officials by leading American and multinational corporations have long made international headlines.[147] At the end of May 1978 the secretary general of the Thai government's inter-departmental 'Anti-Corruption Committee' in Bangkok made the astounding disclosure that 'over one third of the national budget finds its way into the pockets of unscrupulous government officials each year', that hundreds of cases of corrupt practices among senior officials had been discovered, and that the Committee through its anti-corruption investigations had salvaged some seventy-five million baht in national budget funds during the past two years. Thai premier Kriangsak Chamanand asserted when this report was made that 'it would take considerable time' to eradicate corruption in Thailand because it 'has become deeply rooted in the bureaucracy for quite a long time'.[148]

'Kickbacks', 'key money' and other bribes are commonly viewed by many observers as necessary grease for the wheels of enterprise in most of non-Communist South-east Asia. It has been so for a long time – a matter of student rage and public resignation. But in the Communist segment of the region, the official ascendancy of Marxist-Leninist morality and the advent of a new bureaucracy and élite have not had all that much of an impact on the old practices either. More than three years after the consolidation of Communist power throughout Vietnam, corruption, not just in the 'liberated' South, still appears to be rampant:[149]

Refugees repeatedly complain that in order to sustain themselves they were forced to sell possessions – everything from television sets, refrigerators and motorbikes to wristwatches and clothes – to officials and soldiers from the North. The Secretary General of the Communist Party, Le Duan, said not long ago that 'a lot of property belonging to the revolution in the newly liberated areas was under loose management'. The Communists have sometimes attributed the corruption to the loose and decadent ways intro-duced into the South by the Americans, as if it was a kind of infection, but it seems to exist in Hanoi too. A West German chemical salesman who recently made his first visit to Hanoi, was surprised to be asked by Vietnamese officials for pens, watches and cartons of cigarettes. 'After we finish our negotiations,' they would say 'If you want to take a picnic to the country on Sunday, it will cost you so many cartons of cigarettes.' They even had their favorite brands – Marlboro and Salem.

Organised political reaction to corruption and mismanagement, whether in the Communist or non-Communist segments of South-east Asia, may take a while to make itself felt. But it is here perhaps that the more significant differences between the two segments are likely to become apparent. Political dissent, for whatever reason, in the non-Communist part of the region, after all, can operate in national environments that are relatively more accessible to ideas, goods and services from abroad, that have more media that are willing, if not always able fully or successfully, to articulate criticism of prevailing regimes, and that, however grudgingly, are more likely to be tolerant of the formation of partisan opposition groups than in the Communist Party. Suharto's 'New Order' is sharply taken to task by various observers for its repressive authoritarian features, and rightly so. But one must ask what would have happened if the SRV counterpart of a General A. H. Nasution publicly began berating the government for its insensitivity to student critics. President Ferdinand Marcos' 'martial law with a smile' has its vocal opponents the world over, and with good reason. But one is entitled to query whether in Ho Chi Minh City or in Vientiane, in 1976 or today, one would encounter the same kind and extent of press coverage of domestic and foreign events one could and would find in Manila. Malaysia's sweeping internal security laws understandably provoke condemnation in many quarters. But one wonders if there are, as in Malaysia, half a dozen opposition parties in Cambodia that are regularly contesting seats in open parliamentary elections. Some might regard such queries and comparisons as unfair, in light, for example, of the decades' long period of war and upheaval in Indo-china, but the differences in political ambience between non-Communist and Communist South-east Asia today remain vital just the same.

3

Party programmes and tactics

A. Class, race, and religion

Fundamental to all tactics of Communist parties is their particular
perception of the social class structure of the country in which they
operate, and, concomitantly, of the stage of historical development
attained by the country's ruling élite, according to Marxist-Leninist
precepts. Even in that part of South-east Asia where Communist
parties now rule, the class struggle is by no means considered to have
ended, nor, of course, the evolutionary process toward Communism.
On the contrary, the rigours of class struggle, and the problems of
pushing the transformation of economy and society toward the
Communist goal, can be as severe as in circumstances – prevailing in
the rest of South-east Asia – in which the party is considered
illegitimate and/or in a state of open insurrection against the prevailing non- and indeed anti-Communist government.

To be sure, the advent of Communist rule soon brings a diminution
in the size and scope of the class enemy. The case of Cambodia is
perhaps illustrative. The sweeping changes initiated by the leaders of
the Communist Party of Kampuchea (KCP) and of Cambodia in the
ancient Cambodian socio-economy, according to official sources,
enlisted the overwhelming support of the population, '90 percent' of
whom are described as 'of good quality and firmly revolutionary'.
This ninety per cent of the population is made up out of 'the poor
peasants, the lower middle peasants, the middle peasants in general,
the working people in general', plus 'revolutionaries of other revolutionary class elements' such as 'former intellectuals, students,

petty bourgeoisie, national capitalists and progressive personalities'. This population group of ninety per cent is described as 'strategic', and it 'can accomplish anything' ('Look at the vast ricefields covered with rice in the rainy season').[1]

But what of the remaining ten per cent of the Cambodian population? According to official analysis four-fifths of this remaining ten per cent is a 'middle force', which, though 'revolutionary' in character also, is 'not powerful', and is capable only of making a 'medium revolution' of 'lesser importance'. Just who, in terms of class or occupation, comprises this four-fifths segment official Kampuchean analysis thus far has not disclosed. Finally, one-fifth of the remaining ten per cent consists of the 'hesitant and undecided', who are uncertain as to whether the Kampuchean revolution will succeed, or whether Cambodia can fight the Vietnamese as it now in fact is doing. The small 'middle of the road' group must be 'built up' and given confidence in the revolution. This can be done by explaining the meaning of the revolution to it ('Making revolution means defending the country and preserving the Kampuchean race forever, without becoming anyone's slaves'). Apparently there are no class formal enemies left in Cambodia according to this analysis, only 'medium' revolutionaries and the 'hesitant' – a particular formulation that may well be considered to conform with the results of the bloodbath in Cambodia since the KCP fully assumed power in 1975.

Though innovative in emphasis, perhaps, it might be noted that the above Kampuchean class analysis, first by grouping together the 'workers' with the poor and 'middle' peasants, and secondly, by explicitly recognising the revolutionary potentials of representatives of other social strata, including the petty and 'national' capitalists, is, in broad terms, in agreement with Leninist and Maoist class concepts. The revolutionary potentials not only of the peasantry and workers, but also those of the bourgeois strata were appreciated both by Lenin and Engels and were elaborated upon further by Mao Ze Dong. They subsequently found extensive application in the class analysis of such leading Communist theorists in South-east Asia as Dipa Nusantara Aidit, during the heyday of the Indonesian Communist party (PKI) in the nineteen fifties and early sixties.[2]

For Aidit, writing in 1957, the unfinished tasks of the Indonesian revolution were the completion of a 'national' revolution that would overthrow imperialism, and a 'democratic' revolution that would overthrow the powers of the 'feudal landlords'.[3] In outlining this 'national' and 'democratic' revolution for Indonesia, Aidit hewed closely to the Leninist concept of 'national democracy' as a phase preliminary to the establishment of Communist Party supremacy in a given country. Such variant concepts as 'people's democracy', 'new democracy', and 'bourgeois democracy', originating with Lenin and used extensively by among others Mao Ze Dong and his associates in the Chinese party, describe the same initial stages on the road to Communist hegemony before Socialism can be properly implemented.[4] The proletariat, the poor, middle and even rich peasants (the latter with certain limitations), the petty bourgeoisie (including intellectuals, traders and fishermen), and sometimes too the 'national' bourgeoisie can join in a common front to achieve the tasks of the Indonesian revolution, according to Aidit. Landlords and the 'compradore' bourgeoisie (those with foreign capital connections) are the class enemy because they are the mainstays of feudalism and imperialism, respectively.[5]

Aidit's analysis may be compared to that of Jusuf Adjitorop published more than twenty years later. Adjitorop, then in Beijing, had escaped the anti-Communist holocaust following the failure of the abortive 1965 coup attempt in Indonesia which had been organised by a handful of leaders and cadres of the PKI and dissident Indonesian military (see chapter 2). Ever since then Adjitorop has been a spokesman for a pro-Peking faction in exile of the PKI, periodically issuing statements variously identified as coming from the 'Central Committee' of the PKI or from a 'Delegation' of the 'Central Committee'. On 23 May 1978, on the occasion of the fifty-eighth anniversary of the PKI's founding, Adjitorop issued a statement entitled 'Unite and Carry on the Struggle to Smash the Fascist Military Dictatorship and Build a Free and Democratic New Indonesia'.[6] After castigating the present Suharto government's allegedly 'anti-democratic and anti-people behaviour' in general terms, this statement notes specifically the struggle of three groups which throughout South-east Asia today are viewed by theorists and leaders of non-ruling Communist parties as comprising their revolutionary vanguard: workers, peasants (and fishermen), and students. The latter of course never have formally constituted a social class in Marxist-Leninist theory, and their appearance today in South-east Asian Communist literature and policy statements, sometimes to the exclusion of any discussion of other 'petty bourgeois' groups (as in Adjitorop's 23 May 1978 statement), testifies to the significance of anti-government student movements in the non-Communist segment of the region.

Flexibility in class analysis so as to permit enlistment of as many as possible in a mass united front against limited targets has especially characterised recent programmes of the two wings of the Communist Party of the Philippines. The currently more important Maoist wing of this party, the CPP (Marxist-Leninist) (or 'Mao Ze Dong Thought'), in a policy statement issued in early October 1972, reaffirmed the need to lead a revolutionary struggle against the 'US-Marcos dictatorship'.[7] The statement asserts that because of its 'revolutionary politics', the party can be relied upon not only to meet the interests of the mass of 'workers and peasants', but also to 'respect the legitimate interests of the petty bourgeoisie and national bourgeoisie'. The party describes itself as able to 'mobilize the biggest mass force' in order to overthrow the 'tyrannical government of Marcos'. This mobilisation of the masses is said to involve, *inter alia*, (1) the building up of 'revolutionary trade unions' through insistence on better living conditions for workers; (2) appealing to peasant support by raising demands for reduction of land rent and elimination of usury, and by instituting 'mutual aid and exchange of labor' among the peasants; (3) 'vigorously' arousing the 'student masses' including the formation of 'underground co-ordinating committees' among students in order to 'defy the fascist ban on basic democratic rights' (e.g. the right to demonstrate); (4) encouraging other sections of the petty bourgeoisie, including the intelligentsia (teachers, physicians, nurses, journalists, lawyers and government civilian employees should be won over to the 'anti-fascist united front'); and (5) finding supporters even among the national bourgeoisie whose members, though they cannot bear arms against 'the enemy', nevertheless can be persuaded to give their help through 'support in cash or kind or use of their facilities'.

Apart from the preceding strata, however, the Philippine party's October 1972 policy statement takes note of other groups that should be appealed to or should be 'welcomed' by the party as efforts are made to 'join up with all forces' opposed to Marcos. Such groups include (1) 'officers and men of the reactionary armed forces' who have turned against Marcos, (2) the half million or so expatriate Filipinos working in the US, (3) religious and semi-religious groups, and (4) various partisan political figures from the old parties, the Liberals and Nacionalistas.[8] One might note that the Philippine party indeed has had some success in winning support among these four groups. For example, Philippine army lieutenant Victor Corpus defected to the Communists and before his 1976 capture by the government had become a principal commander of the Communists' 'New People's Army' (NPA). In the US a number of periodicals such as *Philippine Liberation Courier* and *Ang Katipunan*, published in California by anti-Marcos Filipinos, regularly report on and appear to favour the cause of the NPA. And on repeated occasions (for example on 23 December 1974 and 18 December 1976) Philippine defence secretary Juan Ponce Enrile denounced 'radical' clergy for 'consorting' with the NPA rebels or with their sympathisers.[9] The Philippines is the only country in the non-Communist segment of South-east Asia today with a pro-Moscow-oriented Communist party, which, though tiny, has a developed and regularly articulated programme. Comparing the programme of the pro-Moscow party (which continues to call itself *Partido Komunista ng Pilipinas* or PKP) with that of the earlier mentioned Maoist wing, shows certain similarities, especially as regards class analysis. The PKP's programme, adopted at its Fifth Congress (held in 'conditions of illegality' somewhere on Luzon) on 11 February 1973, urges the revolutionary transformation of society by means of a 'national united front of all oppressed masses' struggling together in order to establish a 'national democratic government' that will overcome 'imperialism, feudalism, and monopoly capital'. The 'major' social forces behind the 'national democratic revolution' are the 'working class, the peasantry, the working intellectuals and the progressive ranks of the studentry'.[10] However, the national bourgeoisie and petty bourgeoisie are not forgotten in this analysis, and the PKP programmes hold that a 'progressive outlook' is now also developing in these strata. Hence, all manner of bourgeois cottage industry and small grocery store owners, fishermen and 'low salaried government employees', and even members of the 'big bourgeoisie' not linked to 'foreign monopoly capital', can all be 'objective allies' of workers and peasants in the common struggle for national independence and democracy. As did the programme of the CPP(M-L), so that of the PKP notes the revolutionary potential of dissident Philippine military ('patriotic and anti-imperialist consciousness is developing among young officers and servicemen', as the 1973 PKP programme puts it) and of the clergy (in the Roman Catholic church in the Philippines, 'patriotic young members of the Filipino clergy', deeply feeling 'the plight of the working masses under the yoke of imperialist and feudal exploitation', today are aligning themselves against 'foreign monopoly cap-ital').

One hastens to add that next to these similarities there are of course also significant tactical differences between the programmes, of the Maoist and Moscow-oriented wings of the Philippine party. The 1973 PKP programme, for example, stresses the importance of a 'peaceful revolutionary transformation' of society, including by means of the electoral process, although the people have the right to meet force with force. As early as November 1974 the PKP found words of praise for the Marcos regime's basic land reform programme, though it promised also to continue to struggle for the interests of the peasantry. The PKP has also expressed support for the government's policies of trade union restructuring, increases in workmen's compensation, and development of co-operatives and mutual help associations among the peasantry.[11] The PKP particularly has condemned what it per-ceives as an exclusive stress on 'protracted people's war' and on the tactic of 'encircling the cities from the countryside' to which the CPP(M-L) and NPA policy statements frequently refer. José M. Sison, until his capture in November 1977 the principal CPP(M-L) theoretician and NPA tactician, has criticised as 'revisionist' the CPP(M-L)'s readiness to walk the parliamentary path, and in turn has been attacked in PKP literature for espousing a 'cowboy ideology' by having 'turned the gun into a fetish'.[12]

While there is no denying the CPP(M-L)'s and NPA's heavy tactical emphasis on guerrilla war and on armed struggle as the central experience for all party cadres, it would not be correct to say that the Philippine Maoists have no interest in political action, for example through united national front activity. Their persistent outreach among Philippine students and clergy is evidence of this. But the Philippine Maoists' front building too, it would be fair to say, serves the ultimate purpose of more effective violent confrontation of, and armed struggle against, the Marcos government. Certainly for Sison and his associates, coming to maturity as they did in the nineteen sixties, when parliamentary and other constitutional pro-cesses in the Philippines seemed particularly ineffective and corrupt, the power that flows from the barrels of guns, to use the Maoist adage, always has seemed more appealing than the non-violent variety. At the same time, leaders of the PKP (as distinct from the party as such) appear to be acquiring a new semi-legitimacy in Marcos' 'New Society' establishment. PKP secretary general Felicisimo Macapagal has said that the PKP's readiness to co-operate with the Marcos government serves the purpose of implementation of the reforms of the government and also to strengthen the Marcos regime's 'independent posture' in domestic politics and foreign relations.[13] Encouragement of such an 'independent posture' by the Marcos government (that is, less dependence on the US) is, it may be observed *inter alia*, also a matter of official Soviet policy today. Such violence as exists in the Philippines today is not being caused by the PKP, according to Macapagal, but rather by 'Maoists, plain bandits' and others. As an indication of the relative acceptability in the Philippines today of the PKP's non-violent and collaborationist posture it may be observed that Macapagal and other PKP Politburo members 'have at times even attended occasions at Malacanang, the Philippine White House'.[14]

A special tactical problem for Communist parties is occasioned by the demands of distinctive ethnic or racial minorities in the various South-east Asian countries. An example is Burma. In the nineteen fifties, the badly harassed Burma Communist Party (BCP) under the leadership of Thakin Than Tun formed a coalition with restive, autonomy-seeking or secessionist-oriented ethnic movements in the Union of Burma. Thus the BCP joined the Karen National Union, the Karenni National Progressive Party and the New Mon State Party in a 'National Democratic United Front' (NDUF). With this NDUF, considered subversive by the government, some other secessionist groups such as the Kachin Independence Army and the Shan State Independence Party established a working co-operative relationship, even though they did not formally join the Front.[15]

However, in 1963 the NDUF failed to win concessions in its negotiations with the military junta led by General Ne Win which had seized power in Rangoon on 2 March 1962. The BCP's 'ethnic' allies soon went their own way, leaving the NDUF a hollow shell. A general amnesty issued by the Ne Win 'Revolutionary Council' government on 1 April 1963, for many, including Communist and ethnic secessionist political prisoners, had had little effect on the resistance; and the failure of the NDUF negotiators to win for the various insurgent armies government recognition of their control over the territories they occupied helped to produce a violent intra-party struggle within the BCP. The struggle was instigated by the so-called 'Beijing returnees' in the party. These were cadres who had received their training in People's China and, strongly influenced by Maoist ideology, denounced 'revisionism' and compromise or negotiations with the government, and demanded a militant line. There ensued a protracted intra-party power struggle, marked by expulsion and execution of a number of BCP leaders, including the assassination of Thakin Than Tun on 24 September 1968. According to documents released by the Ne Win government, Than Tun had allowed himself and the BCP to become wholly dominated by the 'Beijing returnees'. During this period the question of future tactical collaboration with the ethnic secessionist armies of the Shans, Karens, Kachins, Mons and others seemed to recede into the background for a while.[16]

By the early nineteen seventies, however, a seemingly more unified BCP, under new leaders, and with extensive aid in weapons and trained cadres from People's China, had staged a remarkable come-back, growing to an army of some 5 000 by 1973 and controlling much of the Shan state region east of the Salween River and the China border.[17] Collaboration (in a changing kaleidoscope of *de facto* alliances with different ethnic armies) continued with secessionist minorities. But the latters' own strength and aims increasingly presented difficulties for the BCP. The much smaller, increasingly Moscow-oriented Communist Party of Burma (CPB) or 'Red Flags', even before the capture of its principal leader Thakin Soe on 8 November 1970, in the context of stepped-up government security campaigns, had already announced its opposition to the ethnic separatist movements in the country.[18] This reflected the Soviet position toward Burma's regional problems. The pro-Peking BCP, perhaps more fully realising the long-term united front advantages inherent in the continuing nationalities' opposition to the Ne Win regime, was loath to follow suit, however. Instead, the BCP developed (as did the NPA with respect to the secessionist Moro National Liberation Front in the Southern Philippines) the position that amelioration of ethnic grievances and 'true' autonomy would be possible once the party's reforms for the country had been implemented.

The BCP's point of view was exemplified in an address by party chairman Thakin Ba Thei Tin in May 1975. After reviewing all potential support groups of the party, Tin declared that the BCP would indeed form a united front 'with the armed forces of various nationalities' fighting the Ne Win government. But, he added, the BCP believed in 'equal rights' for all Burmans, and this meant that the 'liberation' of the majority lowland Burmans was 'correlated' with the liberation of the Shan, Kachin, Karens and other minority groups.[19] The latter phrase was taken to mean that the era of Communist style 'liberation' for majority and minority groups in Burma would be the same, and that political secession for ethnic rebels was not being contemplated. And so, despite united front appeals, the relations between the BCP and the nationalities' resistance in Burma has often been an uneasy one, despite their common opposition to Ne Win's government.

In recent years some Burmese ethnic independence movements have particularly resented alleged BCP territorial encroachments and infiltration. It is well to note also that the Communists' unwillingness to endorse explicitly the ethnics' political aims stems from the paramount position of the class struggle concept in Marxist-Leninist thought. In Marxism-Leninism the all-pervading class struggle encompasses, and is deemed more important than, racial or minority conflict. As the history of ethnic minority problems in various Communist states, whether the USSR or Yugoslavia, People's China or the SRV, shows, official policy is essentially a thinly disguised assimilation, accelerated by ideological training no less than by common work experience. Secession or even 'autonomy' in the manner advocated by some Burmese ethnic movements such as the Karen National Union and by the Moro National Liberation Front in the Philippines or even 'autonomy' would simply not be tolerated.

On occasion the tactical shifts made by a Communist party in South-east Asia on this question may seem particularly blatant. At its first National Congress in 1935 the Indochinese Communist Party adopted a resolution which recognised the 'right of all nationalities to full liberty', pledging that after the overthrow of imperialism, 'each nationality will have the right to self determination' and would be permitted to choose either to adhere to the new Communist state in Indochina (then apparently envisaged as including Vietnam as well as Laos and Cambodia), or to proclaim a 'separate state'. By 1951, however, with Communist power consolidated in at least one part of Vietnam, the programme adopted by the Lao Dong (Workers', i.e. Communist, Party) no longer talked of the right to separation of Vietnamese nationalities. Instead, the programme put emphasis on the need of the nationalities to unite and help each other, and 'resolutely' to struggle against 'chauvinistic nationalism' and all 'imperialist' manoeuvres that might create dissension among the ethnic minorities. Then, by 1960, after several 'autonomous zones' for minorities had been in operation for a number of years in the Democratic Republic of Vietnam (North Vietnam), the DRV's amended constitution declared the country to be a 'unified multi-national state'. The constitution said further that such 'autonomous zones as may be established' in the nation are 'integral and inalien-able parts of the Democratic Republic of Vietnam'.[20] And so self-determination for ethnic nationalities seems to have disappeared in the unified Socialist Republic of Vietnam, and the same constitu-tional principle as that of the DRV is being applied with respect to the place of minorities.

Where the racial composition of a South-east Asian country is somewhat more evenly divided, however, as in Malaysia, the Com-munist Party's ethnic policy position can be particularly hard to define. Malays and ethnic Chinese comprise about 53 per cent and 36 per cent respectively of Malaysia's total population of twelve million, and as the Communist movement both in east and west Malaysia historically has been largely Chinese, finding a basis of appeal to Malays has been rendered all the more difficult for the Communist Party, also because for the past two decades successive governments have been attempting to provide educational and economic advan-tages to the Malays in order to equalise their chances in life with the Chinese. In an environment of continuing conflict over such Malay-Chinese equalisation, the various factions of the Communist Party of Malaya (CPM) reflect and, indeed, help to accentuate their nation's communal tensions. The private Chinese schools, historically a re-cruiting ground of Malaysian Communists, have remained of special concern to Malaysian Communism, and charges that through policies of standardisation of the school curricula and general use of the Malay language the Malaysian government 'is frantically carry-ing out its policy to eliminate Chinese language education' in the country have remained the CPM's stock in trade over the years until this very day.[21]

Yet it is precisely such CPM defence of Chinese language education that rivets the ethnic Malay's stereotyped conception of 'Chineseness' ever firmer to Communism. In turn anti-Communism has popularly often come to be identified not just with a defence of the Malay language and the broader Malayan cultural heritage, but also with Islam as the quintessential quality of 'Malayness'. Toward the close of 1974, after several weeks of student demonstrations in various localities, and police raids on the campus of the University of Malaya in Kuala Lumpur, the Malaysian government published a White Paper (presented to the Malaysian parliament on 19 December 1974) entitled 'Communist Party of Malaya – Activities within the University of Malaya Chinese Language Society'. This paper sought to demonstrate that the student 'Chinese Language Society' on the Kuala Lumpur campus was an integral element of the CPM's underground recruitment campaign and that 'under the guise' of studying Chinese literature and culture the society was really a conveyor belt for Mao-flavoured CPM propaganda. It is to be noted also that it was the University of Malaya 'Malay Language Society' which had been in the van of the local student counter-attack on the allegedly subversive activities of the 'Chinese Language Society'.

The interplay of racial and religious communalism with pro- and anti-Communism in Malaysia is further exemplified by the CPM's front organisation, the *Parti Persuadaraan Islam* (Islamic Solidarity Party), usually referred to by its acronym Paperi. Originally formed in 1965 as a unit of one of the 'regiments' of the CPM's 'liberation army', Paperi seeks to capitalise on Malay identification with Islam, and on orthodox Muslim demand for greater recognition of Islamic law, up to and including in effect advocacy of a wholly Islamic state embracing present-day multi-racial Malaysia. Such a state would straddle the Thai-Malaysian border, because among Thai Muslims in southern Thai provinces like Yala (long estranged from the central Thai government in distant Bangkok) a sense of unity with their more orthodox Muslim Malay co-religionists across the frontier has at times been pronounced.

Although Paperi's cadre core is quite small (numbering perhaps no more than one hundred led by a five-man Central Committee of CPM veterans), the group is not just a mere paper Communist front. The effects of its appeal in present-day Malaysia should not be minimised. In various statements by Paperi's Central Committee, the Malaysian governments of the 'puppet Abdul Rahman' and of other premiers like Abdul Razak and Hussein Onn are described as having been 'hostile to Moslems', as 'brutally exploiting' those Malay Muslims going on the *hadj* (pilgrimage to Mecca), and, in its foreign policies, as being guilty of 'the betrayal of the struggle of Moslem Palestinians against Zionist Jews'.[22] The aim of Paperi is a 'Malayan democratic republic', a phrase of CPM vintage, reflective also of the kind of tactical and ideological union of left of centre republicanism and

Islamic purism encountered in such contemporary Middle Eastern regimes as those of Libya, Syria and Iraq.

In reaching out to the Malay mass with this Islamic centred approach, the CPM-Paperi not only seeks to overcome the Communists' liability of being anti-religious (the favourite theme of pro-government Malay Muslim leaders) but also facilitate a transition to a new class consciousness among the Malay masses. Such a class consciousness, in the Marxist-Leninist perception, presumably transcends communal loyalties. For next to its Islamic focus, Paperi emphasises the plight of the Malay rural population, the world of the rubber tappers and smallholders, small rice farmers and agricultural labourers. It is not just to the religious sentiments of these people, but to their economic problems as well that Paperi appeals address themselves. In a broadcast statement in the middle of March 1976, Paperi for example spoke of the problems of the 'Islamic believers in our country' who 'can hardly keep from starving':[23]

> More and more peasants in the country have gone bankrupt, and tens of thousands of them have been deprived of their land under the fabricated accusations of illegal land occupation. Several hundreds of thousands of acres of their land have been seized and controlled by the Federal Land Development Bureau and other bureaucratic organizations. All this has aroused the strong indignation of the Islamic believers and their resolute resistance to the reactionary regime.

The Malaysian government's Federal Land Development programme (FELDA), while fostering the land acquisition and resettlement of hundreds of impoverished landless Malays and smallholders over the years, has also aroused leftist criticism because of its loan provisions for peasants and the peasants' inability to pay land taxes.[24] In recent years, moreover, Malaysian rubber producers (about 48 per cent of whom according to the Malaysian government have holdings under five acres, and only 12 per cent of whom hold plots from ten acres on up, while 25 per cent have no land of their own at all, but are tenants and sharecroppers)[25] have been badly hit by price fluctuations of latex. This, even as the annual inflationary rate (24 per cent in March 1974), saw the cost of standard consumer goods skyrocket. On 21 November 1974, in Baling, in East-Central Kedah state, not far from the guerrilla-infested Thai-Malaysian frontier, it came to violent protest demonstrations by thousands of smallholders. To this Baling 'rising' both Paperi and the CPM's 'Peasant Front' have frequently referred in recent years as marking a 'new phase' in the 'struggle' of the Malay peasantry.

On 20 December 1975, the CPM Central Committee adopted a new 'draft land program', based on the party 'new democratic' policy of working for the abolition of 'feudal' and 'semi-feudal' characteristics in Malayan agrarian relations and dedicated to the principle that land should 'go to the tiller'. With this new land programme Communism in western Malaysia strengthened its tactical approach to the ethnic Malay community, and as one illustration of Communist agrarian policy in South-east Asia today, the main features of this 1975 CPM land programme may perhaps be summarised below:[26]

(1) The heart of Malayan land reform, according to the CPM programme, is the confiscation of all lands belonging to the 'British monopoly capitalists', for example rubber, palm and tea estates, and their transfer to the control of the Malayan 'People's Republic'. After the transfer of control, estate and farm workers will participate in the management of the taken-over estates. The lands of 'other foreign monopoly capitalists' will be dealt with on the basis of their owners' attitudes 'toward our revolution'. *Inter alia* one may note that, of the foreign-owned estates in West Malaysia today, those held by predominantly British capital remain the largest.

(2) All land, including rice fields and agricultural implements, held by 'bureaucratic organs' (such as Malaysian government development agencies) or by 'bureaucrat capitalists and national traitors' (presumably all those Malaysians opposed to the CPM and the new 'People's Republic') will also be seized. The taken-over rice fields are to be distributed free of charge to landless or landpoor peasants.

(3) Uncultivated 'wastelands' now under government control will also be distributed free of charge to landless or landpoor peasants.

(4) Varying treatment is to be accorded to lands held by different groups of owners, for example, 'tyrannical landlords', 'enlightened landlords', 'middle' and 'small national capitalists', and 'poor peasants'. In passing one may note perhaps the Maoist flavour of these ownership distinctions, particularly as between 'tyrannical' and 'enlightened' landlords.[27] 'Tyrannical' landlords will have their land confiscated outright. But only the 'surplus' land of 'enlightened' landlords is to be seized ('requisitioned and purchased through consultation') and then is to be freely distributed to the landless and

landpoor peasantry. The lands of the 'small' and 'middle' national
capitalists (for instance, lands held as investments by retired lower
officials or by merchants) will be 'protected' by the 'People's Republic'. But the living and working conditions of the tenants and/or
workers on these lands will be 'improved' through 'consultations',
presumably with the officials of the CPM and new 'People's' government. As for 'poor peasants', their 'legitimate rights' to such land as
they now hold will be protected. Presumably 'poor peasants' stand to
benefit from the distribution of lands confiscated from 'British
monopoly capitalists' and 'bureaucratic organs'.

(5) Lands owned by religious organisations, temples, public welfare
organisations and religious teachers are to be 'respected' by the new
'People's' government. One may note *pari passu* that, as in Indonesia
and in the southern Philippines and southern Thailand, private
Islamic schools and foundations in Malaysia, as well as Muslim
scholars of the writ (*ulama*), may have considerable holdings; indeed,
in some areas ulamas are among the richest landowners in Malaysian
rural society. It is noteworthy that the CPM, recognising ulama
influence, is not anxious to offend Islamic leaders and institutions in
Malaysia.

(6) 'Usurious' debt transactions will be cancelled, and interest rates
charged to the peasantry will be reduced greatly; meanwhile the
CPM also opposes all 'exorbitant taxes and miscellaneous levies'.
Rural commercial transactions should be fair to all concerned, and
government agricultural services and co-operatives may not exploit
the peasant through the sale of farming tools, fertilisers and other
needed implements.

(7) 'In sum the party's general line on land reform is to rely fully on
the poor peasants and farm workers; to unite closely with the middle
peasants; to win over the rich peasants; to abolish the neo-colonialists
and feudalist land system step by step; to liberate the productive
forces in the countryside, and to develop agricultural production.'

With suitable adaptations the main themes of the preceding land
reform statement of the CPM are found also in the programmes of
other Communist parties throughout the South-east Asian region. In
the current programme of the Maoist wing of the PKI, the Indonesian
Communist Party, for example, which was first announced in
November 1967, Indonesia is described as being in the grip of the
'vestiges of feudalism' all through the countryside, as landlords
exercise a 'monopoly' on land holdings, and as an extensive debtor

bondage of the peasantry prevails that reduces the latter to mere 'slaves of the usurers and landlords', with all manner of feudal labouring and service duties (*pologoro*) being required of them.[28]

The worsening economic plight of the mass of the Indonesian rural population, according to this same Indonesian Maoist perspective, results in 'ever greater numbers of peasants' losing their lands, and going to the cities in an attempt to make an uncertain living. But in the cities they usually sink into vagrancy. The way out of all these problems is a sweeping agrarian reform: 'all lands owned by foreign and indigenous landlords' will be confiscated 'without any compensation' and the taken-over lands will be 'distributed to the farm labourers and poor peasants free of charge, individually', to be 'their individual property'. Modern estates shall be owned by the state, *pologoro* and other 'feudal' duties shall be abolished, and 'all debts the peasants owe to usurers and landlords shall be cancelled'. Like the CPM land reform programme, that of the pro-Chinese wing of the Indonesian party is not committed to taking over the holdings of relatively wealthy peasants. For example, in the Indonesian party's programme one reads that 'lands and other properties of the middle peasants shall be protected from infringement'.

As in Malaysia, so in Indonesia (where organised Communism is much weaker and has been driven far more deeply underground than in west Malaysia), a gradually spreading polarisation of landholdings, along with the steady growth of the landless rural proletariat, adds appeal to Communist agrarian tactics. The Marxist concept of *verelendung* ('immiseration') fully applies to Indonesian rural society. A recent case study of land tenure patterns in one *kabupaten* (district) in densely populated central Java province shows nearly 30 per cent of rural households not to have any land at all. At the same time nearly 20 per cent of the best land is reserved for local officials or government use.[29] According to a January 1976 statement of Indonesian agriculture minister Thayib Hadiwijaya, landownership in Java now *averages* only 0.6 to 0.8 hectares per farmer family, which is said to make it 'impossible' for most farmers to raise their incomes even though they take part in government sponsored production intensification programmes.[30]

Other calculations suggest that only one in three farm families in Java now own sufficient land to support a family. Some 48 per cent of Java's rural labour force is either unemployed or works less than 35 hours per week, or has an income below the poverty level of 20 kilograms of rice per month. Many have been forced to sell their land so that the number of landless is increasing. Even the spread of inexpensive tools such as the sickle is reducing the demand for farm labour.[31]

Work on estates also offers little prospect. Trade union analyses demonstrate that some estate workers receive wages as low as 50 Rupiah (1 US dollar equals 415 Rupiah) a day. Industrial wages are not always much better. A study of the wage levels in 114 enterprises in central Java showed that as many as 59 paid a minimum wage of under 5 000 Rupiah a month.[32]

As the population continues to increase, a rootless, impoverished, semi-vagrant 'floating mass' of people also grows in numbers, an appropriate target for Communist tactics throughout the region. The steady growth of the rural proletariat in Java has reached the point, in the view of one observer, where 'literally thousands of landless families crisscross the Javanese countryside, following the harvest from West to East, and then returning for the next season as the paddy (rice) starts to yellow on the fields again'.[33] What the present writer has elsewhere called a 'scavenger economy'[34] in Indonesia is certain to be aggravated by 1985 when, as public works and power minister Sutami predicted in a gloomy forecast in December 1976, some twenty million people on Java alone will have no place to live either in villages or in the urban areas, and will be consigned to exist as mere 'loafers'.[35] There is no indication that, despite its significant financial stabilisation efforts and strongly development-oriented policies over more than a decade, Indonesia's Suharto regime is any nearer to being in a position to contain the spread of extensive pauperisation.

On occasion Communist agrarian analyses address themselves not just to the peasants' problem, but also offer a wider scope on the general effect of the transformation of the agrarian socio-economy as a result of growing inputs in the region by the present day multinational corporations. The PKP or Moscow-oriented branch of the Philippine Communist Party is virtually alone in the South-east Asian area in having attempted to analyse what it calls the 'neo-colonialist' transformation of the old, family oligarchy-ruled Philippine estate economy into the modern system of multinational-operated 'agro-businesses', linked to the raw materials needs of Western and Japanese industries, as well as to the new processing industries in the Philippines themselves. As one PKP analysis has put it:[36]

In agriculture, the new imperialist strategy entails the expansion of processing industries, and thus the reduction of land and labour resources devoted to rice and corn production so that these resources could be employed in a widely diversified agricultural production to provide a constantly adequate supply of materials for the processing industries, including vegetable and fruit canning, poultry and meat packing and small scale cottage industries. These industries will be adjuncts of multi-national companies and will each concentrate on a particular complementary stage of the whole productive process. . . . Land reform in the hands of foreign monopoly capital becomes a method of breaking up the land monopoly of the old landlord oligarchy to pave the way to the development of raw material and food processing industries, as well as to small scale adjunct manufacturing.

The triple interlocking of multinational corporations, new Filipino small-scale and adjunct industries (such as food processing), and large-scale 'agro-business' food and raw materials production, on the one hand encourages the growth of the Filipino bourgeoisie, not just in the traditional entrepreneurial but also and more particularly in the modern managerial sense. This development will also help to weld the Filipino professional groups from lawyers to accountants closer to the 'neo-colonialist' business establishment. At the same time the transformation of old estate agriculture into modern, 'corporate farms' and more diversified 'agro-business' production is seen by the PKP as turning the 'impoverished' tenant farmer more and more into 'half peasant and half proletariat', thus providing labour for the new multinationally ruled domestic industries.

This whole process, however, according to the PKP's perception, cannot but aid, in the long run, a polarisation of social strata and class consciousness in the Philippines. Such polarisation is facilitated in the bourgeois strata, for instance, by the deliberate fostering of 'various schemes of corporate shares dispersal for raising capital resources of monopoly corporations from the savings of employees and wage earners'. While on the opposite end of the social scale, the *sisantes* or landless rural semi-proletariat rapidly grows in numbers (according to the PKP the sisantes are 'now a bigger army than the tenants'), finding an existence in wholly proletarian employment in the cities or else with the better situated peasantry who in turn are benefiting from the new small-scale agriculturally oriented processing industries and enterprises. The expansion of modern 'agro-business' or 'corporate farming' (for example, '13 new sugar mills opened in the last 4 years have absorbed an additional 5000 hectares for sugar production', and the labour force in the sugar-producing areas now totals more than 400 000 according to PKP analyses) further absorbs but also heightens the proletarian class consciousness of the rural working masses.[37]

In keeping with Leninist (and Maoist) precepts, Communist party programmes do not perceive the above noted accelerating class polarisations as occurring without the emergence of internal strata nuances that can be tactically important to a particular party. For example, the new dynamism provided by the multinational corporations today to indigenous bourgeoisie in the South-east Asian region has a 'boomerang' effect, in that some segments of this bourgeoisie for ideological or business reasons begin to find themselves coming increasingly into conflict with foreign capital and corporate interests. Two decades ago such prominent Communist theoreticians in South-east Asia as the late chairman of the Indonesian party, D. N. Aidit, following Leninist precepts,[38] had already made a point of stressing the vacillating but also the potentially 'revolutionary' attributes of the 'national' Indonesian bourgeoisie, competing as it did with foreign business interests in the import-export sector of the economy.[39] More recently Francisco Balagtas, PKP Central Committee member, has noted that the 'left wing' of the Philippine bourgeoisie today, reformist in outlook, is not linked with foreign 'monopoly' capital. According to Balagtas the 'ruling bourgeoisie' in the Philippines has, in fact, a shifting centre and today is composed of those who are 'chafing' under the country's partnership with the 'foreign monopolists'.[40]

In light of the preceding, the 'anti-imperialist' and 'anti-feudal' programme focus, standard among Communist parties in the non-Communist segment of South-east Asia at present, can perhaps be better understood. Operating in conditions of illegality these parties seek to build as broad a united front appeal as possible. In this effort the 'national' or 'left' bourgeoisie, including its intellectual-professional elements for whom a shift away from prevailing martial law or 'emergency' rule toward democratic constitutionalism is particularly attractive, can be mobilised in the struggle to reduce foreign political and economic ('monopoly capital') interests. At the same time, and especially in the context of the Communist perception of a 'neo-colonialist' transformation of the multinational-dominated economy, growing ranks of the landless rural proletariat and semi-proletariat are believed to be particularly susceptible to the old Communist battle cry: 'Land to the tillers!' The PKP's concept of the modern big 'agro-business' and 'corporate farming' rural economy, with its mass of proletarianised *sisantes*, also lends new colour to the old idea of the 'anti-feudal' struggle against the landlords as Communist parties for more than half a century have sought to propagate it in the Asian countryside.

Emphasis on a presumably intensifying social stratification and class consciousness is, of course, not confined to PKP analyses. Also in South-east Asian nations with particularly extensive racial and other communal group loyalties the class approach prevails in Communist theory and class consciousness is said to be deepening as a result of the dynamics of foreign 'monopoly'- and 'imperialist'-dominated national economies. Even in Malaysia where, as we have seen, there are blatant Communist attempts to play on communal grievances, whether racial or religious, the principle of class solidarity is not lost sight of. In west Malaysia, in June 1978, an important CPM statement, commemorating the 'thirtieth anniversary of the national liberation war against Britain', declares that in order to develop the revolutionary armed struggle in Malaya it is necessary to 'solve the nationality problem'. However, the 'nationality problem' must be viewed from a 'proletarian, not a bourgeois viewpoint', which means that it is necessary 'to emphasize class unity, not disparity among nationalities' in Malaya. The class unity approach means an essential stress on 'the idea that workers and peasants of all nationalities belong to one family and that the working people of all nationalities are class brothers'. Poverty is not confined to, nor a problem of, a particular nationality, but 'of class', according to this CPM precept.[41]

The revolutionary mass movement in Malaya is viewed by the CPM in at least some of its policy pronouncements in standard, broad-based, intergroup terms. However, even more than other Communist parties in South-east Asia today, the Communist Party of Malaya and its two rival offshoots have had little use for explicit class appeals to the 'national' or even the 'petty' bourgeoisie as such, preferring to couch programmatic proselytising among the bourgeoisie in terms of the latter's specific components or interest groups. Thus while 'workers', or 'peasants', are customarily mentioned that way in class terms in CPM policy statements and appeals, the 'petty' and 'national' bourgeoisie are not. Instead reference is made in CPM statements to owners of 'medium-sized and small enterprises' or to 'medium and small businessmen' who are said to be 'dissatisfied with the reactionary ruling clique' or who have 'condemned' the Malaysian government's economic policy which, it is alleged, 'only serves the plundering activities of the foreign monopoly consortium' in the country.[42] For the CPM the term 'bourgeois' appears to be essentially an epithet of opprobrium, as, for example, in its references to 'bureaucratic bourgeois' who, along with the 'landlord class', are agents of 'imperialism' and 'feudalism' against which the party is struggling.

One may perhaps note that South-east Asian Communism's tactical stress on a class consciousness that transcends racial or other communal loyalties is, even in the Malaysian environment, not misplaced. To be sure, significant racial differences remain evident in the Malaysian economy and CPM tactics clearly are designed to exacerbate group grievances. It has been estimated, for example, that only 2 per cent of the corporate sector of the Malaysian economy is owned by ethnic Malays, while Indians own 1 per cent, Chinese 22 per cent and foreigners 61 per cent. Household income per month averages M$387 for the Chinese, M$310 for the Indians, and only M$179 for the Malays. Even in agriculture, the main general employment category of Malays, the Malay share of ownership in rubber production is only one-third of 1 per cent (as compared to 1.3 per cent for the Indian, 13.2 per cent for the Chinese, and 77.7 per cent for foreigners), and only 3.6 per cent for all other forms of agriculture taken together (one-fifth of 1 per cent for Indians, 9.2 per cent for the Chinese, and 66.8 per cent for foreigners).[43] In the aftermath of the bloody clashes between Malays and Chinese in Kuala Lumpur in May 1969, the Malaysian government, through its 'new economic policy', made explicit attempts to accelerate a more rewarding Malay participation in the country's national economic development – a policy which, in turn, further aroused Chinese apprehensions.

And yet, there is no doubting the signs that communal cleavages and Malay-Chinese antagonisms are increasingly being crossed by intra-communal polarisations of wealth and class identities, as is the case elsewhere in the region. As one observer has noted, 'At one time it was believed that poor Malays would be happy to see rich Malays being driven around in luxury', presumably deriving 'vicarious prestige' from it, but 'increasingly this is thought to be no longer so'.[44] Current official economic policy is to lift the standard of living and the level of economic participation for the poor of all racial groups, not just Malays. Here one may observe that stereotypes of 'poor' Malays and 'rich' Chinese are particularly misleading. Toward one end of the scale the slowly growing middle class of Malays (recently estimated as comprising some 50 000), with intermediate income levels and modern consumer aspirations, now 'tend to identify themselves with the better-off Chinese'.[45] Meanwhile some 300 000 Chinese farmers, many of them rubber smallholders, are confronted by the same pressures of fluctuating prices and inflation as the Malay small-holders. Indeed, the plight of thousands of poor rural Chinese relocated in some 400 'New Villages' during the Emergency of the nineteen fifties today plays a role in CPM tactics, as it is to a degree among these Chinese rural poor that the party has developed its support group (Min Yuen). The Chinese poor in Malaysia also comprise unemployed youths often with above average education – another CPM recruiting ground. Today, in part because of these Chinese educated unemployed, 'there is more sympathy for the "underground"' of the CPM 'in the towns and cities than before'.[46] It is noteworthy, however, that unlike in the older generation, the beginnings of a new inter-ethnic class or group consciousness generally have not got hold of the youthful poor; the young Malay and Chinese educated unemployed do not appear to be converging, on the contrary. Perhaps, as a legacy from their experience at university where Malay and Chinese students are apt to strengthen their separate identities through their respective Malay and Chinese lan-guage societies on campus, recent university leavers, especially when struggling to find employment, retain, at least initially, a strongly divisive sense of ethnicity. This is why recruitment of young, educated Malays by the CPM has remained so difficult, since the party frequently continues to be stereotyped among Malays as essentially being a vehicle for Chinese ethnic interests. After more or less satisfactory employment has been achieved, however, and the mem-bers of Malaysia's major racial groups have been drawn into the modern, consumer-oriented urban culture, then, as has been indi-cated, a Sino-Malay convergence based on a mutuality of class interests and tastes can become evident. Conversely, the harsh realities of the rubber smallholder's life can make for a convergence of interests among Chinese and Malays at the lower end of the socio-economic scale.

And so CPM tactics, in a way, try to have the best of two tactical worlds: to recognise and appeal to the separate religious (that is,

Islamic) and ethnic identities of Malaysia's major racial groups, and, at the same time, to insist in conformity with Marxist-Leninist orthodoxy that common class interest transcends these divergent group loyalties. No opposition Communist party in South-east Asia has developed quite to the same extent such a dual tactical approach as that of the CPM.

The divergence of orthodox theory and social reality demands other adjustments. All Communist parties in South-east Asia, including the ruling parties in the Indochina area, insist, in line with standard Leninist doctrine, that the 'working' class, that is by implication the industrial proletariat, leads the revolutionary transformation of society and economy. Certainly in the non-Communist segment of South-east Asia this is to a large extent mere fiction, because apart from the small size and underdeveloped state of the industrial proletariat, any organised activity of the industrial proletariat, for example, typically through trade unions, is closely controlled by the prevailing regimes. It has not always been so. But today not a single labour organisation of any size or operational significance exists in non-Communist South-east Asia that can be said to be an arm of the Communist party, in the manner, say, that the Central Labour Organisation of Greater Indonesia (*Sentral Organisasi Buruh Seluruh Indonesia* – SOBSI), for more than two decades and until its demise in 1965, was an agitational and recruiting arm of the Indonesian Communist Party. The role of organised labour, under the no-nonsense security-conscious and development-minded regimes of non-Communist South-east Asia, is exemplified by the characterisation in a Singapore government publication a few years ago which speaks of a 'radical' transition in the life of organised labour in the island republic in the recent past, 'from a period of traditionally militant trade unionism' to the present era of 'tripartite co-operation' of labour, business entrepreneurs and government, 'with modernization and economic growth as the primary concern'.[47] Singapore's National Trades Union Congress (NTUC), with which more than three-fourths of all unionised workers are affiliated and which rarely deviates from the wishes of premier Lee Kuan Yew's ruling People's Action Party, certainly represents this tripartite co-operative philosophy.

Not all countries in non-Communist South-east Asia have achieved the relative sophistication in trade union organisation and programmes, combined with efficiency in surveillance, intelligence-gathering and preventive control exercised by the government, as is the case in Singapore. In Thailand, for example, the labour movement is still comparatively in its infancy (there were only 153 trade unions in July 1976, with an estimated membership of about 80 000).[48] Effective, nationwide organisation or co-ordination of programmes and policies have been difficult to develop. Though a few ethnic Chinese cadres of the underground Communist Party of Thailand (CPT) have long been active in some of the Bangkok unions, the Thai labour movement generally is as yet too undeveloped to play a 'vanguard' proletarian role in Communist tactics. In 1974, a 'Labour Co-ordinating Centre' was established by more radical trade union activists in Bangkok. The Centre functioned briefly as an 'informal labour federation' for local unions, but it increasingly became infiltrated by student militants who urged strikes and other disruptive actions primarily for political reasons, apparently perceiving unions as organisational weapons against the Thai government. The Soviet embassy in the Thai capital, as part of its reportedly general tactics at this time of supporting students and other anti-government militants, is said to have subsidised a number of strikes initiated by the Labour Co-ordinating Centre. Increasingly more conservative or apolitical affiliates turned away from the embryo federation and after 1975 it soon began to fade away.[49]

Yet the Centre's brief alliance with Thai student radicals had been a not unimportant tactical indicator for the CPT. After 1976, when the party's ranks began to swell with several hundreds of former students who had fled an expected crackdown in the wake of the advent of the strongly anti-Communist Thanin Kraivichien government, new attempts would be made by the CPT to develop a united national front with the (as yet uncertain) help of the more militant trade union leadership.

B. The special case of the students

The Thai case illustrates that students, rather than industrial workers or peasants, can be the more immediately useful 'vanguard' of revolutionary change for the Communists. Thus it has become an imperative organisational task for most parties in the region to transform quixotic student posturing into disciplined cadre-directed activity. The task is not easy for many reasons, not least because on occasions of high student militancy, workers and peasants may often already and unsuccessfully have been approached by student leaders to join in anti-government action. Inappropriate student behaviour may well have left a legacy of revulsion among workers and peasants alike. Thus, in 1973–4, in the first few heady weeks and months after Thai student demonstrations had brought down the regime of premier Thanom Kittikachorn, student activists linked with such organisations as the National Student Centre of Thailand or NSCT (which has been Communist-infiltrated since its inception in 1970, according to claims made in 1974 by high-ranking Thai police officers in conversation with this writer), attempted to 'energise' workers, trade unions and farmers. For example, the Bangkok students went into Thai village society, where, in the words of one observer:[50]

> They preached vague notions of socialism which they themselves understood barely or not at all; confused villagers with tales of the evil designs of 'the CIA'; urged them to resist corruption at the village level without any suggestion (or knowledge) as to how that might be accomplished; and finally returned to Bangkok, some for good.

Still, as a revolutionary seedbed, the student-worker-peasant alliance is increasingly being recognised in Communist policy pronouncements in South-east Asia. But the problem of freewheeling student militancy is not overlooked either, and class solidarity is seen as the solution to it. On 23 May 1978, in his annual commemorative statement on the founding of the PKI, Jusuf Adjitorop, who from Beijing leads the Chinese-oriented wing of the Indonesian party, reviewed the recent 'movement of college and other students' against the 'Suharto fascist regime'. He deplored the repressive action taken against the students by the Indonesian government, but provided a prescription as to how the students might overcome such repression in the future: 'So long as they [i.e. the students] unite closely with all the democratic patriotic forces – *especially with the workers and peasants* – the Indonesian people will certainly be able to continuously develop the struggle to overthrow the Suharto fascist military clique and to win final victory.'[51] And in its statement on 1 December 1974, commemorating the thirty-second anniversary of the Communist Party of Thailand, its Central Committee declared that 'University

and middle school students and intellectuals must closely and completely integrate their struggle with the struggles of the workers and
peasants *before* they can promote the struggle to achieve independence', democracy and a new educational system.[52]

Historically the revolutionary potential of students in South-east
Asia is well established and Communism's tactical interest in them is
understandable. Since a number of Rangoon University students
were killed in July 1962, four months after the regime of General Ne
Win took power in Burma, periodically flaring student opposition in
the country has been directed against 'political repression' as well as
rising prices, shortages of goods and general economic stagnation – all
targets also of the Burma Communist Party. During the great student
rising in Rangoon between 6 and 11 June 1975, students marched and
demonstrated along with workers against the lack of jobs, and
skyrocketing prices, and for a 'democratic Burma'.[53] Official sources
later claimed that the underground Communist Party of Burma was
among the instigators of this workers-students rising, but proof has
not been supplied. Malaysian authorities, meanwhile, always quick
to see the hand of the Communist Party of Malaya in any display of
organised public opposition to the government, declared that demonstrations by University of Malaya students in September and
October 1974, on behalf of peasant squatters driven from their
illegally occupied lands at Tasek Utra in Johore Bahru, had been
'Communist instigated'. In this connection the allegedly Communist
complexion of the University of Malaya's Chinese Language Society
at this time has already been noted earlier in this chapter.

But perhaps the most obvious instance of the melding of student
militancy and Communist tactics in recent years has been provided in
Thailand. University student militancy has a decades' long history in
the Thai kingdom. In 1947, during the fall of the Pridi Panomyong
government, again in 1957, during the disputed general election of
that year, and once more in 1962, when the World Court ruled in
Cambodia's favour in a case involving a temple located on the
Thai-Cambodian border, Thai university students, especially those
of Bangkok's Thammasat University, had taken to the streets, sometimes provoking bloody confrontations with the police.[54] More recent
student demonstrations have come in 1968, against the arrest of a
'free speech' advocate, a former member of parliament, and against
the martial law rule of premier Thanom Kittikachorn generally,
again in 1972, against Japanese products and alleged Japanese

financial manipulations, and once more in 1973 in favour of a new constitution and the Thanom regime, the latter campaign eventually culminating in the fall of Thanom's government.

The cascading student protests in Thailand in recent years have come in the context of the rapid expansion of the Thai educational establishment during the very decade (1963–73) that Thanom was in power. For example, from 1960 to 1970, higher education enrolments in Thailand leaped from 23 896 to 52 464, a 120 per cent increase. New universities were established in all parts of the country (such as Chiang Mai University in northern Thailand in 1964, Prince of Songkla University in the south in 1967, and new Colleges of Education in Mahasarakam in 1968, and in Pra Nakorn in 1969).[55] Indeed, the inauguration of some new institutions, such as the Pra Chom Klao Institute of Technology, and the Ramkamhaeng University, coincided with the closing months of the Thanom regime. But as significant impetus was being given to an expansion and a 'democratisation' of higher education, the problem of university graduate unemployment also became steadily more acute, especially for graduates in the arts and social sciences.[56] At the same time, the character of the Thanom regime was increasingly felt to be more repressive and authoritarian. The Thanom era thus significantly contributed to a radicalisation of the younger Thai and to sowing the seeds of the regime's own destruction. As we have seen, already in 1971, in a study on 'Urbanization in Thailand', prepared for the Ford Foundation, one reads that 'competition in the urban economy is increasing strains among students that occasionally erupt in acts of group violence'.[57]

The student radicalisation process has been difficult to stop, and particularly the CPT has benefited from it. Shortly after the Thai student movement's successful overthrow of the Thanom regime, such prominent student activists as Seksan Prasertkul, leader of FIST ('Federation of Independent Students of Thailand'), could still place 'preservation of democracy, the country's religion, and the King' at the head of his programme, in this way no doubt reflecting a broad range of Thai student sentiments.[58] But between 14 October 1973, when the Thanom regime fell, and 6 October 1976, when the Thai military, after an uneasy and turbulent era of parliamentary democracy, re-established their authority, Thai student opinion became both more polarised and radicalised. An ideological split in the Thai student movement between a more radical egalitarian wing on the one hand, and a military-backed, conservative and militantly anti-Communist wing on the other, became prominent. The October 1976 military coup brought to the premier's office the strongly anti-Communist Thanin Kraivichien and Thanin's premiership eventually saw some 2 000 Thai students, affiliated with the NSCT and other groups, take to the hills to join the Communist insurgents.

Student leaders now began calling for a Maoist style, rurally based revolutionary war. In Thai Communist media, the NSCT executive urged the 'heroic struggle of youths, schoolchildren, students and the Thai people' against the 'arch feudalists, fascist warlords and reactionaries' in power in Bangkok.[59] On 1 April 1977, Thirayu Bunmi, one-time NSCT secretary general, declared in a broadcast interview over the CPT's 'Voice of the People of Thailand' that unlike the Thai nation and the Buddhist religion the Thai monarchy had become 'obsolete' and 'was deteriorating', so that 'if our people were to destroy it there would be no adverse effects'. In subsequent months Communist broadcasts castigated the king as an 'archfeudalist' and his wife as a 'female feudalist'.[60] Such views of the Thai monarchy would have been unthinkable a few years earlier.

The influx of students into the CPT posed serious organisational problems for the party leadership, as a number of distrustful cadres looking askance at student posturing wanted nothing to do with them.[61] Moreover, after the Thanin Kraivichien regime itself was overthrown in a bloodless coup on 20 October 1977, and replaced with a more moderate, less stridently anti-Communist regime led by the Thai supreme commander, General Kriangsak Chamanand, several hundred students eventually left their CPT abode and returned to their homes under an official promise of amnesty. But others remained and today not only several scores of former students and young Thai intellectuals have become a permanent, if as yet not altogether trusted and integrated, part of the CPT, but Thai student participation is now also an essential element in the new united front organised by the CPT. First and preliminarily, there was the 'National Democratic United Front' (NDUF), and then, in the course of 1977, a new major front group was formed, called the 'Patriotic and Democracy Loving Peace Forces Co-ordinating Committee' (PFCC). The Co-ordinating Committee and its NDUF predecessor are by no means the CPT's first try at national front building. As early as November 1964, Thai Communists had announced a broad-based organisation called the Thailand Independence Movement (TIM) which in theory would bring together all opponents of the Thai government. TIM, and its 1965 successor, the Beijing-sponsored 'Thailand Patriotic Front' (TPF), though reflecting the escalating 'people's war' being waged by the Thai Communists, remained essentially shadow organisations.[62] But the Coordinating Committee not only has a solid core of student militants, gradually and formally permitted to be active in CPT policy decisions, but also such principal leaders of the Socialist Party of Thailand as its one-time parliamentary spokesman Bunyet Wothong, its present chairman Khasaen Suksai, and its secretary general, Chmani Sakset, as well as other intellectual dissidents, labour activists and veteran officials of farmers' organisations.[63]

The trickle of former student dissidents who have left the CPT, confident of premier Kriangsak's amnesty, has not affected the CPT's persistent praise of, and outreach to, the Thai student community. The founding anniversary of the NSCT each 1 February is always marked by laudatory statements over the CPT's radio transmitter; student leaders who have gone 'into the jungle' to join 'the people's struggle', as the CPT media put it, continue to be regularly interviewed by the Communist media, and the role of 'patriotic students and people' in various risings against 'US imperialism' is regularly commemorated in the same media as well.

Clearly the Co-ordinating Committee has a depth which the TIM and TPF did not have and, whatever its qualms, Thai Communism seems prepared to accommodate its new friends. The CPT is at pains to provide continuous recognition to Socialist Party of Thailand meetings and decisions. For example, a 'special meeting' of the Socialist Party of Thailand on 6 April 1978 was extensively reported by CPT media and remarks of party leaders were given publicity as if they had been made by CPT officials. This April meeting marked, in fact, the Socialist Party's integration with the PFCC and according to Socialist leaders who had visited various areas of insurgent operations 'the Thai people's armed struggle in the north, north-east and south has constantly advanced', so that the 'reactionary power' is said to be no longer able to stop it.

The role of students, moreover, appears to have stood Thai Communism in good stead as it attempts to strengthen its hold on the community of Muslim dissidents in the southern part of the kingdom, referred to earlier. On 7 August 1977, a spokesman for the so-called 'Thai Muslim People's Liberation Armed Forces' (TMPLAF) announced that his group had been formed and was under the 'full

leadership' of the CPT, in order to accelerate the struggle for 'democracy for all nationalities' in Thailand.[64] While the Communist Party
of Malaya has long been proselytising among Thai Muslims, the
announcement of the TMPLAF's formation was an indication that
the CPT henceforth meant to articulate Thai Muslim aspirations as
well. A major impetus for the TMPLAF's founding, however,
appears to have come from some young Thai Muslim students,
who have ties with student dissidents now active on behalf of the
Co-ordinating Committee and Thai Communism's new 'patriotic'
front building effort. Inspired by left-leaning youthful Muslim activists in the 'Moro National Liberation Front', Thai Muslim students
claimed an identity between the Muslim struggles in southern Thailand and in the southern Philippines. To what extent the TMPLAF
is, in fact, a variant of the 'Moro' movement, and whether or not the
CPT has established more than a paper front in the TMPLAF,
remains to be seen.

The Thai case, and particularly the formation of the Co-ordinating
Committee, underscores a Communist party's constant need to
identify and bring together those strata segments and special groups
who can be dialectically aligned and mobilised in the revolutionary
cause. To be sure, 'revolutionary cause' may often be too grandiose a
term. When operating under conditions of deep cover and total
illegality, as is the case with parties in the non-Communist part of
South-east Asia, narrowly defined and limited objectives – such as
restoration of full parliamentary functions, and of political and press
freedoms, implementation of agrarian reform legislation, or recognition of the rights of minorities – enable party-inspired or -infiltrated
front organisations to win a following. The aim is to bring about a
general change in the prevailing political climate through a realisation of limited but cumulative reforms, also with a view to achieving
or restoring the legitimacy of the Communist Party in the country
concerned. Additional pressure for change may be exerted and a loss
of credibility for the government may result through the steadily
eroding effect of an insurgency and terrorist campaign. But the effects
of such 'people's war' cannot always be calculated with certainty. As
the Malaysian case in particular suggests, the threat to a nation's
security, and the victims which a seemingly unending and inconclu-
sive guerrilla war leaves in its wake, may well eventually help solidify
most of the body politic against the insurgents.

Of particular advantage in the Communist front-building process
can be the support of another political party, even if small. Socialist

parties in South-east Asia have sometimes fulfilled such a role (for example, the 1938 'merger' of the Socialist Party of the Philippines with the PKP, which to a degree relegitimised the latter) although it is to be emphasised that Socialists in Indonesia (including its now banned *Partai Sosialis Indonesia*), and today, also in Singapore (where the People's Action Party nominally remains Socialist), have been avowed anti-Communists. The Socialist Party of Thailand offers a current illustration of such fellow travelling. The Socialist Party of Thailand in recent years led a shadowy life until it won fifteen parliamentary seats in the January 1975 general elections. But shortly, in the April 1976 elections, it lost most of its seats again, and in the rapid polarisation of Thai politics during the 1973–6 period, the Socialists not only had competitors on the left but manifestly were also no match for the larger, conservative or moderately conservative parties. Socialist Party general secretary Boonsanong Boonyothayan, the party's ablest leader, was assassinated and party candidates were frequently intimidated by the terrorist tactics of their opponents. The advent of the Thanin regime was the last straw for the Socialists, and their merger with the CPT in 1977 in a new Vietcong style 'patriotic' front of the left, seemed a logical step.[65] The CPT has thus acquired a number of intellectuals with some practical parliamentary experience and with a potential following in some Bangkok trade union and provincial political circles. The Thai polity is changing, the monarchy and the Buddhist establishment have become tarnished because of alleged partisan political involvements in recent years, and the alliance with the Socialist Party has given the CPT an added outreach to a frustrated and disillusioned citizenry.

In non-Communist South-east Asia, then, parties and front activists, where they are able to function, aim for the condition which party literatures usually designate as 'national democracy'.[66] This is a leftward movement of limited political and economic changes in which the party usually, but not necessarily, is relegitimised and is enabled to control the government, eventually establishing a dictatorship of the 'people', that is a true 'people's democracy'. A 'dictatorship of the people', rather than the orthodox Marxist 'dictatorship of the proletariat' is envisaged, because the 'proletariat' is a concept traditionally more suitable to industrial societies. Relying on Lenin, it was Maoist thought that developed the concepts of the 'dictatorship of the people' and of 'people's democracy' in Asia, and South-east Asian Communists have relied heavily on these concepts as well.

According to Communist theory, the stage of the 'people's dictator-

ship' and 'people's democracy' is essential *before* the stage of 'Socialism' can be entered. In the stage of 'Socialism' the last vestiges of the
class struggle can be considered to have been eliminated. In most of
South-east Asia, of course, even 'national democracy' remains to be
realised. But in Indochina, to which we now briefly turn our attention, the 'people's dictatorship' has been completely established with
the 1975 consolidation of Communist power. Here the transformation
of the country into a Socialist society can begin, or, as in the case of
North Vietnam, can now be accelerated.

C. Vietnam and Laos

An outline of the principal policies to be followed, both by the
Vietnam Communist Party or VCP, the new name of the Lao Dong or
Workers' Party, and for the new, unified, Socialist Republic of
Vietnam (SRV) as a whole, was offered by various speakers at the
Fourth Congress of the Workers' Party held in Hanoi (14–20
December 1976). It had been sixteen years since the meeting of the
Third Workers' Party Congress in September 1960. The Third
Congress had promulgated the party's general line of building Social-
ism in the North and of uniting Vietnam and achieving 'national
salvation' through armed struggle.[67] In his lengthy address on 17
December 1976 to the Fourth Congress, Politburo member and party
theorist Le Duc Tho reviewed party achievements and shortcomings
since the Third Congress. He noted that the party had grown from
31 448 'chapters' and 16 340 'organizations at the grassroots level' in
1960, to 95 486 chapters and 34 545 organisations in 1976, and that
the party now had more than 1.55 million members, or 3.13 per cent
of the population.[68]

   In accordance with various evaluations of future party responsibilities Le Duc Tho recommended (and the Congress duly adopted)
amendments to the party statutes allowing for, among others: (1) an
intensification of the 'ideological task' (that is, ideological training)
by and in the party and an upgrading of the overall quality of party
members; (2) an improvement of the party's organisation so as to
assure a 'regime of collective mastership and the building of a new
economy, a new culture and new men'; (3) the promotion of party
solidarity, democracy and party discipline, and (4) a development of

cadres in keeping with the demands of 'the new stage'. Le Duc Tho
and other speakers also repeatedly referred to the 'three revolutions'
which are to be carried out in the now unified SRV and which are an
expression of the 'labouring people's right to collective mastership'.
These three revolutions are: 'the revolution in production relations,
the scientific-technical revolution, and the ideological and cultural
revolution of which the scientific-technical revolution is the key.'
Flowing from this triple revolutionary process are specific policy
concerns for the party in the SRV, such as the development of 'large
scale socialist production', the wiping out of oppression, poverty and
backwardness, and, generally, the building of a 'peaceful, independent, unified and socialist Vietnam', which in turn will contribute to
the struggle of the 'world's people' for the same objectives.

Particularly noteworthy was Le Duc Tho's stress on the need to
build up and improve the party's leadership ('leadership in several
aspects of construction', and 'economic planning' was said not to
have caught up with 'developing political duties', and the 'organizational structure for guaranteeing collective ownership' was criticised
as being 'weak in many respects'). Evidently the demands of building
a unified, Socialist Vietnam require an overhaul of national leadership selection and training procedures through the mechanism of the
expanding party organisation.

In this connection, Le Duc Tho's social class and party support
group analysis attracted attention also as a harbinger of a new
tightening of ideological training and party discipline. According to
Le Duc Tho, the Lao Dong throughout its history has 'always
affirmed' that it is the party of the 'Vietnamese working class', that its
stand is the 'stand of the working class – the class which is closely
linked with the production in large scale industry' and the class which
is armed with scientific Marxism-Leninism. Putting emphasis on the
working class, according to Le Duc Tho, will definitely not lead to a
separation between the party and the working class on the one hand,
and the Vietnamese nation on the other. On the contrary, such
emphasis will enable the party to serve people and nation still more
effectively. But as Le Duc Tho put it, such emphasis also means
'drawing a clear line' between the party and 'the stand of the petty
bourgeoisie and bourgeoisie'. To draw such a line is 'very important',
according to Le Duc Tho, because the Workers' (or Communist)
Party in the past derived such 'a large number of its members from the
peasantry and the petty bourgeoisie' who achieved their 'revolutio-

nary consciousness' first by developing 'patriotism'. In other words, according to Le Duc Tho, it has become necessary for Vietnamese Communism now, with unification completed, to emphasise the more orthodox, traditional proletarian and vanguard character of its party, in contrast to the earlier period of the struggle for national unification and independence, when 'patriotism' was put in the foreground and, when in the interests of the united front, concessions could be made perhaps to 'petty bourgeois' and peasant influences.

In the Workers' Party's Central Committee report to the Fourth Congress this same theme is also apparent. The social composition of the party is to be changed so as to strengthen its 'working class' composition. Recruitment of workers from larger industries is to be emphasised, along with thoroughly 'collectivised' peasants and with those military and intellectuals of demonstrated 'revolutionary' views.[69] The struggle for 'national democracy' is now at an end, 'people's democracy' is here, and the stage of Socialism is about to begin. And while party secretary general Le Duan, in October 1977, could still speak of the party as a party of 'the great majority of the people' advancing under the banner of national independence and socialism,[70] with the actual achievement of national independence and national unification, the 'great majority' representation in the party is apparently to be narrowed. As Le Duc Tho again put it:

> The primary question of principle is to strengthen and develop the party and select cadres from the ranks of workers who constitute a class basis of the party. This is in line with the requirement for strengthening the leading role of the working class in the period of transition to socialism.

In conformity with this new class perception of the VCP, Le Duan in his political report to the Fourth Congress delivered on 14 December 1976, referred to the pivotal role of trade union organisations in integrating the political responsibilities and economic managerial roles of workers, requiring an increasingly solid union organisation under labour leaders who are 'thoroughly conversant with the party line and policies'.[71] Le Duan also drew a distinction between North and South Vietnam in respect of the role of the peasantry. The North Vietnamese peasantry, having become 'the collective peasant class', can and must concentrate on implementing the 'three revolutions' already mentioned earlier; they, along with the workers, now constitute the 'main force' in the 'construction of socialism'. The Southern peasantry, however, is not yet so far advanced: they must still be drawn into various associations in order to be educated and 'enhanced' in their patriotism and their love of Socialism and it is still necessary to 'motivate' them in order to help in rehabilitating and increasing production for the state. One may note *inter alia* that while poor and middle peasants are recognised as having revolutionary potential, and the importance of the worker-peasant alliance is always emphasised, the peasants are not a 'vanguard' class, comparable to the workers, according to Vietnamese Communist theory.[72] The Southern peasantry is comparatively even less developed in discharging its revolutionary responsibilities from this point of view.

Important too, according to Le Duan, is the role of the 'intelligentsia', which must be united with workers and peasants. Large numbers of intellectuals must be trained, also with the aid of party and mass organisations and through state bodies, so that the intellectuals' talents can be best used in Socialist reconstruction. Evidently the intelligentsia, like the peasantry, are, in the new stage now confronting the VCP, to be moulded and directed under a reconstituted party much more rigorously 'proletarian' and orthodox Socialist than in the earlier 'national democratic' stage when the accent was on achieving national 'salvation' and independence by enlisting the 'patriotic' sentiments of broad social strata.

Supporting as well as encompassing the VCP, and integrally involved in developing the worker-peasant-intelligentsia alliances, is the new 'Fatherland Front of Vietnam' (FFV). The FFV is the successor to the 'National Unity Front', founded in 1976, which itself was a merger of previous fronts such as the old 'Fatherland Front of Vietnam' (in existence between 1855 and 1976), the 'National Liberation Front of South Vietnam' (1960–76), and the 'Alliance of National Democratic and Peace Forces of Vietnam' (1968–76). The National Unity Front evidently served as a transitional organisation, and the founding congress of the FFV, meeting in Ho Chi Minh City (formerly Saigon), adopted a programme on 4 February 1977 stipulating as the organisation's principal aim to 'unite all the people in the name of building a peaceful, independent, united and socialist Vietnam'. Such unity is to be put in the service of the 'socialist industrialisation' process, the abolition of poverty, and the transformation of the economy 'from small scale into large scale socialist production'. Popularising Marxism-Leninism, teaching courses to the masses on the programme and policies of the VCP, and on the national traditions and 'outstanding works of culture' are also to be part of the FFV's efforts. Organisationally, the FFV is officially described as including not only the VCP but also such minor and 'fraternal' parties as the 'Democratic Party of Vietnam' and the 'Socialist Party of Vietnam', which seem to exist primarily to foster the illusion of political pluralism in the SRV, as well as federations of trade unions, women's and youth groups. A 191-member Central Committee, Presidium and Secretariat direct the FFV's daily affairs.[73]

Conspicuous in the organisational policies of both the FFV and the VCP is 'expertness' – the recruitment and development of technical and economic specialists capable of providing leadership in the country's Socialist stage. This is in keeping also with the heavy stress on educational expansion in the SRV as projected by the 1976–80 Five-Year State Plan, and on the creation of a new Socialist 'culture' and of a 'new man'. A goal of 13.7 million school children has been set for 1980, and party and FFV are both closely involved in supervising and assisting in broadening a range of cultural activities and experiences – from books and plays to radio programmes and motion pictures – for all those attending schools.[74] Another characteristic of both VCP and FFV organisation is its 'civilian' focus. The proportional share of seats held by the 'People's Army of Vietnam' in the VCP Central Committee has declined since the Fourth Congress, and while there is some military participation in the FFV, it tends to be minor and peripheral. In the SRV today, 'the party firmly commands the gun in spite of the latter's importance for so long.'[75]

Socialist transformation of the class and economic structure away from the comparative socio-economic pluralism and individualism still permitted in the 'national democratic' stage of development is no mere rhetoric in the SRV. In March 1978, the SRV government began implementing a policy designed to destroy the class of small entrepreneurs and traders insofar as it still existed, particularly in South Vietnam. A government decree, issued on 7 April 1978 by SRV premier Pham Van Dong, declared that 'on the basis of developing the socialist trading network' the state would 'encourage' most small traders 'to switch to production'.[76]

'Switching to production' has meant compelling traders to adopt new modes of living and to become 'productive laborers useful to society'. It is believed that the 'petty urban bourgeoisie', while

different from landlords and the big bourgeoisie, nevertheless is
linked with a system of private ownership. And it is considered to be
'historically inevitable' that all systems of private ownership 'are
eventually destroyed', as one Hanoi editorial has put it.[77] Toward the
end of June 1978, it was reported that '95 percent of the bourgeois
trader households in Ho Chi Minh City' had registered for 'productive work', meaning that in many cases entire households had left for
other districts in order to engage in various state projects such as
peanut oil and cattle fodder production.[78]

The decree ordering a 'switching' of traders to 'production' accelerated a massive forced resettlement programme whereby some 1.33
million people, mostly from the cities, were relocated to uninhabited
rural areas in so-called 'New Economic Zones'. In these zones the
settlers particularly are to engage in food production and in opening
new farm land, but their relocation has also been seen as providing for
more effective security controls over an urban population whose
loyalties to the new regime are still suspect. According to premier
Pham Van Dong, eventually four million, mostly urban Vietnamese
from the South are to be relocated in the New Economic Zones, an
undertaking which is proportionally one of the largest 'social en-
gineering' ventures ever undertaken by any Communist state, and
illustrates the depth of official commitment to creating a 'new man' in
the SRV. The anti-trader decree especially aroused the fear and ire of
South Vietnam's 1.2 million ethnic Chinese, many of them historically engaged in middleman entrepreneurial and commercial activities. Tensions developed between Hanoi and Peking, as hundreds of
thousands of the Hua (Hoa) (that is, Chinese in Vietnam) fled across
the border into China, and others departed by specially sent vessels,
all carrying tales of confiscation of their property and brutal treatment by Vietnamese officials. However, the SRV seems prepared to
weather Beijing's enmity for the sake of implementing the vision of a
new 'Socialist' structure for the Vietnamese human community and
its economy.[79]

'Socialist' transformation is also the main thrust of Communist
Party policy in the SRV's ally, the Laotian People's Democratic
Republic (LPDR). Established on 2 December 1975, after the Lao
monarchy formally ended with the abdication of King Savang, the
LPDR's development today is in the hands of the People's Revolutionary Party of Laos (*Phak Pasason Pativat Lao* – PPPL), and a forty-
four-member Supreme People's Council. Kaysone Phomvihan,

PPPL secretary general and concurrently LPDR premier, declared in March 1978 in an address to the Supreme People's Council and cabinet that 'our revolution has entered the period of socialist revolution', and that 'socialist transformation and construction' were now being implemented in the country.[80] On another occasion he noted that the LPDR, while now 'bypassing the stage of capitalist development' and closing the stage of the 'national democratic revolution in Laos', had established a 'progressive political system', in which the Marxist-Leninist party (i.e. the PPPL) was now 'steadily enhancing' its 'class nature'. The formation of a worker-peasant alliance, as a matter of Marxist-Leninist principle according to Kaysone Phomvihan is necessary for every revolution led by the working class. However, in Laos, which is a 'backward agrarian country with strong survivals of feudalism', the working class is still in embryo form and the level of economic development, moreover, not only varies from region to region but from ethnic group to ethnic group. The development of a united front, also supported by the 'intermediate social forces' (not further identified by Kaysone Phomvihan), nevertheless has been possible, and the front organised by the Communists, namely the 'Patriotic Front of Laos', was used as a 'special' mechanism of establishing an alliance with 'neutralist strata'.[81]

If the above observations suggest a certain tactical subtlety and deliberation, and, indeed, some care in the mobilisation of popular support for the PPPL, then it must be noted that Lao party leaders appear to have learned their lesson that the 'Socialist' transformation of society cannot be stamped out of the ground. The 'National Congress of People's Representatives', which on 2 December 1975 had declared Laos a People's Democratic Republic, had been impatient to effect rapid 'Socialist' changes. In his address to that Congress, Kaysone Phomvihan had laid down a kind of 'who is not for us is against us' hard line of solidarity and patriotism. The vanguard role of the minuscule Laotian proletariat was put in the foreground, peasants were exhorted to form co-operatives and to produce more, the military were urged to defeat imperialist intrigues, students were told to 'integrate theory and practice', and monks were commanded to mobilise and educate the people, and so on.[82]

But the attempt made in the course of 1976 radically to change the character of Laotian society, somewhat in the manner being tried in South Vietnam, proved a failure. Sharp popular resentment and even organised resistance arose, which included dissatisfied party cadres and military personnel. While official media might stress the 'new and brilliant life style' being adopted by town dwellers,[83] PPPL cadres, outdoing each other in dour petty officiousness, focused on Laotian hairstyles, dancing and singing at religious festivals, and even at private celebrations. Official censure visited on the public by party 'investigating squads', the alleged arrogance and even brutality in treatment of the masses, all provoked such adverse reactions that by July 1976 the PPPL Central Committee felt compelled to declare that recent party decisions had not been in accord with the 'earnest desires and needs of the people' in the new Socialist stage. Bureau-cratic supervision diminished, folk festivals were no longer interfered with, political indoctrination courses were reduced, and the planned Socialist transformation of the LPDR assumed a less grim appearance.[84]

The official recognition – noted earlier – of the as yet nascent state of the Laotian proletariat and of the wide differences in development levels among ethnic groups probably also provides further justifica-tion of SRV guidance of a 'backward' Laos, exemplified not least by the continuing presence of tens of thousands of Vietnamese military in Laos. This continuing Vietnamese presence may well be the new dynamic in domestic Laotian politics. Already in February 1976, various Laotian groups, among them former party cadres, had formed the 'Lao Popular Front' including guerrilla insurgents against the PPPL regime, and declared that the Laotian people has been misled by the so-called 'Patriotic Front of the Pathet Lao', and that the anti-PPPL resistance would harass the 'traitors and their Viet-namese masters without respite'.[85] So long as Hanoi retains its overwhelming presence in Laos, the few-hundred-man force of the Lao Popular Front, reportedly supported in secret by some Thai military, is unlikely to dislodge the PPPL. But the fact remains that Laotian Communism today is polarised between an avowedly anti-Vietnamese group, and a group tolerant of Hanoi's dominance of the country. The future development of Lao politics will most likely hinge on this conflict.

D. Cambodia

More than two years passed after the Khmer Rouge final conquest of Phnom Penh on 17 April 1975, before the mystery-shrouded Cambodian Communist Party (KCP) fully revealed itself. On 27 September 1977, Pol Pot, KCP secretary general and concurrently premier (since January 1976, when a new constitution established the new state of 'Democratic Kampuchea', it will be recalled), in a lengthy address offered his retrospective analysis of Cambodia's political revolution, starting from the 'era of slavery' in the past and going through the KCP's official founding in 1960, and the subsequent 'national democratic' revolution and struggle for independence from 'imperialist' domination.[86] Within the 'national democratic revolution', according to Pol Pot, there also occurred the class struggle against 'feudalism', for example, between peasants and landlords. The feudal problem was extensive. According to Pol Pot, in the Thmar Koul region of Batambang province in 1957–8, for example, ninety per cent of the farm land 'belonged to the landowners', and among 'tens of thousands of peasants one could count only four or five landowners'. Peasant impoverishment, as a result, was common. Yet the rural conflict remained 'hidden', in the view of Pol Pot, because 'the minions of the landlord and ruling class', the 'functionaries and teachers', deliberately sought to minimise and bury the conflict and mislead the peasants about their miserable plight.

The KCP, however, educated and mobilised the peasants, and, as Pol Pot put it, made them a fundamental revolutionary force based on the 'worker-peasants alliance' under party leadership. Through different modalities of struggle, legal as well as illegal, political as well as economic, and operating all the while from guerrilla and other support bases in cities and the countryside, 'total liberation' was finally achieved with the capture of Phnom Penh. Three basic tasks confronted Democratic Kampuchea, according to Pol Pot. First the country must be defended, and its independence and sovereignty must be retained. Secondly, the Socialist revolution must be improved, and the 'socialist collective system' must be strengthened 'in all fields'. Thirdly, and possibly reluctantly, great attention must be paid to building Socialism in every area of endeavour.

Only two years after total liberation, significant achievements could already be noted, as Pol Pot saw it: (1) the old 'repressive' order of production 'has been completely wiped out'; (2) the labour power of the working people had now been wholly liberated and 'is being nursed, fed and promoted into a seething, vigorous, vivid grand production movement with the highest sense of ingenuity and initiative', and (3) peasant village and commune (called respectively *sahakor phum* and *sahakor khum*) co-operatives were expanding, comprising hundreds of households each and being organised into a collective force, through a communal support system called *phkot phkong*. *Inter alia* one may note that the *phkot phkong* system facilitated creation throughout the country of production units of men and women, recruited from all social strata, and harnessed their labour to the collective production of food. For this system and for the commune co-operatives, Phnom Penh and other cities were virtually emptied of their populations, and urban inhabitants were forcibly marched into the countryside to begin 'socialist production and construction'. The socially levelling effect of the co-operatives and the *phkot phkong* system was deliberate. As Pol Pot put it, 'contradictions' between those from the cities and those from the countryside, between workers and peasants, between 'physical workers and the intellectuals' were 'solved' as all worked and lived together.

The educational system was also geared to the new mode of mass collective labour. As Pol Pot put it, 'Theory should be learned at the same time as it is being applied to actual work.'[87] The team of Yugoslav reporters which visited Cambodia in 1978 was introduced to a young man described as a surgeon. When the young man was asked where he had completed his medical studies the young man replied: 'We do not require studies. Linking the experience of the masses with the direct requirements of the revolution, we train surgeons and other experts we require.'[88] The Yugoslav news team also noted that in Cambodia 'There are no universities, higher, secondary, or elementary schools in the country, with the exception of elementary reading and writing lessons in cooperatives.'

As the work-oriented, 'learn by doing' and socially levelling co-operative and *phkot phkong* systems made their impact felt, the KCP leadership anticipated that 'life and death contradictions' would persist in the country. These contradictions involved not so much the formerly wealthier peasants and bourgeoisie (some twenty per cent of the population) because they too, according to Pol Pot, were now 'content' with the collective system of co-operatives. Rather it was a 'handful of reactionary elements' (not further specified) aided by 'various spyrings working for imperialism and international reactionaries' who are 'the enemy' and who were said to be actively attempting to sabotage the Cambodian revolution. Yet even these elements were held to be educable and only 'the smallest possible number' of them, in Pol Pot's view, needed be isolated and 'eradicated'.[89] At that stage, however, there were few exact details about the remaining 'class enemy' in Democratic Kampuchea other than that tens of thousands appeared to have been executed. In August 1977, according to Thai intelligence, there were widespread revolts in the Siem Reap and Undon Meechai regions of western Cambodia, including extensive arrests and executions of political and military cadres.[90] At the end of May 1978, it was announced that the government, army and people of Democratic Kampuchea under the KCP's leadership had 'smashed another plan to stage a coup d'état' by the Vietnamese Communist Party and the SRV, aimed at 'toppling' Democratic Kampuchea.[91] Six Vietnamese nationals who had allegedly co-ordinated their activities 'with the CIA' had been seized in connection with this foiled plot. Such charges against the SRV have been common particularly since the end of 1977, when Cambodian-Vietnamese relations sharply deteriorated amidst continuous and extensive border fighting. According to Hanoi, there were uprisings against the Pol Pot regime in Cambodia's Prey Veng, Svay Rieng and other provinces and parts of these provinces may well have been under control of pro-Hanoi Cambodian forces. An internal power struggle within the KCP, involving among others information minister Hu Nim and public works minister Toch Phoeun against premier Pol Pot and foreign minister Ieng Sary, was also presumably linked to the frequent official reports of smashed spy rings and 'reactionary' plots, but there is little certainty.[92] By May 1978, some 14 000 Cambodians from all walks of life had sought refuge in Thailand since the advent of the Communist regime in Phnom Penh.[93]

The Pol Pot regime's total reorganisation of Cambodian society on the basis of military style co-operatives and work collectives was accompanied by an extremely puritanical outlook on personal morals in which the death penalty has been exacted for such infractions as the use of liquor, gambling, and any unapproved sexual activity. As in Vietnam and Laos, the Socialist stage in Cambodia demanded a zealous 'new man' who had wholly submerged his identity in the demands of the party's 'proletarian dictatorship'.[94] The proletarian emphasis and the 'learn by doing' philosophy also put a premium on absolute self-reliance while breaking new ground for the new society. Not only did Pol Pot claim with pride that Democratic Kampuchea was 'building socialism without a model' (although, at least in spirit, Cambodia's Socialist revolution emulates People's China's 'Great Leap Forward' and 'Great Proletarian Cultural Revolution'), but as the earlier mentioned Yugoslav reporting team noted:[95]

The main slogan of the Communist party is: 'Building and development with our own resources.' This was repeated to us in almost
every region of the interior, where we visited large building
sites. . . . No one mentions or asks for aid from outside. Everything
is done with spades and pickaxes and manual irrigation pumps.
Kilometers of dikes are built with earth carried in baskets. The only
mechanisation we saw on all these worksites were a few dump
trucks and dredgers left over by the former regime and a few dozen
tractors and trucks which the new authorities have bought from
Yugoslavia.

By the middle of 1978 there were signs that Democratic Kampuchea
was intending to moderate its extreme isolation. Foreign minister
Ieng Sary, at a Belgrade Conference of Foreign Ministers of Non-
Aligned Nations in July 1978, defended the closing of his country at
the time of the Communist takeover in 1975 'because otherwise we
would have had a civil war', and even 'more would have died' because
of 'our complexities and difficulties'. He claimed that 'now the
situation is better' and that the food problem had been completely
solved so that now 'we can use people for international activities'.[96]
By the end of 1978, however, the Pol Pot regime was in serious
difficulties, as tens of thousands of Vietnamese troops pushed ever
deeper into Cambodia, and on 3 December 1978 a Hanoi-supported
'Kampuchea National United Front for National Salvation'
(KNUFNS) was proclaimed. On 7 January 1979, KNUFNS's chairman, Heng Samrin, a former member of the KCP Executive Committee for the country's eastern region and former political commissar
and commander of the Kampuchean 'People's Army' Fourth Division, became head of a new 'Kampuchean People's Revolutionary
Council Government' as the Pol Pot regime fled from Phnom Penh to
take up a guerrilla struggle in the western part of the country. To rally
his scattered forces and continue the fight against the Vietnamese
occupation forces and their allies, Pol Pot proclaimed the formation
on 18 January 1979 of a 'Democratic and Patriotic Front for National
Unity' (DPFNU), but repeated Vietnamese offensives and 'mop-up'
operations against the Pol Pot remnant suggested that the DPFNU
would be hard-pressed to maintain itself. On 18 February 1979 the
Heng Samrin government signed a 'treaty of peace, friendship and
co-operation' with the Vietnamese government, and on 22 March a
Laotian delegation headed by President Souphanouvong signed a

'statement of cooperation' with the Heng Samrin Revolutionary Council Government. These agreements, denounced by People's China and the Pol Pot government, confirmed not only Cambodia's satellite status vis-à-vis Vietnam, in a manner comparable to that of Laos, but also lent substance to fears of Hanoi's expansionist policies and that an 'Indochinese Federation' had in fact now come into existence.

Although the underground Pol Pot government claims that its guerrillas are continuing to battle the Vietnamese occupation forces in Cambodia, the Heng Samrin regime has simultaneously been attempting to maintain food production and mitigate the harsher features of the Pol Pot era's enforced mass collectivisation system. 'Freedom of residence' has been promised Cambodians, as well as a 'planned economy' with markets, while 'backbreaking forced labour' has been declared abolished. Now called the 'People's Republic of Kampuchea', the new Cambodia under Heng Samrin is also committed to restoring national social traditions and a somewhat more permissive social system generally. Redoubled emphasis is to be placed on developing a modern, scientific educational system. It remains to be seen, however, whether Cambodians, though 'liberated' from the harsh repression of the Pol Pot regime, will long tolerate a continuing Vietnamese military presence. A deepening crisis over food shortages may well bring the new Cambodian relationship with Hanoi to the breaking point, and already by April 1979 there were signs of popular Cambodian discontent over extortionist practices of Vietnamese military in the country, prostitution, and over a general sense of being treated as a 'colony' by the SRV.

Whether the Heng Samrin regime and the People's Revolutionary Council Government will eventually prove to be but a transition to a regime ultimately acceptable to People's China (which remains adamantly opposed to the SRV presence in Phnom Penh) remains to be seen, but in the meantime spokesmen for the 'Council Government' emphasise that they firmly adhere to 'Marxism-Leninism' and urge party cadres not to adopt an élitist view in leading the masses or to enrich themselves at the masses' expense. New 'management committees' and 'production teams' were formed by the Heng Samrin government to increase food production in the collectives, but the emphasis is to be on persuasion and exemplary cadre behaviour, not on liquidation of all manner of enemies. Family and village structures, demolished by the extensive social levelling and collectivisation programme of Pol Pot's Democratic Kampuchea, are to be restored. Obviously the new Phnom Penh government will have to rely heavily on Soviet bloc financial and technical assistance if it is to accomplish a sustained and significant rate of economic growth.

In summary, the Indochina states, unlike non-Communist South-east Asia, have officially said farewell to the 'national democratic' stage of their revolutions, and have begun to enter the phase of 'Socialist construction' and development. This has required a searching alteration of the composition and policies of the dominant party. The formal 'proletarian' and Bolshevised character of the party has had to be emphasised so as to make sure that only the dedicated and thoroughly trained remain members. Socialist transformation also means the removal of the last vestiges of class structure and class consciousness. In the SRV the campaign against bourgeois traders is an example of such removal, while in Democratic Kampuchea the social levelling of the co-operatives and the *phkot phkong* systems as well as the extermination of tens of thousands of real or imaginary opponents of the regime and of class enemies was designed to accomplish the same end. The Laotian case suggests that sooner or later popular resentment and indeed organised resistance to these more draconian dimensions of Socialist transformation rise to the point that the party finds it necessary to become more moderate in keeping (as the PPPL Central Committee put it in July 1976) with the 'earnest desires and needs of the people'. Internecine frontier conflict in the region, raising for the Indochina regimes the spectre of 'imperialist' plots and subversion by 'reactionary elements', may well be an obstacle to a future softening of Socialist stage reforms.

4

Party organisation and appeals

A. The organisational outreach

A recent proclamation of the Burma Communist Party Central Committee declared that the three principal weapons in the defeat of 'the enemy' were: (1) a disciplined, self-critical party, properly grounded ideologically (in this case in 'Marxism-Leninism-Mao Ze Dong thought'), and in touch with the masses; (2) a 'people's army' wholly under the party's control; and (3) a united front, headed by the Communist Party, and composed of all 'revolutionary classes' and groups.[1] *Pari passu* this prescription serves as the organisational model for all Communist parties in South-east Asia today, even if, as in the case of Indonesia, the two wings of the Communist Party (oriented toward Moscow and Beijing respectively) consist largely of a few, furtive, underground cadres. In the Philippines, Thailand, Burma, and Malaysia the Communist organisational triad now exists in varying degrees of development and strength, however, and the focus of party life typically is on the strengthening of and development of successful tactics for the component units of the triad.

BCP media, currently, seem in an especially exhortatory mood, but all Communist parties in the region attempt to define the scope of and build their structure. Although, not surprisingly, party organisational directives are customarily counsels of perfection, they do tend to convey something of the special quality sought for in the units of the triad. Thus, the BCP's 'People's Army' today is described in party media as typically being 'a whole with the people', and as moving about 'skilfully' in the region where it fights, because its superior intelligence derives, presumably, from close interaction with the

177

people. On the other hand, the Burmese government's army (the 'mercenary army', as the BCP calls it) has no support from the people and hence 'does not know the rough and intolerant terrain'.[2]

As for preserving party unity and strength, the BCP's directives are similarly specific: individual opportunism, attempts to form cliques or 'mini-parties', a display of exclusiveness stemming from bigotry or racism – all these must be resisted.[3] The sure test, it would seem, is whether an act or contemplated policy enhances or detracts from party unity, and the BCP leadership appears to feel that firm adherence to 'Marxism-Leninism-Mao Ze Dong thought' provides an infallible guide in such cases. Hence the stress on proper ideological preparation, which is believed able to combat schismatic, individualising and separatist tendencies. Such tendencies are of course an old problem in the history of Communist parties, but the BCP appears to believe that it has found the answer. That answer is for party members to be both 'red' and 'expert' at the same time. Cadres therefore are reminded that technology *serves* politics (not the other way around) even though, to be sure, technology is an indispensable ingredient of the 'proletarian revolution'.[4] 'Proletarian politics' is able to give proper direction to 'technical and other tasks'. In short, just as the 'party must command the gun' (that is, the army) in Maoist parlance, so proper ideas and thoughts must command the use of all tools. Diligent study of proper theory, and a correct grasp of ideology 'in all areas', are therefore essential, but the BCP (as do some other Communist parties in the racially and ethnically so heterogeneous South-east Asian environment) note the special difficulties arising from the 'even lower' educational level of 'comrades' who belong to various ethnic and nationality groups.[5] Racism, 'belittlement and oppression' are responsible for this lower educational standard (indeed 'some minorities do not even have their own literature'), and the task of ideologically and organisationally integrating members and cadres from the minority groups thus is seen as being all the more difficult.

South-east Asia's Communist parties are characterised by a number of common organisational impulses. For example, all parties have relied on and benefited from recruitment from the ranks of organised labour. The Philippine Printers' Union (*Union de Impresores de Filipinas*), founded in 1906, from whose ranks came Crisanto Evangelista, the founder of the Philippine Communist Party, and the Philippine Workers' Congress (*Congreso Obrero de Filipinas*), established in 1913, are important seedbeds of Philippine Communism.[6]

The establishment in Singapore in 1924 of the Nanyang Federation of Labour was to be a significant dynamic in the development of Malayan Communism.[7] From its inception in the first years of the present century much of the Indonesian labour movement developed a radical political orientation. Such unions as that of government pawnshop workers, founded in 1916, were to offer a recruiting ground later on to the fledgling Indonesian Communist Party.[8]

Sometimes race has served as an organisational common denominator. The early development of both the Malayan and Thai Communist parties is inseparable from the political aspirations of ethnic Chinese, for example. Then again we must consider South-east Asian parties as expressions of the strivings of a common new élite throughout the region. This élite in turn is a distinctive social consequence of the spread and acceptance of modern Western style schooling. This is not to say that peasants and industrial workers are lacking in the early South-east Asian parties. It is to note that the petty bourgeoisie of traders and lower to middle rank officialdom as often as not was the social environment of future party leaders – indeed in Indonesia leadership recruitment from the lower aristocracy was to be not uncommon. To what extent were the parties and the nationalist organisations as well but vehicles for the often highly charged unassuaged aspirations of this new élite, 'burning to govern'?

To see the pattern of organisational impulses at work it may perhaps be useful to focus briefly on a case study of one party, its origins and its appeals. The organisational development of the Communist movement in the east Malaysian state of Sarawak can serve as a springboard for a consideration of Communist organisational problems elsewhere in the region.[9] Today Communism in Sarawak, a state whose total population is estimated at 900 000, is structured by the North Kalimantan Communist Party (NKCP). The NKCP is, however, only the current organisational vehicle of a movement that has known a number of different forms. Historically durable, though at the moment fallen on difficult times because of recent defections under the government's amnesty offer, Communism in Sarawak may be said to have received its first major organisational impetus as a result of the anti-Japanese resistance in the area during World War II. This it had in common with other parts of South-east Asia, such as the Philippines and Malaya, where the Japanese Occupation also breathed new life into the local Communist movement. In 1942, at the beginning of World War II in Asia, a 'Sarawak Anti-Fascist League', elements of which later changed their name to 'Races' Liberation

League', came into existence. From this predominantly Chinese resistance organisation, there was to emerge in the post-war period a series of small Communist-oriented groups such as the 'Sarawak Liberation League', founded in 1954 and its successor, the 'Sarawak Advanced Youths' Association' (SAYA), established in 1956. The first of these two groups had, perhaps, no more than thirty hard-core members, with an additional three or four score of sympathisers mainly in Kuching. But as Sarawak Communism's principal organisational vehicle, SAYA soon developed a potentially wider outreach through organisational 'sections' for workers, farmers, students, 'racial work', cultural activities and so on. From SAYA's sections impetus was given first to the formation in 1961 of a Communist front labour group, the 'First Division Trade Unions Congress', and in 1962 to the 'Sarawak Farmers' Association' (SFA).

The private Chinese schools, centres of the cultural pride and unappeased frustrations of Sarawak's 350 000 ethnic Chinese inhabitants, had been a recruiting ground for Communist organisers since the days of the Sarawak Liberation League and they continued to provide much of the early organisational matrix of what the Sarawak government, by the early nineteen sixties, was beginning to call the 'Clandestine Communist Organisation' (CCO) and later the 'Sarawak Communist Organisation' (SCO) in the state. The basic organisational unit of the SAYA in the Chinese schools in Kuching and Sibu was the cell, usually composed of three students, only one of whom (for security reasons) would know and have contact with other cells.[10] The cell concept eventually came to be applied also inside the SFA, in friendly trade unions, and eventually also in the left wing of the Sarawak United People's Party (SUPP), a party widely regarded as having become Communist infiltrated during the nineteen sixties, though no longer so today.

The cell was and is not only an action unit, for SAYA documents also indicate that it was and is a study and self-criticism entity (*Xue Xi (Hsueh Hsih)*). Formally a number of cells constitute a branch, with several branches establishing a district committee. In the latter half of the nineteen sixties, when the CCO (SCO) had reached its greatest extent, a number of district committees elected an interlocking hierarchy of higher executive committees at the town and division level, but this is no longer the case, although the North Kalimantan Communist Party (NKCP) today claims to have a functioning Central Committee.

From the start SAYA's and the CCO's concern was with the united-front-building process, even as a formal Communist party for Sarawak *per se* remained undeveloped at this time and even as the government's term 'Clandestine Communist Organisation' denoted less a party as such but rather a complex of more or less distinct Communist or Communist-oriented groups. The name NKCP does not appear until 1972. Still, the CCO (SCO) in Sarawak was in this respect not altogether atypical of Communist organisations in South-east Asia. For in conditions of illegality, as most Communist parties in South-east Asia have historically found themselves, the separate party front organisation, loosely allied with other front groups, has often been tactically more effective than a Communist movement dominated by a single defined party and known to be formally Communist. Vietnam offers a well known illustration. But also in the Philippines, during the early nineteen sixties, the pattern of radical and/or Communist-infiltrated youth, labour, and farmers' organisations laid the agitational and proselytising foundation from which the Maoist Philippine Communist Party and its New People's Army could later develop.[11]

CCO (SCO) front-building was effected through a range of recreational, cultural, and sports groups. Informal, but carefully organised picnics, parties, dancing and singing classes served the same purpose. One CCO (SCO) document released by the Sarawak government describes the recruiting process as follows:[12]

(1) Single out targets among the masses through investigation and circumstances.
(2) Understand the targets through winning their acquaintance and confidence, to be followed by investigation into their family and social backgrounds.
(3) Unite them with the Organisation through helping them in the name of welfare activities through the medium of some open organisation.
(4) Groom them for absorption into the Organisation through ideological education – studies of elementary materials such as 'Revolutionary Views of Life', etc., in Hsueh Hsih (self study) cells of a low order.

After this preparation the candidate would begin reading more advanced indoctrination materials, and in preparation of candidate membership the candidate would be required to write an autobiography giving personal data on family, education, social circumstances, and so on. Finally, after months, or even years, of candidate membership status, entry into full membership could then be accomplished upon the taking of an oath. In this oath the candidate member identifies himself as a member of the Sarawak Advanced Youths' Association and as 'one of the elite of the people of Sarawak'. The candidate also promises to assist in the realisation of 'the democracy and freedom of Sarawak', to study 'the theories and principles of Marxism/Leninism and the ideology of Mao Ze Dong', and to adhere closely to the organisation and central authorities of SAYA. The candidate declares also by this oath that 'there is no title more glorious than being called a revolutionary', and that he will gladly lay down his life if need be for the 'service of the organisation and the great enterprise'.[13]

Douglas Hyde has observed that when the SFA was formed in 1962 there was overwhelming interest and response – in one Third Division area, near the town of Sibu, some 1 000 members were enrolled in a month's time. Relatively the SFA had little to offer, enrollees knew that they were joining an illegal organisation, and yet they joined.[14] It is as if the Chinese rubber and pepper planters and rice farmers of Sarawak had a void in their lives which only the SFA, as *their* organisation, somehow, could fill. *Mutatis mutandis* the same observation applies to the youths that flocked to SAYA's carefully planned recreational and cultural events: the basketball games, the singing groups and dancing classes, the concerts and the picnics, organised by SAYA's and later by the SUPP's younger activists, filled a vacuum in the lives of restless and frustrated Chinese youths. These youths had been educated in Chinese language schools, with the result that, as their English was deficient, they were cut off from much of the English medium and culture of their state's élite, and saw their employment opportunities restricted mainly to that of shop assistant or clerk in provincial Chinese stores.[15]

Shortly, Chinese political aspirations were to be thwarted with Sarawak's absorption into the Malaysian Federation in 1963. Many Chinese would have preferred an independent Sarawak, in which they would have become the dominant population group in relation to Dayaks and Malays, and not just the Communists made capital out of the charge that the whole idea of the Malaysian Federation was but a scheme to 'contain' the potential political power of the ethnic Chinese. Even before Malaysia was formally created on 16 September

1963, SAYA activists had already been crossing the border into Indonesian Borneo where they received guerrilla training in special camps supervised by Indonesian military and cadres of the Indonesian Communist Party.[16] The latter party had led the way in Indonesia's official opposition, at the time, to the formation of the Malaysian Federation. Once trained the young Chinese guerrillas returned to Sarawak, there to join the CCO's people's army and its new overcapping front, the 'North Kalimantan National Liberation League' (NKNLL). On 8 December 1962, a brief revolt led by A. M. Azahari, an ambitious Brunei politician with Indonesian connections, had broken out in the Sultanate of Brunei. The revolt, which soon fizzled out, had the covert support of the Indonesian government, and had as its presumed aim the creation of a 'revolutionary government' for North Kalimantan (Borneo) that would include all or most of Sarawak, Sabah and Brunei. Though the objectives of the revolt remained hazy, there was nominal CCO (SCO) support for Azahari's revolutionary government and its *Tentara Nasional Kalimantan Utara* (National Army of North Borneo – TNKU).

But after the abortive 1965 coup in Indonesia, the consequent collapse of the Indonesian Communist Party and the erosion of President Sukarno's power, Indonesia's 'Confrontation' campaign against, and opposition to, the Malaysian Federation ended. Soon the Sarawak guerrillas no longer found themselves welcome on the Indonesian side of the frontier, although Indonesian Chinese in border villages continued covertly to supply the insurgents. Despite increasingly better organised counter-insurgency measures, some 2 000 young Chinese, formally members of SAYA and/or the NKNLL, went on with their intermittent guerrilla struggle, developing a network of jungle camps and arms caches, and retaining a measure of support among the Chinese planters and farmers of the upriver country. Notwithstanding strenuous government efforts at supervising teachers and curricula in the private Chinese schools, the guerrillas continued to draw a trickle of sympathisers from these schools. In the later nineteen sixties, and increasingly during the early seventies, special programmes called 'Operation Petik' (Persuasion) aimed at weaning students away from what the Sarawak authorities said was Communist propaganda in the schools were being instituted, and in 1974 the Sarawak government claimed that in this way some 800 students had been 'successfully prevented' from 'being won over to the Communist side'.[17]

The Sarawak guerrillas kept on operating in two overlapping

groups, however, one called the 'North Kalimantan People's Army' (*Pasokan Rakyat Kalimantan Utara – Paraku*), and the other the 'Sarawak People's Guerrilla Force' (*Pergarakan Gerilya Rakyat Sarawak – PGRS*). Sometimes both were collectively referred to as the 'North Kalimantan People's Armed Forces' (NKPAF). No major doctrinal or tactical differences separated these two 'people's armies', rather the division seems to have been dictated by logistical and geographic-operational considerations. As the long years of jungle fighting and the lack of one-time Indonesian support across the border began to make their effects felt, however, defections became more numerous, both from the ranks of SAYA-SFA, and from the guerrilla groups. In October 1973, the Sarawak government began a new peace and amnesty campaign for the insurgents, the so-called 'Operation Sri Aman' (Peace), which by March 1974 had seen Paraku's 'political commissar', Wong Kie Chok, a former employee of the Chinese embassy in Djakarta in the early 1960s, as well as more than 480 of his guerrilla followers, lay down their arms.[18]

The NKPAF thus seemed at first to have been virtually wiped out. But some 100 followers of SAYA-SFA and the NKNLL remained, eventually augmented by several scores of young NKPAF Chinese who had, at first, accepted 'Sri Aman' amnesty but then redefected back to the guerrillas in the jungle. By March 1974 the NKCP had a new chairman, Wen Min Chuan, a veteran of the guerrilla fighting of the early sixties and a new Central Committee. By 1978, its ranks had grown again to about 250, and it vowed to carry on with 'armed struggle as the main form of struggle'. The NKPAF was renamed the 'North Kalimantan People's Guerrilla Force' (NKPGF), and in the jungly interior of Sarawak's First Division has been slowly building its base areas and community networks again, even in the face of stepped-up joint Malaysian-Indonesian border surveillance. SAYA and the SFA still exist, but to all intents and purposes have become paper adjuncts, at least for the moment, of the main NKCP-NKPGF organisation. The latter is likely to be a more tightly organised central party structure in the future than the CCO (SCO) of the past.

The Sarawak case among other things points up the problem of maintaining effective central organisational control in conditions of illegality and insurgency. The Philippines offers a different perspective on the same problem. The 'Communist Party of the Philippines (Marxist-Leninist)' (CPP(M-L)), also called 'Communist Party of the Philippines (Mao Ze Dong Thought)', at the time of its founding congress near Capas, Tarlac province, between 26 December 1968 and 7 January 1969, adopted a party constitution providing for the customary 'democratic centralism' (defined as 'centralism based on democracy and democracy under centralised leadership'), and placing highest authority in a National Congress and Central Committee.[19] Decentralisation involved regional, provincial, district, section, and branch organisations and committees. Top level day-to-day management of the party, between plenary meetings of the Central Committee, is placed, again in standard fashion, in a Political Bureau (Politburo), and its Executive Committee. All this is in keeping of course with the usual organisation of Communist parties around the world.

The Maoist Philippine party's constitution, however, has a separate article on the 'territorial organisation' of the party by which presumably is meant the party organisation at the regional, provincial, district, and section levels, and which provides for regular meetings and for the execution of central party decisions at these lower hierarchical planes of the party. One is mindful that the Philippines is an archipelago and that conditions of insurgency, counter-insurgency, and later martial law impede smooth communications. In any case, 'territorial organisation', for the CPP(M-L), has come to mean over the years an increasing degree of, and eventually openly acknowledged, self-government of local party units. There are nine 'regional' party organisations throughout the Philippines which in many though not all respects are autonomous and exercise wide executive control over the front groups ('mass organisations') and, in considerable measure also over the guerrilla units of the New People's Army (NPA) in their respective areas. In December 1975 the CPP(M-L) expressed the hope that it would lead the Philippine revolution 'more effectively' by expanding the party organisations, the NPA and the 'democratic unified front'.[20] But to what extent the hope was realised may be questioned. For by the following year, in an eighth anniversary party statement, the CPP(M-L) Central Committee, noting that 'no complete ready made plan for solving our specific issues exists in books or foreign countries' (a swipe also at the alleged 'revisionism' of the Soviet Union), admitted that the NPA and the mass organisations were unable to break through the 'enemy's large scale encirclement and oppression'. Instead of breaking through, it was said attempts were being made to 'sabotage' the enemy. The same statement also revealed something of the autonomy of regional party organisations by asserting that these organisations were now 'financially independent', and that, indeed, the time had arrived when the regional organisations should be sending their cash surpluses to the Central Committee.[21]

A few weeks earlier CPP(M-L) chairman Amado Guerrero (José Maria Sison) had already declared that though the party practised the principle of centralised leadership, this was accompanied by 'dispersed operations'. When 'we have difficulty communicating with each other,' Guerrero said, 'we will resolutely act according to the general line' as laid down by the Central Committee. However, 'party organisations of various areas may take the initiative and carry out their difficult tasks according to local conditions'. [22]

The importance of developing local support for NPA operations, in accordance with the need for autonomy by separate units of the party, also became apparent in a 26 March 1977 CPP(M-L) statement commemorating the NPA's eighth anniversary. Claiming that in the preceding year the mass base of the NPA had expanded rapidly, this statement described the use of so-called party 'liaison teams' between the masses and the NPA. The teams apparently are charged with establishing close contact with the public at large 'through various flexible methods' and the conducting of 'social investigation' (not further specified). Through the local liaison teams recruits and followers are evidently won to support the party and the NPA, and thus eventually a network of 'secret organisational cells and committees' springs into existence.[23] The same statement refers also to the development of 'armed and unarmed propaganda teams', as well as to 'full fledged guerrilla units' and training units as further dimensions of this localised mobilisation effort, all of which is primarily designed to help the NPA develop in the region.

The initial organisational dynamic thus seems to have come from 'liaison teams' with their presumably special intimate knowledge of particular conditions in a given area. The building of mass support proceeds around the work of these local liaison groups, until the party and front organisational structure in the area is sufficiently developed so that it can take over the 'mass operations' in support of the NPA. The focus on the NPA in the 29 March 1977 CPP(M-L) statement is not a tactical aberration but follows, in fact, CPP(M-L) constitutional directives. Article IX of the CPP(M-L) constitution declares the NPA to be the 'main weapon of the party in the people's democratic revolution and in the subsequent socialist stage'. It is the

NPA, according to the same article, which is seen as welding together 'most profoundly' the 'basic alliance' of the workers and the peasants. Indeed, in the countryside, the NPA is charged with creating 'an independent regime' (that is, a liberated zone) by making agrarian revolution and establishing rural base areas through its armed struggle.

But crossing the movement toward autonomy in localised operations in accordance with the Maoist Philippine party's 'territorial' organisation is another trend, that of building a nationwide united front against the Marcos regime. The development of such a front as one element in the triad of organisation is always a tactical necessity for any Communist Party, as we have seen, but varying circumstances dictate the priority and intensity of the effort. Currently the priority for the Philippine Maoists is not in question. Comparatively, the CPP(M-L) finds itself today in the position summarised by a recent Burma Communist Party exhortation to the effect that 'simply establishing a party is not enough to insure that our party wins the people's democratic revolution, or after that is reached that the great historic task of marching toward socialism and communism is accomplished. A party serves only as a core and it needs the masses of the people.'[24] Already before, but particularly since, the 1972 Marcos proclamation of martial law in the Philippines did the CPP(M-L) begin urging the fusion of 'all forces that are opposed to the fascist dictatorship of the US-Marcos clique', and in October 1972 party media reported that a 'National Democratic Front' (NDF) was being formed by the party with its own distinctive programme.[25] Six years later, if Marcos himself is to be believed, the CPP(M-L)'s National Democratic Front had become the heart of the party's organisational efforts in his country. For example, addressing a visiting US congressional delegation in January 1978, Marcos reportedly said that 'the active Communist movement in the Philippines is now centred around the National Democratic Front, a relatively new organisation serving as an umbrella for all subversive groups.'[26]

Marcos' statement is surprising for, as has been noted, the NDF is not a 'relatively new organisation', having been announced formally in the CPP(M-L) literature at the time that the Philippine president placed his nation under martial law. But it is true that only since 1975, or so, has there been a seemingly significant, slowly increasing, if informal coalescing of the anti-Marcos opposition, ranging from Protestant and Catholic clergy and missionaries, to students and intellectuals and political groups like the *Laka ng Bayan* ('People's Force') and the *Katipunang Kalayaan at Katurangan* ('Freedom and Justice Party') which were active in the 1978 general elections for the interim national legislature (*Batasang Pambansa*). The pattern of this opposition convergence is in some way similar to and in other respects different from that of the period of the middle and late sixties, when the PKP (as yet untroubled by a rival Maoist Communist Party) was by itself a far less significant radical force than the combined effect of a number of Communist-infiltrated and -oriented fronts, some though by no means all with Maoist leaders, such as the *Kabataang Makabayan* (KM) or 'National Youth', the *Lapiang Manggagawa* (LM) or 'Labour Party', the *Masaka* (*Malayang Samahang Magsasaka*) or 'Free Peasants Union', the AKSIUN (*Ang Kapatrian Sa Ikauunlad Natin*) or 'Brotherhood for Our Development', a federation of the unemployed, and so on.

To be sure, there was in the sixties no 'umbrella' organisation for these and other separate groups. But there was considerable overlap of memberships and a remarkable similarity in major political objectives, particularly as regards the need to loosen the Philippine dependency on the US, and to alleviate the great disparities in wealth and access to social services among the population. In a sense the CPP(M-L) was an attempt to crystallise the radicalism of the sixties, just as the CPP(M-L)-created NDF, amorphous as it still is, to be sure, is an attempt to crystallise the further radicalisation and widening anti-government resistance induced by the ongoing martial law regime. And so the CPP(M-L), under running attack by the government's security campaign, has decentralised itself extensively for purposes of carrying on its insurgency, but it is also hiding behind the 'umbrella' of the NDF at a national level. However, there is a difference, it seems well to note, between the radical movement of the sixties and that of the seventies in the Philippines. The separate, anti-government groups of the sixties, such as the KM, were designed to stimulate and create a national movement of opposition, in which the various interest groups of society such as students, workers, peasants, and so on, could each find their own particular organisational haven (infiltrated and led in most cases by Communists like Sison and his lieutenants). The CPP(M-L)'s NDF of the seventies, on the other hand, is not so much designed to stimulate another opposition movement, rather it is meant to be the movement itself. Instead of having to join separate organisational components (such as KM or

LM), those against Marcos and the martial law regime can now essentially remain with their own principal institutional or other affiliations, such as the church, trade unions, or political parties, not least because martial law makes formal identification with a separate and distinct opposition group more difficult than in the sixties.

The NDF, then, gives the CPP(M-L) an opportunity to operate nationally in, and attempt to capture control of, an essentially loosely structured nationwide anti-government mass movement, while at the same time developing many different foci of dispersed guerrilla resistance throughout the country, supported by local front organisations. The latter in turn can invigorate the NDF. The NDF's 'manifesto', developed by a CPP(M-L)-supervised 'Preparatory Commission' in April 1973, is cast in the generalities of politically liberal and 'progressive' language that can appeal to the many, regardless of institutional affiliation, who are weary of Marcos martial law government. Thus the NDF manifesto speaks of uniting all 'anti-imperialist and democratic forces' in order to establish a 'coalition' government that will be truly democratic. The manifesto also talks of restoring freedom of speech, the press and association, of improvement of people's livelihood and of land reform, and so on.[27] But not all points in the manifesto are likely to be acceptable to all of Marcos' critics. For example, the point urging that all support 'the armed resistance and the underground' against the 'US-Marcos dictatorship' may dovetail with the CPP(M-L)'s tactical emphasis on the New People's Army guerrilla war and its local front supporters. But not all Filipino opposition elements − for example, some in the Roman Catholic church − are convinced that 'liberation' or 'people's war' is the way to go about changing matters, though some clergy, reportedly, have made common cause with the NPA insurgents. Still, on the whole, the NDF's programme fits the mood of the gradually rising anti-Marcos opposition, and as such it is, perhaps, the best example in South-east Asia today of the well known Marxist-Leninist tactic of 'national democracy', with its priority of front-building, which must be successful before Communists can seize power and the stage of 'Socialist' reconstruction can begin. The 15 June 1978 issue of *Liberation*, a publication of the NDF's Preparatory Commission, claims that an 'underground movement' consisting of a 'broad association of revolutionary people' is spreading throughout the Philippines. This 'movement' is building 'a strong, determined and organised force' which 'one day' will 'crush the Marcos dictatorship',

Liberation notes, however, that for the time being the 'movement' must remain secret as it would be 'suicide to fight the enemy unprepared'.

The NDF, it seems well to emphasise again, is only one dimension of CPP(M-L) tactics. The other remains the waging of the guerrilla struggle through the NPA and its decentralised territorial 'command structure', backed by local mass and front organisations. In continuing this guerrilla opposition the CPP(M-L) also persists in drawing the line between itself and its rival, the Moscow-oriented PKP. The latter too is all in favour of united front and 'mass organisation' building. But it sees any such front effort essentially in parliamentary, non-violent terms, as part of a gradual change in the constitutional climate in the Philippines that will not only put an end to martial law, but, in the process, legalise the PKP as a political party as well. As the PKP's Central Committee put it in November 1974, the party wants to submit its programme to the voters in an open election, and hence it does not seek to overthrow the government by force of arms but rather 'aims to make that government truly serve the interests of the broadest ranks of the Filipino people', through 'mass struggles, electoral means and the exercise of democratic rights'.[28] A 'truly democratic political economic and social order' in the Philippines, according to the PKP, would also legitimise the PKP. 'Mass struggles' from this perspective appear to refer to militant popular agitation campaigns, short of violence, through which the united front and its supporters compel the Marcos regime of its own will to end martial law. Thus, by rejecting NPA style people's war the PKP has made its future wholly dependent on the success or failure of the anti-Marcos united front which its rival, the CPP(M-L), is also trying to capture. Whether such organisational dependency is tactically wise for the PKP remains to be seen.

Both Sarawak and Philippine Communism tell us something of the difficulty of maintaining organisational coherence and control in times of party illegality. There are also contrasts in the development of the two movements. The formal establishment of the NKCP, out of the separate remaining components of the CCO (SCO), came essentially at a time – in the early seventies – when the movement would shortly be confronting its deepest crisis, and thus when a single, clearly defined organisational rallying point became most essential. In the Philippine case the ongoing insurgency of the NPA and resistance to Marcos' martial law regime eventually had something of an effect on public opinion, even if prominent CPP(M-L) leaders, like

José Sison, fell into government hands. By November 1977, when Sison was captured, the anti-Marcos resistance in the Philippines, of Communists and non-Communists alike, was already beginning to assume the dimensions of a 'popular front', reminiscent of the anti-Hitler days of the late nineteen thirties in Western Europe. The CPP(M-L)'s National Democratic Front was designed to capture this anti-Marcos dynamic, also permitting the badly battered party to hide behind its own NDF. In Sarawąk however the front-building process, after the defections of 'Operation Sri Aman' in 1974, must begin all over again, and the party can only hide in the jungle for the time being.

Even so, the Sarawak Communist organisation, including the rudiments of SAYA and the North Kalimantan National Liberation League, is comparatively still better off than the Indonesian Communist movement at present. The latter, divided between pro-Moscow and pro-Beijing wings and organisations, now has no functioning party, united front, or guerrilla army operating in Indonesia itself. Such organisation as exists in Indonesia today is confined to a few scattered, deep cover cadres, primarily of the Beijing party and a handful of insurgents along the Sarawak-Indonesian border. These insurgents function primarily as adjuncts of the North Kalimantan People's Guerrilla Force across the border in Sarawak. Most of the activity and publications of the two wings of the Indonesian party are carried on by a few scores of Indonesian émigrés in Beijing, Tirana, Moscow and other East European capitals. These émigré wings of the PKI regularly criticise each other's policies, in conformance with the nuances of the Sino-Soviet dispute. Their mutual accusations are not without some insight value as to some of the problems which party organisations in South-east Asia in general, and in Indonesia in particular, have faced in the recent past, and so they may perhaps be briefly noted here.

B. The problem of armed insurrection

As is known, the PKI or Indonesian Communist Party in the early sixties grew to be the largest party organisation outside the Communist bloc countries, with more than a million formal members and candidate members and with additional hundreds of thousands in youth, labour, women's, veterans' and other front organisations. This huge party and united front complex appears to have had little internal coherence and discipline, however, and after the débâcle of the 1965 coup, which soon saw the formal demise of the PKI, one authoritative analysis by the Moscow wing of the party attacked the 'lack of order in the admission of new members' and the consequent gradual 'mass penetration of petty bourgeois ideology' into the party in the days before the coup. While new membership figures were 'impressively high', according to this same critique, actually the 'number of people versed in Marxist-Leninist ideology was rather slender'. The party and its leaders became too 'bourgeois', seeking and receiving 'golden sops' thrown them by their enemies, as they indulged themselves meanwhile in a 'leftist phraseology', and thinking themselves true revolutionaries gave in to petty bourgeois 'adventurist' influences in their ranks. In consequence of their organisational errors, party leaders completely miscalculated the strength of their party and the political situation in the early months of 1965. The 'recklessness' of party leaders led them to plunge into the disastrous coup attempt of 30 September 1965.[29]

The unfolding of the 1965 coup itself, in which scattered and uninformed party leaders were evidently unable to rally the rank and file at the critical time of counter-coup action by General Suharto and his associates, may perhaps lend some substance to these Moscow-wing criticisms. But it is noteworthy that the Beijing-oriented branch of the PKI, too, in its own assessment of the 1965 coup débâcle that overtook the party, has had much to say of organisational weaknesses, 'bourgeois' influences, and the like.[30] However, not just the defects of party organisation undid the PKI. The deficiencies of united-front-building contributed even more to the holocaust that destroyed the Indonesian Communists in the aftermath of the 1965 coup, according to the current interpretation by the Beijing oriented wing of the party today. This united front problem of the PKI is particularly associated with a critique of the so-called 'two aspects' theory of the party as developed by the Beijing wing of the PKI in its *otokritik* or self-criticism of September 1966. According to this critique the party in the years immediately before the 1965 coup, when its united front complex grew so enormously, and when the PKI was wheeling and dealing with other parties and interest groups in the Indonesian arena of power, developed the theory that there was a 'people' (or 'pro-people') aspect to the internal dynamics of the Indonesian Republic, as well as an 'anti-people' aspect. Party chairman D. N. Aidit and the PKI leadership are accused in the *otokritik* of merging party policies wholly with this so-called 'people aspect', even though the 'people aspect' of state power in Indonesia was allegedly dominated at the time by the untrustworthy national bourgeoisie with which the party had allied itself.[31]

This criticism of the party's supposed identification with the 'pro-people' aspect of the political forces then prevailing in the Indonesian Republic in fact is a criticism of the party's whole united front policy in the early nineteen sixties. For it was in the early sixties that the PKI sought to blend its doctrines as much as possible with the teachings of then President Sukarno and other official Indonesian national philosophies. It was then also that, in conformance with Sukarno's stress on the need for national unity during the campaign to acquire Dutch-held West New Guinea and, later, during the Indonesian 'confrontation' against the planned Malaysian Federation, that the PKI attempted to mitigate some of its more militant domestic demands and ventures (for example, in connection with the land reform campaign of the early sixties). PKI policy at this time stressed that the party was a national party, integrated with national beliefs and institutions. Some foreign observers, also in light of the new respectability that the party was acquiring through its collaboration with the establishment, spoke of a 'domestication' of the PKI. Aidit and other party spokesmen meanwhile vehemently denied that the party thought of a possible future coup d'état. As an establishment fixture in the closing days of the Sukarno era, the party took comfort from the fact that it was on the side of 'the people', that is, the broad mass of Indonesians presumably being driven in progressive directions under Sukarno's revolutionary tutelage. The few Muslim and other anti-Communist diehards who had been denounced by Sukarno and who officially had been placed beyond the pale of accepted political life constituted the 'anti-people' aspect of the state and against these the PKI and Aidit could rail as lustily as any other member or group of the Indonesian establishment.[32]

Thus having sunk into the mire of 'opportunism' because of its 'domesticated' policies and close identification with Sukarno, as the *otokritik* has it, the party was unprepared for the temptation of the coup and recklessly plunged into it without having the revolutionary means, either in the way of trained cadres or effective united front strength, in order to be successful. Despite its huge numbers, then, and the large complex of front groups, the PKI organisation was weak and lacked thorough ideological training and party discipline.

It is difficult to resist the impression that the *otokritik*'s negative evaluation of the 'two aspect' policy of Aidit and of the PKI is a kind of *ex post facto* rationalisation of defeat. Considering that the *otokritik* comes from the Beijing-oriented wing of the party, it must be emphasised that at least at one time the 'two aspect' theory must have been acceptable to Chinese and Indonesian Maoists: some of Aidit's fullest explanations of the theory came during addresses which he gave to various audiences in People's China during a visit there in September 1963. These addresses, including an exposition of the 'two aspects' theory, were even considered important enough to have been disseminated subsequently by Beijing's own Foreign Languages Press.[33] If the 1965 coup had succeeded then it seems likely that the 'two aspects' theory would have achieved a more positive appreciation in Indonesian Maoist circles than is the case these days.

Even so the episode of the 'two aspects' theory is not without some probative value for Communist party organisations. Just as the PKP in the Philippines is doing today, so the PKI in Indonesia yesterday foreswore the path of systematic insurgency and guerrilla resistance, largely relying on a groundswell of opinion and slowly evolving political consensus, as reflected in a broad-based popular movement, in order to effect desired political changes. Whether under these circumstances PKI leaders should have considered at all entering a conspiracy looking toward a coup d'état may well be questioned. In any case, the reliance on 'movement'-oriented, united front tactics proved insufficient to achieve party goals, or indeed even to insure party survival after the coup, because the whole huge PKI and front group complex rapidly crumbled. In contrast to the PKP, and, being Maoists, perhaps having the PKI's experience and the 'two aspects' theory in mind, the CPP(M-L)'s leaders today are apparently not relying on the National Democratic Front or any other front movement alone.

In addition to the situation in Sarawak at the moment, in at least one other case of South-east Asian Communism today broadly based movement style appeals and united front tactics evidently are of secondary importance when compared to the perceived value of armed struggle. Perhaps more than any other party in the region today, with the exception of the NKCP, the Communist Party of Thailand (CPT) and its 10 000-man 'Thai People's Liberation

Armed Forces' (TPLAF) seem utterly convinced of Mao's dictum that political power flows from the barrel of a gun. This is not to say that, at various times, and with the aid of its Beijing and Hanoi friends, the CPT has not attempted to promote a number of front groups; it is to say that such efforts have had little if any durable and effective results and that development of a front complex does not seem to be an organisational priority in the CPT. This is the more remarkable because the present CPT, it will be recalled, developed in fact out of what could essentially be called a front group, namely, the largely Chinese Thai 'Communist Youth Organisation of Siam' established in 1927. And even after the CPT's formal founding in 1942, some effort was made to establish front style affiliates in the trade union movement.

But it was not until December 1964 that the CPT, apparently at the instigation or upon the advice of the Chinese Communists, briefly decided to commit itself fully to a 'movement' strategy. It was on 8 December 1964 that the 'Voice of the People of Thailand', the clandestine radio transmitter located either in China's Yunan province, or in Pathet Lao-held territory in Laos, announced that a 'Thailand Independence Movement' (TIM) had been established in Beijing, and *Ekharat*, a CPT publication, similarly announced the formation of TIM.[34] In its 'manifesto', TIM employed standard 'national democratic' themes, calling for the expulsion of 'US imperialists' from Thai territory, the establishment of a 'genuine democracy', and the implementation of a policy of peace and prosperity for all Thais.[35] Whether in an attempt to create an impression that a groundswell for change was beginning in Thailand and hence the birth of yet another 'movement' was a natural development, or whether as a result of a doctrinal or tactical conflict within the TIM, at any rate on 1 January 1965, the establishment of a 'Thailand Patriotic Front' (TPF) was announced in Beijing. Its programmatic statement closely paralleled the national democratic themes of TIM, including demands for 'democratic rights', for a turning away from the policies which allegedly had made Thailand into a 'new type colony' of the US, and for improvements in general living standards. By November 1965, TIM leaders, according to Chinese media, had announced they were merging their organisation with the TPF, but the tactical significance of this merger and indeed the nature of the front leadership remained obscure.[36]

Meanwhile, however, attempts had been made to develop the

united front structure and Beijing's New China News Agency again announced that on 1 May 1965 a 'Thailand Federation of Patriotic Workers' (TFPW) had been established. A TPFW statement, allegedly issued first in Bangkok, pledged full support to the TPF and its programme called for the overthrow of the 'US imperialist'-oriented regime in Thailand. A 'Thai Patriotic Teachers and Professors Group' similarly announced its adhesion to the TPF in March 1965, and a 'Thai Patriotic Youth Organisation' was to do the same thing in a proclamation issued on 15 February 1966. During 1965–6, the 'Voice of the People of Thailand' and/or the Chinese press announced the birth of a number of other front organisations ranging from a 'Poor People's Federation' to a 'Self-Liberated Farmers' and Planters' Association', while CPT publications called attention to declarations of adhesion to the TPF from exiled intellectuals, student leaders, Buddhist clergy and other individuals. The TPF in the later sixties seemed particularly anxious to portray itself as being an informal, embryo government in exile, maintaining 'foreign representatives' in Beijing and London, as well as roving emissaries.[37]

Yet even as the impression was being created that there was a broad-based Thai united front movement, similar in intent, one might suggest, to the NDF in the Philippines today, the CPT was beginning to flex its own organisational muscles, claiming increased insurgency action and recruitment of peasant followers in the northeast. As early as its third anniversary message on 1 January 1968, the TPF urged Thais particularly to rally around the CPT.[38] The component support groups of the front, like the Thai Patriotic Youth Organisation, began doing likewise. The CPT in turn gradually began referring less and less to the TPF, and began propagating its own 'national democratic' line, including establishment of a 'people's government' of workers, peasants, petty and national bourgeoisie, and, especially, insisting in various press releases on the primacy of guerrilla struggle and on the need for a military solution to Thailand's problems. By the early seventies this military emphasis all but overshadowed CPT tactics. At the same time, People's China seemed to become less blatantly involved in supporting the Thai Communist movement. Between 1973 and the fall of the Thanom Kittikachorn regime, and 1976 and the advent of the new, strongly anti-Communist military-dominated government of premier Thanin Kraivichien, Thailand experienced a return to an era of party-focused parliamentary government under cabinets led by the Pramoj brothers. Though new opportunities existed in this turbulent period for united front action, the CPT stuck to its guerrilla-oriented, uncompromising hard line. When the Thanin regime assumed power, some 2 000 student activists, fearful of reprisals, sought refuge with the CPT. The 'Voice of the People of Thailand' subsequently began broadcasting that students were joining the TPLAF and engaging in 'mass struggles' among the peasantry. These 'mass struggles' seemed to be primarily proselytising and volunteer construction work, but did not include much united-front-building effort. With the fall of the Thanin regime on 20 October 1977, and a return to a more moderate, though still militarily dominated government, the students reportedly left their CPT patrons and began going back home. Thus neither in the 'democratic' era under the Pramojs, nor, subsequently, in the authoritarian and semi-authoritarian period of Thanin and Kriangsak, were CPT efforts at united-front-building, national democratic style, much in evidence.

Still, it would be a mistake to say that Thai Communism has formally and wholly abandoned such efforts, for party media claim that 'revolutionaries' continue to propagandise and lead 'the people of various strata' in a struggle for national independence and democracy, and that great success has been achieved in 'awakening the political consciousness of the masses' amidst 'vigorous struggle' and through 'widely publicising revolutionary theory'.[39] But while such 'consciousness raising' processes through proper indoctrination are acknowledged, one finds few if any references in the CPT media releases to standard united front tactics such as the need to unify diverse social strata, including peasants, workers, petty and national bourgeoisie, in common action. Rather, the focus of CPT operations is the insurgent war of the TPLAF, just as in Sarawak the focus of the North Kalimantan Communist Party is the North Kalimantan People's Guerrilla Force.

In its recently published brief historical sketch of Communism in Thailand, the CPT again and again returns to the theme of armed struggle, as if this is the only organisational purpose of movement and party.[40] Only dates and events related to this theme receive mention. Thus, after the third CPT Congress in 1961, one is informed, leading party cadres began living in the rural areas in order to 'mobilise farmers to prepare for armed struggle' and to develop new cadres. And in 1969, in conjunction with a new policy issued by the 'Supreme

Command' of the TPLAF, there was yet another pledge by the party 'resolutely [to] pursue the path of armed struggle to the end'. When united front tactics are discussed at all in this party history it is in conjunction with the insurgency, and so one reads that on 1 December 1976 the party issued a statement calling for unity among all 'patriotic and democracy loving forces' – a standard 'national democratic' line – but 'so as to wage the people's war to the utmost' and in order to topple the 'fascist' Thai government.[41] Broadcasts of the 'Voice of the People of Thailand' particularly concern themselves with claimed successes in the armed struggle (for instance, one broadcast, in early August 1978, asserted that since August 1977 the TPLAF had fought '810 battles in various regions', killing more than 1 350 enemy troops and had seized 'hundreds of firearms' and much ammunition),[42] saying that since the 'flame of the people's war' is now 'raging' throughout the country 'we must step up mass mobilisation and mass organisation work'.[43] The latter formulation almost suggests that the tactic now is that *because* people's war is spreading, united front organisational activity must also be intensified, instead of the other way around.

Even when support is obtained for the CPT from other groups and organisations the focus in CPT media remains on the value of such support for the Thai people's war. Thus, the dissent of Thai Muslims, in the southern provinces of the kingdom, became officially significant for the party when in August 1977, under CPT tutelage, a 'Thai Muslim People's Liberated Armed Forces' organisation was formed, which though under party control is reportedly independent of the TPLAF. By the formation of their own liberation army, the Thai Muslims, according to CPT media, 'have now learned a lesson gained at the expense of their blood and tears', and this lesson is that 'only by taking up arms' can Thai Muslims succeed in toppling the 'fascist dictatorial' Thai government.[44]

The CPT, of course, has not been relying exclusively on Thai Muslim dissent in order to develop the Communist armed struggle in Thailand's southern provinces. During 1977–9 in particular, the CPT's cadres were active in Songkhla, Surat Thani and Nakhon Si Thammarat provinces. After a Thai military offensive against Communist guerrilla encampments in the last two named provinces early in February 1979, Thai military sources, according to the Singapore daily *The Straits Times* on 12 February 1979, declared that the CPT 'recently' had organised a general party conference in southern

Thailand and adopted a new seven-point programme for going on the offensive. The programme ranged from the customary attacks on government posts and personnel and impeding highway construction projects, to intensifying propaganda work in rural areas and obtaining their financial support. By 21 April 1979 a spokesman for the Thai Internal Security Operations Command declared that Communist insurgent activities along the southern Thai border with Malaysia had continued 'unabated'. The Communist guerrillas were reported to be engaged in 'eliminating' government officials, as well as collecting intelligence, food and financial funding for their operations. That the CPT in southern Thailand means business and intends to develop a disciplined regional organisation became apparent at the close of March 1979, when the Bangkok daily *World* reported that eighteen Thai students who had earlier joined the CPT in Nakhon Si Thammarat province had been summarily executed by party cadres because the students had attempted to break with the party and defect. Though the party is geographically scattered, the CPT's regional operations, particularly those in the southern provinces, do exhibit increased co-ordination and planning, as the focus on implementing 'people's war' tactics permeates party ranks.

Meanwhile, members of the Socialist Party of Thailand and of dissident students' organisations who have joined the CPT and its forces, are described in the CPT media from the same 'people's war' perspective. Recently the 'Voice of the People of Thailand', in connection with the activities of the Socialist Party of Thailand, duly noted some of the united front efforts of Socialist cadres, for example, in 'art, and culture, education, the military and people's state power', but major attention was focused in the 'Voice' broadcast on Socialist assistance to the 'Thai people's armed struggle'.[45] Another recent broadcast over the 'Voice' recounts the work of the National Student Centre of Thailand, a student dissident organisation, and begins by reporting that students, youths and intellectuals have now flocked to the 'armed struggle areas' of Thailand, where they are said to be contributing in many ways and where they are being 'tested and tempered amid the flames of people's war which is engulfing the entire country'.[46] Again, it is to be stressed that for none of these groups is united front activity to be ignored. But the thrust of their efforts is principally channelled, either directly or indirectly, toward guerrilla insurgency.

This military emphasis has brought the CPT advantages as well as

new problems. The CPT's twenty-man Central Committee is headed
by a veteran of the Vietnam fighting, Charun Wangam, and most of
his Committee colleagues have received 'people's war' training in
Hanoi or Beijing. CPT organisational structure, especially in the
'armed struggle areas' in the north-east, now has become somewhat
like that of the Philippine NPA, in that TPLAF 'battle commands'
increasingly become synonymous with and assume the work of
local party committees. Moreover, a growing degree of operational
autonomy is evident, similar to that met with among CPP(M-L)
units in the Philippines, especially among the CPT and TPLAF
organisations in the north and south of the kingdom. Though CPT
Central Committee directives have repeatedly warned against the
dangers of failing to screen applicants and newcomers to party ranks,
and insist on the primacy of ideological training, the influx of students
and others in the wake of Thanin's appointment as premier was for a
while so considerable that the real test of suitability became an
applicant's readiness to join a guerrilla unit almost at once. Later, in
order to facilitate the process of absorption of new CPT recruits,
training camps reportedly were established in nearby Laos. In August 1978, two defectors told the Thai government's chief counter-
insurgency agency, the Internal Security Operations Command, that
Phonsay village, Sayaboury province in Laos, a five kilometre walk
from the border of Thailand's Nan province, had become a centre for
weapons-training for new CPT recruits.[47]

Even with this training, however, the youthful new guerrillas of the
TPLAF appear to have become the cause of some friction in party
ranks, because the newcomers, allegedly anxious to emulate Che
Guevara right away, were unfamiliar, according to party veterans,
with the logistical and other problems of fighting a protracted guerrilla war. On the other hand, the influx of the students, along with
numbers of labour activists, peasant leaders and others, provided, as
one analysis has put it, 'a union of urban intellectuals and rural
guerrillas similar to that wrought by the exodus to the "liberated"
areas of China in the 1920s and 1930s'.[48] There is little question that
the CPT-TPLAF now has a number of 'liberated' zones in several
Thai border provinces. Already in September 1975, the Bangkok
government admitted that some 640 of its villages, with a total
population of about 200 000, were wholly controlled by the CPT.[49]
Since that time, as the TPLAF 'battle command' and military
operational network has spread, the number of CPT villages has

grown still further. The plight of the Thai farmer in the north-east, of the hill tribe settler in the north, and the grievances of the Thai Muslim in the south, all offer the CPT future toeholds in the countryside, as meanwhile urban recruits give the TPLAF a new organisational character reminiscent of the early influx of Philippine city youths and university students to the NPA in the late nineteen sixties and early seventies. There is no indication that CPT appeals in the rural north-east of Thailand are being effectively undercut by land reform and other ameliorative measures of the Bangkok government, nor does it appear that the substitution of serious student and intellectual dissent with the modified authoritarianism of the Kriangsak Chamanand regime is being dissipated.

The pattern of armed insurrectionary activity by Communist guerrillas in South-east Asia can be deceptive, however, because on a day-to-day basis the incidence of such activity may appear to be limited. It is therefore not the extent of armed insurrection, or the numbers of combatants involved, but the staying power of the insurgents over the months and years that is the important factor in assessing the question of incidence. As reported by military authorities or in the press the scope of armed conflict may seem limited. Even as the Bangkok press, for example, used such expressions as 'intense fighting' (in connection with clashes in the Khao Klo mountains in Petchabun province in June 1976) or Communist insurgents going 'on a rampage' (in Ubon Ratchatthani province in the previous months), in reality no more than three or four dozen guerrillas and less than a score of Thai military and officials were killed in such encounters. Overrunning a rural police station here, ambushing a convoy of military there, capturing some weapons or 'liberating' (that is, intermittently occupying) a village yet elsewhere – the CPT's force at first blush does not create the impression of posing a major threat to continued Thai central government authority. Moreover, often the incidence of guerrilla activity is clouded by simple brigandage and extortion: in April 1979 Thai military sources reported that the 2 000 or so Communist insurgents in northern provinces like Loei and Petchabun relied heavily on extracting 'protection' money from sawmill owners exploiting the forests where the insurgents hide.

It is not different in the Philippines, where – as in May 1979 – Defence Department officials issued firebreathing pronouncements that measures would be taken to halt a 'rising' incidence of guerrilla insurgency on Samar Island province. In fact, the New People's

Army on Samar had briefly entered a number of small Samar towns in recent months, firing shots and acquiring provisions. But the total casualty rate of several months of such shoot-ups was described as three police and two militiamen killed. More disquieting, perhaps, was the Philippine Defence Department report that the mayors of a number of towns on Samar were working in collusion with the NPA – a pattern of symbiosis between officials and insurgents common to Luzon since the earliest days of the post-war Huk insurgency in the Philippines.

Considered by themselves all such incidents of Communist 'armed insurrection' seem insignificant. But they do go on, month after month, year after year, eroding public confidence and security, creating 'counter-governments' that must be dealt with by a cowed local population, slowing economic development, diverting precious resources to continuing military campaigns, and – not least – providing South-east Asian governments with a justification to maintain extensive controls over political activity and freedom of expression. The imposition and application of such controls has a polarising effect, as non-Communist critics of prevailing regimes feel compelled to join the radical opposition groups among which Communist proselytisers do their work.

C. Three models for the search for power

With the foregoing case studies in mind, we can now perhaps suggest that Communist organisation in non-Communist South-east Asia today tends to follow three basic models. One is typified by the NKCP in Sarawak, by the CPT in Thailand and, though much less is known about it, also by the BCP in Burma. It is the model in which 'the gun' does not so much seem to command the party, rather it is all but synonymous *with* the party. That is to say liberation war so wholly envelops Communist organisational activities that a distinctive party organisation, apart from the guerrilla force, operationally at least hardly seems to exist, if at all. United-front-building, in this model, though by no means wholly lacking, does not seem to be a priority of party policies. It is noteworthy that this model does not require a particular party organisational magnitude in order to be operational: the Sarawak insurgents of the NKPGF number less than 200, their

Thai counterparts in the TPLAF more than 10 000 – thus setting the range of guerrilla organisational size in South-east Asia today. Both organisations, however, are growing, if at different rates.

The second model is exemplified by the Moscow-oriented PKP in the Philippines today, and by the Indonesian Communist Party (PKI) in Indonesia under party chairman D. N. Aidit in the nineteen fifties and early sixties. In this model, insurgency is not operationally in existence as a party tactic and revolutionary violence is specifically eschewed, while the party formally identifies with militantly political but essentially constitutional and parliamentary means of coming to power. Front-building, either in the form of a more or less co-ordinated, broad-based 'movement' (as the CPP(M-L)'s 'National Democratic Front' also suggests), or else in the form of separate party-dominated youth, women's, farmers', trade union, and other interest groups (as Aidit's PKI succeeded in developing), has tactical and organisational pride of place in this model. In the third model, finally characterised by an organisational straddling of the first two models (as exemplified by the CPP(M-L)), the party attempts, though not always successfully, to separate itself organisationally from its guerrilla force and so makes an effort to 'walk on two legs', that is, develop next to its liberation army a broad-based united front in order to win a following and bring about 'progressive', leftward changes in the political arena. Apart from the CPP(M-L) already discussed, it is the Communist organisations in western Malaysia today that seem to correspond more closely to this model than any other, and concerning which a word should now be said.

As has been indicated earlier, west Malaysian (or Peninsular Malayan) Communism today is divided into three organisations: the parent Communist Party of Malaya (CPM), and two rival offshoots, one of which developed in February 1970, and is called the Communist Party of Malaya (Marxist-Leninist) or CPM(M-L). In terms of formal membership, as distinct from informal supporters who are considerably more numerous, all three organisations are small, with the CPM according to government sources having fewer than 2000 members, and the CPM-Revolutionary Faction (CPM(RF)) and CPM(M-L) each less than 300. Yet the three organisations appear indestructible and have for years now kept engaged a sizeable segment of Malaya's security forces; they pose a significant threat to Malaysia's domestic security, if various government circles are to be believed.

According to the CPM's May 1972 constitution (the constitutions of the other two parties have not been published, although 'basic party rules' are said to be in existence for each), the party's supreme leadership body is the National Congress, which, when not in session, is 'replaced' by the Central Committee (article 13).[50] The latter, along with the Central Committee's Politburo, secretary general and deputy secretary general are the chief executive organs of the party (article 15). The basic unit of the CPM is the branch, which may be established 'at every mill, mine, estate, village, school, platoon and within the armed working units of the National Liberation Army' (article 19). Among the principal responsibilities of branches are to lead party members in the study of 'Marxism-Leninism-Mao Ze Dong thought', to 'unite closely with the masses', and supervise their work, and to implement party decisions (article 20).

There are two particularly noteworthy features of the CPM constitution. One is the explicit prohibition (article 12) against the formation of 'cliques', or the engaging in other activities 'violating the organisational principles' of the party. This is probably a reference to the schismatic movement that has plagued the party since January 1970, when resistance arose against a Herodian Central Committee order issued to 'liberation army units' directing the liquidation of recent recruits because of alleged untrustworthiness. The other feature relates to the organisational integration of the 'Malayan National Liberation Army' (MNLA), the CPM's fighting arm. Provision for the formation of party branches within the 'liberation army' has already been noted, but it must also be observed that party organisation may and does take place at the 'company level' of the MNLA, and as such it is said to correspond to the party organisation at the 'district' or 'area' levels of the CPM. Article 16 provides that the formation of party leadership bodies, including congresses, at the area, district, or MNLA 'company level', will be convened by the party organisation of a higher level 'in accordance with the Congress's situation'. The practical meaning of the latter phrase is not apparent. But it is evident that above the branch level, and below the plane of the Central Committee of the CPM, the most commonly met with and functionally active intermediate party organisation today is the 'company level' MNLA party organisation. In fact, it is at this point that the similarities between the CPT-TPLAF in Thailand and the CPM-MNLA in west Malaysia are particularly noteworthy in that military and party organisation all but seem to merge.

However, in this connection it is also well to remember that the

CPM organisation is distinctive in two ways. First, it has made considerable efforts to develop its branches, the bottom rung of the organisational ladder, also outside the MNLA, so that the party is not wholly swallowed up by the army and thus the really important point of party and 'liberation army' merger tends to occur higher up on the organisational scale, for example, at the party 'district' and MNLA 'company' levels. However, branches do serve as recruiting funnels for the MNLA, since among their duties (article 20, sub. 2) is to arouse the masses to launch 'people's war'. The second distinctive feature of the CPM organisation, which it also has in common with its rivals, the CPM(RF) and CPM(M-L), is the use of a separate political action front, as well as a guerrilla force. Because of the small number of formal members in all three parties, considerable membership overlap between individual parties, their fronts and their insurgents may be assumed, although the CPM's action front group reportedly has members who are not at the same time members of the CPM as well. Similarity of the names of the political fronts and of the guerrilla organisations has made for a good deal of confusion in various news reports as to which party faction is involved in a certain action. The following table presents the principal affiliations:[51]

Party Organisation	Political Action Front	Guerrilla Army
CPM	Malayan National Liberation League (MNLL)	Malayan National Liberation Army (MNLA)
CPM(RF)	Malayan People's Liberation League (MPLL)	Malayan People's Liberation Army (MPLA)
CPM(M-L)	Malayan People's Liberation Front (MPLF)	Malayan People's Liberation Army (MPLA)

Thus the fighting forces of the CPM(RF) and of the CPM(M-L) both bear the same name, Malayan People's Liberation Army (MPLA). The CPM's MNLL has been described by the Singapore government as having its followers in that island republic too, and indeed it is known to be operational throughout peninsular Malaya. The fronts and armies of the CPM(RF) and of the CPM(M-L), however, appear to be active mainly in southern Thailand or in the Thai-west Malaysian border area.

As in the case of the CPP(M-L) and its NDF and NPA, so west Malaysian Communism is organisationally 'walking on two legs', as the Maoist phrase has it, by projecting both a united front as well as a 'people's war' tactic at one and the same time. There appears to be a recognition in principle, at least, in all three west Malaysian Communist Parties, that 'mass struggles' should be encouraged also outside a military context. Considering the relatively small size of its party hard-core membership, which official Malaysian sources, in any case, tend to equate with the size of its liberation army, the parent CPM in particular has encouraged front proliferation developing, in addition to its political action front, a number of other front groups with specific appeals to youth, the more orthodox Muslim community, peasants, and others. Critics and official quarters allege that these front groups are largely paper organisations, designed to create the impression of a widening public dissatisfaction with the Malaysian government. Programmatic emphasis in these front groups tends to fall on the importance of armed struggle, however, in a manner comparable to that of the CPT's tactic in Thailand. Discipline, grounded in thorough ideological indoctrination, is considered to be indispensable to success in 'people's war'.[52]

The MNLL is seen in CPM media as pledged to 'fight shoulder to shoulder' with 'various' other 'fraternal revolutionary organisations' in order to enhance the 'developed armed struggle in our country'.[53] The 'Malayan National Patriotic Youth and Student Movement', founded by the CPM in 1975, appears similarly persuaded of the necessity of the path of violence. In a recent statement on this movement's work over the CPM's clandestine transmitter, 'Voice of the Malayan Revolution', it is alleged that 'all legal channels' and 'legitimate expression of any opposing views' have become 'blocked', so that it may be asked: 'Is there any way for us ... other than resorting to illegal and secret methods?'[54] As for the earlier described Paperi, the CPM's 'Fraternal Islamic Solidarity Party', its Central Committee's messages emphasise too that 'the revolutionary armed struggle' of the people in various South-east Asian countries 'is developing rapidly and vigorously' and that 'it is imperative to rise up and fight against the brutal government' in order to achieve true freedom and democracy. The Malaysian government's alleged 'betrayal' of the struggle of Muslim Palestinians against Zionism, its 'brutal exploitation' of the pilgrimage to Mecca, and transformation of the government's land development programme (FELDA) so as to make thousands of Muslim Malay families into 'slave farmers' – all these are favourite themes in the CPM appeals to the more observant and orthodox Muslim Malays, but always with an ultimate view to expanding 'people's war' and to 'serving the Malayan National Liberation Army'.[55]

In its quarrel with its rivals, the CPM(RF) and the CPM(M-L), the CPM has also put tactical differences over the use of armed struggle in the foreground. Thus, in one extended critique, the CPM accuses the 'socalled Marxist-Leninist faction' of opposing the Maoist dictum of using the countryside in order to encircle the cities and thus ultimately seizing power by means of armed force. The CPM (M-L)'s call for armed struggle is designed to 'mislead the people and mix the genuine with the fictitious', according to the CPM.[56]

Organisationally, however, there appears to be very little difference between the three west Malaysian Communist parties, though little enough is known of claimed party structures like a national 'Congress', a Central Committee, Politburo and the other legislative and executive organs of the two smaller CPM offshoots. All three parties actively proselytise among ethnic Chinese rural residents and Chinese small town youth in Malaysia, but whatever the radicalisation of their political consciousness that may be provided by roaming cadres and 'self study' cells, the degree of the neophyte's political maturity tends to be gauged by and large in terms of his or her readiness to leave home and engage actively in the 'liberation' armed struggle. As early as 1971, in its White Paper entitled 'The Resurgence of Armed Communism in West Malaysia', the government of Malaysia had noted that genuine united front activity in the west Malaysian Communist movement had to all intents and purposes ceased to exist, in favour of a concentration on building a network of underground supporters connected with the struggle tactics of the CPM, then still the only Communist party. So considered, one could make a case that even the CPM's distinctive united front efforts are made in order to serve the ultimate success of guerrilla war. It remains to note that despite periodic reports of Politburo leadership rifts, particularly dissatisfaction over some of the policies of the CPM's long-time secretary general, Chin Peng, the central party leadership of the CPM has been remarkably stable, and continuing accommodations are being made, both at the Politburo and at MNLA 'regimental command' levels, for close participation of ethnic Malays and Thai Muslims, side by side with Chinese.

D. Indochina

Analysis of the organisation of the ruling Communist Parties in the Indochinese states today is possible only to a limited extent, in large measure because relatively little is known for sure of the present-day structure and operations of government which the party of necessity dominates. In the Socialist Republic of Vietnam (SRV), the Vietnam Communist Party (VCP), at its important Fourth Congress in December 1976, expanded its Central Committee from 53 full members and 24 alternates to 101 full members and 32 alternates, many of the additions being economic specialists whose skills will be needed as the SRV embarks on the 'Socialist Revolution' in the present stage of its development.[57] At the Fourth Congress, too, party first secretary Le Duan cited as 'the biggest shortcoming and weakness' in the party an inadequate grasp of the role of the party at this time 'when the party leads the state to carry out the socialist revolution'. Among the organisational mistakes listed by Le Duan were 'empiricism' in party building and in methods of leadership (not further specified), inappropriate work styles, 'loose' procedures in the admission of new members, and inadequate political and ideological preparation.[58]

Future party building, according to Le Duan, should strive for the close integration of ideological and political training with organisational development, and it should be carried out through strengthening of 'the revolutionary mass movement'. Enhancing the quality of party cadres or members should go hand in hand with general improvements in party branches and in the 'primary organisations' of the party. The latter, it was said, are 'the basic fighting units' of the party, where contact with the masses is most direct. According to Le Duan, a party branch or primary organisation 'cannot be considered a good one' unless production increases, the life of the masses is improved, and the revolutionary purposes of the SRV are fully articulated. Continuing with his counsel of perfection for the meetings, tasks and efforts of branches and primary party organisations, the VCP first secretary declared:[59]

> Their meetings must have a concrete and rich political content; they must engage in discussions on the party line and policies, on the tasks assigned to their localities and units, on the plans to fulfill these tasks; they must distribute work and apportion responsibility to each party cadre and member, and review the performance of party branches and members. Efforts must be made to create in the party organisations, in their daily activities as well as in their meetings, a seething and militant atmosphere, and promote the collective wisdom, initiatives and the high sense of responsibility of every party member.

Following the Fourth VCP Congress, and as attempts to transform the South Vietnamese socio-economy intensified, cadre training and indoctrination were greatly stepped up. A reported rescreening and 're-evaluation' of party members, particularly those with official responsibilities in the South, who had allegedly succumbed to bribery and other corruption, helped instill new discipline. It might be emphasised that party leaders have been quite candid about their organisational shortcomings. In his address to the Fourth VCP Congress, Politburo member Le Duc Tho for example spoke of 'corruption, bureaucracy, arbitrariness, autocracy and lack of devotion' among some party members, as well as of the 'abuse of their powers', their commission of 'fraudulent and unlawful acts', their bullying tactics, and other malversations.[60] In keeping with the demands of the new Socialist stage in the SRV, a proper class background for the VCP membership is now seen as increasingly important as a safeguard against 'deviation' and other supposedly weakening tendencies. Thus Le Duc Tho described as a 'primary question' for the party the selection of cadres 'from the ranks of workers', and, as far as South Vietnam is concerned, recruitment also of 'labouring peasants, especially poor peasants and hired labourers'. Efforts should also be made, according to Tho, to give the proper training to, and utilise the services of, intellectuals in the rebuilding of the party, and in this regard the party has attacked 'narrow and prejudicial views' which do not consider the intelligentsia to be 'a fundamental class'.[61]

Organisational implementation of all these and other admonitions has taken several forms. For example, in line with the directive to improve the quality of party branches and of the party's 'primary' level contacts with the masses, there has been a campaign of 'vigorously turning toward the grassroots', meaning special attention to be given by the party to the performance of rural co-operatives and other village enterprises. In 1978, Hanoi's leading daily editorially charged that 'many villages and agricultural cooperatives', even though they control sufficient land and have a large enough work force, have failed to intensify cultivation. This was ascribed among other factors to the low level of organisational and managerial competence of 'grassroots cadres'.[62] Shortages in the manufacture of ordinary tools and implements, and inadequate supplies of industrial and trade materials are also problems whose solution is perceived as requiring greater concern for what the same editorial termed, with a curious expression, 'streamlining the grassroots'.

Le Duan's demand voiced at the December 1976 Fourth VCP Congress for a strengthening of the 'revolutionary mass movement' was reflected also in his emphasis at that time on a further consolidation of 'the union of the nation' within a new, broad-based national front. It will be recalled that, historically, Vietnamese Communism has been quite adept in developing a number of such fronts (for example, the Vietminh Front was founded in 1941, the Vietnam Fatherland Front was established in 1955, the National Front for the Liberation of South Vietnam in 1960, and the Vietnamese Alliance of National Democratic and Peace Forces in 1968), in keeping with its persistently emphasised 'national democratic' tactics of building a widely based popular following, within which the Communist Party, generally concealed, acts as the principal organisational dynamic.

The 'Socialist stage' upon which the new SRV is now embarked doctrinally requires a break with the approaches of the earlier stage of the 'national democratic' struggle. And so Le Duan's call for a new national front was to result in the birth, in February 1977, of yet another new Vietnamese front organisation, the Fatherland Front of Vietnam (FFV). That same month the FFV's new programme and the merger of all other fronts with the FFV was approved by the SRV's Constituent Assembly. The main aim of the FFV is to 'unite all the people in the name of building a peaceful, independent, united and socialist Vietnam'. According to the FFV programme, conditions must be created allowing all citizens to participate in public affairs, and for the mobilisation of all people in order to develop the nation toward 'socialist industrialisation', and to transform the economy generally toward 'large scale socialist production'.[63]

Meanwhile the 'revolutionary' role of the People's Army of Vietnam (PAVN) has been changed to that of a more organisationally tightly structured force concerned with defending the unified Vietnamese nation's 'peace and independence'. At a level of 600 000 regulars the SRV army is the largest in South-east Asia.[64] There is also an armed militia of about 1.5 million, altogether a sizeable military establishment whose ideological preparation is also the party's concern. While the number of army representatives in the Central Committee of the VCP increased at the Fourth Party Congress, proportionally the share of army representation in the Central Committee has declined, and 'From this one may conclude that the party firmly commands the gun in spite of the latter's importance for so long.'[65]

The party-directed mobilisation of the Vietnamese nation is expected to absorb PAVN also, as well as be targeted at specific social groups. An example of the latter is the so-called 'Three Assaults' youth movement, formally launched early in 1978, for the dual purpose* of assisting in the development of the country's 'New Economic Zones' and in aiding the PAVN in the Cambodian border conflict and in the maintenance of domestic security generally. On the one hand 'assault youth units' have been reported to be operating jointly with PAVN in dealing 'appropriate punitive counterblows' to the Cambodian 'invaders'. On the other hand they have been praised in the Hanoi media for launching irrigation projects, constructing roads, working on state farms, and so on.[66] Next to an 'assault' on problems of defence and economic life, the 'Three Assaults' youth movement is designed to meet constructively needs of youth for study, recreation, cultural and sports activities, and it is noteworthy again that SRV media emphasise that the 'tasks' of the 'Three Assaults' groups must be fulfilled 'in the grassroots organisations'. The socially transforming impact of the 'Three Assaults' movement presumably is expected to make itself felt also on a 'number of youths' who according to official sources 'still indulge in unhealthy activities and an unhealthy lifestyle'.[67] In the new unified SRV, the VCP-supervised pattern of social controls evidently means that no one is to escape the demands of the revolutionary new stage of Socialism in the country. This stage, as Vietnam's Fourth National Trade Union Congress, meeting in Hanoi in May 1976, pledged itself to do, has as its immediate objective the fulfilling and 'overfulfilling' of the nation's second five-year (1976–80) plan.[68]

In the Laotian People's Democratic Republic (LPDR), meanwhile, the organisational accent is also on the needs of economic reconstruction. It is recognised, at least in theory, that compared to solving 'the problem of materials as well as manpower' in national development, 'the human factor remains primordial', as Laotian vice premier Phoumi Vongvichit put it at the Conference of Socialist Countries on Technical Training held in Ulaanbaatar, Mongolia, in early September 1978. 'Technical and managerial cadres', according to the Laotian vice premier, 'must become the model socialist working people of Laos.' Both the 'People's Revolutionary Party of Laos' (*Phak Pasason Pativat Lao* – PPPL), the ruling Communist Party, and the 'Lao People's Liberation Army' (LPLA) are considered to be the principal organisational means of mobilising the Lao masses toward

national reconstruction, under the watchful eyes of some 40 000 SRV
military still stationed in the LPDR. The latter's presence continues
to feed on the scattered anti-Vietnamese resistance movement of
former Pathet Lao.

The organisational imperatives for the PPPL and the country were
outlined by premier Kaysone Phomvihan to a joint session of the
LPDR Supreme People's Council and the Council of Ministers late in
July 1978. Each province in the LPDR is to become 'an all round and
complete strategic centre', according to the premier, capable of
solving 'various local problems'.[69] Emphasis is to be placed on
maximising production and services at each local level of government, and the development of co-operatives in villages or districts or
state-run agricultural and forestry enterprises is believed to require
first of all an 'urgent' improvement in the quality of local and district
party committees, as well as the consolidation of all auxiliary work
organisations. Cadres and government officials may have to be
assigned new tasks, and in this connection Kaysone Phomvihan
called for careful leadership assignments:[70]

> In transferring and rearranging cadres and officials the various
> ministries and branches must democratically hold group discus-
> sions, study and firmly grasp the level of capabilities of each cadre
> official; and appropriately and reasonably put them in the right
> sections.

The care and nurture of intellectuals is not to be overlooked:[71]

> Regarding those young fraternal cadres and officials who have
> maintained a certain level of cultural understanding, it is necessary
> to arrange for them to attend long term training courses. Regarding
> those fraternal intellectuals, specialists and skilled workers, it is
> necessary to provide appropriate political training and material aid
> for them so as to help them promote and expand their intelligence,
> capabilities and vocational education.

As in the case of the SRV, the 'grassroots' is expected to become a
PPPL focus too, and Kaysone Phomvihan has cautioned that 'im-
practical' bureaucratic procedures that are 'not linked to the grassroots level' must be avoided. At the same time, 'leading cadres' in
various ministries and departments of government 'must find time to

go to the grassroots level' in order to understand the reality of local conditions and in order to help 'expand local initiative'.[72]

And as in the SRV, so in the LPDR today, mobilisation of youth for both defence and reconstruction work has top priority. Vientiane media have taken note of 'youths in the armed forces and in guerrilla ranks' who have successfully 'countered armed provocation' by 'enemy bandit bands' (presumably a reference to dissident former Pathet Lao who, along with Meo tribesmen, form much of the anti-government insurgent resistance movement in various parts of Laos today) who are said to be 'engaged in sabotage activities against our young republic'.[73] 'Youths in workers' ranks' are reported by the same media to have taken control of factory production and meanwhile 'youths in peasants' ranks' have become a 'vanguard' in rice cultivation. Not all Lao youth appear to have been persuaded by the call of the new order in their country, however, and there are official complaints that 'some youths living in various towns' still 'live sluggishly' and that even 'generally speaking' the work performance of youths in the recent past 'remains unenthusiastic'.[74]

To many outside observers, familiar with the traditional, easygoing Lao life style the alleged lack of enthusiasm for the new regime among the youth of the nation is but a dimension of a general impression that the advent of the Socialist revolution in the three Indochinese states perhaps has been gentlest thus far in Laos. In fact, were it not for the pervasive Vietnamese presence in the LPDR today it is doubtful if the demands for greater cadre efficiency and party organisational discipline and growth would be heard with the same urgency from PPPL leaders. Just the same, however, Laos, like the SRV and Cambodia, has been in the grip of a 're-educational' revolution, involving thousands whose ideological *bona fides* or past political behaviour has been called into question by party cadres. There are an estimated 40 000 political prisoners in Laos (a large number for a country with only about three million people), held in camps near the Chinese border, and there are milder camps as well for the 're-education' of those guilty of relatively minor infractions of the new rules of morality such as kissing in public, or wearing Western dress.[75] And not a few have escaped Laos' new Socialist revolution: by May 1978, there were at least 82 000 Laotian refugees in Thailand.[76] Unlike Cambodia, however, the possibility of personal rehabilitation through the national reorganisation process at least seems to exist in the LPDR. Initially much was made of the periodic release of former senior officials of the pre-Communist regime who, after having attended what were euphemistically called 'teach-ins' at various camps, experienced what they termed a 'new consciousness' and who, as a result, reportedly were able to 'deepen our hatred for the enemy'.[77] But such announcements have become much rarer since 1977.

The planned mass mobilisation and party organisational and bureaucratic tightening in Laos have not as yet focused on the formation of a new national front, similar to the SRV's Fatherland Front of Vietnam. However, there have been organisational changes in the Lao People's Liberation Army (LPLA), including introduction of a new code of internal discipline and new regulations for dealing with the Laotian population. Reminiscent of the well known Chinese Communist 'people's liberation army' directives during the nineteen thirties are the admonitions in the LPLA's new code of discipline 'not to take a single needle or piece of thread from the people, pay fairly for what is bought, and pay for anything that is damaged', and 'to behave correctly and speak politely to everyone'.[78] Among the new regulations governing the LPLA's contact with the civilian masses are the following:[79]

1. *The Four 'Respects':* respect people of all nationalities as our own parents or blood brothers; respect the customs and traditions of people of all nationalities; respect Buddhist monks and other people's right to belief; and respect and fully assist local administrations or committees.
2. *The Four 'Don'ts':* don't intimidate or scold the people; don't take the people's property or trouble them or their administration; don't destroy temples, Christian churches or other public buildings; and don't take liberties with women.
3. *The Four 'Helps':* help the people earn their living and repair and build their homes; help the people study cultural and political affairs; help the people by giving medical treatment; and by aiding them keep their houses clean; and help the people attack the enemy and defend the country.

The degree to which the LPLA is now being relied on by the PPPL to act as a galvaniser of popular reconstruction and national defence efforts in conjunction with the Vietnamese presence is a matter of conjecture for the moment. But the implications of the new codes of discipline and population contact seem to be to use the army at least to some extent as an instrument of mass mobilisation at a time when the PPPL's own cadre development still leaves much to be desired, according to the admission of party leaders themselves. The *de facto* Vietnamese military occupation of Laos today also makes the LPLA's role all the more important as a go-between with the Laotian civilian population.

Finally, there is the Cambodian case. Little reliable information has penetrated the curtain of isolation and bloody mayhem with which the *Angka Leou* ('Organisation on High') of the Kampuchea Communist Party (KCP) has surrounded their country since Communist forces occupied the Cambodian capital of Phnom Penh on 17 April 1975. The border conflict with the SRV and reports of attempted pro-Vietnamese coups in the capital appeared to have accentuated a pattern of intra-party power struggles and bloody purges at all organisational levels, as well as in the armed forces.[80] Province officials, village chiefs, Khmer Rouge army veterans, party district leaders – all these and others fell victim to killing waves of retribution unleashed by the Pol Pot regime, as the premier himself meanwhile kept denouncing 'imperialism and foreign reactionaries' who allegedly 'harbour the strategic and fundamental intention of threatening and attempting to grasp our Cambodia'.

To what extent a cadre structure still functions in Cambodia, and to what extent also, in light of the continuing regimental strength fighting with the Vietnamese, there is an increased militarisation of all operating party and government structures, can only be speculated upon at present. At a 'mass meeting' in Phnom Penh on 27 September 1977, commemorating the seventeenth founding anniversary of the KCP, premier Pol Pot outlined a comprehensive programme for the party in leading the nation toward modern agriculture, industrial growth and educational expansion ('our party's aim is to have the people learn and at the same time serve the movement to defend and build the country'). Various 'seething mass movements', ranging from the collection of natural fertiliser to the building of major dams, are the party's responsibility, and 'under the correct and clearsighted leadership of the Cambodian Communist Party', according to Pol Pot, a steady improvement in the conditions of life and health of the nation was assured. At the same time the party 'must exert utmost efforts' to help the historical tide of 'revolutionary and progressive people' around the world.[81]

The latter admonition was not altogether rhetorical; during 1978, for example, some half dozen 'friendship' delegations from parties and regimes around the world sympathetic to Democratic Kampuchea were received in Phnom Penh. The Pol Pot regime clearly meant to cultivate an international following for the KCP and its national experiment. Perhaps in part designed to overcome the global condemnation of its domestic holocaust, and in part designed as a counterweight to Hanoi's own stepped-up diplomatic efforts to win friends and influence in South-east Asia, the organisational responsibilities of the KCP appeared to involve the encouragement of such international 'friendship' and 'solidarity' organisations, supplementing the government's still limited formal diplomatic contacts.

In summary we may note that both in Communist and non-Communist South-east Asia Communism's primary organisational weapons remain (1) the party, (2) the united front or 'mass movement', and (3) the 'people's liberation army'. Other support groups, especially those involving youth, are usually made to interact with and serve the latter two, as for example in the SRV or in the organisational structure of the CPP(M-L) in the Philippines. As we have seen, however, while in principle party, front, and army are all acknowledged to be indispensable, tactical variations may dictate emphasis on one of the three to the virtual exclusion of one or both of the others. Such exclusion, it may be noted, is not confined to the 'liberation army' or the front organisation: one could make the case, for example, that in the Philippines, during the middle and later nineteen sixties, even the PKP seemed to 'underemphasise' its own tactical presence in favour of the new left and radical nationalist complex of front groups then becoming prominent, while a party self-effacing technique and the use of fronts have also been a particularly prominent feature of Vietnamese Communist history. Sometimes the role of a liberation army is altogether eschewed (as in the case of the PKI in Indonesia under D. N. Aidit's leadership in the nineteen fifties and sixties), sometimes the army all but seems to dominate the party, as would seem to be the case with the CPT-TPLAF in Thailand, at present, and, then again, the army must do double duty, acting in a formal military role but also as a mass mobilisation device more appropriate to a united front organisation, as appears to be true for Laos. Constantly shifting organisational emphasis, now building new interest groups and fusing them into a 'movement' only then to funnel all energy into a new 'people's liberation army' – these and other variations and combinations are demands that are made of Communists on the road to power.

5

Between Peking and Moscow

Replying recently to an allegation that his party was 'pro-Moscow', the secretary general of the *Partido Komunista ng Pilipinas* (Communist Party of the Philippines – PKP), Felicisimo C. Macapagal rejected that particular characterisation. He emphasised instead that the PKP is an 'independent' Filipino party and does not take orders from Moscow. He added, however, that the PKP has supported the Soviet point of view, because the USSR 'has consistently taken a progressive and principled position' on various world issues, in contrast to the position of the Chinese Communist Party which, according to Macapagal, not only has a 'chauvinistic and pro-imperialist' point of view, but, indeed, allegedly has attempted to interfere in the affairs of 'fraternal parties', including in the Philippines.[1]

Macapagal's views, *mutatis mutandis*, may be taken as suggestive generally of positions taken by various Communist parties in Southeast Asia today. Not in the sense that these parties necessarily endorse the 'principled position' of the USSR, on the contrary; it is rather that they formally view themselves, like the PKP, as 'independent' or 'national' parties, which are not beholden to any one of the major international power centres of Communism. At the same time, however, their 'national' orientation is deemed quite compatible with obvious preferences for either the policies of the USSR or of People's China. Avowals of such a particular preference again as in the case of the PKP are usually accompanied by less than complimentary references to the policies of the other international Communist major power.

217

A.　Relations with People's China

On balance, in the line-up of such preferences among South-east Asian Communists, People's China appears to have somewhat the better of it at the moment. With the exception of the PKP, and the Communist parties of the Socialist Republic of Vietnam and of Laos, Communists in South-east Asia itself today tend to be primarily Beijing-oriented, although the USSR can count also here and there on the sympathies of small handfuls of émigrés – like those from Indonesia, who even have a Moscow-sponsored, and usually Prague-domiciled, group called the 'Leadership of the Central Committee of the Indonesian Communist Party' (*Partai Komunis Indonesia* – PKI). But, certainly where Communism is most active in South-east Asia at present, for example in the form of ongoing guerrilla insurgencies in Burma, Thailand, Malaysia and the Philippines, it is Beijing that is the international lodestar and, at least formally, it is Maoist military theory that is the inspiration of the insurgents' tactics.

The point is worth stressing because this dominant Chinese orientation among South-east Asian Communist parties prevails today even though in recent years there has occurred a gradual normalisation in diplomatic relations between Beijing and the South-east Asian governments confronted by the hostility of these Communist parties. For instance, Malaysia, the Philippines and Thailand established formal diplomatic relations with People's China on 31 May 1974, 9 June 1975 and 1 July 1975, respectively; yet all of them have experienced and continue to face Communist guerrilla movements whose adherents tend to turn toward Beijing and Mao's thought. But then so is the Burmese government confronted by the armed rebellion of the Burma Communist Party (BCP) which Beijing has been assisting with arms and trained cadres for more than a decade. And yet when the Chinese Communists came to power in 1949, Burma was the first non-Communist country to recognise the Beijing regime.[2]

Conversely, Indonesia and People's China extended mutual diplomatic recognition as early as 1950 (although it took four years before an Indonesian ambassador arrived in Beijing), and at no time has the Djakarta government ever confronted within its national boundaries a Chinese-oriented Communist insurgency comparable to that which confronts Rangoon or Kuala Lumpur today. Yet since

October 1967, Sino-Indonesian diplomatic connections have been suspended (though not formally broken) when relations between the two countries sharply deteriorated in the aftermath of the 30 September 1965 coup in Indonesia. For more than a decade now Indonesian spokesmen from time to time have held out the promise of an eventual normalisation of relations with People's China. But uncertainty over the status and loyalties of Indonesia's 3.5 million ethnic Chinese inhabitants is currently given by the Suharto government as the official reason for delay in full resumption of diplomatic ties with China. As we shall see, other considerations of Indonesian domestic policy figure in this delay as well. Meanwhile Singapore's premier Lee Kuan Yew has repeatedly said that his island republic will be the 'last' state in South-east Asia to establish formal diplomatic relations with Beijing, and in any case will do so only after Djakarta has normalised her relationship with the Chinese. Yet Singapore too does not confront a Beijing-oriented insurgent movement, although the island state has known repeated flare-ups of student and trade union unrest in the nineteen fifties and sixties. Such unrest Singapore authorities have attributed to undercover adherents of the Beijing-oriented Communist Party of Malaya across the Causeway. And so paradoxes and anomalies continue to abound in South-east Asia's relationships with People's China even as the region's governments face Beijing-oriented insurgencies or otherwise articulate strongly anti-Communist domestic policy positions.

Appreciation of the incontrovertible reality of People's China's existence, plus periodic apprehension over its policies in South-east Asia, particularly in relation to local Communist parties, and over the place of local Chinese minorities, have all caused Sino-South-east Asian relations to gyrate wildly from time to time. Indonesia offers a case in point. Already in 1951, only a few months after the Sino-Indonesian mutual diplomatic recognition and consular exchanges, there arose Indonesian fears over the large and growing size of the Chinese diplomatic establishment in Djakarta and over the seemingly unauthorised entry of, presumably, Chinese diplomatic personnel.[3] Later, during the nineteen fifties, it was widely suspected that the large Chinese embassy in the Indonesian capital was actively assisting the Indonesian Communist Party with funds in the party's political comeback from the débâcle of the party's attempted coup in Madiun in 1958. The PKI sharply denied receiving such help, however. The Asian-African Conference in Bandung, Indonesia, in

April 1955, offered Chinese premier Zhou En-lai (Chou En-lai) an opportunity to allay fears of alleged Chinese subversive intentions in Asia. The Conference's own commitment to principles of peaceful coexistence, and professed respect for national sovereignty and territorial integrity, as embodied in the Conference's final communiqué, was believed to act as an inducement to Beijing to 'scale down' such support as the Chinese might in fact be giving to local Communist parties in the region.[4]

In subsequent years, at least in Indonesia, Beijing officially not only ceased to be viewed with suspicion and hostility, but indeed by the early nineteen sixties a kind of Sino-Indonesian partnership in international affairs, particularly in relations with the Third World, and in fostering more radical nationalist movements in that world, appeared to be developing.[5] By January 1965, Indonesia had withdrawn from the United Nations and Beijing was encouraging Sukarno in forming a rival 'Conference of New Emerging Forces' (CONEFO). A wide-ranging agreement, signed in Beijing on 28 January 1965 between Chinese and Indonesian representatives, declared that they shared a common view of the polarisation of world political forces between 'imperialist' and 'old established forces', on the one hand, and 'anti-imperialist' and 'new emerging forces' (which included the Communist states) on the other, and that no 'peaceful co-existence' between these two camps was possible.[6]

China, despite opposition from the Indonesian army, also encouraged Indonesia's President Sukarno in the development of a 'Fifth Force', the arming of workers and peasants as a military organisation independent of the regular armed forces establishment. Covert agreements ostensibly unknown to the army were made between Sukarno's emissaries and the Chinese to arm this 'Fifth Force' with Chinese weapons.[7] The PKI meanwhile, by now grown to the largest political party in Indonesia and seeing itself as heir apparent to the ailing Sukarno, hewed closely to the Chinese line, even as it retained officially correct relations with Moscow. Whether the Chinese in the early months of 1965 encouraged, or at least knew of, the plot of a number of Indonesian Communist leaders and dissident military commanders to seize power, remains controversial, although it is likely that they did. Certainly some of the Chinese arms shipments eventually wound up in the hands of Indonesian Communist rebels during and after the coup. Two weeks before the PKI-military plot unfolded on 30 September 1965, the Malaysian press, drawing on Thai and Hong Kong sources, was reporting the following:[8]

Communist China is reported to be sending secret supplies of arms, explosives and military equipment to the Indonesian Communists who are getting ready for a showdown with armed forces.

The Bangkok newspaper *Democracy* reported yesterday that clandestine shipments of arms were being unloaded at various places along the Java coast.

It quoted Hongkong sources for these disclosures which coincided with reports from Jakarta about unusual activity around Baten and Pulabutan Batu in West Java and some smaller ports in East Java.

The Indonesian police are reported to have stepped up their investigations into these reports. Political observers say that the Indonesian Communist Party (PKI) are fully aware that the Indonesian armed forces will resist any Communist bid for power, and it is getting ready for the inevitable clash.

In view of President Sukarno's declining health, the PKI has intensified its efforts to build a secret military force with Communist Chinese help.

Widespread suspicion, also in official Indonesian circles, that Peking had encouraged the abortive 30 September coup attempt, fanned endemic anti-Chinese public feeling in Indonesia, and in the months after the coup there were frightful anti-Chinese pogroms. Mutual bitterness, exchanges of hostile diplomatic notes, and recriminations led to the new nadir in Sino-Indonesian relations, when embassy staffs and consular personnel were mutually withdrawn and diplomatic ties were formally suspended in October 1967. The 1955 Sino-Indonesian Dual Nationality Treaty, which had sought to regularise the citizenship position of Indonesian Chinese, but which had become much delayed in implementation, now became a dead letter altogether.[9] The legal and civil status of most Indonesian Chinese, even those who in obedience to government directive sought to assimilate themselves by adopting Indonesian names and life styles, once again became uncertain.

Officially, too, China remained part of the new post-coup Indonesian demonology. President Suharto in an address to the Indonesian parliament on 16 August 1967, for example, declared that 'it is an established fact that the People's Republic of China has directly or indirectly supported the September 30 movement' (that is, the coup), and Suharto added that even after the coup there was 'evidence of subversive activities' by Beijing against the Indonesian government.[10] Even after the mutual withdrawal of their diplomatic personnel Djakarta continued to accuse Beijing of sending agents into Indonesia in order to instigate an uprising against the Indonesian government. The Indonesian army press, in November 1967, claimed that Chinese Communist nationals had recently landed in secret near Tandjong Priok, the port of Djakarta, in order to aid in the underground Communist resistance movement in Indonesia, including in West Kalimantan (Borneo).[11] Local Chinese were subsequently accused of aiding the Communist underground in Blitar, East Java.[12]

By the early nineteen seventies, however, apart from periodic Indonesian complaints over China's anti-Indonesian 'propaganda campaign' (Beijing was permitting pro-Maoist PKI émigrés in the Chinese capital to use the Chinese media for their anti-Suharto statements), the focus of official Indonesian concern in relations with People's China primarily became the question of the present and future loyalty of the 3.5 million Indonesian Chinese. In April 1973, for example, then Indonesian foreign minister Adam Malik said that he had turned down a recent Chinese suggestion to resume regular diplomatic relations with Indonesia, on the grounds that the Djakarta government needed time 'to educate its Chinese population to be loyal to Indonesia and not have their orientation towards Beijing'. According to Malik, Chinese officials even agreed with him on this matter, and Malik estimated that 'it might take five to ten years' before the Chinese in Indonesia were, in fact, thus 're-educated'.[13]

The involvement of young local Sarawak Chinese in Communist insurgency, as well as the allegedly surreptitious entry of Chinese into Indonesia, were being offered by Indonesian officials as representative reasons for concern. The Indonesian West Kalimantan (Borneo) military district commander, Brigadier Seno Hartono, declared in June 1974, for example, that the involvement of ethnic Chinese in the local Communist insurgency in Sarawak was to be viewed as 'a link in the struggle of the overseas Chinese in this region to try and become a class grouping of their own, which seeks power over the native born in a social and political sense'.[14] At about the same time the Central Java Prosecutor's Office noted with alarm the alleged 'smuggling' into Indonesia of Chinese from the Chinese mainland, and indicated that the Chinese in question had originally left Indonesia a few years earlier because of their pro-Beijing sympathies but that they were now surreptitiously returning via the Communist guerrilla-infested West Kalimantan region.[15]

Even as, in the aftermath of the Vietnam war and with the advent of the more pragmatic Hua Guo feng (Hua Kuo-feng) regime in China itself, most South-east Asian regimes appeared to be interested in letting bygones be bygones, Indonesian reluctance to normalise relations with Beijing remained. The civil status of Indonesia's Chinese officially continued to be the stumbling block, as far as the Suharto regime was concerned. By June 1978, Indonesian foreign minister Mochtar Kusumaatmaja was saying that the Indonesian government did not mean to 'reneg' on its intention to restore normal relations with People's China. But, he added, 'some matters' had to be settled first. The position of the Indonesian Chinese was 'an obstacle', Kusumaatmaja said, for the Chinese in Indonesia might become 'an issue as in Vietnam'.[16] *Pari passu* one may note here that informed estimates place the number of those Chinese in Indonesia who can claim People's Chinese citizenship at about 972 000, while only some 1 750 are said to hold Republic of China (Taiwan) passports. Estimates of those Indonesian Chinese who are 'stateless' fluctuate greatly (for example, between 79 000 and 800 000).[17] The remainder of the 3.5 million Indonesian Chinese group presumably holds Indonesian citizenship.

As Indonesian civil and military officials in general appear to differ on the desirability of normalising relations with Beijing (with the military having reportedly a much more negative attitude), the real issue in the normalisation controversy is probably being masked by the official emphasis on the citizenship status and concern over the loyalty of Indonesian Chinese. That real issue is the preservation of the set of Indonesia's post-coup domestic policy priorities as determined by the military-business establishment that favours the ruling Golkar (the government party) and the Suharto regime. In particular, the benefit which the Indonesian military-business élite derives from the Suharto government's policy priorities is involved. Rapid economic development, supported by huge foreign development capital and stabilisation inputs, and requiring optimum conditions of domestic tranquillity and stability: this is the primary policy desire of the Suharto regime. To realise that desire the authoritarian mechanisms of national security must continue to be preserved and must remain in the hands of the Golkar-oriented military; and the threat of the allegedly 'latent' danger of Communism and the PKI must be and is being raised by the spokesmen for the regime.[18] The fact is that Suharto's *Orba* (*Orde Baru* – New Order), as many of its supporters feel, has done well enough without a normalisation of relations with Beijing. And who knows what political dynamics might be set in motion with the reopening and restaffing of the Chinese embassy in Djakarta – not just in terms of the Indonesian Chinese, whose business competition, as always, is sharply resented by influential Indonesian entrepreneurs, even as others in this entrepreneurial group join hands with the Chinese merchant and financial world, but also in terms of the student, intellectual and other dissident groups that have already confronted the Suharto government in recent years?

In short, the question of Sino-Indonesian diplomatic normalisation pivots on the problem of maintaining *Orba's* policy 'style', and on the fear of introducing new variables into the Suharto government's priority formula for stable economic development. Needless to say, Soviet perceptions of the reasons for Indonesia's resistance to a normalisation of her relations with Beijing push just this question of Chinese 'subversion' into the foreground. In October 1978, for example, one commentary over Moscow's 'Peace and Progress' Radio, noting that Indonesian foreign minister Kusumaatmaja had rebuffed a suggestion of normalisation, declared that it had been People's China's 'crude interference' in Indonesia's internal affairs in connection with the 1965 coup attempt that had led to the suspension of diplomatic relations in the first place. The same commentary went on to raise the spectre of continuing Chinese 'interference' in Indonesian affairs, alleging that the number of Chinese illegally entering Indonesia had recently increased and that Indonesian media were expressing concern over the 'Chinese agents' among the country's Overseas Chinese community.[19] Thus, though official Indonesian circles hardly intend it to be so, their characterisation of the Chinese question and of the diplomatic normalisation problem is remarkably consistent with Moscow's portrayal. It, of course, also tends to ignore Beijing's own frequent assurances, in recent years, that it has no intention of meddling in the internal affairs of its neighbours.

On the other hand, the Indonesians may be forgiven perhaps if they do not forget too quickly the lessons of history and the experience of their regional neighbours. In 1954, for example, Burma and People's China adopted a joint declaration of 'Peaceful Co-Existence', and in 1960 the two nations signed a ten-year Friendship and Non-Aggression Treaty, providing for Chinese technical assistance. All seemed well. In 1967, however, Sino-Burmese relations suddenly and sharply deteriorated, when in the context of China's 'Great Proletarian Cultural Revolution' Chinese embassy officials in Rangoon began inciting the Chinese community in Burma, especially Chinese students, against the Burmese government. Violent clashes resulted in the deaths of scores of Chinese, and Beijing was soon accusing the 'reactionary' Ne Win government of 'sabotaging' friendly relations.[20]

China meanwhile also began stepping up her assistance to the insurgents of the Burma Communist Party (BCP), the so-called 'White Flag' faction. During 1968–9, several hundred Chinese military reportedly crossed the border to begin helping the Burmese Communist guerrillas operating in the eastern part of Burma's Shan state.[21] China's ideological and tactical training of 'White Flag' cadres, and her supplies of weapons to the guerrillas continued in subsequent years. The BCP 'liberation forces' had grown to nearly 10 000 when, in early 1974, they overran the garrison town of Mongyang and began threatening Kengtung.[22] As one report put it at the time:[23]

In particular, the Burmese government is increasingly worried about China's apparent support for the Communist insurgents of the White Flag army.

Operating from bases along the Chinese border in the Shan area east of the Salween [river], a guerilla force of the pro-Chinese Burmese Communist party estimated to number between 4,000 and 10,000 men has been making periodic forays southwards to the strategic Kentung plateau, which overlooks Laos on one side and Thailand on the other. They are equipped with Chinese infantry weapons and communications equipment, as the Working People's daily in Rangoon now acknowledges in its guarded references to 'foreign assistance.' Some reports say that Chinese involvement extends to the supply of hundreds of officers and technicians carefully selected from ethnic groups which live on both sides of the border.

Formally, with the ending of the 'Cultural Revolution' in China, relations with Burma slowly began improving once more, and already in August 1971, General Ne Win visited Peking again where Chinese premier Zhou En-lai told him that the 'Chinese government has consistently pursued a friendly and good neighbour policy' with the government of Burma.[24] Chinese support for the 'White Flags' has continued until this day, however, even as new Sino-Burmese diplomatic exchanges take place and new avowals of mutual friendship are made. Though Burmese government forces, in the course of 1977–8, were successful in dispersing the BCP from some of their strongholds, the 'White Flags' sanctuary and major supply base across the Chinese border has not vanished with the more moderate, pragmatic policies of China's chairman Hua Guo feng. Good 'government to government' relations, as in the case of Rangoon, still do not prevent Beijing from extending aid, if at a low key level, to other Communist Parties and their insurgent forces on a 'party to party' basis, even if the distinction between such 'government to government' and 'party to party' relations can at best be only a rhetorical one as far as People's China's uneasy neighbours in South-east Asia are concerned.

Burma is not the only instance which the Indonesians could cite as reason for their hesitation. Considering Democratic Kampuchea's (Cambodia's) close relationship with Beijing in the period after 1975, particularly in the face of Hanoi's pressures, it is ironic to note that not so long ago Prince Norodom Sihanouk, then still trying to maintain his country's independence and neutrality, was accusing the Chinese embassy in Phnom Penh of attempting to subvert the local Chinese through their propaganda.[25] These alleged activities by the Chinese embassy replicated events in Burma, and Chinese diplomatic personnel in Phnom Penh were obviously inspired by the 'Cultural Revolution' in their homeland. By the middle of 1967, Sihanouk also charged the 'Khmer-Chinese Friendship Association' which maintained close connections with the Chinese embassy in the Cambodian capital of subversive activity and dissemination of Maoist materials, and with giving aid to the Cambodian Communists.[26] Shortly before the Phnom Penh visit of Marshal Josef Broz Tito in January 1968, Sihanouk revealed an alleged plot of local Chinese Communists to assassinate the Yugoslav leader. Meanwhile President Ferdinand Marcos of the Philippines and other official Philippine sources had been claiming for some time that People's China was also actively aiding Communist insurgent activity and the Communist movement generally in the Philippines. Lax enforcement of Philipine immigration laws was said to have permitted the entry into the Philippines of hundreds of Chinese who were Communist agents giving aid and advice to the Philippine Communists.[27] As early as September 1965, Philippine armed forces' intelligence reported the alleged discovery of Communist insurgent training centres in Bicol and the Visayas run by Chinese Communists.[28] And a year later, during a visit to the US, Marcos declared in a nationwide television interview that he knew 'for a fact' that the recent resurgence of Huk guerrilla activity in the Philippines was being assisted by 'agents' from Peking.[29] The scope of Chinese Communist activity in the Philippines, at least according to Philippine sources, had been as great or even greater in the nineteen fifties. For example, in 1952 it was claimed that Chinese Communists in the Philippines had their own 'Politburo' and had an organisation of some 3 000 members and that this organisation in recent years had received the equivalent of about $200 000 in funds from the China mainland.[30]

Even before June 1975, and the formal establishment of Sino-Philippine diplomatic relations, as well as the increasing trade volume between the two countries, such earlier charges of alleged Chinese subversion had begun to pass from the public limelight in the Philippines. Occasional instances of tension between Beijing and Manila these days are no longer the prelude to a new barrage of stories in the Philippine press about Chinese subversive activity in the country and in South-east Asia generally. For example, the extension of Philippine control, early in 1978, over a portion of the Spratley Islands in the South China Sea, sovereignty over which is disputed not only by Beijing and Manila but also by Hanoi, led to a relatively mild Chinese rebuke. But already by 15 March 1978, Marcos could announce that his government had come to an agreement with People's China and the Socialist Republic of Vietnam on the 'peaceful settlement' of the dispute over the Spratleys, though the details of the settlement have not been revealed. Philippine government sources criticised Western media for allegedly creating an 'insidious plot' to drive a wedge between People's China and the Philippines over the Spratley Islands issue.[31]

On 25 September 1970, Radio Beijing, in an official commentary entitled 'Flames of Revolutionary Armed Struggle Rage All Over South-east Asia', could still eulogise the Philippine Communists for developing 'a new vigorous situation' in the country, singling out the Maoist New People's Army (NPA) for particular praise.[32] Such public encouragement became a rarity in the mid-seventies, however. The tone adopted by Chinese leaders in their relations with the Philippines and the rest of South-east Asia (a current exception is Vietnam) these days was well exemplified by two other developments in Sino-Philippine relations in this period. On 28 November 1977,

Chinese ambassador Ko Hua declared in Manila that although China 'has contacts' with foreign Communists, his government never interferes with the activities of Communists in other countries. The ambassador made his remark in reply to a question about the recently arrested chairman of the Beijing-oriented CPP(M-L), José Maria Sison. On 12 March 1978, Chinese vice premier Li Xian-nian (Li Hsien-nien), during an official visit to Manila, once again expressed support for the Association of South-east Asian Nations (ASEAN), declaring that China favoured 'the just struggle of South-east Asian countries to safeguard their independence, combat superpower interference, and their efforts to protect their natural resources and economic interests'.[33] With statements like these People's China appears to have come full circle and to have returned to the conciliatory gestures of Zhou En-lai at the Asian-African Conference in Bandung in 1955.

And yet Manila, like its other South-east Asian neighbours, remains wary of China. President Ferdinand Marcos told a US congressional mission visiting the Philippines in early January 1978 that it is the view of the Philippine government that 'as in Malaysia, Thailand and Indonesia, Communist insurgents' in the Philippines 'are being assisted by the Communist Party of the People's Republic of China'.[34] And the problem of the Overseas Chinese remains, too. With almost clockwork regularity various Philippine administrations over the past two decades have sought to regularise the civil status of the half a million Chinese in the Philippines, announcing new measures, some of which facilitate the legalisation of their immigrant status and/or their naturalisation procedures. Yet, even when naturalised as Filipino citizens, the Chinese continue to experience popular antipathies. The Manila paper, the *Daily Express*, in early November 1978, for example editorially charged that 'In the rush to attain a dominant position in the economy some naturalised Filipinos tend to think only of material gain, availing themselves of the benefits given by the government as a result of their new status.' These naturalised Filipinos, that is, Chinese, said the *Daily Express*, should remember that they 'must also share the burden of nation building'. Public criticism of Chinese Filipinos for their alleged dominance of such fields as banking and the entertainment industry, and even of their involvement in a recent rash of suspected arson cases involving commercial establishments, all suggest potential new sources of conflict, also with Beijing.[35] Because while Beijing's policy is officially to encourage Overseas Chinese to become good citizens of the country where they live and work, the Chinese government also takes the position that it cannot be indifferent to their maltreatment, as recent tensions in Chinese relations with Hanoi prompted in part by the problems of SRV Chinese residents again show.

By the close of 1978, however, Beijing, mindful that Moscow and Hanoi were doing the same, was seeking South-east Asia's goodwill in a deliberate way not seen since Zhou En-lai sought to charm his fellow Asian-African Conference-attenders at Bandung more than two decades earlier. The formal basis for the new Chinese rapprochement with South-east Asia, a rapprochement quickened by the SRV's and the USSR's own diplomatic initiatives in the region, to be discussed presently, was the Sino-Malaysian communiqué, issued in Beijing on 31 May 1974. This communiqué appeared on the occasion of the visit of Malaysian premier Tun Abdul Razak to the Chinese capital, when Sino-Malaysian diplomatic relations were officially established. The communiqué contains an affirmation of the cordial relations between the two nations on the basis of the 'five principles of peaceful co-existence', including (1) 'mutual respect for sovereignty and territorial integrity', (2) 'mutual non-aggression', (3) 'non-interference' in internal affairs, (4) 'equality and mutual benefit' of and for the signatory parties, and (5) 'peaceful co-existence'. The prevailing 'social system' in a country is a matter for the country's 'own people', according to the communiqué and all forms of external aggression or 'subversion' in the affairs of another the signatories regard as 'impermissible'.[36] Just as China recognises the 'independence and sovereignty of Malaysia', so the Malaysian government acknowledges the government of People's China as 'the sole legal government' of China, and declares Taiwan to be an 'inalienable' part of People's China's territory. It is worthy of mention, perhaps, that Razak, upon his return to Malaysia from signing this communiqué in Beijing, addressed a mass rally in the Malaysian capital in which he made a point of stressing that he had been assured by the Chinese government that the problem of the Communist guerrillas in Malaysia, most of whom, it will be recalled, are ethnic Chinese, was a matter for Malaysia to settle as she saw fit. Beijing, Razak said categorically, would not help the insurgents.[37]

The developing Sino-Malaysian rapprochement, it might also be noted, had given Malaysian Communists some difficulty. Before Razak's 1974 visit to Beijing the Communist Party of Malaya (CPM) appeared to prefer to ignore completely the various indications of a warming trend in Sino-Malaysian relations. When for example in August 1971, a Chinese trade delegation had visited the Malaysian capital, the CPM's clandestine transmitter, 'Voice of the Malaysian Revolution', had merely repeated its standard theme that 'Razak and his ilk' were 'faithful lackeys of US imperialism' and that Malaysia still subscribed to the 'myth of creating two Chinas'. When it became apparent, however, that the establishment of diplomatic ties between the two countries would be but a matter of time, the CPM's policy position became that the new warmth in Sino-Malaysian relations was due to the pressure of domestic opinion within Malaysia itself, and that the Malaysian government, because of the demands of Malaysian public opinion and because of significant changes in the international balance of forces, was now compelled to move closer toward Beijing. The 'Razak clique's' preliminary negotiations with the Beijing government, the 'Voice of the Malayan Revolution' now regarded as reflecting a 'world trend' as well as the 'will of people'.[38]

Pari passu it should be observed that a tack essentially similar to that of the CPM was taken by the CPP(M-L) in the Philippines when Manila and Beijing, on 9 June 1975, announced formalisation of their diplomatic relations, and that Thai Communists, in light of the Sino-Thai diplomatic rapprochement of 1 July 1975, have also followed a similar, face-saving line. In the Malaysian case Kuala Lumpur's significant trade relations with the Beijing government even *before* diplomatic normalisation (in 1972, for example, 70 per cent of the 190 000 tons of rubber which China imported came from Malaysia)[39] had already given the CPM problems of doctrinal rationalisation. There is little doubt that with the stepped-up 1977–8 Chinese diplomatic offensive in the region as a whole, for example, Chinese vice premier Deng Xiaoping's visit to Thailand, Malaysia and Singapore in November 1978, as a counter to Moscow's and Hanoi's moves and with further commercial, technical, and cultural exchanges with South-east Asia, as well as affirmations of 'non-interference' in domestic affairs, the region's Beijing-oriented Communist parties may sometimes demonstrate particular strain in their ideological loyalties. In its current policy phase of attempting to provide leadership to the Third World, People's China will probably be ready and even anxious for broad 'united fronts' with South-east Asian nations in various international questions.[40]

Noteworthy in this context has been Beijing's avowed endorsement of ASEAN. Thus China media praised ASEAN's 1977 Kuala Lumpur 'summit' conference because of what Beijing called the conference's 'positive role' in opposing 'super power' expansion and aggression, and in protecting the 'national independence' of the ASEAN member states.[41] On the occasion of the visit of the Thai premier, General Kriangsak Chamanand to China in early April 1978, China's vice premier Deng Xiaoping not only found kind words for ASEAN's idea of the 'neutralisation' of the South-east Asian region, but he also noted the organisation's efforts in the 'common struggle' for a new and more equitable 'international economic order'.[42] Deng repeated his praise for ASEAN and its stand for peace, freedom and neutrality during his visit to Bangkok on 6 November 1978.

And yet, while there is moderate pleasure in most South-east Asian capitals, if not necessarily among South-east Asian Communist parties, over China's current policy of 'government to government' rapprochement, scepticism remains. After all, ASEAN states domestically follow a relentless anti-Communist policy, and the 'Declaration of ASEAN Concord', signed at Denpasar, Bali, Indonesia, on 24 February 1976, pledges each ASEAN member state 'to eliminate threats by subversion to its stability' and to strengthen both its own national as well as ASEAN 'resilience'.[43] China's endorsement of ASEAN, under such conditions, requires some verbal legerdemain, not lost on Communists in the region. On the other hand, there are ASEAN states which still do not see the need for normal diplomatic relations with Beijing. As one analyst of changing Sino-Singaporean relations has put it in describing the island republic's continuing reluctance for such a normalisation of relations:[44]

> With approximately 76 percent of the population being Chinese, Singapore still needs time to convince its citizens, especially the older generations, to be true and loyal to Singapore and not China. Moreover, Singapore is not too sure if China is sincere in keeping her hands out of the domestic politics of Singapore. Finally, the lack of formal ties between China and Singapore does not hamper the profitable trade for both countries.

For some prominent officials in the Singapore as in the Indonesian government today, China's long-term intentions to dominate the South-east Asian region have not really changed. Already in June 1971, Singapore premier Lee Kuan Yew noted that China had not altered its pro-revolutionary position and for this and other reasons urged the necessity for the smaller Asian nations to develop a long-term countervailing force, in order to offset Chinese power and militancy.[45] Commenting on the Deng Xiaoping visit to Singapore in early November 1978, one Singapore official-participant in the talks with the Chinese visitor reportedly declared that the Singapore government still believed that 'in the long run China will be its main problem': 'China is the longer term player.' Indeed in Singapore Deng Xiaoping suffered, in fact, his bluntest rebuff during his Southeast Asian tour. During a banquet honouring Deng, Singapore's premier Lee Kuan Yew, on 12 November 1978, said that Singapore's inhabitants 'know enough of geopolitics to know that their future directly depends on Singapore's future in South-east Asia', not on China's place among the industrial nations. Lee added that Singaporeans have come to recognise that they cannot afford to sacrifice their national interests for China's, after which Deng reportedly struck from his own prepared reply a remark thanking Lee for his address.[46] As Adam Malik, now Indonesia's vice president, remarked some years ago, it is not the Chinese military potential as such that constitutes a threat to security and peace; it is China acting as a source of 'ideological and political subversion', as the 'main pressure centre for the shaping of discontent' and for the training of professional revolutionaries in the region – in short, it is the problem of China which on a 'party to party' basis is still committed to continue to encourage, however quietly and modestly at present, the Beijing-oriented Communist parties and their guerrilla insurgencies in the various South-east Asian countries.[47]

It did not go unnoticed in the region that, when asked to comment by a Thai journalist on SRV premier Pham Van Dong's promise made to the Thai government in September 1978, that the Vietnamese would not support the Thai Communist insurgency, China's vice premier Deng Xiaoping not only branded Dong's pledge as mere hypocrisy, but he also refused to commit China to a similar promise. Deng's refusal to do so reportedly contributed to the coolness of his reception in Malaysia on 9 November 1978, when the Chinese vice premier visited there.[48] Thai observers in particular were reminded in this connection of the statement of then Thai premier Kukrit Pramoj after his journey to Peking in early July 1975. Kukrit, at pains, at the time, to put newly established Sino-Thai diplomatic relations on a good footing, told the Thai press that he believed Chinese government leaders to be sincere in not wishing to interfere in Thailand's internal affairs by helping the Thai insurgents. However, Kukrit added, 'Chairman Mao agrees that the government is something and the Communist party something else – they don't interfere with each other',[49] a somewhat disingenuous and not altogether reassuring formulation.

Toward the close of 1978, the deepening quarrel between the SRV (backed by Moscow) and Democratic Kampuchea (supported by Beijing), as well as the border conflict between the SRV and People's China, had added new and troubling uncertainties to the South-east Asian regional scene. In 1970, Chinese premier Zhou En-lai had elicited a verbal pledge, given by Pham Van Dong to Cambodia's Prince Sihanouk, both then in the Chinese capital, that after the Vietnam war Hanoi would not interfere in Cambodia's choice of government and would withdraw her own forces from Cambodian soil.[50] Five years later, with the Communist Vietnamese in control of Saigon, Zhou's hope for stable post-war Cambodian-Vietnamese relations had already begun to turn to ashes, even as Zhou and other Chinese leaders and media meanwhile were warmly praising and congratulating Hanoi on its 'liberation' of South Vietnam.[51] SRV clashes with the Cambodians over strategic islands in the Gulf of Thailand, and in Cambodian border provinces, set the stage for a Sino-Soviet 'proxy' conflict, in which Hanoi increasingly turned to Moscow and Phnom Penh to Peking for aid and security assurances. As we have seen, the 1978 'de-bourgeoisisation' of the SRV socio-economy particularly affected Vietnam's 1.2 million ethnic Chinese inhabitants, and by May 1978, about 90 000 Vietnamese Chinese had fled across the border into People's China amidst rapidly deteriorating Sino-SRV relations (see chapter 3 above). In early August 1978, Sino-SRV discussions over the Chinese émigré problem came to naught, as the Chinese demanded that Hanoi stop 'persecuting and expelling' Chinese from the SRV, while the Vietnamese countered with the assertion that it was 'the enticement and forcing' of ethnic Chinese to leave Vietnam by the Chinese government that had to cease.[52]

The SRV's decision to join COMECON (the Soviet-dominated Council of Mutual Economic Assistance in Europe) led China to end its $300 million aid programme to the Hanoi government and, toward the close of August 1978, Beijing accused Hanoi of sending its troops into the Chinese frontier territory with the aim of 'nibbling' Chinese

land.[53] In subsequent weeks the rhetoric of mutual denunciation
between Hanoi and Beijing seemed to become almost routine. With
the signing on 2 November 1978 in Moscow of a Soviet-SRV treaty of
'friendship and co-operation', during the visit of Vietnamese Communist Party secretary Le Duan and SRV premier Pham Van Dong
to the Russian capital, a new escalation of the 'proxy' conflict took
place. The Soviet-SRV treaty provides that in the event one of the
signatories is attacked, or is threatened by attack, mutual consultations will begin at once to counter the danger and 'appropriate and
effective measures' will be taken to ensure the 'peace and security' of
the parties. On 8 November 1978, the visit of a Chinese mission in
Phnom Penh led to strong expressions of Chinese support for Phnom
Penh and at the same time during his Bangkok visit, Chinese vice
premier Deng Xiaoping described the Soviet-SRV friendship treaty
as a threat not only to the security and peace of Asia but also to the
whole world. He also branded the SRV the 'Cuba of the Orient' as it
allegedly now was carrying out Moscow's designs in Asia. The Soviet
'hegemonists', Deng warned, were stepping up their 'expansionist
activities' particularly in South-east Asia.[54]

By this time some twelve SRV army divisions, totalling more than
100 000 men, were confronting about 40 000 Kampuchean forces
along their border. There was also growing evidence that Beijing was
increasing its aid to the beleaguered Phnom Penh government,
including the construction of new airport facilities usable by jet
fighter aircraft to be given to Kampuchea in the future, it was
rumoured. Neither the Soviets nor the Chinese, however, seemed
particularly anxious to become directly involved in the SRV-
Kampuchean fighting.

The accelerating Vietnamese invasion of Cambodia, however, and
the establishment on 8 January 1979 of a Hanoi-backed 'Kampuchean People's Revolutionary Council Government', even as Pol
Pot's regime was now reduced to an underground guerrilla struggle,
prompted a vigorous Chinese response. On 16 February 1979, Chinese forces invaded and occupied a border zone in Northern Vietnam,
an exercise intended as a 'punitive lesson'. The Chinese withdrew
after about four weeks, as fears deepened that there would be an
inevitable Soviet response, perhaps along the Sino-Soviet frontier.
But notwithstanding the 2 November 1978 Soviet-SRV treaty, Moscow's reaction was relatively mild, consisting mainly of verbal bar-
rages and additional military supplies for her Vietnamese ally. The

Chinese, despite their subsequent withdrawal from Vietnam, and intermittent discussions with Hanoi's representatives over various issues ranging from the exact location of the frontier, to the question of territorial control over the Xisha and Nansha Islands, remained basically irreconciled to the SRV's occupation of Cambodia, and the emergence of a Soviet-backed Indochinese power bloc. As Vietnam is likely to attempt eventually to improve its relations with its neighbours, it may well be that the Heng Samrin regime of the new 'People's Republic of Kampuchea' will prove to be a transitional government, and that a new political arrangement, more acceptable to the Chinese, will eventually emerge. The redoubtable Prince Sihanouk, once again resident in the Chinese capital, could play a pivotal role in such a transition.

Meanwhile, the Chinese-Vietnamese conflict and the Vietnamese occupation of Cambodia have brought about a – probably temporary – realignment of the interests of Hanoi's South-east Asian neighbours with those of People's China. Both Beijing and the ASEAN states are concerned over the implication of a Soviet-supported Indochinese power bloc led by Hanoi. But the common concern is also a source of embarrassment to both. Chinese assurances of support for Thailand, given in April 1979 in the face of the Vietnamese 'mop up' offensive against the remnants of Pol Pot's regime, discomfited the Bangkok government of premier Kriangsak Chamanand, anxious to maintain Thai neutrality amidst the fighting around it. In turn South-east Asia's Communist insurgents, from Burma to the Philippines, remain essentially Chinese-oriented, and the Chinese government can hardly wholly disavow them, thus having to have increased recourse to drawing distinctions between relations at the 'government to government' and at the 'party to party' levels when dealing with the non-Communist South-east Asian states.

B. ASEAN and Indochina

The intensity of the SRV-Kampuchea conflict as it unfolded during 1977–9, as well as its rapidly impacting international ramifications, took the South-east Asian region by surprise and affected its various post-Vietnam war policy scenarios. There is at the moment much less talk of 'falling' South-east Asian 'dominoes' in the wake of the

Vietnam war, although one hastens to add as in the case of People's China, scepticism and wariness regarding Hanoi's intentions in the region remain. At first, in the aftermath of the Communists' victory in Indochina, South-east Asia's leaders tried to put as pleasant a face upon their regional prospects as possible. Thus the then Malaysian premier, Tun Abdul Razak, in July 1975, for example, declared that the emergence of Communist governments in Cambodia and Vietnam would not pose a threat to Malaysia or to other South-east Asian countries. Indeed, according to Razak, the end of the fighting in Indochina had even brought 'new prospects for a durable peace and stability' to South-east Asia.[55] Officially this hope was frequently reiterated in subsequent months, even as there developed sharp SRV criticism of ASEAN and, by implication also, of the policies of individual ASEAN members.

During much of 1976, for example, Hanoi media seemed to stress that with the consolidation of Communist victories in South-east Asia 'two paths' now lay open to the other countries of the region, one of which, based on alliance with the 'US imperialists', and reflecting the interests of local big landlords and comprador capitalists, could lead only to inevitable 'defeats'. Especially Thailand, and Indonesia (the latter country Hanoi media chose to characterise as the US 'regional policeman') were seen as taking this road. The second path, according to Hanoi, is the path of 'true independence, peace and non-alignment', a formulation which Hanoi was to reiterate in various forms also in the future. The second path appeared to refer in the first instance to the need for a diminished US military and political presence in the region.[56]

ASEAN had been for some time a source of suspicion to Hanoi. As early as 1971, when ASEAN had issued its so-called 'Kuala Lumpur Declaration', in which its members pledged to work for international recognition of the South-east Asian region as a 'zone of peace, freedom and neutrality' from outside interference, a Hanoi comment had seemed to link ASEAN to 'US' aggressive and interventionist policy' and said that only total withdrawal of American forces could open the door to genuine peace and neutrality in the region.[57] On the eve of the ASEAN heads of state conference near Denpasar, Bali, Indonesia, on 23 February 1976, the Vietnamese army newspaper *Quan Doi Nhan Dan* described the forthcoming meeting as actually having been prompted by the US, with the aim of realising the new post-Vietnam war American strategy of maintaining its military bases in order to block the 'revolutionary movement in South-east Asia'.[58] Repeatedly Vietnamese media have said that 'the Vietnamese fully support the struggle of the peoples of the South-east Asian nations for independence, democracy, peace and social progress', a formulation which some worried commentators have taken to mean a Hanoi pledge to aid the Communist insurgents in the area. Even in the context of diplomatic normalisation such a pledge has been heard. In March 1976, for example, the Hanoi daily *Nhan Dan* said again that peaceful coexistence should be the basis of future Vietnamese relations with Thailand, adding, however, the Vietnamese people's support for the Thai people's 'struggle for genuine peace and national independence'.[59]

The US military bases in the Philippines, as well as the Djakarta government's alleged readiness to become the 'main prop' of American strategy in the South-east Asian region, all have been severely criticised by Hanoi, as has Indonesia's occupation and annexation of formerly Portuguese East Timor. The latter action was described in the SRV media as a trampling on the 'East Timorese people's sacred right of self determination'. As late as the middle of July 1977, when Vietnamese government and party leaders visited Vientiane, a joint SRV-Laotian communiqué condemned the allegedly 'feverish efforts' being undertaken by some ASEAN states to strengthen their bilateral military alliances under the aegis of their common anti-Communist policies. These efforts, according to the communiqué, were threatening to turn ASEAN into a 'de facto military alliance'.[60]

Considering the markedly more conciliatory tone which Hanoi began to adopt toward its South-east Asian neighbours in subsequent months, as meanwhile its difficulties with Phnom Penh and Beijing began to mount, it seems well to stress that the basic SRV objective of seeking a diminished US strategic presence in the South-east Asian region has not changed. On 5 July 1976, SRV foreign minister Nguyen Duy Trinh – at a time when sharp SRV criticism of ASEAN still was *de rigueur* – had already indicated that his country was prepared for a policy of good relations with its South-east Asian neighbours, essentially on the basis of the 1955 Bandung Conference formula, namely, principles of mutual non-aggression, peaceful co-existence, non-interference in each others' affairs, equality and mutual benefit. Throughout 1978 Trinh's principles began to be frequently referred to by other SRV officials. In January 1978, at a time of increasingly more frequent Vietnamese visits to South-east Asian countries, SRV vice foreign minister Vo Dong Giang, while in Kuala Lumpur, declared that his government was prepared to discuss a new form of regional co-operation with her South-east Asian neighbours. As for ASEAN, Giang said that it was well known under what conditions the organisation had been formed, and 'We do not want to talk about its past.' Because of the 'deep changes' in South-east Asia, according to Giang, 'we feel it is necessary and there is great possibility to promote cooperation, bilateral and regional relations.'[61]

Even as Soviet commentary began noting that 'the peace loving policy' of the SRV and Laos was producing positive results in the ASEAN countries,[62] Vietnam's new approach started to crystallise in a new 'peace zone' plan for the region, presumably as a replacement for the concept of South-east Asia as a 'zone of peace, freedom and neutrality' adopted by ASEAN in its 1971 Kuala Lumpur Declaration. The SRV proposal embraces the concepts of 'peace' and neutrality, but substitutes 'independence' for the Kuala Lumpur Declaration's concept of 'freedom'. At a meeting of ASEAN foreign ministers in New York in June 1978, Giang explained his government's proposal further, noting that Burma and Laos would also be invited to subscribe to the new doctrine (Democratic Kampuchea's exclusion was obvious). Respect for sovereignty and territorial integrity, rejection of all foreign bases, establishment of mutually advantageous relations, and regional co-operation for the benefit of 'true independence' were the essential ingredients of the SRV plan, as Giang explained it.[63] The SRV's substitution of 'independence' for ASEAN's 'freedom' is, of course, not mere semantics, since 'independence' is for the SRV a code word for a diminished US military and strategic influence through the ASEAN organisation, specifically the elimination of US military bases (as in the Philippines) and of further US military 'advisory' relations and other military co-operation (as with Indonesia and Thailand), also through the ANZUS Treaty mechanism.

Phan Hien, SRV vice minister for foreign affairs, in a Kuala Lumpur visit shortly after Giang's formulation, seemed at pains to put forth the SRV's flexibility in presenting 'our suggestions, not proposals' in turning South-east Asia 'into a zone of peace'.[64] But ASEAN reaction predictably was, and continues to be, guarded, not least because these SRV diplomatic initiatives have come at a time of Vietnam's increasing difficulties with Phnom Penh and Beijing. The ASEAN states do not wish to create the impression that they have been co-opted by Hanoi in its conflict with China and Cambodia.

Undaunted, however, the SRV pressed its diplomatic offensive. Thus SRV premier Pham Van Dong, during a Bangkok visit in early September 1978 – part of yet another Vietnamese goodwill tour through ASEAN capitals – apparently proposed a treaty of friendship and co-operation with Thailand, an offer which the Bangkok government, after due consideration, rejected.[65] Dong agreed however to the Thais' insistence that he give a firm commitment that Vietnam will cease its support for the Thai Communist guerrillas. Dong's pledge to this effect had a positive effect throughout the region, although, given the geographic realities, SRV assistance to the Thai Communists can and doubtless will continue to funnel through neighbouring Laotian territory. A similar pledge was given by Dong to Philippine President Marcos; indeed, Marcos announced on 21 September 1978 that the Philippines and the SRV had agreed not to 'support, encourage or initiate subversion against each other'. Marcos also confirmed that the two countries would settle peaceably their dispute over control of the Spratley Islands in the South China Sea.[66]

Vietnam's obvious gestures of friendship to its South-east Asian neighbours, though appreciated, did not alter their domestic anti-Communist posture, however, and Malaysia's home affairs minister, Tan Sri Ghazali bin Shafie, on 18 October 1978 in Kuala Lumpur, warned that the SRV's assurance of not supporting subversion should not cause a false sense of security among Malaysians. 'Weapons from Vietnam will not be out to destroy us . . . but let us not be lulled into a position of complacency simply because we receive such assurance,' Ghazali said.[67] Elsewhere in the region Hanoi's diplomatic initiatives have been perceived as genuine concessions to the reality of ASEAN, though understood to be dictated as much by the need for regional friends, in the light of Chinese and Kampuchean hostilities, as by the SRV's urgent requirements of trade and economic development. Malaysian willingness to assist Vietnam with the rehabilitation of the SRV's war-ravaged rubber industry has been the kind of ASEAN response which, along with improved, including commercial, relations with the US, Hanoi is anxious to elicit as it seeks to accelerate its economic growth.

But SRV diplomatic initiatives in South-east Asia were of course taking place when, as indicated, Chinese gestures of friendship also abounded. Meanwhile Democratic Kampuchea, not to be outdone, also attempted to improve its relations with its neighbours as well as attract broader international recognition and respectability (in light of the bad publicity its domestic turmoil has received) and gradually

abandon its isolation. In October 1978, Kampuchea's deputy premier for foreign affairs Ieng Sary visited some ASEAN capitals
hoping to improve the adverse impression which his own country had
been making of late. In a joint statement issued on 20 October 1978,
at the conclusion of Ieng Sary's visit to Manila, Kampuchea and the
Philippines promised to refrain from acts of aggression against each
other, agreeing further that 'an independent Cambodia', as well as
ASEAN's plan to establish a zone of 'peace, freedom and neutrality'
in South-east Asia would both contribute to the cause of peace in the
region. Earlier Ieng Sary had said that Cambodia was not supporting
the Communist Party of Thailand, but that Cambodia 'sympathised'
with 'people's liberation' movements abroad. The revolution in each
country, according to Ieng Sary, 'has to be carried out by the people of
the country themselves'. [68] During his Djakarta visit later in October
1978, Ieng Sary stressed that his government and country's current
struggle to maintain themselves as 'an independent and nonaligned
nation' (an allusion to Phnom Penh's conflict with Hanoi) had a
significance that went beyond the borders of Kampuchea. [69] Djakarta
officials like those in other ASEAN capitals refused at that point to be
drawn into the SRV-Kampuchean quarrel, however. Yet as an *acte de
présence*, Ieng Sary's goodwill journey was certainly significant, adding yet another suitor to the current row of nations wooing South-east
Asia.

The closing months of 1978 then, while certainly not characterised
by the collapse of Communist movements and insurgencies in South-
east Asia, did see a relative profusion of protestations of goodwill by
Communist powers for the South-east Asian nations which historically have confronted the South-east Asian Communist Parties
and which have been supported by those Communist powers. The
presence of Chinese vice premier Deng Xiaoping during the
religious ceremony in Bangkok, in early November 1978, marking the
entry of Thai Crown Prince Vajiralongkorn into Buddhist monk-
hood, produced this immediate reaction among some foreign observers: '"What will the boys in the jungle think of this?" – a reference to
the guerrillas of the Communist Party of Thailand (CPT).' [70] At least
at the close of 1978 it almost appeared as if the vision of some ASEAN
leaders a few years ago of a South-east Asian region in which 'all
countries, indigenous and major powers alike, have a vital stake in the
peaceful progress' of the area 'towards higher levels of economic
prosperity and political harmony' [71] might yet become a reality. The

formalisation of relations was another indication of this. On 29 May 1976, Vietnamese officials arrived to open up their embassy in the Malaysian capital, and on 12 July 1976, the Philippines and Vietnam agreed to immediate establishment of diplomatic ties. On 6 August 1976, diplomatic relations were concluded between Thailand and Vietnam. With Indonesia and Burma Hanoi has had diplomatic ties since the fifties (though Indonesian relations notably weakened in the aftermath of the 1965 coup attempt). Other components of Communist South-east Asia were also normalising their relations with the rest of the region – for example, on 18 June 1976, Thailand and Democratic Kampuchea agreed to exchange embassies.

These promising developments were crossed, however, by the Vietnamese invasion in force of Democratic Kampuchea, the capture of Phnom Penh and the fall of the China-backed Pol Pot government, and the subsequent Chinese invasion of Vietnam in order to administer Hanoi 'a lesson'. By 13 January 1979, at their special foreign ministers' meeting in Bangkok, the ASEAN states reminded Vietnam of its 'pledge to ASEAN countries scrupulously to respect each other's independence', and calling for the 'immediate and total withdrawal' of all foreign forces from Cambodia. Especially in Thailand, increasingly confronted with a stream of tens of thousands of Cambodian refugees and Pol Pot military crossing its borders, concern over the Vietnamese-installed 'People's Revolutionary Council Government' in Phnom Penh grew. After People's China's invasion of Vietnam on 16 February 1979, the ASEAN states attempted yet another initiative, this time through the United Nations Security Council, where they introduced a resolution calling, in effect, on Vietnamese forces to withdraw from Cambodia, and the Chinese (who by then were already pulling back their forces) to do the same in Vietnam. The resolution was defeated in the Security Council because of a Soviet veto, and Hanoi's daily *Nhan Dan*, on 18 March 1979, declared that the ASEAN attempt in fact had added 'to the slanders' of the Chinese 'reactionaries'. The Hanoi daily recalled pointedly that during the American-Vietnamese war some ASEAN states had sided with the US. 'We are prepared to forget this debt', *Nhan Dan* said, because of a desire to look to an improved future in the region, but the paper warned the ASEAN states not to make 'another mistake', and conspire with the Chinese.

The effect of Hanoi's reaction was a new nadir in relations with its non-Communist neighbours, particularly as ASEAN states for the

time being continued to recognise the underground Pol Pot government in Cambodia as the only legitimate regime of that country.
Increasingly ASEAN states, confronted with a *de facto* Vietnamese
dominance of both Laos and Cambodia, despite Hanoi's continued
disavowals that an 'Indochinese Federation' had come into being,
began to assess their regional security requirements in terms of still
further intelligence and military co-operation, if, formally, on a
bilateral basis. By the middle of 1979 the polarisation between
Communist and non-Communist South-east Asian governments
seemed to be growing worse, and prospects of the earlier hoped-for
co-operation had faded. In a difficult position too were some of the
Communist guerrilla insurgent movements in the ASEAN states, for
instance in Thailand, where formal adhesion to the Chinese ideological position remained the CPT's lodestar, even as the proximity of a
Soviet-oriented, aggressive Vietnam began to loom larger, promising
new possible tactical assistance in the future.

C. The influence of the USSR

Partly because it has an active following among South-east Asian
Communist parties as such (as already indicated at the beginning of
this chapter, the Philippine PKP, the Communist Parties of Laos and
the SRV, and a faction of Indonesian PKI émigrés generally can be
said to be in Moscow's camp) but perhaps more because of its global
strategic considerations, does the USSR today continue to be a factor,
along with other major powers, in this new post-Vietnam war system
of South-east Asian intra-regional relations. The Soviet position in
South-east Asia at present appears to be motivated by a number of
long-term political and strategic perceptions as well as by the legacy
of its direct bilateral experiences with some of the nations of the region
such as Burma and Indonesia. As to the former, it is the Soviet
perception that in the present era of détente, revolutionary, anti-
colonial, and anti-racist movements in Asia and Africa will continue
their respective drives to power. Détente, in the view of one recent
Soviet analyst, 'creates the best conditions' for solidarity and 'international assistance' to ongoing 'national liberation' struggles in the
Third World.[72] South-east Asia, to be sure, is not a major theatre of
Soviet strategic concern at the moment like the Indian Ocean or

portions of Africa. Nevertheless it is for the Soviets a region where, as a result of the decisive defeat in Vietnam of the US policy of 'aggression, imperialist piracy and support for reactionary regimes', the international revolutionary struggle has received an important boost, also because of the assistance Hanoi received from Moscow, and hence new initiatives now can and should be taken there.[73]

Like Hanoi, Moscow sees both negative and positive features in the currently increased regional self-awareness of the members of ASEAN. The desire for an atmosphere of peace, neutrality and freedom from foreign interference, Soviet commentators see as 'closely bound up' with the international struggle for peace and security, indeed, even with détente.[74] On the other hand, 'imperialist circles' are said to be attempting to persuade ASEAN's members to turn their organisation into a military alliance, a *de facto* successor to the now defunct SEATO (South-east Asia Treaty Organisation).[75] Moscow also shares with Hanoi a concern over alleged US attempts to build a new strategic network in the Western Pacific (involving Japan, elements of US-controlled Micronesia, the Philippines, Australia and New Zealand, and, covertly, also Indonesia), in the context of which, as another Soviet analyst has put it, efforts are being made 'to introduce military activity in ASEAN, through the back door so to say'.[76]

While Soviet comment does take note of ASEAN's professed concern for peaceful coexistence and mutual co-operation with all countries, the Association's commitment to developing a 'regional resilience' (for example, as provided for in the ASEAN 'Treaty of Amity and Co-operation' of February 1976) is sometimes perceived by the Russians to have an aggressive implication which, it is held, prevents, among others, the SRV from endorsing the Amity Treaty. Still, Soviet media, on the whole, seem determined to find a silver lining in ASEAN's development. The Association's member states these days, particularly the Philippines and Thailand, are finding themselves praised for beginning to see regional and world developments 'more realistically' (for example, in supporting the SRV's membership in the United Nations), and for seeking better relations with the Indochina states.[77]

Such Soviet ambivalences toward South-east Asia, it could be argued, are not without some justification. From Moscow's point of view there is good reason to be warily sceptical about developments in the region. On balance, Soviet diplomacy and aid policies in most of

South-east Asia over the past three decades can hardly be called a success – indeed, Indonesia is a showcase of a Soviet policy débâcle. On the other hand there is the warmth in Soviet-SRV relations, illustrated by, for instance, Soviet naval usage of refuelling and refitting facilities at the SRV's Cam Ranh Bay. Were it not, however, for its strained relations with Cambodia's Pol Pot regime and China's backing for the latter, one should question whether Hanoi's leaders really desire so close and dependent a relationship with Moscow as the 2 November 1978 Soviet-SRV treaty symbolises. One is mindful that, in 1976 and early 1977, before the SRV-Kampuchean border conflict escalated to the new and troubling heights of a supposedly Sino-Soviet 'proxy war', Hanoi was unmistakably signalling Washington that it desired a rapprochement with the US which would in part assist it in meeting Vietnam's urgent economic development needs and also keep it from being wholly driven into Moscow's arms. For the new Carter administration in a US still traumatised by the Vietnam war's aftermath and by the US prisoner of war-missing in action issue, such a rapprochement would, however, have required too bold a diplomatic initiative too soon.

An opportunity thus was lost and Moscow seized it, as doubtless some rather mixed feelings prevailed in Hanoi. Given the Vietnamese reluctance it hardly seems likely that the SRV will begin playing in South-east Asia the role which Castro's Cuba has eagerly assumed in Africa. The Soviet Union's current alliance with the SRV should not obscure the fact that notwithstanding its historic inspirational and training role for South-east Asian Communism, and despite some thirty years or more of occasionally ardent courtship of South-east Asian governments, the USSR today is as far as ever from having acquired hegemony or even decisive influence in any country of the region, probably not even in the SRV. From this perspective there is for the Soviets nothing comparable to Afghanistan or Cuba in South-east Asia.

Soviet experience with individual South-east Asian countries has often been disappointing. Russian-Burmese diplomatic relations were established as early as 1951. Although in subsequent decades Moscow consistently found praise for Burma as a 'national democratic' state, whose domestic and foreign policies were said to be keeping it on the path of 'non-capitalist' development and of 'peaceful co-existence', the Rangoon government, despite Beijing's support for the Burma Communist Party (BCP) insurgents, has kept the Russians at arms' length. Proffered Soviet military assistance has been refused, and Russian economic aid has been kept at a relatively low level. In the later seventies, though in great need of foreign loans if its 'Burmese Way to Socialism' programme was to succeed, Rangoon has sought only some $200 000 in Soviet credits, compared to about $5 million from the US, and $19 million from Japan.[78] And undaunted by Beijing's 'party to party' support for the BCP, the Ne Win regime continues to seek and maintain a friendly *modus vivendi* with People's China.[79]

Meanwhile the small and ineffectual 'Red Flag' Communist Party of Burma, with its mainly Arakanese following, pursues its own obscure and faction-ridden course. There is no indication that the Soviets have wanted to support it or any other party or group of their own, even if one could be developed in Burma's officially one-party system.

With Indonesia too, Soviet relations developed relatively early (in 1954 Indonesia opened its embassy in Moscow). In the later nineteen fifties and early sixties, Indonesian President Sukarno's militant nationalism and aspirations to Third World leadership seemed to the Soviets a particularly promising tactical opportunity to win influence among African and Asian nations. Between Sukarno's first visit to Moscow in 1956 (he was to visit the Russian capital three more times in subsequent years) and the turning point of the *Gestapu* coup attempt in 1965, prominent Soviet figures like Nikita Khruschev and K. Voroshilov and others went to Djakarta to demonstrate their government's apparent approbation of Indonesian policies. Moreover, Soviet economic assistance to Indonesia of some $365 million, plus a military aid programme valued at $1.25 billion (including missiles, destroyers, submarines and MIG-21 aircraft) had got under way. These made Indonesia, next to People's China, probably the recipient of the largest amount of Soviet aid to any nation.[80]

Yet, already by 1963, the Russians had good reason to regret their largesse and earlier encouragement of Sukarno. The latter, locked in a complex power struggle with the Indonesian Communist Party (PKI) and with the army, turned not only toward seemingly ever closer relations with Beijing, but also toward risky foreign gambits like the 'confrontation' campaign against the Malaysian Federation. At the same time, despite huge injections of aid, the Indonesian economy sank into chaos. As China's influence in Djakarta seemed to grow, the Soviets, demonstrably, appeared unable to moderate Sukarno's adventurism and their huge Indonesian investment clearly was turning out disastrously. In the 1965 coup's aftermath formal Soviet-Indonesian diplomatic relations were preserved, but the stridently domestic anti-Communist tenor of the Suharto regime hardly suggested any speedy improvement of relations.

By November 1966, the Soviets were evidently ready to make the best of a bad job, and agreed to a financial protocol fixing Indonesia's total indebtedness to the USSR at $804 million (including some $523 million in military debts) with final repayment set for 1 July 1981. Still, during much of the later sixties relations remained strained, as the Soviets reacted sharply to the Suharto regime's campaign against the underground PKI, and the execution of prominent PKI leaders. The Djakarta government in turn took offence at anti-Suharto broadcasts over Radio Moscow. With the December 1973 visit to Djakarta of Soviet minister for culture Ekaterina Furtseva there began an improved diplomatic climate, however, and on 23 March 1974, a new Indonesian-Soviet trade agreement was signed.[81]

Recent Soviet assessments of Indonesian affairs, on the one hand, highlight the danger of Djakarta's alleged military co-operation with the US, the lingering problem of political prisoners, and the influence of 'ultra-Right political circles' in the country, while, on the other hand, there is praise for Djakarta's 'international initiatives', including those made through ASEAN, in order to achieve 'peaceful co-existence' in the world.[82] Between 1975 and 1976 alone, according to the Soviet news agency *Novosti*, trade between the two countries grew by 48.2 per cent (from 28.6 million roubles to 42.4 million), and in November 1975 Moscow announced a technical and financial assistance programme for the development of two hydropower plants in west and central Java.[83] The post-coup Indonesian political climate remains at best one of warily cool correctness when it comes to relations with Communist states. The Djakarta government today, like those in the rest of ASEAN, values the Soviet diplomatic, trade, and assistance relationship primarily as a necessary, cautiously used balancing factor in the region, not as an invitation to a possible new and warmer rapprochement or international partnership.

Moscow cannot be faulted, however, for failing to keep on trying and asserting its presence. Agreement to establish diplomatic relations was reached with Malaysia in 1967, and with Singapore in 1968, but it was not until 2 June 1976 that the Philippines finally agreed on mutual diplomatic recognition with the USSR. Malaysian premier Tun Abdul Razak's visit to Moscow in October 1972 elicited the kind of Soviet reaction which may be taken as characteristic of official Russian perceptions of non-Communist South-east Asia generally today: guarded and aware of 'many complex problems', yet optimistic, praising 'achievement', and seeing opportunities for a further warming of relations.[84] Next to trade the Soviets seem inclined particularly to push agreements on cultural and scientific cooperation (including scholarships to study in the USSR) with the South-east Asian countries, and also organise semi-formal mutual 'friendship' societies. At the close of November 1971, a spokesman for the Malaysia-Soviet Friendship Society in Kuala Lumpur announced that a counterpart Soviet-Malaysia Friendship Society had just been formed in Moscow headed by USSR minister of oil and refineries, V. Federov. In Thailand and the Philippines there are similar organisations.

But Soviet media persist in underscoring the ambivalences of progress in the South-east Asian countries. Thus such media comment in recent years on the Philippines has focused on the dangers of the US military bases in that country. However, there has also been praise, in keeping with similar comments by the pro-Moscow PKP in the Philippines, for some of President Ferdinand Marcos' agrarian policies and for his attempts to develop a more independent foreign policy, particularly in improving relations with the Communist bloc.[85] Then, too, the frequent changes in Thai government since the overthrow of the Thanom Kittikachorn government in 1973 are perceived in the Soviet media as indications of a domestic Thai struggle against 'reactionary', pro-US and 'rightist' elements entrenched in the armed forces' establishment by 'new democratic' forces who seek a turn toward a more 'realistic' and 'independent' foreign policy. The complete withdrawal of lingering, covert US military influence, speedy elections, and a legitimisation of the political left are all viewed in the Soviet media as desiderata for the Thai state. Soviet perceptions today thus seem to stress a long, transitional stage toward an eventual triumph of less authoritarian, less US- or Western-oriented regimes in South-east Asia, and already in 1975, for example, Soviet commentary hopefully put it that 'in the confrontation of the democratic and reactionary forces, a foundation is being laid for a new, peaceful and independent Thailand'.[86] Whatever its reservations about the resolute domestic anti-Communist stance of a particular South-east Asian government, Moscow is determined to use every channel of contact. Thus the Russians were eager to open a branch of their Narodny Bank in Singapore although the regime of premier Lee Kuan Yew in the island republic should rank high in the Soviets' political demonology.

Continuing also as part of its long-term policy interests in the region is the Soviets' suggestion for a new security framework in Asia, announced first, almost casually, during an international conference of Communist and Workers' Parties in Moscow on 7 June 1969 by Soviet party secretary Leonid Brezhnev. Brezhnev said on that occasion, without further elaboration, that he was 'also of the opinion' that 'the course of events' was 'putting on the agenda the task of creating a system of collective security in Asia'.[87] Initially, in subsequent years the Soviets provided few details of just what kind of security system they had in mind, although they appear to have made a special effort to enlist the interest of the Indonesians. But on 7 March 1970, after talks in Moscow, the then Indonesian foreign minister Adam Malik, during a Singapore stopover, declared that 'All Asian countries, including Indonesia, have rejected the Soviet Union's proposal for a regional security arrangement', adding that his talks in the Soviet capital had convinced him that the Russians, in fact, had 'no blue prints' at all of their security plan for Asia. As Malik put it, 'All the Russians want to do is sell the idea and, if given the backing of the Asian countries, they will think out something.' The impression that the Soviet proposal was and is essentially but another anti-Chinese ploy concocted by Moscow remains widespread. As Malik again said it: 'What do we want these pacts for – to fight who? China? I don't think China will want to attack us.'[88]

Despite such rebuffs, Soviet spokesmen nevertheless kept referring to their collective security proposal without at first fleshing out its frame. Then, on 27 February 1972, after US President Richard Nixon's historic China visit, the Nixon-Zhou En-lai communiqué issued in Shanghai may have given the Russians some further impetus to develop their security concept. The Shanghai communiqué rephrased and reiterated the old 1955 Asian-African Bandung Conference formula (in turn based on the even earlier Sino-Indian so-called Panscheel 'peaceful co-existence' concept), stressing respect for sovereignty and territorial integrity of all states, non-interference in internal affairs, mutual restraint and abstention from attempts to seek 'hegemony in the Asian Pacific Region', and so on. On 20 March

1972, no doubt buoyed by the new twenty-year Indian-Soviet treaty of peace and co-operation (signed on 9 August 1971 in New Delhi), Brezhnev, addressing the Fifteenth Congress of Soviet Trade Unions, provided some details of his original Asian collective security concept. Renunciation of the use of force, respect for sovereignty and inviolability of borders, co-operation on the basis of mutual benefit, non-interference in internal affairs – these were the elements which Brezhnev now proposed as appropriate to his Asian security design. Malaysian premier Tun Abdul Razak, during his Moscow visit in October 1972, declared that these principles of the Brezhnev concept and ASEAN's own neutralisation idea were in harmony with each other. As one Thai daily was to editorialise later, the Brezhnev proposal turned out to be just a 'reactivation' of the Panscheel and Bandung Conference principles.[89] Soviet commentators asserted, however, that the 'steady growth' in the opportunity to realise such policy principles as 'territorial integrity' and sovereignty were the result of the emergence of Socialism in the 'international arena' and the 'favourable' effect of that emergence 'on the world situation'.[90]

In the later seventies, as Chinese critics were quick to point out, less came to be heard of a Soviet 'collective security' proposal as such.[91] Instead, emphasis was placed in Soviet pronouncements on the principles of the old Panscheel-Bandung formula. An analysis of South-east Asian events appearing in *Pravda* in October 1978, for example, said nothing of the Brezhnev proposal, referring instead to the fact that the USSR was supporting the efforts of ASEAN states to make their region and continent one of 'peace, friendship and co-operation', and asserting that the Soviet Union had 'consistently' advocated the 'strengthening of ASEAN states' independence, sovereignty and territorial integrity'.[92] To Beijing the whole Brezhnev proposal however has been merely 'a pretext for expansion'. And, according to the Chinese, the Soviets' current 'smiling diplomacy' toward the ASEAN nations has been forced on them by the impossibility of ignoring the 'ascending position' of these nations any longer.[93]

It remains to note that Soviet spokesmen deny that Brezhnev's proposal was but an anti-Chinese ploy. Thus on 25 June 1975, the Soviet ambassador to Thailand, Boris Ilyichev, declared in a Bangkok address that 'one should be void of common sense' to presume that there may be any international Asian arrangements 'without participation of the People's Republic of China' and that it was up to China to involve herself in any new security arrangement, presumably even one proposed by Moscow. Meanwhile, Soviet Commentators have called into question China's peaceful intentions in South-east Asia, raising the spectre of continuous Chinese subversion in the region.[94] But some of the South-east Asian press, having taken due note of China's protective attitude toward ethnic Chinese fleeing the SRV, has also been quick to observe Soviet readiness to exploit China's sensitivity to the plight of Overseas Chinese.[95]

These days the USSR makes sure not to lag behind other Communist powers in courting ASEAN. Within approximately the same time frame that the SRV's Pham Van Dong, People's China's Deng Xiaoping, and Democratic Kampuchea's Ieng Sary made the rounds of South-east Asian capitals (between September and early November 1978), so too did USSR deputy foreign minister Nikolai Firyubin. Whether in Manila, Bangkok, or Djakarta, as one Thai news analysis pointed out, Firyubin declared that the Soviet Union considers ASEAN and its concept of a 'zone of peace, freedom and neutrality' to be a 'positive' idea, but as Thai foreign minister Uppadit Pachariyangkun noted, Firyubin did not use the word 'support' in this connection: 'Expressing full support of ASEAN and the zone of peace concept from Moscow's point of view would appear too much like following the lead of China,' while 'sticking to the old ploy that ASEAN is a US backed military bloc would not, at the present time, hold water.' So 'Firyubin took the middle course of calling it a positive idea which leaves room for us to call it "support".'[96]

Leaving semantic niceties like this aside, Firyubin in Djakarta stressed that his country's relations with Indonesia 'were appreciably progressing', while in discussions with the Soviet leader in Manila, even the possibility of Soviet military aid to the Philippines was apparently mooted in the event the US should prove reluctant to meet the Marcos government's needs.[97]

Still, there are no illusions about the new Soviet presence. Not forgotten in South-east Asia are allegations that two former top Malaysian officials, Abdullah Ahmad, one-time deputy minister of science and technology, and Abdullah Majid, another deputy cabinet minister and previously a senior foreign affairs official, at the time of their arrest in November 1976 in Kuala Lumpur on poorly specified charges of pro-Communist activity were said to have acted in the interests of the USSR.[98] Nor, as the Soviet Union presses its diplomatic initiatives in the region in the months ahead, will the implication of the Soviet-SRV Friendship Treaty be ignored. Moscow clearly means to push a less than totally willing Hanoi into broadened 'peaceful co-existence' ventures with its ASEAN neighbours, turning the region away from US and Chinese influence as much as possible, in a complicated three-way power play. The theme of long-term Soviet policy intentions in the region was perhaps revealed at the close of yet another recent *Pravda* analysis of ASEAN's future:[99]

> The recent visits by the prime minister of the Socialist Republic of Vietnam to Thailand, the Philippines and Indonesia and the agreements concluded attest that the establishment of neighbourly relations among countries with different social systems reveals opportunities for achieving economic progress with greater efficiency.

Local South-east Asian Communist parties have thus become only one and not necessarily the most important policy channel for either Moscow or Beijing as they seek to affect the future course of events in the region. Indeed, despite – perhaps one should say because of – their recent respective diplomatic initiatives in the area, neither Moscow nor any of Asia's Communist regimes have made a point of affirming their adhesion to a particular Communist party or faction of its choice. During his South-east Asian journey in November 1978 Deng Xiaoping's unwillingness to disavow 'party to party' relations came in a negative rather than a positive formulation, from which it would be difficult for local Beijing-oriented parties to derive a sense of wholehearted Chinese enthusiasm. This is not to say that, as in the case of the Beijing-supported BCP in Burma, or in the more complex instance of a divided CPT in Thailand, receiving aid from both the SRV (via Laos!) and from Beijing-backed Pol Pot underground guerrilla regime, the wellsprings of foreign assistance have now dried up. It is to say rather that South-east Asia's relations with the dispensers of such foreign aid are increasingly structured by diplomatic, strategic and commercial variables not evident ten or even five years ago.

D. The Indochina question and the world

On 14 November 1979, the United Nations' General Assembly, by a large vote (91 in favour, 21 against, and 29 abstentions) approved a

resolution introduced by the ASEAN states calling for the withdrawal
of all 'foreign' military forces from Cambodia – a measure clearly
aimed at Hanoi and indirectly also at Moscow, since Soviet military
advisers had been operating with the Vietnamese forces in Cambodia
as of the end of 1978. Two months earlier, the UN General Assembly
already had handed the Vietnamese another diplomatic defeat, when
it voted (71 in favour, 35 against) to give Cambodia's seat in the
Assembly to the now underground government of 'Democratic Kampuchea' headed by Pol Pot and Khieu Sampan, despite SRV and
Soviet protests that the only legitimate government in Cambodia
today is that of the 'Kampuchean People's Revolutionary Council',
and 'Peoples Republic of Kampuchea' headed by Heng Samrin.

Meanwhile, international attention came to be focused not only on
the plight of the Cambodian refugees (an estimated 120 000 of whom
were in various centres well inside Thailand by the beginning of 1980,
with perhaps as many as 500 000 camped on both sides along the
Thai–Cambodian frontier), but also on the determined Vietnamese
effort, backed by Soviet advisers and technical personnel, to wipe out
the 25 000-man guerrilla army of Pol Pot mainly operating in Western
Cambodia near the Thai border. On 26 January 1980 the Carter
administration in Washington publicly expressed concern that the
Vietnamese offensive, around Poipet on the Thai–Cambodian frontier, would not only drive the Cambodian border refugees into
Thailand, but also could lead to a Vietnamese crossing of the border,
with unforeseen consequences. Thai military forces, strengthened by
stepped-up US military supplies, have greatly increased in the tense
frontier zone. In the background remained the question as to whether
People's China would permit the destruction by the Vietnamese of
Beijing's client, the Pol Pot–Khieu Sampan regime of 'Democratic
Kampuchea', or whether the Chinese would resort, at some future
time, to a second 'punitive' military strike against Hanoi.

To be sure, the first such Chinese military attack against the
Vietnamese, beginning on 16 February 1979, though lasting less than
a month, had pointed up logistical and tactical weaknesses in the
Chinese armed forces. Moreover, Beijing and other nations that
continue to recognise and/or support the underground regime of
'Democratic Kampuchea' had long been embarassed by the odious
international reputation of Pol Pot. The latter, though relinquishing
his post as 'Democratic Kampuchea's' premier to President Khieu
Sampan, in mid-December 1979, has remained commander of the

guerrilla forces. On 6 December 1979, the United Kingdom withdrew diplomatic recognition of 'Democratic Kampuchea'. However, London stressed that this did not mean that such recognition would now be accorded the Heng Samrin government in control of Phnom Penh, because, as a British spokesman put it, 'The dependence of the Heng Samrin regime on the Vietnamese occupation army is complete', adding that there was 'no reason to doubt' that without the Vietnamese, Heng Samrin's 'People's Republic of Kampuchea' government 'would be swept away by resurgent Cambodian nationalism'.[100]

No amount of international criticism, not even in the context of controversial charges that Hanoi, Heng Samrin, and the Soviets, have been blocking efforts to aid the diseased and malnourished Cambodian border refugee population, appears to be able to dissuade Hanoi (and by implication its Soviet ally) that it not only will ultimately triumph in Cambodia militarily, but also that the rest of the world will come to accept the existence of a *de facto* Indochinese Federation under Vietnamese leadership as a *fait accompli*. Hanoi has sharply criticised ASEAN's 'crude interference' in the Cambodian problem, and has let it be known that it will never accept an alternative, 'neutral' Cambodian regime, for example, one headed by Prince Norodom Sihanouk.[101] SRV premier Pham Van Dong, when queried about critical international reaction to the Vietnamese intervention in Cambodia, responded that 'I believe' that as the 'situation' in Cambodia becomes 'increasingly clear', everyone will be brought to 'a correct assessment of the new developments there'.[102]

Hanoi and the Heng Samrin regime rather seek to draw world attention to People's China's allegedly warlike designs against them. Simultaneously they stress the evils of the Pol Pot era for the mass of Cambodians, and the readiness with which the Pol Pot 'clique' allegedly lent itself at an early date to China's 'attack on Vietnam in their program of expansion and hegemony'.[103] By attempting to discredit Pol Pot, for example, through a much publicised trial on charges of genocide before a 'People's Revolutionary Tribunal' in Phnom Penh in the middle of August 1979, the Vietnamese and its ally, the Heng Samrin government in Cambodia, evidently seek to discredit Beijing and others who continue to recognise 'Democratic Kampuchea' as well.

Meanwhile, and with the Soviets' political, economic and military encouragement, Hanoi remains also intent on closely supervising the domestic governing structures of Laos and Cambodia and integrating

the latter two countries as much as possible into a single strategic
entity with which the world, and particularly non-Communist South-
east Asia will have to reckon. Not just Vietnamese military, party
officials and technical advisers in Cambodia are the mainstay of the
Heng Samrin regime, but, reportedly Vietnamese in a non-official
capacity, for example, farmers, artisans and professional people were
during 1979 and since being sent to such Cambodian provinces as
Kompong Speu, Kompong Cham and Takeo, as settlers. This arrangement is part of a supposedly 'sister province' relationship
between Cambodia and the SRV, as the latter engages in a *de facto*
'colonizing' of the new 'People's Republic of Kampuchea', as Beijing
now is charging.[104] A corollary process is to be found in Laos, where,
in addition to at least 50 000 troops, and 6 000 SRV government and
party officials, there are now reportedly also about 100 000 Vietnamese civilians, some from South Vietnam, who have been settled in a
3 000 square mile area that comprises the region of Saravane, At-
topeu, the Bolovens Plateau, and Sam Neua.[105] In Laos there are at
least one thousand Soviet personnel, including 'ministry advisers'
and air force specialists, who supervise use of the 22 MiG 21 aircraft
Moscow has delivered to Laos since September 1978.[106] In Heng
Samrin's 'People's Republic of Kampuchea' there are an estimated
800 Soviet 'technicians' and 'advisers', some seconded to the Vietnamese armed forces, others having been engaged in unloading
vessels at the Kompong Som port, in transportation maintenance, in
harbour and road construction, and so on.

Both in Laos and Cambodia, however, there is nationalist resentment of and even organised resistance to the heavy Vietnamese
dominance. As early as February 1976, various self-described
nationalist groups, including former Pathet Lao elements, organised
themselves into a 'Laotian Popular Front' and issued an appeal to the
United Nations demanding withdrawal of all 'foreign military, notably the north Vietnamese'.[107] By November 1979, this ongoing resistance against the present Lao People's Democratic Repulic, especially among the Hmong (Meo) mountain tribes, reached the point that
the Vientiane government and the Vietnamese felt it necessary to
resort to the delivery or air delivered toxic gas attacks against the
Hmong.[108] People's China reportedly has been active in organising
and supplying the Hmong resistance movement in such Laotian
provinces as Phong Saly, Oudomsay and Nam Ta near the Chinese
frontier. In fact, Beijing reportedly has equipped a regular 4 000 man
insurgent unit, the so-called 'Lanna Division', mainly composed of

Hmong and disenchanted former Pathet Lao,[109] and despite Laotian requests has refused to withdraw all Chinese 'technicians' engaged in road building and maintenance in Northern Laos since 1961.

In Cambodia, the 'People's Republic' of Heng Samrin probably could not maintain itself for a day without the presence of the 200 000-man Vietnamese military force now estimated to be in Cambodia. Despite its odious reputation, the Pol Pot–Khieu Sampan 'Democratic Kampuchean' regime is a beneficiary of the Cambodian nationalist sentiment, although among the tens of thousands of Cambodian refugees, riven by various nationalist 'Free Khmer' factions and would-be 'liberation' leaders, Cambodia's former ruler Prince Norodom Sihanouk remains a clear favourite.[110] Anti-Vietnamese resistance in Cambodia remains as ill-equipped and poorly organised as in Laos, however, and Sihanouk has sought to keep his distance not only from the Pol Pot–Khieu Sampan forces, but from Beijing and Washington as well, in an effort to appear as 'neutral' as possible. As indicated, neither Hanoi nor for that matter Moscow, has any intention of permitting any regime other than one compliant to Vietnamese wishes to prevail in the Indochina region.

Under Hanoi's aegis, meanwhile, the alliance solidification, if not unification, between the three Indochina states, continued apace during 1979–80, and at the conclusion of the conference of the Foreign Ministers of the SRV, Laos and Cambodia, held in Phnom Penh on 5 January 1980, it was noted that the 'parties saw eye to eye with one another on all points', and that the ministers had noted 'with satisfaction and pride' that the 'militant solidarity between the three peoples' had been 'further consolidated and developed' through 'new trials' during the 'previous year'.[111] The Soviets' interest in maintaining their new proxy foothold in Asia, that is, the Hanoi-dominated Indochinese alliance, is exemplified by the aid that they have poured into the three Indochinese states. Estimates of annual Soviet aid to the SRV during the 1977–80 period alone run to at least $750 million, and on 27 December 1979 the Heng Samrin government's Trade Minister, Tang Saroem, on a visit to Moscow, signed an economic aid agreement reportedly worth $250 million over the next three years. On 8 January 1980, Soviet Education Minister M. A. Prokofyev, during a Phnom Penh visit, asserted that during 1979 alone Russian aid to the Heng Samrin regime had amounted to $85 million, including rice, pharmaceuticals, textiles, cement, vehicles, and paper.

Not surprisingly, Vietnamese media staunchly defended the Soviet intervention in Afghanistan. And the Indochina states as a unit, even as Hanoi receives emissaries from her non-Communist South-east Asian neighbours, who seek to improve relations, sometimes seem to give the impression that the world community must choose between having good relations with the Hanoi – Vientiane – Phnom Penh – Moscow axis, or with Beijing, but that it cannot have both.[112] Certainly in some military and media circles among Hanoi's ASEAN neighbours such an impression in turn has led to a hardening of attitudes toward both Vietnam and Moscow. Talk of 'beefing up' the South-east Asian regional collective security implications of the Manila Treaty of 1954, indeed even of reviving a SEATO-like organisation, have been accompanied by sharp criticism of the USSR, for example, Singapore Foreign Minister S. Rajaratnam's acerbic remark, early in January 1980, that it was a 'tribute to the skill of Soviet propaganda' that the world continued to view the invasion of Cambodia as a Vietnamese war, while in reality it was 'a Soviet war through Vietnamese proxy'.[113]

Nevertheless Hanoi's leaders also appear to believe that their hold on their Laotian and Cambodian neighbours will inevitably be accepted by the world, and that ASEAN and other Asian states will not wish to forego indefinitely the diplomatic and economic advantages of closer relations with the Indochina bloc. Even so, that bloc's internal difficulties, especially its development needs, eventually may generate political dynamics of change which may prove too strong for Hanoi, even with Moscow's help, to contain. The Heng Samrin regime's national defence minister, and concurrently commander of the armed forces of the Kampuchean 'People's Republic', Pen Sovan, admitted in an address to a national conference of Cambodian 'intellectuals' in November 1979, that having been led astray by 'the nationalists', some of 'our brothers still have dust in their eyes'. He urged his audience particularly to be on guard against the various ways in which the 'enemies' of the nation, from People's China to US 'imperialism', were seeking to destroy 'the unity' between Cambodia and Vietnam.[114] Still, Nationalist Cambodian resentment of the SRV's heavy hand is likely to grow in proportion that the Heng Samrin regime and its mass front organisation, the Kampuchean National United Front for National Salvation (KNUFNS), continue to conceive of the remaining Cambodian populace as a 'sheet of white paper' that somehow can be painted beautifully with colours of the KNUFNS's policies. 'Thus we are proceeding from zero', said Pen

Sovan, 'We must teach the people and indoctrinate them in the true line leading to genuine rights of freedom, democracy and happiness'. Such assertions are likely to recall for most Cambodians the horrors of the Pol Pot era's economic and social reforms.

While by the beginning of 1980 the threat of mass starvation in Cambodia, both among the hundreds of thousands of refugees straddling the Thai border and among the remaining population in the country, had been blunted by the strenuous relief efforts of UNICEF, OXFAM, the Red Cross, and other organisations, as well as by Soviet and Vietnamese aid, staggering problems of social rehabilitation and economic development continued to confront the Communist regimes in Cambodia and the other Indochinese states. At the ceremonies in Phnom Penh marking KNUFNS' first anniversary on 1 December 1979, KNUFNS' president Heng Samrin declared that with the economic reorganisation of the country following the fall of the Pol Pot regime, Cambodians had 'finally returned to their home villages and been reunited with their families' and that 'They now have decent shelters and clothing and sufficient food rations'.[115] Other reports indicated, however, that at the close of 1979 there still was no currency in Cambodia, all work was still being paid for with food (a meager basic ration of 28 pounds of staples a month consisting mainly of rice, corn, some fish and vegetables was the 'wage' for a sedentary worker, 35 pounds for a heavy labourer, and 46 pounds for a soldier) and there was 'constant hunger' among civilian workers, even those with steady jobs.[116] Industrial production and transportation facilities were still minimal, and heavy flooding reportedly had made the rice fields uncultivable, while irrigation canals remained 'silted over from disuse'.[117] Taking a leaf from Vietnamese policies the Heng Samrin regime, in the middle of 1979, began with a purge of the half-million ethnic Chinese inhabitants of Cambodia, resulting in growing numbers of Chinese seeking refuge in Thailand, and doubtlessly adding to the further dislocation of the distributing trade and crafts in the country.[118]

In Vietnam, during the first three years after the Communist reunification of the country in 1975, there were severe economic reverses. Alternating floods and drought, as well as cadre mismanagement admitted by party leaders themselves had led to serious shortfalls in grain production (for example, a reported shortage of about 2 million tons in 1977 alone), to damage to arable land, and to serious population dislocations. Industrial production lagged, as more than a third of the nation's 22 million total labour force remained unemployed, and skilled Chinese manpower began fleeing the SRV.[119] On 16 January 1980 Hanoi Radio reported that a long drought again threatened the winter rice crop and that though 1979 rice production was 8 per cent higher than the previous year, and another 2.5 million acres had been brought under food crop production, nevertheless '1979 was a most difficult year for Vietnamese agriculture'.[120] The SRV's already noted continuing heavy dependence on the USSR (for example, 65 per cent of Vietnam's total trade is with the Soviet Union), and the Soviet's funding of 60 per cent (or $3.2 billion) of Vietnam's 1976-1980 Five Year Plan)[121], have their corollary in the Lao People's Democratic Republic. Soviet assistance in key Laotian public and military services is extensive.[122] Direct Soviet economic and technical assistance to Laos now runs to about $150 million a year, but the figure may be higher as it is apparent that Moscow prefers to extend its influence in the country through its Vietnamese proxy. Laotian premier Kaysone Phomvihan's claims, made at the end of December 1979, that dry season rice land acreage had increased by 30 per cent over the previous year, and that average rice production per hectare had risen to 1.5 tons, are difficult to verify, as are claims of improved industrial production (for example, an increase in electricity production to 840 million kilowatt hours in 1979, or 2.6 times the amount in 1978).[123]

As in the case of the hundreds of thousands of Cambodian refugees, however, and the defection of such prominent Vietnamese leaders as Hoang Van Hoan (a founding member of the Vietnam Communist Party and Vice-Chairman of the Vietnamese National Assembly) to People's China in July 1979 the real attitude of Laotians toward their government, is best illustrated perhaps by the numbers of them who have 'voted with their feet', that is, those who have sought to escape the Lao People's Democratic Republic. By early 1979 there were already some 120 000 refugee Laotians in Thai camps,[124] and by the beginning of 1980 their number seeking safety in Thailand as well as in other South-east Asian countries and in the rest of the world had risen to at least 200 000.

There is as yet little indication of domestic stability in the Communist party leadership of the Indochinese states. 'Massive purges' of old cadres and their replacement by 'technocrats' and military personnel in the Communist Party of Vietnam were reported during the first weeks of 1980. Suspicion of pro-Chinese sentiments, declining cadre morale, and efficiency and inability to provide modern managerial style leadership presumably were among the reasons for the shake-up.[125] Even revered military figures like General Vo Nguyen Giap, the hero of the battle of Dien Bien Phu, were affected (the sixty-nine-year-old Giap lost his Defence Minister's post amidst speculation that the Soviets desired a more pliable figure in that post). In Laos, in the closing weeks of 1979, earlier defections of party leaders (like Sisanan Saignanouvong, editor of the Lao People's Revolutionary Party newspaper *Sieng Pasason*) were followed by arrests of prominent officials, like Khampeng Boupha, Communications Minister, and Kampo Phongkeo, Education Vice Minister, apparently because of their dislike for the Vietnamese dominance of Laos. Seven senior civil servants in various other ministries were also reported to have been arrested.[126] Not surprisingly, the Lao People's Revolutionary Party's Central Committee, on 2 December 1979 appealed to 'cadres, combatants and compatriots' throughout the country to 'strengthen unity among the entire people,' and to oppose all 'divisive' campaigns launched by unnamed 'imperialists and reactionaries'.[127]

In the SRV, not only the persistent exodus of refugees, but the continued detention of some 50 000 people in 're-education' camps, and the compulsory relocation of thousands of others to distant and barren 'New Economic Zones', suggests that popular support for the Communist regime is dubious. Nevertheless, in 'the spirit' of what the SRV party daily editorially has called 'collective mastery', in Vietnam, as well as in Laos and Cambodia, significant 'infra-structural' changes in production methods are going forward.[128] The larger and socially more disruptive communes and collectives established during the Pol Pot era in Cambodia have been dismantled. But the concept of 'public ownership of the means of production', is always held up as the ideal, and there is a steady broadening of the network of cooperatives and communal controls in farm and factory production. Particularly in Laos, however, extensive allowance is made for various 'private' sectors of the economy, including some in food crop production. 'Misguided revolutionary zeal' in working out the gradual transformation toward a collectivist economy is specifically cautioned against, also in the SRV.[129] At least in theory official recognition is given to the need for local popular controls over production and mangement. Thus the new SRV Constitution, announced in August 1979, provides for elected 'people's councils and people's committees' as the 'local organs of state authority' charged, among others, with meeting the 'demands of production and life' in their local constituencies.[130] Whether such mechanisms are likely to be effective in winning broader domestic support for the Hanoi regime, particularly in the southern part of the SRV, or whether the best intended structural reforms in public administration and economic affairs will be thwarted by the continuing suspicion of the SRV and its Indochinese allies among their regional South-east Asian neighbours and in much of the rest of the world remains to be seen.

6

Conclusion: a look ahead

In an address, given only one year or so after the consolidation of Communist power throughout the Indochina area, Singapore's able foreign minister S. Rajaratnam nevertheless felt encouraged to enumerate what he regarded as a series of Communist defeats in South-east Asia since World War II. He noted, for example, that since the war's end the Indonesian Communist Party (PKI), 'the largest Communist party in Asia outside China', twice had attempted to seize power, failing 'disastrously' however on both occasions. In Burma, Rajaratnam went on, two Communist Parties have been seeking the key to success for three decades but to no avail, 'and they are still at it'. As for the Communist Party of Malaya, it too attempted to seize power. The first time was after the collapse of the Japanese Occupation authority during World War II and before the British could re-establish their governance in the Malay Peninsula. This attempt was unsuccessful. But according to Rajaratnam, Malayan Communists tried again during the struggle for independence, when Communists sought to join with non-Communists in the hope of achieving dominance as Malaya eventually acquired its independence. This also however 'did not happen'. As for Singapore, there as well Communists tried to forge a united front tactic with non-Communists, in the same hope that they would 'inherit' an independent state, but 'this time too they failed', as Rajaratnam put it.[1]

Singapore's foreign minister regarded it as 'ironic' that 'the domino theory, once upheld by the Americans and repudiated by the Communists is now being embraced by the Communists'. As evidence he asserted that Samad Ismail (the former managing editor of Kuala Lumpur's *New Straits Times*, arrested on 22 June 1976 and currently

being held on charges of pro-Communist activity) had assured
Hussein Dahidin (detained on 16 June 1976 and former editor of the
Singapore daily *Berita Harian*) that after Indochina, 'Thailand would
be the next domino to fall, followed by Malaysia and Singapore'.
Rajaratnam declared that Communist irresistibility and invincibility
was a 'myth', but that even so acceptance of the Communist 'threat'
was 'realistic'. In turn, he argued that once the Communists in
South-east Asia became aware of the 'invincible power' of the non-
Communists, the Communists themselves would cease being a
threat, becoming instead 'at worst a nuisance'.[2]

Pace Rajaratnam, there remains the reality that with the turn of
events in Indochina much of South-east Asia is now Communist.
Moreover, even with 'peaceful coexistence' in the air at the moment,
and with official Communist visitors and delegations becoming a
frequent sight in non-Communist South-east Asian capitals, the
effects of the Indochina conquest are making themselves felt in the
region in deeply tragic, human terms. By the end of November 1978,
the United Nations' High Commissioner for Refugees estimated that
since the end of the Vietnam war in 1975, some 75 000 people had
escaped in all manner of vessels from Indochina, mostly Vietnam,
and sometimes after incredible hardships had landed in Thailand,
Malaysia, Singapore, Indonesia and the Philippines.[3] By that time
some 22 000 Vietnamese 'boat people' refugees faced a gloomy future
in temporary camps on Malaysia's Pulau Bidong Island alone, their
miserable plight rapidly becoming an international scandal. In May
1978, the US Central Intelligence Agency reported that since the
Communists acquired power throughout Indochina in 1975, an
estimated 160 000 refugees from the latter area have streamed into
Thailand.[4] Although about 50 000 of this group were subsequently
resettled in third countries, the remainder (comprising some 82 000
Laotians, 14 000 Cambodians and nearly 4 000 Vietnamese) are still
in Thai camps. While stricter and more selective entry requirements
have been imposed by the Thai government since November 1977,
the refugee flow, overtly and covertly, continues.

To be sure, among the refugees are those motivated less by
concerns of political repression and more by the desire to improve
their living conditions in Thailand. But whatever the Communisation
process in Indochina may mean, tens of thousands evidently want no
part of it. One physician who has worked in the Indochinese refugee
camps in Thailand has offered a vignette of their condition not likely
to be lost on others living in the region:[5]

The horror and misery of their flight to safety is etched in their blank, tear stained faces. Men and women weep readily at the nightmarish memory of their ordeal. Husbands, wives, children, parents have been lost in the process. Gone is the familiar look of initial elation found among newcomers. One is ready to assume that they know very little of the difference between Communism and freedom. Their main concern is to escape oppression and annihilation of their tribes.

Communist writers, with justification, have been quick to point out that many of those currently so concerned with the fate of 'boat people' and other refugees from Indochina had precious little to say as the US war machine left devastation in its wake in the rice fields and villages of Vietnam and Cambodia a few years earlier. Just so. But the point is that as each day or each week has brought another harrowing tale of refugee escape, the determined domestic anti-Communist policy posture of the governments in the rest of South-east Asia is easily reinforced in the popular mind.

Not that the refugees as such automatically arouse widespread sympathy. Ethnic hostilities between host population and some refugees are abundantly evident. Yet, not least because of the psychological effects of the refugee stream, the suspicions and hostility between Communist and non-Communist South-east Asia are likely to remain strong even as official gestures of rapprochement continue to be made. And it is the force of such suspicion and hostility that also is likely to structure the role of local Communist movements and their future relationship with Communist governments in and near the region. The dynamics of this problem do not always appear to be understood. For example, while chiding the pundits on South-east Asia who only a few years ago were predicting dire consequences from a Communist victory in Vietnam, the US under secretary of state for political affairs, David Newsom, recently noted that, on the contrary, 'the dominoes which were to have fallen in South-east Asia, in fact did not fall', adding on the basis of this observation that 'there is much to suggest that the carrying of the revolution to the states of South-east Asia beyond Indochina was not a priority objective in Hanoi'.[6] To admit that indeed this was not a priority objective of Hanoi's not only does not alter, say, Hanoi's historic aid to the Thai Communists, but more importantly, it probably also misreads the significance of the ongoing bifurcation of South-east Asia today between Communist and non-Communist segments and of the problem of their interaction, for example, the SRV's quicksilver posture toward ASEAN. Neither a solution to the problem of the human misery caused by the aftermath of the Communist ascendancy in Indochina, nor to the question of defining the relationship between the two segments of South-east Asia today seems greatly advanced by talking of the unsuitability of the domino theory at the moment.

Other recent analyses perhaps came closer to the mark. One perceptive Filipino writer, for example, sees South-east Asia as passing through a 'two tier confrontation-consolidation phase' in the near future.[7] The first or upper tier of this phase is likely to be a time-consuming process, as 'revolutionary and traditional passions' will first have to 'subside' in the SRV, Laos and Cambodia, even as the USSR and People's China meanwhile 'jockey for political leverage'. At the second or lower tier of this confrontation and consolidation process, is ASEAN, at present, according to this analysis, 'far ahead' in terms of its own political stability. Only an upsurge of Communist guerrilla activity in such countries as the Philippines, Indonesia or Malaysia, or the acquisition of considerably increased power by the Thai Communist insurgents now 'can derail ASEAN'. This, one might comment, seems unduly optimistic, but the surprising picture presented by South-east Asia at the beginning of 1979 is, on the one hand, 'a settling down' for purposes of increased economic and other co-operation among the non-Communist countries of the area, even as their domestic insurgent problem is under control, while, on the other hand, there is a 'fierce scramble for power' among the Communist powers within the region.[8]

One hastens to add that the 'two tier' development process in South-east Asia of course should not be taken to mean that the two tiers do not influence each other – for instance, that the power struggle in the Communist orbit will necessarily leave the ASEAN area unaffected, on the contrary. There is a certain sense of bewildered reluctance in official circles from Bangkok to Manila as Communist emissaries come and go to woo and entice support for the respective sides in the Moscow-Beijing power play. One Bangkok editorial in November 1978 summed up the prevailing mood:[9]

Just as [Thai] Prime Minister Kriangsak Chamanan was discussing Southeast Asian affairs with Chinese Senior Vice Premier Teng Hsiao-ping yesterday, the New China News Agency in

Peking lashed out at the Soviet-Vietnam treaty of friendship, accusing Hanoi of staging a bloody border incident to coincide with the visit of Vietnamese leaders to Moscow. At the same time Chinese Communist Party Vice Chairman Wang Tung-hsing, now in Phnom Penh, has pledged full support for Cambodia against Vietnamese 'aggression'. To top it all Soviet Ambassador to Malaysia Boris T. Kulik voiced at the same time in Kuala Lumpur Soviet support for ASEAN.

Each one of these incidents taken by itself is extremely important to Thailand and to Southeast Asia but all of them taken together the significance only boggles the mind. It appears as if there is a new ballgame going on in Southeast Asia and naturally Thailand is in the middle of it. We had wishfully thought that we will not be drawn into the Sino-Soviet dispute but have we been willy nilly drawn into it?

The ASEAN or non-Communist 'tier' can only feel uneasy as the conflict of Communist powers in the 'upper tier' of the region develops further. One critical point of the interaction between the two tiers will be the future of Cambodia. As it became evident by early 1978 that Hanoi intended to maintain military and political pressure until a Phnom Penh regime more to its liking would be established, both Peking and the ASEAN powers were affected. It has come to be anticipated that a change of government in Cambodia and the ascendancy of Vietnamese influence there would provoke a new intra-Communist power struggle in the country as the adherents of the Beijing-supported Khieu Sampan-Pol Pot regime would begin resorting to guerrilla resistance. Already toward the close of 1978, People's China was reportedly preparing for an 'inevitable' collapse of the Pol Pot government and a continuation of the fight against an SRV-installed regime in Phnom Penh. Beijing's anticipated counter-move would also involve a strengthening of its hand in Laos, either by encouraging a pro-Chinese faction in Vientiane or by consolidating its long-time influence in northern Laos where Chinese road construction has been a historic conduit.[10] Though in a White Paper on Kampuchea published in April 1978, the SRV government declared that in 1954 it had given up the original notion of the Indochina Communist Party to form an 'Indochinese Federation' (composed of Vietnam, Laos and Cambodia), Hanoi currently advocates what is called a 'confederated approach' among the three Indochina governments. The concept of such a 'confederation' suggests a somewhat less strict form of unity. But it may well be considered by the Vietnamese merely as a phase toward ultimate complete federation in the manner envisaged by the early Indochinese Communists in 1930.[11]

Whatever the formalities of its merger arrangement, a unified Communist Indochina, allied with Moscow, would have seriously disquieting security implications, not only for China; such a unified state would be the military colossus of South-east Asia as well. Particularly Indonesia, geographically the region's largest state, has been concerned to find and preserve a balance to the SRV's already significant regional military power. A Cambodia free from Hanoi's influence and acting as a potential diplomatic counterweight is therefore important to Indonesia's strategic concerns.[12]

The Cambodian question also interacts with Djakarta's reluctance to normalise its relations with Beijing. Rightly or wrongly, the Suharto regime by the beginning of 1979 still did not feel ready for such normalisation. Keeping People's China diplomatically at arms' length while at the same time strategically acknowledging the desirability of its presence in Kampuchea, or alternatively and if it were to come to that, in Laos, is as much a part of Djakarta's balance of power considerations as a desired residual US military presence on Philippine bases. But a Hanoi-oriented Kampuchea, let alone an Indochinese 'confederate' arrangement, would probably impel the kind of Sino-Indonesian rapprochement which Djakarta thus far has been anxious to avoid. Such a rapprochement might well become the South Asian pendant of the informal Beijing-Tokyo-Washington alliance in North Asia that some observers already saw in the making at the close of 1978. In relation to this, moreover, the Soviet-SRV Friendship Treaty offers part of a new confrontational context that ASEAN leaders, perhaps vainly, hope will not further develop in their region.

Yet, as such an alignment of forces develops, the Communist parties and factions in South-east Asia now less than flourishing would become the important ganglia of the intra-regional power struggle. They would thus acquire a new significance as developments in the 'two tiers' increasingly interlock. The Communist parties in South-east Asia would thus seem to have a stake in the Moscow-Beijing 'proxy' conflict. One might speculate that in the long run an important impulse in the resurgence of South-east Asian Communism would come from the hardening of the national alignments led by Moscow and Beijing.

For ASEAN and Burma such a prospect is not a pleasant one. It is therefore noteworthy that at no time in the recent past have the ASEAN states so loudly sung the virtues of 'non-alignment' (despite their respective individual military ententes with the US, the Commonwealth or even with each other) as at the time that the 'new ballgame' in South-east Asia, to use the phrase of the above-cited Bangkok editorial, has been attempting to enlist various regional players. As one news commentary over Kuala Lumpur radio put it:[13]

> Some political observers see the current visit of China's Teng Hsiao-ping to ASEAN countries as an attempt to counter the earlier visit of Vietnam's Pham Van Dong. While this may be so, the countries of ASEAN are very clear on their stand which is derived from their desire to see South-east Asia a zone of peace, freedom and neutrality. This means that while we will listen to both sides, neither side can expect any support from ASEAN. ASEAN in general and Malaysia in particular have made it very clear that peace in this region will not be the peace imposed by dominant power but rather a peace arrived at by mutual respect for each of the South-east Asian nations' right to existence.

Concern that instability in the 'upper tier' of South-east Asia will inexorably affect developments in the 'lower tier' has been evident in Indonesian foreign minister Mochtar Kusumaatmaja's reaction to the deepening SRV-Kampuchean crisis. The ASEAN countries are hoping, according to Kusumaatmaja, that the major powers will recognise that South-east Asian countries wish to concentrate their efforts on peaceful development, so that these major powers should not take any action that could aggravate the hostility between Cambodia and the SRV. It was perhaps particularly noteworthy that the Indonesian foreign minister linked this expression of hope to a statement expressing continued reluctance on Djakarta's part to normalise relations with Beijing in view of Deng Xiaoping's refusal to suspend China's connection with various Communist movements in South-east Asia.[14] As indicated, a Cambodia that has become an SRV (and Moscow-aligned) satrapy may well eventually accelerate the future new Indonesian rapprochement with Beijing. But until then, non-alignment Indonesian style will keep Djakarta apart from Beijing. As the pro-Suharto Djakarta daily *Suara Karya* put the official line: 'China will surely use diplomatic privileges to help openly or secretly the local Communist movement.'[15]

But is ASEAN, according to our Filipino analysis, really at present so far ahead in terms of 'internal stability' that only a resurgence of Communist guerrilla activity would 'derail' the association? Chances for a guerrilla 'derailment' of this kind seem relatively slim, to be sure. There is no doubt that, at the beginning of 1979 and viewed superficially, organised Communism in the non-Communist 'tier' of South-east Asia could not be considered a significant threat to domestic stabilities and/or principal development policies. In two countries of the non-Communist segment, Singapore and Indonesia, terrorist and/or insurgent activity is so limited and sporadic as to be negligible, and furtively moving, deeply underground cadres are confined to laborious united-front-building under strict surveillance that effectively boxes in any manifestation of permissible 'leftist' tendencies. In the Philippines, the minuscule Moscow faction of the party has made its own separate peace with the Marcos regime, while the Beijing wing of Philippine Communism, suffering from the loss of José Maria Sison's capture in November 1977, keeps up its scattered, continuous, but hardly decisive guerrilla confrontation.

In Malaysia the party is weakened by its division into three factions, and although the periodic terrorist attacks of the largest group, the parent CPM, are disruptive and intimidating, from the point of view of Malaysia's national development they can scarcely be considered lethal. In Thailand the CPT's developing cadre structure, logistical base, steady numerical growth and frequency of attacks have made it, to be sure, a serious danger to the kingdom's future stability. A genuine attempt at a Communist power seizure is as yet out of the question however, and the moderate Kriangsak government's efforts to win back disaffected youth have had a measure of success and are continuing. Still, while Thailand is not a 'tottering domino', and even allowing for official hyperbole, there is a persistent and even a gradually increasing level of CPT insurgent pressure through guerrilla and terrorist activity. In November 1978, for example, the Thai Internal Security Operations Command (ISOC) reported that the frequency of 'terrorist insurgency' during the past month had risen by almost half over the previous month alone. An insight into the slow haemorrhaging effect of the insurgency can be gleaned, perhaps, from an ISOC spokesman's analysis of government counter-guerrilla activity during the brief period from 13 October to 9 November 1978 alone. During that time, throughout Thailand, 22 insurgents were reported killed, 37 surrendered, 1 was wounded and 9 were arrested, while Thai security forces also 'destroyed 19 terrorist strongholds and seized a large number of arms and ammunition'. Clashes along the Thai-Cambodian border, despite high-level mediation discussions in previous weeks, were, according to ISOC, also said to be continuing.[16]

A monthly rate of a few score terrorists killed and captured and some 'strongholds' seized may seem to suggest the existence of but a minor security problem. Yet year after year, as in the cases of Malaysia and the Philippines, the same problem persists, ebbing and flowing in intensity with other changes in domestic stability, a drain on precious resources, a cause of rural coercion and intimidation, a focus for unassuaged urban political dissent. The two or three thousand Thai insurgents of the mid-sixties, have grown at present to a force four or perhaps even five times as large, aided now by Hanoi then by Beijing, sometimes by both at the same time, becoming a seemingly chronic disability of the Thai (as *mutatis mutandis* of the Malaysian or Filipino) body politic. Above all it is the persistent, Phoenix-like ability of South-east Asian Communism to rise again and again from disorganisation and defeat; its long haul staying power historically has proven perhaps the most remarkable characteristic about it.

Burma affords another example. In the middle of 1978 the fragile alliance of the BCP with the rebel Shan state army and other ethnic dissident groups was once again reported to be collapsing. Burmese security forces, meanwhile, buoyed by a seeming weakening of Chinese support for the BCP, were steadily on the offensive, pushing forward deeply as rarely before into insurgent territory. By early December 1978, however, the picture had changed again. The BCP guerrillas recovered from cadre losses, were making ready to recapture lost ground in the western Pegu Yoma region, and the Shan state insurgency generally was flaring up again, with the Communists seeking new allies among ethnic splinter groups.[17] The 'Voice of the People of Burma' claimed new victories for the 'people's army' as meanwhile the Burmese government announced an anti-rebel 'suppression campaign' near the Thai border (across from the Mao Sot district of Thailand's Tak province) not previously considered an insurgent-infested area.[18] And so it seems that no sustained government military offensive, no new suitably code named counter-insurgency 'operation', or yet another campaign, seems capable of finally and wholly crushing the Communist guerrilla movements or

the political party organisations within it. Communist guerrilla
activity in the lower South-east Asian 'tier' seems to have become an
endemic, multi-generational problem for which no one appears to
have a solution.

Moreover, and contrary to our earlier-cited Filipino 'tier' analysis,
it is probably not even the insurgency within their borders as such, the
'derailing' effects of which the non-Communist governments of
South-east Asia have cause to fear. It is, rather, what might be called
perhaps the aggravating effect of such insurgencies when considered
in relation to other, non-Communist, dynamics of dissent and opposition presently confronting the various authoritarian or quasi-
authoritarian regimes of the region. While the trappings of constitutional democracy and the rule of law are outwardly maintained,
nowhere in non-Communist South-east Asia are formal ground rules
of political opposition to, or public criticism of, prevailing regimes
securely founded or generally understood and accepted. Experimen-
tation with political formats still continues. Prevailing parliamentary
systems are not well equipped to handle the resentments and frustrations of younger, increasingly better educated electorates, or to
balance or channel the competing claims of ethnic or religious interest
groups. Functioning opposition parties, circumscribed in their operational freedom in varying degrees, exist to be sure, but usually offer
few prospects for the meaningful articulation of policy alternatives.
The role of the apolitical, conforming technocrat or specialist, quietly
allied with the ruling military or dominant government party élites,
seems to be the best that is open to the cautious, would-be reformer
who is unwilling to join the Marxists in the hills or jungles. For some
time to come, to play such a role and reap its benefits will be enough
for the burgeoning ranks of university graduates and the skilled. But,
inexorably, the philosophy of 'don't rock the boat because you'll
endanger our development policy' on which the Lee Kuan Yews and
Suhartos in South-east Asia have capitalised and which forms the
consensus political culture of the ruling élites, is likely to become less
and less credible if the inequalities in the benefits of various social and
economic policies emerge more sharply.

In all the whirl of international conferences that are being held in
Manila these days, and with multinationals opening their branches in
Makati, and 'New Society' favourites wheeling and dealing along
Roxas Boulevard, there remain Tondo and the nagging question if, in
the Philippines, after nearly a decade of Marcos martial law style

national development, 'Juan de la Cruz' is now any better off. For example, real wages of Filipino workers (1972 is 100) fell to 71.2 in 1976, and to an estimated 69.3 in 1977. In 1976 only about 26 000 tenants (a mere 6 per cent of the total number originally anticipated) had actually begun the payment of amortisation instalments to the Land Bank, ending their dependence on their landlords and marking the actual implementation of the basic land reform process undertaken by the Marcos regime.[19] In March 1978, their numbers, as reported to this author by various Filipino sources, had doubled – progress, to be sure, but still leaving a long way to go in solving the country's tenancy problem. The rural society's 'immiseration' has not been dramatically reversed in the Marcos era. To the Filipino peasant mass, throwing in one's lot with the scattered, currently seemingly leaderless NPA and its urban hothouse intellectual cadres, may not be much of a choice. But the deficiencies of the Marcos economic reform programme and its apparent confidence that sooner or later new wealth will trickle down to the bottom of society, are not therefore any the less demonstrable.

The Philippine case is, unfortunately, not an isolated one. Nowhere in the lower, non-Communist 'tier' of South-east Asia has the march toward tenancy, landownership concentration, landlessness of the rural population and proletarisation and the pervasive peasant indebtedness to landlord-creditors been notably reversed. Yet despite their extensive and often incisive analyses of the social consequences of these problems, Communist parties in South-east Asia, with the possible exception of the Aidit era in Indonesia in the early sixties, thus far have remained successful in very limited measure in harnessing peasant discontent. As often as not, initial peasant mobilisation today takes place outside party or party front auspices, though governments are quick to see the hand of Communist organisers in such peasant movements.

Thai Communists have never wanted for peasant supporters, but effective organisation of peasant discontent has not, thus far, been Thai Communism's forte. In 1974, Thai farmers in the central provinces, long restive over enforced land dispossessions and their exploitation by landlord-creditors, began a series of demonstrations, also in Bangkok, culminating in the formation of a militant Peasants' Federation of Thailand (PFT). Largely because of PFT pressures, caps were eventually placed on land rents, and emboldened by their success, the organisation in subsequent years has been winning significant followings among the hill tribe and minority groups of the north (e.g. in Chieng Mai province) and in the impoverished Isan (north-east). Since 1975, turning increasingly more active politically, PFT leaders have also denounced military rule, the ineptness of parliament, official corruption, as well as the continued exploitation of the peasantry by landlords. Violent clashes with police and with conservative political youth groups such as the 'Red Gaurs' also became more common. Prominent PFT leaders, like Intha Sribunruang, editor of the PFT's principal paper, were assassinated. When the conservative Thanin Kraivichien government came to power in October 1976, the PFT was proscribed. Shortly, along with many other opponents of Thanin, the remaining PFT leadership drifted into the orbit of the Communist Party of Thailand (CPT). The vast majority of the PFT rank and file today are almost certainly not Communist, but they and their leaders are still wary of the reform promises of, and amnesty offers made by, the present more moderate government of premier Kriangsak Chamanand. The relationship between the CPT and the TPF seems at best an uneasy marriage of convenience, whose possible future split is likely to depend on the extent to which new elections, party configurations and parliamentary processes can address themselves effectively to the problems of the growing members of landless peasants and agricultural labourers.[20]

Thus far, the root problems of the Thai farmer particularly but not exclusively in the north and north-east – the exploitative landlord-tenant relationship, with its exorbitant land rents and usurious credit transactions – have all thus far only been minimally addressed. This is not to say that Thai agriculture overall has declined in past decades. Expansion of cultivated areas and crop diversification in provinces east and west of the Central Plain had brought by 1978 a doubling of real farming income since 1960 for some 2.5 million farmers (about 10 per cent of the national total), according to a World Bank analysis. But in parts of the north, south and virtually all of the north-east, crop diversification and irrigation improvements have been retarded, and certainly for these major sections of Thai rural society prospects are bleak. Putting the poverty line at a household income of 500 Baht (about US$25) per month, one Thai government agency already in 1969 calculated that half the households in the south and north, and three-quarters of those in the north-east, were living in 'absolute poverty', and conditions are described as worsening since then: 'Recent visitors to the more remote areas of the Upper North and North-east have reported more frequent cases of subsistence farmers turning to scavenging and hunting in forests to supplement their declining rice yields.'[21]

The operational focus of the CPT precisely in the north and north-east of Thailand is hardly accidental: the rural poverty and politicised discontent in these long neglected regions continue to provide Thai Communism with some of its best potential recruiting grounds, although the party, as we have seen, is still far from properly utilising that potential. The CPT can continue to find followers in these areas, notwithstanding the fact that the Isan problem has been increasingly recognised during the past two decades in distant Bangkok as a possible threat to the existence of the Thai government itself. Already in 1961 the Thai government formulated a five-year development programme for the region, and in subsequent years, with the financial assistance of the US (equally alarmed about the Communist danger in Isan) still further schemes were drafted.[22] Yet the region remains a public administrative stepchild of the Thai government and it is not just the easy access for Communist infiltrators from Laos across the Mekong River which leaves Isan today as it was yesterday and likely will be tomorrow: a seriously disaffected periphery zone, eventually ready to be 'rolled up', as Communist parlance has it, in a concerted Communist move toward the parasitic 'primate city' of Bangkok.

Reference has been made above to subsistence farmers in northern and north-eastern Thailand resorting to a 'scavenger' existence in the forested areas adjacent to their fields. The 'scavenger' simile is appropriate to describe other life styles elsewhere in rural South-east Asia. More than two decades ago it was so used, for example, to denote the economy of landpoor farmers in Indonesia, tilling their own small, fragmented and often widely scattered plots, alternately with sharecropping, petty trade and wage labour, in a catch as catch can struggle for an income.[23] Population pressure and land shortages in Java have made such rural 'scavenger' economies common: already nearly thirty years ago one case study of Tjibodas village in west Java, for example, showed how the majority of villagers, including those holding insufficient amounts of land to live on, became sharecroppers of land held by others, or performed agricultural wage labour, or engaged in petty trade, usually on a commission basis.[24]

Accurate occupational statistics are difficult to obtain in many rural areas of Java because of the prevalence of the 'scavenger' economy, as some peasants, for example, in Djabres village, central Java, work on their own plots, but also labour on others' land for a wage or part of the crop, while occasionally earning extra income as well from labouring in a nearby small roof tile manufacturing plant.[25] Landlord and 'seigneurial' rights vis à vis landless labourers and tenants are well entrenched in rural Java, despite periodic ameliorative and anti-usury legislation and the undoubted growth of the peasant co-operative movement. Labour-saving devices at harvesting time are adding to the armies of the rural unemployed. The land shortage in Indonesia inexorably accelerates both the rural and urban proletarisation process:[26]

> The World Bank, for example, recently reported that landlessness had increased 'rapidly' in the 1970s, forcing increases in unemployment and underemployment levels. More and more rural people driven off farms are looking for work as laborers, turning to urban areas when it isn't available in the countryside. On Java some studies estimate as much as 75 percent, possibly 80 percent of the population is landless.

Meanwhile 'ecological deterioration' – the stripping of remaining wooded areas by land-hungry peasants who thus aggravate the already serious dangers of erosion and land depletion – proceeds apace, as, at the same time, government-assisted programmes to move Java's surplus population to less densely crowded regions in the Outer Islands have met with only indifferent success: 'So far more than 50 years of experimenting with various transmigration schemes have yielded meager results.'[27]

Java appears to be moving toward something of a proletarisation explosion. However, the political mechanisms of Suharto's *Orba* ('New Order') seem unlikely to be able to deal with it when and if it comes. As in the Philippines, the dazzle of modern corporate business structures, and the gloss of the capital city élite, for a while longer may obscure the misery of the mass. But even the most general formulations of a democratic left in Indonesia today would be suspect, leaving suggestions of any incisive structural economic reforms or socially meliorative programmes tainted with 'Communism'. Indonesia's two parliamentary opposition parties, the Muslim Unity Development

Party (*Partai Persatuan Pembangunan* – PPP) and the Christian confessional *cum* nationalist Democratic Indonesia Party (*Partai Demokrasi Indonesia* – PDI) can hardly be considered likely implementors of agrarian reform or workers' welfare programmes.

At least in Singapore, whatever the non-Communist left's strictures on Lee Kuan Yew's authoritarianism, the still nominally Socialist PAP measures its achievements at election time in the quantifiable tangibles of Marxist appeal: so many standpipes with running water built for the people, so many new apartment houses, or clinics, or community centres, and so on. Suharto's Golkar Government Party cannot match such techniques. On the contrary, even in its ASEAN environment the plight of the Indonesian worker attracts unfavourable attention. In July 1978, for example, Augus Sudono, chairman of the All Indonesia Trade Union Federation, noted that the average wages for Indonesian workers are the lowest in the ASEAN community. Some basic daily wages in east Java, for example, according to Sudono, are as low as 75 Rupiah (about US$0.18) and in north Sumatra 150 Rupiah (about US$0.32). In the Philippines, Sudono pointed out the average basic daily wage is 600 Rupiah (US$1.28) and in Malaysia and Singapore substantially higher still. Sudono complained that 'many employers', though alleging business reverses, actually had made significant profits but were exploiting their workers, as meanwhile labourers were still further gouged by so-called *pungli* or illegal levies demanded by corrupt military and civilian officials.[28]

If Sudono's assertions might be dismissed as coming from a partisan source, this would not be easy to do with the results of a survey of workers' wages and employment conditions conducted in March 1978 by the east Java provincial office of the Indonesian government's Directorate General of Manpower Care. The survey was conducted among 210 companies in the province comprising 15 different types of business. Nearly 37 000 workers responded to the survey's questionnaire. Among the principal findings were that 93 per cent of the workers in the 210 companies surveyed were not receiving enough in wages 'to restore energy, muscles and thought spent in their work', and that several companies still paid their workers as little as 100 Rupiah per day (about US$0.22), while the maximum pay was 800 Rupiah per day (US$1.76). The method used in the survey included calculations covering all minimum physical needs (KFM) of a worker per month, as well as the KFM needs of his children. The survey concluded that the KFM per day for an unmarried worker in 1977 was 464.64 Rupiah (about US$0.92). If this were used as the standard, then 93.74 per cent of all workers in the 210 companies surveyed by the Directorate General of Manpower Care received wages below the required KFM.[29]

Will ASEAN be 'derailed' because of intensified Communist insurgency? Or will it be because, notwithstanding the currently heavily accentuated Communist phobia in official public policies, the prevailing system of political economies simply is no longer going to be acceptable to an increasingly better educated and sophisticated younger electorate? Criticism that national economies have inadequate benefit delivery systems and faulty development priorities are becoming more frequent even as huge foreign credits and investments continue to pour in. Commenting in mid-1978 on the structure of Indonesia's industrial development, Permadi S. H., spokesman for the national Consumer Foundation in Indonesia (YLK), noted in his testimony before a parliamentary committee that luxury goods continued to be produced in quantity, while the populace, meanwhile, was doing without adequate supplies of basic necessities. Referring to official exhortations – made by Indonesian President Suharto on down – that some citizens should be less ostentatious in displaying their wealth and lead simpler lives, Permadi queried how such official admonitions could mean much 'if industries in Indonesia produce luxury automobiles, colour television sets and luxury mansions'. According to Permadi, the present industrial structure does not serve the needs of the majority of Indonesians, 80 per cent of whom have low incomes. Some 15 per cent have a medium income and only 5 per cent a high income, as he put it. Industrial development, Permadi urged, should be more geared to serving the interests of the low income 80 per cent of the population who continue to suffer from shortages of such basic commodities as rice, coconut oil and sugar, which must be imported. Indonesia, he said moreover, was becoming a 'waste basket' of foreign products which continue to be imported even though warnings or even bans against them exist in the countries where they are manufactured. Here he referred to some types of insecticides, saccharine and vetsin.[30]

The anomalies and imbalances of the Indonesian economy, despite its overall growth rate and foreign investor confidence, are, in the long run, likely to have a far more devastating effect on domestic political stability than the periodic discovery of an underground 'Communist' front movement or plot. Such anomalies and imbalances form much of the heart of the criticism of the Suharto regime by dissident Indonesian students, active in 1976–8, criticism which spokesmen for Suharto immediately conjoined in their rebuttals with the spectre of the 'latent Communist danger' in the country. After the chaos of the later Sukarno years in the early nineteen sixties the economic stabilisation and development achievements of the Suharto technocracy and its military-business allies have indeed been remarkable. But the rise of the new, foreign-connected business élite has gone on at the cost of miserably slow advances for the Indonesian mass. At the height of the anti-Suharto regime student agitation early in 1978, the Student Council of the prestigious Bandung Institute of Technology published a 'White Book' on the failures of the Suharto regime (literally the 'White Book on the Student Struggle, 1978' or *Buku Putih Perjuangan Mahasiswa 1978*). The 'White Book' lacks balance, often giving the impression here and there of having been put together in the heat of undergraduate sloganeering. But some of its general observations the government of South-east Asia's largest non-Communist state can only ignore at its peril. As the 'White Book' points out, for example, the 'parasitic' capital is absorbing much of the external investment that flows into the country. 'Seventy per cent of foreign capital is invested in the "city" of Djakarta. The other thirty per cent is spread out all over Indonesia. Where is the social justice in that?'[31]

The pattern of investment itself, according to the 'White Book', primarily appears to benefit so-called *tjukongs*, non-indigenous Indonesians, mainly Chinese, who finance leading Indonesian military and business figures. As the 'White Book' puts it:[32]

> The government proudly aggregates the incomes of tjukong with the incomes of the people of Krawang, Boyolali and Gunung Kidul [i.e. poor, food-deficit areas of Java] and then averages them. Next the government loudly proclaims that 'per capita income has skyrocketed.' Is this not manipulation? The people of Krawang, who have been reduced to eating water-hyacinths, have become the victims of a manipulation of the numbers that the government always worships. The people of Krawang have become the victims of statistics. It is said that in 1967 per capita income was US$80, while by 1977 it had increased to US$130. But the fact remains that Krawang, which always used to be a rich granary, where people

never suffered hunger, has today declined into famine area, where people are reduced to eating water-hyacinths. Do you know friends what water-hyacinths are? Water-hyacinths are feed for pigs.

The 'White Book's' charge that the government does not hear the complaints of 'the little people' is but a symptom of the gradually withering promise of the Suharto era.

Confident, however, that its foreign creditors are now financially too deeply committed to the regime's continuance to permit anything to jeopardise it, the Djakarta government also persists in counting on its resources in the international market that may well be dwindling. Indonesia's minister for research and technology B. J. Habibie declared in August 1978, for example, that at its current rate of oil consumption and production, Indonesia would cease to be an oil-exporting country in fourteen years. Domestic oil consumption alone had more than doubled (from 50 million bbl in 1972 to 101.6 million in 1977), Habibie said. Current Indonesian exports were running at 481.8 million bbl per year, mostly to the US and Japan. But if current production remained at about the same level (1.7 million bbl a day) and consumption by 1992 would rise to 686 million bbl, as seems likely, Indonesia would then have to become an oil importer.[33]

While new exploration and development of resources is going forward rapidly, the end or at least the serious diminution of the country's oil boom would undoubtedly adversely affect Djakarta's present international credit relationships. And this would come precisely at a time when the rural 'immiseration' process of the landless, the pressures of the educated unemployed in the cities, and the general lack of balance in industrial expansion would all make themselves even more severely felt. A revived PKI as such, or even an upsurge of insurgency as, for instance, along the Sarawak border or in the manner of Hutapea's shortlived 'People's Republic' at Blitar in early 1968, would not necessarily or automatically be the legacy of such a deterioration of the Indonesian social economy. But it would ring the death knell of the present quasi-authoritarian military-business-dominated political establishment, from the end of which a resurgent left and possibly an eventually relegitimised PKI would probably benefit.

Still another factor is likely to influence such a development. In the race between population growth and a more democratised economic development process, those now living in non-Communist South-east

Asia will not remain unaffected by the eventual accomplishments of the SRV and of the other Communist Indochinese states. In the measure that these achievements become materially tangible and even exemplary, for others in the region the credibility of the domestic anti-Communist posture which is now so much a part of current public policy in the ASEAN segment of the area will probably begin to erode. It could not be said, however, that by the beginning of 1979 the SRV seemed on the way to becoming a model of development for the non-Communist segment of the South-east Asian region at any time soon.

On the contrary. Desperately in need of foreign investments and credits, Hanoi had by its quarrel with People's China at the close of 1978 not only been cut off from Peking's aid, but had also jeopardised possibly important new Japanese and particularly US financial rapprochements. Its friendship treaty with Moscow had cost Hanoi a public expression of concern by President Carter. Over the last two decades Hanoi's 'Chinese connection' was worth between US$12 billion and US$18 billion in Chinese gifts and the new nadir in Sino-SRV relations following the departure of some 100 000 Chinese from Vietnam has cost Hanoi an estimated US$500 million in additional assistance.[34] Vietnam's unemployed currently number 7 million out of a total 22 million labour force, even as the Vietnamese press itself shows little optimism over the future state of the economy. Bad weather, including abnormal dry spells, inadequate efforts to improve soil quality, and above all poor management have had a sharply adverse effect on food production. During the first quarter of 1978 in the southern zone, the amount of rice delivered by the peasantry to the state was only 57 per cent of the comparable period the previous year. Fertiliser supplies are deficient and some 10 per cent of northern fields have been plagued by insects. Deputy premier Le Thanh Ngi, who supervises much of the SRV's economic planning, recently complained of disastrous irrigation failures. He noted that several new dams and a pumping station had collapsed shortly after construction. As for industrial production a recent authoritative analysis notes:[35]

The industrial worker is no more enthusiastic about output than his country cousin. Why should he be when Hanoi has complained that workers can produce 70% to 80% of their daily output norms in four to five hours? Management has established absurd piece

rates which allow a factory employee to earn as much from piece
work in 12 to 13 days as the enterprise guarantees him in regular
monthly wages. 'Negligence and inertia in organising managerial
work' is the sort of language used by the Vietnamese authorities to
sum up the position on the industrial front.

As plans continue to go forward to resettle the SRV population in
new areas of concentration of from 15 000 to 20 000, it is intended that
industrial centres will double in population to 20 million by the year
2000. Meanwhile the increasing SRV dependence on the USSR and
COMECON, the Soviet bloc's Council for Mutual Economic Assistance, may perhaps offset some of the aid losses from Chinese sources.
A number of COMECON members have already promised to take
over some of the aid projects abandoned by the Chinese, and over the
1976–80 period the USSR has agreed to provide Hanoi with some
$2.5 billion in aid. But such welcome impulses neither accord with the
desire of Hanoi's leaders for greater operational independence, especially in national development matters, nor do they necessarily
guarantee the SRV's eventual economic self-sufficiency which its
leaders have for so long espoused. At the close of 1978, Vietnam's
trade was running at an annual deficit estimated at $650 million and
available foreign exchange supplies were low.[36]
    What must obviously alarm the SRV's neighbours, even as Hanoi's
spokesmen visiting ASEAN capitals sing the praises of future regional
co-operation, is the Vietnamese penchant for an aggressive consolidation of their power throughout the Indochinese area, first, in 1975 and
in contravention of the earlier Paris accords by their conquest of
South Vietnam, and, ever since then, by their determination to turn
Cambodia into a Laos-like satrapy and so realise Ho Chi Minh's
dream of an Indochinese Federation. Hanoi radio's announcement
on 3 December 1978, of the establishment of an SRV-backed 'Kampuchean National United Front for National Salvation', intended as a
Vietnamese organisational vehicle for Cambodian dissidents to overthrow the Pol Pot-Khieu Sampan regime, called to mind Hanoi's
similar tactic in creating, in 1970, the 'United National Khmer Front'
as the instrument with which to rally Cambodian Communists
seeking to overthrow the Lon Nol government then holding Phnom
Penh.[37] Thus at a time of its own serious domestic economic disarray,
the SRV courts conflict with People's China, and all but mortgages its
foreseeable political future to the USSR, while engaging in a sus-

tained drive to topple a neighbouring Communist regime. These are moves with potentially serious and incalculable consequences for the region. Even to the more sanguine ASEAN analyst they hardly suggest a model for the rest of the region to follow, or even to become too friendly with. At the very time that Communist parties and factions in non-Communist South-east Asia are in disarray or lacking clear tactical directions, the nearest politically established Communist regimes are in deep conflict among themselves. The SRV-Cambodian conflict, moreover, by drawing the pattern of Sino-Soviet hostilities deeper into the region, tends to erode the charges of South-east Asian Communist spokesmen that South-east Asia remains a target of Western imperialism. As Indonesia's one-time foreign minister Adam Malik, some years ago, already sought to emphasise, ASEAN leaders have had no interest in transforming their association into a military pact because 'In this increasingly interdependent world, the presence of an alien military force whether directly or indirectly, would only invite the presence of another.'[38] A genuinely neutral South-east Asia would require not only, for example, the dismantling of US bases in the Philippines, but also a reconsideration of the SRV-Soviet Friendship Treaty and the withdrawal of Chinese advisers helping Pol Pot's regime in Cambodia.

Bleak though the immediate future of South-east Asian Communist parties is, there remain as valuable assets to these parties the serious domestic difficulties of the countries of the region, no less than the apparently secure base area of the 'Northern tier' of the region, now in Communist hands, namely, Indochina. Future success or failure of these parties, one may perhaps suggest, will depend on their utilisation of these potential advantages.

A bibliographical note:

Suggestions for further reading

Communism in South-east Asia suffers from a paucity of comprehensive studies. There are few recent volumes dealing with the Communist Parties of the region as a whole. Individual country studies are more numerous, but there are notable lacunae with respect to Burma and Thailand, while Indonesia and Vietnam enjoy a relative surfeit. Students of the subject are particularly dependent on press reports, on the Bulletins of the Foreign Broadcast Information Service (FBIS) published in Washington (particularly useful for party statements issued by clandestine Communist radio transmitters like the 'Voice of the Malayan Revolution') and on government reports and memoranda not always accessible to the general reader.

Though now somewhat dated, the trailblazing study of J. H. Brimmell, *Communism in Southeast Asia: A Political Analysis* (London: Oxford University Press, 1959), remains valuable, although its scope is sometimes too narrow to permit understanding of Communism's relationship to economic and social issues in individual countries or to regional security issues. An older, somewhat more superficial account is by Virginia Thompson and Richard Adloff, *The Left Wing in Southeast Asia* (New York: William Sloane Associates, 1950), which has, however, useful thumbnail biographical sketches of early important Communist leaders. Separate country analyses of varying value are assembled in the volume edited by Frank N. Trager, *Marxism in Southeast Asia: A Study of Four Countries* (Stanford: Stanford University Press, 1959). Important also for separate country treatments preceded by a survey of 'Communism in Asia' is the study edited by Robert A. Scalapino, *The Communist Revolution in Asia. Tactics, Goals and Achievements* (Englewood Cliffs, N.J.: Prentice Hall Inc., 2nd edition, 1969). A comparative approach is offered by A. Doak Barnett, *Communist Strategies in Asia: A Comparative Analysis of Governments and Parties* (New York: F. A. Praeger, 1963), which is particularly effective in attempting to assess the effects of the Communist victory in China on Asian Communist movements generally.

The background of Communism in **Thailand** is dealt with in the publication of the now defunct South-east Asia Treaty Organisation, entitled *The
Communist Threat to Thailand*, Short Paper no. 44 (Bangkok: SEATO, August
1967), which also has a brief chronological sketch of major developments in
the history of the Communist Party of Thailand. There is no single com-
prehensive book-length study of Thai Communism. The Royal Thai Govern-
ment's 'Communist Suppression Operations Command' (now called the
'Internal Security Operations Command') has published a report, *Communist
Insurgency in Thailand* (Bangkok: 1973) with versions both in Thai and
English. It particularly notes Vietnamese and other foreign influences on
Thai Communism. There is a historical and analytical background survey by
David Wilson, 'Thailand and Marxism', in the earlier-cited study edited by
Frank N. Trager, *Marxism in Southeast Asia: A Study of Four Countries*,
pp. 58–101. Chinese influence and national front strategies of Thai Com-
munism in the past decade are dealt with by Donald E. Weatherbee, *The
United Front in Thailand. A Documentary Analysis, Studies in International Affairs
no. 8* (Columbia, South Carolina: Institute of International Studies, University of South Carolina, 1970). On the relationship between the Thai Communist movement and constitutional and political changes in recent decades
see especially P. Fistie, 'Communisme et Indépendance Nationale: le Cas
Thailandais (1928–1968)', *Revue Française de Science Politique*, vol. 18 (1968),
pp. 685–714. On the Thai Communist Party's different areas of operation
and on the extent of Chinese and Communist Vietnamese influences in the
development of Thai Communism, see especially Robert F. Zimmerman,
'Insurgency in Thailand', *Problems of Communism*, May–June 1976,
pp. 19–22. For a Thai Communist view see 'Brief History of the Struggle of
the Communist Party of Thailand from 1942 to 1977', a statement broadcast
over the 'Voice of the People of Thailand' clandestine radio transmitter in
Thai, 9 December 1977 (English translation in *Foreign Broadcast Information
Service Bulletin*, 15 December 1977). For the relationship between Communism and recent Thai domestic political developments and problems see Justus
M. van der Kroef, 'Communism and Political Instability in Thailand', *Issues
and Studies*, September 1976, pp. 74–102.

Good synoptic treatments on Communism in **Burma** – among the few
available in Western languages – is the chapter by John S. Thomson,
'Marxism in Burma', in Frank N. Trager (ed.), *Marxism in Southeast Asia: A
Study of Four Countries*, pp. 14–31, and John H. Badgley, 'The Communist
Parties of Burma', in Robert A. Scalapino, *The Communist Revolution in Asia*,
pp. 309–28. On early Communist relations with Burmese nationalism see
also U Ba Maw, *Breakthrough in Burma: Memoirs of a Revolution, 1939–1946*
(New Haven: Yale University Press, 1968). On the origin and operations of
various Burmese dissident groups, some later allied with the Communists,
see chapter 20, 'Insurgent Groups', in Frank N. Trager, *Burma* (New Haven,
Connecticut; Human Relations Area Files, 1956), vol. 3. For the political
background of modern Burmese politics in relation to the rise of Communism

and Marxism consult particularly Hugh Tinker, *The Union of Burma, a Study of the First Years of Independence* (London, New York, Toronto: Oxford University Press, 1957), and John F. Cady, *A History of Modern Burma* (Ithaca, N.Y.: Cornell University Press, 1960). Changing Sino-Burmese relations are described by Frank N. Trager, 'Sino-Burmese Relations. The End of the Pauk Phaw Era', *Orbis*, Winter 1968, pp. 1034–54. For a Soviet view on Burma see, e.g., R. Ulyanovsky, 'Burma's New Path', *International Affairs* (Moscow), May 1972, pp. 17–22.

Vietnamese Communism, its history, organisation and tactics, have produced a veritable mountain of literature in recent years, and suggested readings admittedly become especially selective. In the present author's view the best single volume study is by Robert F. Turner, *Vietnamese Communism. Its Origins and Development* (Stanford, California: Hoover Institution Press, 1975). Highly recommended also is the volume by Douglas Pike, *History of Vietnamese Communism 1921–1976* (Hoover Institution Press, Stanford, California, 1978). John T. McAlister, *Vietnam. The Origins of Revolution* (Garden City, New York: Doubleday Anchor Books, 1971), is a penetrating socio-political analysis of the uses made by Vietnamese Communism of nationalist and political changes in Vietnam in the present century. Jean Lacouture, *Ho Chi Minh, a Political Biography* (New York: Random House, 1968), a skilful and judiciously sympathetic study, should be read in conjunction, for a balanced view, with the incisive and revealing account of Dennis J. Duncanson, 'Ho Chi Minh and the August Revolution of 1945 in Indochina', *The Lugano Review*, 1975, no. 5, pp. 1–23. Duncanson's *Government and Revolution in Vietnam* (Oxford: Oxford University Press, 1968) is recommended for a background understanding of the North Vietnamese strategy of conquest of the South. Well balanced, factual descriptions of North Vietnam prior to unification with the South are to be found in the chapter by Bernard Fall, 'North Vietnam's Constitution and Government', in Wesley Fishel (ed.), *Vietnam: Anatomy of a Conflict* (Itasca, Illinois: F. E. Peacock Publishers, 1968), and in the longer study edited by P. J. Honey, *North Vietnam Today: Profile of a Communist Satellite* (New York: F. A. Praeger, 1962). For a view sympathetic to Hanoi see the account of Wilfred G. Burchett, *North of the 17th Parallel* (Hanoi: 2nd edition, 1957, no publisher).

On the American involvement in Vietnam and on Vietnamese Communist attitudes especially as crystallised in the National Liberation Front, see Frances Fitzgerald, *Fire in the Lake. The Vietnamese and the Americans in Vietnam* (New York: Random House Vintage Books, 1972). Robert F. Turner, 'Myths of the Vietnam War. The Pentagon Papers Reconsidered', *Southeast Asian Perspectives*, September 1972, pp. 1–55, offers a provocative corrective to widely held misconceptions about the origins of the Vietnam war and of the Communist role in it. See also Allan E. Goodman, *The Lost Peace: America's Search for a Negotiable Settlement of the Vietnam War* (Stanford, Calif.: Hoover Institution Press, 1978). Current Vietnamese problems are analysed in Sheldon W. Simon, 'New Conflict in Indochina', *Problems of Communism*,

September–October 1978, pp. 20–36, and Carlyle A. Thayer, 'Dilemmas of Development in Vietnam', *Current History*, December 1978, pp. 221–5. For Vietnamese Communist objectives as seen by the Communists themselves consult especially Le Duan, *On the Socialist Revolution in Vietnam* (Hanoi: Foreign Languages Publishing House, 1965), 3 vols., and Ho Chi Minh, *Selected Works* (Hanoi: Foreign Languages Publishing House, 1960), 2 vols., and for Hanoi's view of the Cambodian conflict see 'Statement of the Government of the Socialist Republic of Vietnam on the Vietnam-Kampuchea Border Issue', *Vietnam Courier* (Hanoi), February 1978, pp. 3–4.

Analysis of Communist developments in **Laos** owes much to the work of Joseph J. Zasloff, in particular to his *The Pathet Lao. Leadership and Organisation. A Report Prepared for Defense Advance Research Projects Agency*, Rand Corporation, Santa Monica, California (Lexington, Massachusetts, Toronto and London: D.C. Heath and Company, 1973). See also Joseph J. Zasloff and Paul F. Langer, *North Vietnam and the Pathet Lao: Partners in the Struggle for Laos* (Cambridge, Massachusetts: Harvard University Press, 1970). A more popular, though informative, account insightful into some of the international dimensions of the Laotian problem and of the Communist role in it is the study by Arthur J. Dommen, *Conflict in Laos* (New York: F. A. Praeger, 1964). A description of the US role in the Laotian struggle, as well as useful background information on Communist strategy, can be found in Martin E. Goldstein, *American Policy Toward Laos* (Rutherford, Madison, and Teaneck, N.J.: Fairleigh Dickenson University Press, 1973). An authoritative Laotian Communist view is that of Kaysone Phomvihan, 'The Victory of Creative Marxism-Leninism in Laos', *World Marxist Review*, March 1977, p. 16, and for a Soviet analysis see M. Kapitsa, 'The Laotian Problem in International Relations', *Far Eastern Affairs* (Moscow), 1977, no. 2, pp. 44–56. On internal Laotian Communist leadership see Martin Stuart Fox, 'The Lao Revolution: Leadership and Policy Differences', *Australian Outlook*, August 1977, pp. 279–88.

The background of Communist penetration into **Cambodia** (Democratic Kampuchea) and its international consequences are dealt with in two studies by Michael Leifer, *Cambodia: The Search for Security* (New York: F. A. Praeger, 1967), and 'Rebellion or Subversion in Cambodia', *Current History*, February 1969, pp. 90–93. For a collection of essays with widely divergent views on the struggle for Cambodia see Jonathan S. Grant (ed.), *et al.*, *Cambodia, The Widening War in Indochina* (New York: Washington Square Press, 1971). See also Douglas Pike, 'Cambodia's War', *Southeast Asian Perspectives*, March 1971, pp. 1–47, and Peter A. Poole, *Cambodia's Quest for Survival* (New York: American-Asian Educational Exchange, 1969), on the efforts of Prince Sihanouk to keep his country on a neutral course. Sino-Cambodian relations are succinctly dealt with in Gao Gan (Kao Kan), 'L'Evolution des relations sino-cambodgiennes (1963–1970)', *France Asie* (Paris), 1974, no. 1, pp. 79–95. For developments in Cambodia since Communist ascendancy see

François Ponchaud, *Cambodia: Year Zero* (New York: Holt-Rinehart and Winston, 1977), Justus M. van der Kroef, 'Political Ideology in Democratic Kampuchea', *Orbis*, Winter 1978–9, pp. 1007–30, and the reports of the Yugoslav journalist Slavko Stanic, relayed over Belgrade's Tanjug news agency from 19 to 22 April 1978, and reprinted in English in the Bulletin of the Foreign Broadcast Information Service for 21 April 1978, pp. H1–H4, 24 April 1978, pp. H1–H4, and 27 April 1978, pp. H3–H4.

Indispensable for an understanding of the position of the Communist regime in Democratic Kampuchea since the time of the 1975 takeover and for the Communist Cambodians' own perception of their party history is the lengthy address by Cambodian Communist Party secretary and premier Pol Pot, at a 27 September 1977 'mass meeting' in Phnom Penh, relayed over Phnom Penh radio, domestic service, 28 September 1977 (reprinted in English in the Bulletin of the Foreign Broadcast Information Service, 4 October 1977, pp. H1–H37).

There is no up-to-date, full length treatment of Communism in the **Philippines**. The origins and early years of the Philippine party, also in its international context, have been dealt with in great detail by Renze L. Hoeksema, *Communism in the Philippines. A Historical and Analytical Study of Communism and the Communist Party in the Philippines and its Relations to Communist Movements Abroad* (unpublished Ph.D. Thesis, Harvard University, Cambridge, Massachusetts, 1956). Details on post-war party operations appear in two reports issued by the Committee on Un-Filipino Áctivities of the House of Representatives of the Republic of the Philippines, entitled *Communism in the Philippines* (Manila, 1952), and *Report on Red Threat* (Manila, 1957). On the question of the interrelationship of peasant discontent and the Philippine Communist Party see especially Benedict J. Kerkvliet, *The Huk Rebellion. A Study of Peasant Revolt in the Philippines* (Berkeley and Los Angeles: University of California Press, 1977). Two useful shorter studies are by Conrado S. Sabelino, *A Study of the Legal (or Parliamentary) Struggle of the Communist Movement in the Philippines* (unpublished M.A. Thesis, University of the Philippines, 1952), and Alfredo B. Saulo, *Communism in the Philippines. An Introduction* (Manila: Atenea Publications, 1969), the latter a journalistic but well written and popular account. On developments especially since the nineteen sixties and the influence of new 'united front' and Maoist insurgent tactics in Philippine Communism, see Eduardo Lachica, *Huk. Philippine Agrarian Society in Revolt* (Manila: Solidaridad Publishing House, Manila, 1971), and two articles by Justus M. van der Kroef, 'Communist Fronts in the Philippines', *Problems of Communism*, March–April 1965, pp. 65–75, and 'The Philippine Maoists', *Orbis*, Winter 1973, pp. 892–926.

An incisive analysis of rural social problems in the Philippines originally reported to be circulating in party circles in 1946 is the unsigned document 'The Peasant War in the Philippines. A Study of the Causes of Social Unrest in the Philippines – An Analysis of Philippine Political Economy', reprinted

in *Philippine Social Sciences and Humanities Review*, vol. 23, no. 2–4, 1958,
pp. 373–436. For an early Philippine Communist view on the party see
especially the unpublished account of one-time Philippine Communist Party
secretary general José Lava, *Milestones in the History of the CPP* (Manila?,
1950). For the views of the leader of the Communist Party of the Philippines
(Marxist-Leninist), i.e. the Maoist wing of the party, see particularly José M.
Sison, *Struggle for National Democracy* (Quezon City: Progressive Publications,
1967), and Sison's work published under the pseudonym Amado Guerrero,
Philippine Society and Revolution (Manila: Pulang Tala Publications, 1971). For
the position of the Moscow-oriented branch of the party, the *Partido Komunista
ng Pilipinas* or PKP, since the martial law era see 'Programme Adopted by the
Fifth Congress of the Partido Komunista ng Pilipinas on February 11, 1973',
Information Bulletin (Prague), 1973, no. 17–18, pp. 14–28, and Francisco
Balagtas, 'Trends of Change in the Philippines', *World Marxist Review*, July
1975, pp. 44–6. Anti-Marcos elements, some sympathetic to the struggle of
the Maoist 'New People's Army', have issued various documents from
outside the country. See, e.g., *Makibaka! Join Us in Struggle* (London: Black-
rose Press, 1978) containing unsigned chapters published by 'Friends of the
Philippines'. For a Marxist view see also William J. Pomeroy, 'The Philippines – Neo-Colonialism in Crisis', *Marxism Today* (London), February 1972,
pp. 54–61, and March 1972, pp. 72–80.

For the historical background and early evolution of Communism in
Malaysia see Gene Z. Hanrahan, *The Communist Struggle in Malaya* (Kuala
Lumpur: University of Malaya Press, 1971, with an introduction by Victor
Purcell and a postscript by Sir Robert Thompson); Victor Purcell, *Malaya:
Communist Menace in Malaya* (New York: F. A. Praeger, 1954). The best and
most comprehensive study of the Emergency period of post-war anti-
Communist struggle and British government policies is 'Anthony Short, *The
Communist Insurrection in Malaya, 1948–1960* (New York: Crane Russak,
1975). See also Lucian Pye, *Guerilla Communism in Malaya* (Princeton, N.J.:
Princeton University Press, 1956), Edgar O'Ballance, *Malaya: the Communist
Insurgent War, 1948–1960* (London: Faber and Faber, 1966), and for various
government reports also on the Communist Party of Malaya's operations
since the Emergency years consult *The Communist Threat to the Federation of
Malaya*, Malayan Government Legislative Council Paper no. 23 (Kuala
Lumpur: Government Printer, 1959), *The Path of Violence to Absolute Power*
(Kuala Lumpur: Government Printer, 1968), and *The Resurgence of Armed
Communism in West Malaysia* (Kuala Lumpur: Government Printer, 1971). A
useful brief survey taking more recent events into account is the publication of
the South-east Asia Treaty Organisation, *The Communist Movement in West
Malaysia and Singapore* (SEATO Short Paper no. 54, Bangkok, February
1972), and on the current split within west Malaysian Communism see
Chandran Jeshurun, 'The Security Situation in Peninsular Malaysia', in
K. S. Sandhu (ed.), *Southeast Asian Affairs 1975* (Singapore: Institute of

Southeast Asian Studies, FEP International Ltd., 1975), pp. 98–108. On Communist developments in **Sarawak** see the publication of the Government of Sarawak Information Service, *The Danger Within. A History of the Clandestine Communist Organisation in Sarawak* (Kuching, Sarawak: Government Printing Office, 1963), and Douglas Hyde, *The Roots of Guerilla Warfare* (London, Sydney, Toronto: The Bodley Head, 1968), pp. 59–128. For **Singapore** see especially Richard Clutterbuck, *Riot and Revolution in Singapore and Malaya, 1945–1963* (London: Faber and Faber, 1973), and Justus M. van der Kroef, *Communism in Malaysia and Singapore. A Contemporary Survey* (The Hague: Nijhoff Publishers, 1967). Leadership and front tactics are ably analysed in Li Ding Hui (Lee Ting Hui), *The Communist Organization in Singapore: Its Techniques of Manpower Mobilization and Management, 1948–66* (Singapore: Institute of Southeast Asian Studies, 1976). For the Singapore and Malayan governments' positions see in particular *The Communist Threat in Singapore*, Legislative Assembly Cmd 33 (Singapore: Government Printing Office, 1957), *Communism in the Nanyang University* (Kuala Lumpur: Government Printer, 1964), and Lee Kuan Yew, *The Battle for Merger* (Singapore: Government Printing Office, 1961).

There are many studies of **Indonesian** Communism. The early years are well covered in Ruth T. McVey, *The Rise of Indonesian Communism* (Ithaca, N.Y.: Cornell University Press, 1965), while further historical developments and tactical changes are considered in Arnold Brackman, *Indonesian Communism. A History* (New York: F. A. Praeger, 1963), Rex Mortimer, *Indonesian Communism Under Sukarno. Ideology and Politics, 1959–1965* (Ithaca, N.Y.: Cornell University Press, 1974), Justus M. van der Kroef, *The Communist Party of Indonesia. Its History, Program and Tactics* (Vancouver: University of British Columbia Press, 1965), Donald Hindley, *The Communist Party of Indonesia, 1951–1963* (Berkeley, California: University of California Press, 1964); Leslie Palmier, *Communists in Indonesia* (London: Weidenfeld and Nicolson, 1973), and Françoise Cayrac-Blanchard, *Le Parti Communiste Indonésien* (Paris: Armand Colin et Fondation Nationale des Sciences Politiques, 1973). On relations of the Indonesian Communist Party with Moscow and Peking see, in particular, Antonie C. A. Dake, *In the Spirit of the Red Banteng. Indonesian Communists between Moscow and Peking* (The Hague and Paris: Mouton Publishers, 1973), and David Mozingo, *Chinese Policy Toward Indonesia, 1949–1967* (Ithaca and London: Cornell University Press, 1976).

A definitive study on the 1965 coup attempt in Indonesia in which both Communists and military dissidents were involved remains to be written. For some of the literature on the subject see Jerome R. Bass, 'The PKI and the Attempted Coup', *Journal of Southeast Asian Studies*, March 1970, pp. 96–105, Donald Weatherbee, 'Interpretations of Gestapu, the 1965 Indonesian Coup', *World Affairs*, March 1970, pp. 305–17, and Justus M. van der Kroef, 'Origins of the 1965 Coup in Indonesia: Probabilities and Alternatives', *Journal of Southeast Asian Studies*, September 1972, pp. 277–98. See also the declassified study of the coup issued under the auspices of the US Central Intelligence Agency, *Indonesia – 1965. The Coup That Backfired* (Washington: December 1968), obtainable from the Photoduplication Service, US Library of Congress, Washington, D.C., and the provocatively critical account of Einar Schlereth and Batjo Daeng Bintang, *Indonesien: Analyse eines Massakers* (Frankfurt: März Verlag, 1970).

For PKI aims before the 1965 coup as perceived by the party leadership itself see, in particular, the 1963 report of party chairman D. N. Aidit, to the Seventh Central Committee of the PKI, published under the title *Set Afire the Banteng Spirit! Ever Forward, No Retreat* (Peking: Foreign Languages Press, 1964), as well as two other publications by D. N. Aidit, *A Short History of the Communist Party of Indonesia* (New Delhi: People's Publishing House, 1955), and *Indonesian Society and the Indonesian Revolution* (Djakarta: Jajasan 'Pembaruan', 1958). On the doctrinal and tactical splits between the two wings of the Indonesian party since the 1965 coup attempt see, as far as the Moscow-oriented faction is concerned, 'Urgent Tasks of the Communist Movement in Indonesia', *Information Bulletin* (Prague), 1969, no. 7 (143), pp. 23–42, and for the position of the PKI's pro-Chinese wing see *Build the PKI Along the Marxist-Leninist Line to Lead the People's Democratic Revolution in Indonesia. Five Important Documents of the Political Bureau of the CC PKI* (Tirana: published by the Delegation of the Central Committee of the PKI, 1971).

Relations between the USSR and South-east Asian Communist movements have been extensively explored in two studies by Charles B. McLane. One entitled *Soviet Strategies in Southeast Asia. An Exploration of Eastern Policy under Lenin and Stalin* (Princeton, N.J.: Princeton University Press, 1966), though comprehensive, occasionally fails to offer much insight into policy nuances of local parties. The other book is part of a larger study by McLane on Moscow's relations with the developing countries and is called *Soviet Third World Relations* (New York: Columbia University Press, 1974), vol. 2 (*Soviet Asian Relations*). Recommended also are two essays by Robert C. Horn, one entitled 'Moscow's Southeast Asian Offensive', *Asian Affairs* (New York), March–April 1975, pp. 217–40, the other 'Soviet Influence in Southeast Asia: Opportunities and Obstacles', *Asian Survey*, August 1975, pp. 656–64. For Soviet involvement in the Vietnam war see especially Donald S. Zagoria, *Vietnam Triangle: Moscow, Peking, Hanoi* (New York: Pegasus Publishers, 1967), and Allan W. Cameron, 'The Soviet Union and Vietnam: The Origins of Involvement', in Raymond Duncan (ed.), *Soviet Policy in Developing Countries* (Waltham, Massachusetts: Gin-Blaisdell, 1970). The significance attached to the Vietnam war from the Soviet point of view is analysed by M. Kapitsa, 'The War in Vietnam and Diplomatic Struggle', *Far Eastern Affairs* (Moscow), 1976, no. 4–1977, no. 1, pp. 18–36.

Soviet perceptions of South-east Asian developments have undergone sometimes significant changes in the past decade, passing from essentially negative and condemnatory assessments of local regimes to more optimistic prognoses. A useful compilation of Soviet scholarly analysis of the region, with chapters on individual South-east Asian countries written by specialists of the Oriental Studies Institute of the Soviet Academy of Sciences, is V. A. Zharov and V. A. Tyurin, *et al.*, *Southeast Asia. History, Economy, Policy* (Moscow: Progress Publishers, 1972). There are various periodically appearing Soviet comments on the state of affairs in individual countries of the region. For example, on early Soviet reaction to the 1965 coup in Indonesia and its aftermath see V. Viktorov, 'Indonesia's Hour of Trial', *International Affairs* (Moscow), December 1968, pp. 43–7. For a non-Soviet, scholarly assessment of Russian attitudes toward post-coup Indonesia consult also 'The Collapse of the Indonesian Communist Party: A Soviet Analysis', *Mizan* (London), March–April 1968, pp. 60–63, and 'Moscow, Jakarta and the PKI', *Mizan*, March–April 1969, pp. 105–18. On a somewhat more positive Soviet assessment of the Indonesian situation today see, e.g., A. Yuryev, 'Indonesia and her Problems', *International Affairs* (Moscow), November 1976, pp. 84–92, which also takes up the role of ASEAN (Association of Southeast Asian Nations). For another synoptic Soviet country view, equally optimistic, see, e.g., Alexander Kakaulin and Ivan Shchedrov, 'Thailand at the Crossroads', *New Times* (Moscow), June 1975, no. 25, pp. 20–22.

There is considerable speculation in Soviet media on the course of post-Vietnam war regional policies in South-east Asia. Soviet analyses of these regional political trends, as well as of their security implications include, e.g., Y. Yuriev, 'Southeast Asia Today', *Far Eastern Affairs* (Moscow), 1976, no. 4–1977, no. 1, pp. 37–44, and Y. Plekhanov, 'ASEAN: Trends of Political Development', *Far Eastern Affairs*, 1977, no. 3, esp. pp. 85–7. On Soviet views of current Chinese policies in the region see M. Kapasov, 'Peking Seeks Hegemony in Southeast Asia', *Far Eastern Affairs*, 1978, no. 4, pp. 29–42, Yuri Plekhanov, 'Peking's Double Game', *New Times*, May 1978, no. 22, pp. 23–5.

Like the USSR, People's China also appears to have altered her perception of South-east Asian developments, particularly since the end of the Vietnam war. For background analyses of People's China's policies toward South-east Asia, including local Communist parties, see Melvin Gurtov, *China and Southeast Asia – The Politics of Survival: A Study of Foreign Policy Interactions* (Lexington, Massachusetts: D. C. Heath, 1971), and Alain-Gérard Marsot, 'The Chinese Perspective', in Sudershan Chawla (ed.) *et al.*, *Southeast Asia Under the New Balance of Power* (New York, Washington, London: F. A. Praeger, 1974), pp. 51–79. See also Joseph Camilleri, *Southeast Asia in China's Foreign Policy* (Singapore: Institute of Southeast Asian Studies, 1975). On the question of the specific interaction between Peking and Communist insurgencies in South-east Asia see Jay Taylor, *China and Southeast Asia. Peking's Relations With Revolutionary Movements* (New York: F. A. Praeger, 1974), 'China's Policy of Revolt in Southeast Asia. Peking Radio Broadcast on 25 September, 1970', *Asia Pacific Record* (Singapore), January 1971, pp. 11–13, and Justus M. van der Kroef, 'Peking, Hanoi and Guerilla Insurgency in Southeast Asia', *Southeast Asian Perspectives*, September 1971, pp. 1–67.

On Chinese relations with some individual South-east Asian countries see, e.g., Shen-Yu Dai, 'Peking and Rangoon', *The China Quarterly*, January–March 1961, pp. 131–44, Ishwer C. Ohja, 'China and North Vietnam', *Current History*, January 1968, pp. 42–7, Gareth Porter, 'The Sino-Vietnamese Conflict in Southeast Asia', *Current History*, December 1978, pp. 193–6, 226. Lee Lai Duo (Lee Lai-to), *China's Changing Attitude Towards Singapore, 1965–1975*, Occasional Paper Series no. 22, Department of Political Science, University of Singapore (Singapore: November 1975), and John Wong, 'The Economic Basis of the Sino-Malaysian Detente', *Asia Research Bulletin*, 31 August 1974, p. 2915. On Beijing's new attitude toward non-Communist South-east Asia see, e.g., 'ASEAN-China. Now, the Southeast', *Asiaweek* (Hong Kong), 10 November 1978, pp. 32–6, Guat Hoon Khaw, *An Analysis of China's Attitudes towards ASEAN 1967–1976* (Singapore: Institute of Southeast Asian Studies, 1977). See also John Wong, 'Southeast Asia's Growing Trade Relations with Socialist Economies', *Asian Survey*, April 1977, pp. 330–44, which is also insightful for the region's economic relations with the Soviet bloc.

On People's China's own views on current South-east Asian problems see, e.g., 'Soviet Social-Imperialist Covet Southeast Asia: The Asian Collective Security System is a Pretext for Expansion', *Chinese Law and Government*, Spring–Summer 1976, pp. 141–5, 'Why Vietnamese Authorities Provoked Viet Nam-Kampuchea Border Conflict', *Peking Review*, 21 July 1978, pp. 5–8, 25, and 'Independence as Trumpeted by Moscow and Hanoi', *Peking Review*, 8 December 1978, pp. 22–4. On Beijing's relations with the Chinese in South-east Asia whose position has frequently been a source of political sensitivities see, e.g., Stephen Fitzgerald, *China and the Overseas Chinese: A Study of Peking's Changing Policy, 1949–1970* (Cambridge: Cambridge University Press, 1972), a comprehensive and informative study which, however, fails occasionally to give adequate weight to South-east Asian concerns over the extent of Overseas Chinese subversion and involvement in local South-east Asian Communist parties.

The Prague-published periodicals *World Marxist Review* and *Information Bulletin* frequently issue statements or articles by spokesmen for the Moscow-oriented factions of the Indonesian and Philippine Communist Parties. *Peking Review* and other Chinese media in most of the last decade have only rarely issued statements by parties or spokesmen for their respective factional groups in South-east Asia (they used to do so much more frequently), although the exploits, particularly of the Communist Party of Malaya, are regularly, if briefly, reported. Among the South-east Asian Communist parties themselves the English language periodical *Indonesian Tribune*, published in Tirana by Beijing-oriented Indonesian Communist exiles, is the best produced and ideologically the most informative. Occasionally it will also carry statements by the Chinese-oriented Communist Party of the Philippines (Marxist-Leninist) and the Communist Party of Malaya. *Ang Bayan* ('The Nation') and *Ang Komunista* ('The Communist') are irregularly appearing periodicals, including in English language editions, of the Beijing- and Moscow-oriented factions of Philippine Communism, respectively.

The student who wishes to keep up with day-to-day developments of the Communist movement in South-east Asia should regularly consult the Bulletins of the Foreign Broadcast Information Service (Washington, D.C.), issued almost daily. They are particularly useful for their extensive English language reproductions of statements and other party policy pronouncements broadcast over the clandestine radio transmitters of the underground Communist parties and factions in the region. They also provide translated local press reports on running clashes between Communist insurgents and government security forces, particularly in Thailand, the Philippines, and west Malaysia. The newsweeklies *Asiaweek* and *Far Eastern Economic Review*, both published in Hong Kong, also provide essential background material and periodic assessments of the strengths of ongoing insurgencies. Indispensable, finally, are the annual issues of the *Yearbook on International Communist Affairs* (Stanford, California: Hoover Institution Press, Stanford University), edited by Richard F. Staar and published every year since 1966. Each yearbook issue covers the most important domestic and international developments relating to Communism or Communist parties in countries around the world, including those in South-east Asia. The country articles are written by specialists in their fields, and each issue of the yearbook also carries a comprehensive bibliography of the most important publications relating to Communism in the countries and regions which have appeared in the preceding year.

Notes

Chapter 1

1. On these nationalist groups see, e.g., Gregorio F. Zaide, *History of the Filipino People* (Manila: The Modern Book Company, 3rd edition, 1964), p. 149; William R. Roff, *The Origins of Malay Nationalism* (New Haven and London: Yale University Press, 1967), pp. 56–90; D. M. G. Koch, *Om de Vrijheid. De Nationalistische Beweging in Indonessë* (Djakarta: Jajasan Pembangunan, 1950), pp. 19–29; William L. Holland (ed.), *Asian Nationalism and the West* (New York: Macmillan, 1953), pp. 33–4 (Introduction).

2. V. I. Lenin, *The National Liberation Movement in the East* (Moscow: Foreign Languages Publishing House, 1957), pp. 59–60.

3. *Ibid.*, pp. 61–2 ('Backward Europe and Advanced Asia', originally published in *Pravda*, 18 May 1913).

4. John P. Haithcox, *Communism and Nationalism in India. M. N. Roy and Comintern Policy 1920–1939* (Princeton, N.J.: Princeton University Press, 1971), p. 11.

5. *The Communist Conspiracy. Strategy and Tactics of World Communism. Part I Communism Outside the United States. Section C. The World Congresses of the Communist International* (Washington, D.C.: Government Printing Office, 1956), pp. 66–73. This is an extremely useful and comprehensive collection of Comintern documents. See also Jane Degras (ed.), *The Communist International, Documents 1919–1922* (London: Oxford University Press, 1956), vol. I, pp. 138–43.

6. J. Th. Petrus Blumberger, *De Communistische Beweging in Nederlandsch-Indië* (Haarlem: Tjeenk Willink, 2nd edition, 1935), p. 18. On the origins of the PKI see also Robert Aarsse, 'Sneevliet et le Début du Communisme en Indonésie', *France-Asie* (Paris), 1970, no. 3/4, pp. 267–82. For the 1924 PKI action programme see Ruth T. McVey, *The Comintern and the Rise of Indonesian Communism* (Ph.D. Thesis, Cornell University, Ithaca, N.Y., 1961), pp. 388–9, note 737.

7. Harry A. Poeze, *Tan Malaka. Strÿder voor Indonesie's Vrijheid. Levensloop van 1897 tot 1945* (The Hague: Martinus Nijhoff, 1976), p. 228.

8. 'Theses on the Eastern Question', in Degras (ed.), *The Communist International*, vol. I, pp. 382ff.

9. Petrus Blumberger, p. 34.

10. *The Communist Threat to Thailand* (Southeast Asia Treaty Organisation, Short Paper no. 44, Bangkok, 1967), p. 44, and Gene Z. Hanrahan, *The Communist Struggle in Malaya* (Kuala Lumpur: University of Malaya Press, 1971), pp. 29–32.

11. Radin Soenarno, 'Malay Nationalism, 1900–1945', *Journal of Southeast Asian History* (University of Singapore), March 1960, pp. 20–21.

12. Truong-Chinh, *President Ho Chi Minh, Beloved Leader of the Vietnamese People* (Hanoi: Foreign Languages Publishing House, 1966), pp. 14–15.

13. Chester A. Bain, *Vietnam. The Roots of Conflict* (Englewood Cliffs, N.J.: Prentice Hall, Spectrum paper edition, 1967), pp. 99–100; Robert F. Turner, *Vietnamese Communism. Its Origins and Development* (Stanford, Calif.: Hoover Institution Press, 1975), pp. 10–12; John T. McAlister, *Vietnam. The Origins of Revolution* (Garden City, New York: Doubleday Anchor Books, 1971), pp. 76–85.

14. In this paragraph I have drawn on the sources cited in note 13 above. See also Jean Lacouture, *Ho Chi Minh, A Political Biography* (New York: Random House, 1968), and Hoang Van Chi, *From Colonialism to Communism – A Case History of North Vietnam* (New York: F. A. Praeger, 1964).

15. Turner, *Vietnamese Communism*, p. 16.

16. Truong-Chinh, *President Ho Chi Minh*, p. 18. See also *Ho Chi Minh On Revolution. Selected Writings, 1920–1966* edited and with an introduction by Bernard B. Fall (New York: F. A. Praeger, 1967), p. 129.

17. 'Vietnam: A Historical Outline', *Vietnamese Studies* (Hanoi), 1966, no. 12, p. 40.

18. *International Press Correspondence* (Inprecorr), 9 August 1924, pp. 569–74; *The Communist Conspiracy* (see notes), p. 167.

19. Jane Degras (ed.), *The Communist International, Documents*, vol. II, p. 311.

20. J. V. Stalin, *Works* (Moscow: Foreign Languages Publishing House, 1954), vol. 7 (1925), p. 154.

21. B. Schrieke, 'The Causes and Effects of Communism on the West Coast of Sumatra', pp. 90–92 in his *Indonesian Sociological Studies. Selected Writings. Part One* (The Hague, Bandung: W. van Hoeve, 1955).

22. On the origins, course and aftermath of the coup see, e.g., Ruth T. McVey, *The Rise of Indonesian Communism* (Ithaca, N.Y.: Cornell University Press, 1965), pp. 290ff.; H. J. Benda and Ruth T. McVey (eds.), *The Communist Uprisings of 1926–1927 in Indonesia: Key Documents* (Southeast Asia Program, Cornell University, Ithaca, N.Y., 1960), esp. pp. 40–2; Jane Degras (ed.), *The Communist International, Documents*, vol. II, pp. 412–14, and J. Th. Petrus Blumberger, pp. 70–150.

23. D. N. Aidit, 'Lahirnja PKI dan Perkembangannja', p. 409, in his *Pilihan Tulisan* (Djakarta: Jajasan 'Pembaruan', 1959), vol. I.

24. Hanrahan, *The Communist Struggle in Malaya*, pp. 32–5. See also René

Onraet, *Singapore – A Police Background* (London: Dorothy Crisp, 1947), esp.
pp. 111–18. Richard L. Clutterbuck, *The Long, Long War. Counterinsurgency in
Malaya and Vietnam* (New York and Washington: F. A. Praeger, 1966), p. 15. I
have also relied on these sources in the following paragraph. The Communist
Party of Malaya in this period was usually referred to as the MCP (Malayan
Communist Party) but in these pages I have used the designation CPM for
reasons of consistency.

25. See in this connection esp. David R. Sturtevant, *Popular Uprisings in the
Philippines, 1840–1940* (Ithaca, London: Cornell University Press, 1976).

26. On the rise of Philippine Communism as described in this and the
following paragraphs I have drawn particularly on Renze L. Hoeksema,
*Communism in the Philippines. A Historical and Analytical Study of Communism and
the Communist Party in the Philippines and its Relations to Communist Movements
Abroad* (unpublished Ph.D. Thesis, Harvard University, Cambridge, Mass.,
1956), and on the unpublished ms. of the one-time Philippine Communist
Party secretary general José Lava, *Milestones in the History of the CPP* (Manila?,
1950).

27. Alfredo B. Saulo, *Communism in the Philippines. An Introduction* (Manila:
Ateneo Publications, 1969), pp. 9–22; Southeast Asia Treaty Organisation,
The Communist Movement in the Philippines (SEATO Short Paper no. 46;
Manila, 1970), pp. 2–3. I have also relied on these two sources in the
following paragraph.

28. Tim Ryan, 'The Revolutionary Upsurge in the Philippines', *International Press Correspondence* (Inprecorr), 12 March 1931, p. 272.

29. S. Carpio, 'First Congress of the Communist Party of the Philippines',
International Press Correspondence (Inprecorr), 25 June 1931, pp. 603–4.

30. José Lava, *Milestones in the History of the CPP*, p. 3; Saulo, *Communism in
the Philippines*, p. 24; Hoeksema, *Communism in the Philippines*, p. 95.

31. Hoeksema, *Communism in the Philippines*, pp. 100–124; SEATO, *The
Communist Movement in the Philippines*, pp. 5–6.

32. S. Carpio, 'The Situation in the Philippines and the Tasks of the
C.P.P.I.', *International Press Correspondence* (Inprecorr), 17 November 1932,
p. 1111.

33. 'Manifesto of the Communist Party of the Philippine Islands', *The
Communist*, vol. 14 (1935), no. 4 (April), pp. 366–80.

34. Royal Thai Government, Communist Suppression Operations Command (CSOC), *Communist Insurgency in Thailand* (Bangkok: English edition,
CSOC, 1973), p. 1.

35. In this paragraph I have drawn particularly on J. H. Brimmell,
Communism in Southeast Asia. A Political Analysis (London, New York, Toronto:
Oxford University Press, 1959), pp. 112–16.

36. Victor Purcell, *The Chinese in Southeast Asia* (London, New York,
Toronto: Oxford University Press, 1951), pp. 171–9.

37. In this and the following paragraph I have particularly relied on John

S. Thomson, 'Marxism in Burma', pp. 14–31 in Frank Trager (ed.), *Marxism in Southeast Asia* (Stanford, Calif.: Stanford University Press, 1959), and Virginia Thompson and Richard Adloff, *The Left Wing in Southeast Asia* (New York: William Sloane Associates, 1950), pp. 82–7.

38. On this period see also Thakin Nu, *Burma under the Japanese* (London, 1954); Maung Htin Aung, *A History of Burma* (New York: Columbia University Press, 1967), esp. pp. 298–303, and John F. Cady, *A History of Modern Burma* (Ithaca, N.Y.: Cornell University Press, 1960), pp. 478–84.

39. See esp. *Dimitroff – Working Class Unity – Bulwark Against Fascism* (New York: Workers Library Publishing Company, 1935), pp. 5–31, 38, 43, 46–71; also cited in *The Communist Conspiracy*, pp. 294–372.

40. Justus M. van der Kroef, *The Communist Party of Indonesia. Its History, Program and Tactics* (Vancouver: University of British Columbia Press, 1965), pp. 21–2, 25–9.

41. On the anti-Japanese underground in Indonesia during World War II see, e.g., B. R. O'G. Anderson, *Some Aspects of Indonesian Politics under the Japanese Occupation 1944–1945* (Ithaca, N.Y.: Cornell University Modern Indonesia Project, 1961), pp. 48–51.

42. 'Brief History of the Struggle of the Communist Party of Thailand from 1942 to 1977', broadcast over the Voice of the People of Thailand, clandestine in Thai to Thailand, 9 December 1977 (*Foreign Broadcast Information Service Bulletin*, hereafter *FBIS*, 15 December 1977).

43. Royal Thai Government, Communist Suppression Operations Command, *Communist Insurgency in Thailand*, p. 3.

44. On the CPT programme and publications in this period see Thompson and Adloff, *The Left Wing*, pp. 61–2.

45. Edward G. Lansdale, *In the Midst of War. An American's Mission to Southeast Asia* (New York, Evanston, San Francisco and London: Harper & Row), p. 7.

46. See, e.g., Major Robert T. Yap-Diangco (edited by V. G. Santiago), *Guerilla Tradition* (Manila: MCS Enterprises, 1971), pp. 78–83.

47. The evolution of Taruc's views can be traced in two books which bear his name as the author, respectively *Born of the People* (New York: International Publishers, 1953), and *He Who Rides the Tiger* (New York: F. A. Praeger, 1967).

48. Onofre D. Corpuz, *The Philippines* (Englewood Cliffs, N.J.: Prentice Hall, 1965), p. 110.

49. Lansdale, *In the Midst of War*, p. 7.

50. The question of PKP control over the Huks is notably discussed in Benedict J. Kerkvliet, *The Huk Rebellion. A Study of Peasant Revolt in the Philippines* (Berkeley and Los Angeles: University of California Press, 1977), pp. 96–104.

51. For the developments described in this and the preceding paragraphs I have relied, besides the works by Saulo, Hoeksema and José Lava previously

cited (see notes 26 and 27 *supra*), also on: Republic of the Philippines, House of Representatives Committee on Un-Filipino Activities, *Communism in the Philippines* (Manila, 1952), and the same Committee's *Report on Red Threat* (Manila, 1957); Conrado S. Sabelino, *A Study of the Legal (or Parliamentary) Struggle of the Communist Movement in the Philippines* (unpublished M.A. Thesis, University of the Philippines, 1952); Republic of the Philippines, Court of the First Instance of Manila, Branch V, *People of the Philippines versus José Lava, et al., May, 1951* (Manila, 1951); and José Crisol, 'Communist Propaganda in the Philippines', *Philippine Studies*, vol. I, no. 3–4, 1953, pp. 208–12.

52. This address is included in an unpublished collection of documents on Philippine Communism assembled by Gene Z. Hanrahan. I am grateful to Mr William Holland for giving me access to this collection.

53. From a PKP document issued in 1952 under the title 'The New Democracy' and included in the Hanrahan collection (note 52 above). For an analysis of the 'New Democracy' concept see Justus M. van der Kroef, 'The Communist Concept of "National Democracy"', *Studies on the Soviet Union*, vol. 4, 1964, no. 2, pp. 39–63.

54. See generally Fortunato L. Crisologo, *The Present Educational Practices of the Huks* (unpublished M.Ed. Thesis, University of the Philippines, 1953).

55. The PKP sharply analysed and attempted to relate itself to this historic Philippine tradition of peasant discontent. See the noteworthy unsigned document, originally circulated in 1946, 'The Peasant War in the Philippines. A Study of the Causes of Social Unrest in the Philippines – an Analysis of Philippine Political Economy', reprinted in *Philippine Social Sciences and Humanities Review*, vol. 23, 1958, no. 2–4, pp. 373–436.

56. Alvin H. Scaff, *The Philippine Answer to Communism* (Stanford, Calif.: Stanford University Press, 1955).

57. Victor Purcell, *Malaya: Communist or Free?* (Stanford, Calif.: Stanford University Press, 1954), p. 46.

58. Lucian W. Pye, *Guerrilla Communism in Malaya. Its Social and Political Meaning* (Princeton, N.J.: Princeton University Press, 1956), p. 67.

59. In this and the preceding paragraph I have relied, besides Hanrahan, *The Communist Struggle in Malaya*, pp. 61–86, and SEATO Short Paper no. 54, *The Communist Movement in West Malaysia and Singapore*, pp. 7–9, also on Harry Miller, *The Communist Menace in Malaya* (New York: F. A. Praeger, 1954) and F. Spencer Chapman, *The Jungle Is Neutral* (London: Chatto and Windus, 1952).

60. Cheah Boon Kheng, 'Some Aspects of the Interregnum in Malaya (14 August–3 September, 1945)', *Journal of Southeast Asian Studies*, March 1977, pp. 48–74.

61. Hanrahan, *The Communist Struggle in Malaya*, pp. 87–107; SEATO Short Paper no. 54, *The Communist Movement in West Malaysia and Singapore*, pp. 9–12; Purcell, *Malaya: Communist or Free?*, pp. 51–8.

62. Anthony Short, *The Communist Insurrection in Malaya, 1948–1960* (New

York: Crane Russak, 1975); *The Communist Threat to the Federation of Malaya* (Malayan Government Legislative Council Paper no. 23, Kuala Lumpur, 1959), and Edgar O'Ballance, *Malaya: The Communist Insurgent War, 1948–60* (London: Faber and Faber, 1966).

63. See W. G. Stefaniak, 'A Reconsideration of British Counter-Insurgency Methods', *Southeast Asian Spectrum*, October 1973, pp. 11–24, for an analysis of MNRLA tactics and British measures.

64. 'The Emergency' (Chapter 22), p. 398, and pp. 404–6 in Federation of Malaya, *Official Yearbook, 1962* (Kuala Lumpur: Government Press, 1962), vol. 2.

65. John S. Thomson, 'Marxism in Burma', pp. 31–4.

66. On the various dissident groups in Burma in this period see esp. chapter 20, 'Insurgent Groups', in Frank N. Trager, *Burma* (New Haven, Conn.: HRAF, 1956), vol. 3.

67. Hugh Tinker, *The Union of Burma. A Study of the First Years of Independence* (London, New York, Toronto: Oxford University Press, 1957), pp. 17–61ff.; John H. Badgley, 'The Communist Parties of Burma', in Robert A. Scalapino (ed.), *The Communist Revolution in Asia. Tactics, Goals and Achievements* (Englewood Cliffs, N.J.: Prentice Hall, 1969, 2nd. ed.), pp. 312–14, and Thomson, 'Marxism in Burma', pp. 37–45.

68. For the role of the PKI during the Indonesian Revolution see esp. Henri J. Alers, *Om een Rode of Groene Merdeka. 10 Jaren Binnenlandse Politiek Indonesië 1943–1953* (N. V. Uitgererij 'De Pelgrim', s. 1, 1956), pp. 64–8, 102–17, 170–96; Anthony Reid, 'Marxist Attitudes to Social Revolution, 1946–1948', *Review of Indonesian and Malayan Affairs*, January–June 1974, pp. 45–56, and the same author's *The Indonesian National Revolution, 1945–1950* (Melbourne: Longman, 1974); and George McT. Kahin, *Nationalism and Revolution in Indonesia* (Ithaca, N.Y.: Cornell University Press, 1952), esp. pp. 210–12, 231–2, 259–77.

69. D. N. Aidit, *Menggugat Peristiwa Madiun* (Djakarta: Jajasan 'Pembaruan', 1964), esp. pp. 17–42.

70. On the rise of the PKI under Aidit see particularly Donald Hindley, *The Communist Party of Indonesia, 1951–1963* (Berkeley, Calif.: University of California Press, 1964); Rex Mortimer, *Indonesian Communism under Sukarno. Ideology and Politics, 1959–1965* (Ithaca, N.Y.: Cornell University Press, 1974); Justus M. van der Kroef, *The Communist Party of Indochina* (Vancouver: University of British Columbia Press, 1965).

71. For a discussion of different views on the 1965 Indonesian coup see Justus M. van der Kroef, 'Origins of the 1965 Coup in Indonesia: Probabilities and Alternatives', *Journal of Southeast Asian Studies*, September 1972, pp. 277–305.

72. Masashi Nishihara, *The Japanese and Sukarno's Indonesia* (Honolulu: University Press of Hawaii, 1976), pp. 170–71. Two weeks before the coup the Thai and Malaysian press reported that the Chinese were supplying arms

to the Indonesian Communists, 'who are getting ready for a showdown with the armed forces', *Sabah Times* (Kota Kinabalu, Sabah, Malaysia), 14 September 1965; *Prachathipathai* (Bangkok), 12 September 1965.

73. On PKI activity in the aftermath of the 1965 coup see Justus M. van der Kroef, 'Indonesian Communism since the 1965 Coup', *Pacific Affairs*, Spring 1970, pp. 34–59.

74. Philippe Devillers, *Histoire du Viet-Nam de 1940 à 1952* (Paris: Editions du Seuil, 1952), p. 97; Frank Trager, 'Vietnam: The Origin and Development of Communism to 1966', *Pacific Community* (Melbourne), Summer 1970, pp. 34–5; Robert F. Turner, *Vietnamese Communism. Its Origin and Development*, pp. 18, 20, 29–74.

75. Hac Hai, 'First Year of the Democratic Republic of Vietnam', *Vietnamese Studies* (Hanoi), 1965, no. 7, p. 33.

76. The ICP instructions appear in *Breaking Our Chains. Documents of the Vietnamese Revolution of August, 1945* (Hanoi: Foreign Languages Publishing House, 1960), pp. 7–21.

77. Chester A. Bain, *Vietnam. The Roots of Conflict*, pp. 109, 111.

78. See in this connection esp. Dennis J. Duncanson, 'Ho-Chi-Minh and the August Revolution of 1945 in Indochina', *The Lugano Review*, 1975, no. 5, pp. 1–23.

79. *The United States and Vietnam, 1944–1947. A Staff Study Based on the Pentagon Papers, Committee on Foreign Relations, U.S. Senate, Study no. 2* (Washington, D.C.: US Government Printing Office, 1972), p. 19.

80. Vo Nguyen Giap, *People's War, People's Army* (Hanoi: Foreign Languages Publishing House, 1961), p. 48.

81. *Ibid.*

82. Hoang Quoc Viet, *Viet-Nam Fatherland Front and the Struggle for National Unity* (Hanoi: Foreign Languages Publishing House, 1956), p. 15; also Robert F. Turner, *Vietnamese Communism. Its Origin and Development*, p. 130.

83. Truong Chinh, 'The Resistance Will Win' (extracts), *Vietnamese Studies* (Hanoi), 1965, no. 7, p. 225.

84. Vo Nguyen Giap, 'The Liberation War in South Vietnam. Its Essential Characteristics', *Vietnamese Studies* (Hanoi), 1966, no. 8, pp. 15–27.

85. Frank N. Trager, 'Viet Nam: The Origin and Development of Communism to 1966', pp. 43–4.

86. Agence France Presse despatch, Hanoi, 18 January 1978 (Foreign Broadcast Information Service Bulletin, 19 January 1978).

87. Vo Nguyen Giap, *Dien Bien Phu* (revised edition, Hanoi: Foreign Languages Publishing House, 1964), p. 153.

88. US Department of State, *A Threat to the Peace. North Vietnam's Effort to Conquer South Vietnam* (Washington, D.C.: US Government Printing Office, 1961), part I, p. 1.

89. *Third National Congress of the Viet Nam Workers' Party Documents* (Hanoi: Foreign Languages Publishing House, s.1.), vol. 1, pp. 60–61; Hammond

Rolph, 'The Viet Cong: Politics at Gunpoint', *Communist Affairs*, July–August 1966, pp. 11–12 (offprint). See also Tran Cong Tuong and Pham Thanh Vinh, *The N.F.L. Symbol of Independence, Democracy and Peace in South Viet Nam* (Hanoi: Foreign Languages Publishing House, 1967).

90. 'Political Programme of the South Vietnam National Front for Liberation', *Viet Nam Courier* (Hanoi), 7 September 1967 (no. 127, Special Issue), pp. 4–5.

91. *Report of United Nations Fact Finding Mission to South Vietnam*. Published by the Subcommittee to Investigate the Administration of the Internal Security Act and other Internal Security Laws of the Committee on the Judiciary, US Senate (Washington, D.C.: US Government Printing Office, 1964); and Marguerite Higgins, 'Saigon Summary', *America*, 4 January 1964. In November 1977, the central Executive Council of the United Buddhist Church in Vietnam smuggled one of its leaders out of Vietnam in order to 'begin a worldwide campaign' against alleged religious persecution in Vietnam (*The New York Times*, 10 November 1977). The interest of US anti-Vietnam war leaders in this development was minimal.

92. *The New York Times*, 17 October 1971. See also, however, Geoffrey Warner, 'The United States and the Fall of Diem', *Australian Outlook* (Canberra), December 1974, pp. 245–59.

93. 'Aggression From the North: the Record of North Viet-Nam's Campaign to Conquer South Viet-Nam', *Department of State Bulletin* (Washington, D.C.), 22 March 1965, pp. 404–27.

94. For these numbers see Chester A. Bain, *Vietnam. The Roots of Conflict*, p. 137.

95. 'Agreement on Ending the War and Restoring Peace in Vietnam', article 5, in US Department of State, Office of Media Services, *Documentation on Viet-Nam Agreement*, News Release (Washington, D.C.), 24 January 1973, p. 34.

96. *The Nation* (Bangkok), 26 January 1973.

97. *The Thieu Régime Put To The Test, 1973–1975* (Hanoi: Foreign Languages Publishing House, 1975), p. 50.

98. Frank Snepp, *Decent Interval. An Insider's Account of Saigon's Indecent End told by the CIA's Chief Strategy Analyst in Vietnam* (New York: Random House, 1977), p. 93.

99. Vo Nguyen Giap and Van Tien Dung, 'A New Development of the Art of Leading a Revolutionary War', *Viet Nam Courier* (Hanoi), August 1975, p. 3. This article was originally published in the Hanoi papers *Nhan Dan* and *Quan Doi Nhan Dan*, 30 June and 1 July 1975.

100. Allan E. Goodman, 'South Vietnam: War Without End?' *Asian Survey*, January 1975, p. 71.

101. Snepp, *Decent Interval*, pp. 122–37.

102. *Amnesty International Report, 1977* (London: Amnesty International Publications, 1978), p. 227.

103. Robert D. Heinl, 'Armed Resistance Is Far From Over In Vietnam', *Sea Power* (Washington, D.C.), October 1977, p. 36. See also *The New York Times*, 28 January 1978.

104. David Rees, *Vietnam Since Liberation. Hanoi's Revolutionary Strategy*, Conflict Studies no. 89 (Institute for the Study of Conflict, London, November 1977), pp. 1–2.

105. William D. Hartley, reporting from Malaysia, in *The Wall Street Journal* (New York), 16 June 1975. See also *New Straits Times* (Kuala Lumpur), 16 December 1975.

106. Joseph J. Zasloff, *The Pathet Lao. Leadership and Organisation* (A Report Prepared for Defense Advance Research Projects Agency, Rand Corporation, Santa Monica, Calif., Lexington Books, D. C. Heath and Company, Lexington, Mass., Toronto, London, 1973), pp. 12–15. I have especially drawn on this source in the present and next paragraphs on Laos, as well as on Paul F. Langer and Joseph J. Zasloff, *North Vietnam and the Pathet Lao: Partners in the Struggle for Laos* (Cambridge, Mass.: Harvard University Press, 1970), and Arthur J. Dommen, *Conflict in Laos* (New York: F. A. Praeger, 1964).

107. Martin E. Goldstein, *American Policy Toward Laos* (Fairleigh Dickinson University Press, 1973), pp. 67–70, and Bernard Fall, 'The Pathet Lao. A "Liberation" Party', in Robert Scalapino (ed.), *The Communist Revolution in Asia. Tactics, Goals and Achievements* (Englewood Cliffs, N.J.: Prentice Hall, second edition, 1969), pp. 188–92.

108. Donald P. Whitaker, *et al.*, *Area Handbook for Laos* (Washington, D.C.: US Government Printing Office, 1972), esp. pp. 179–84.

109. Kaysone Phomvihan, 'The Victory of Creative Marxism-Leninism in Laos', *World Marxist Review* (Prague), March 1977, p. 16.

110. M. Kapitsa, 'The Laotian Problem in International Relations', *Far Eastern Affairs* (Moscow), 1977, no. 2, p. 55.

111. David Andelman, 'Laos After the Takeover', *The New York Times Magazine*, 24 October 1976, p. 54.

112. As reported in *Philippines Daily Express* (Manila), 25 June 1977.

113. *Asiaweek* (Hong Kong), 16 December 1977, p. 16.

114. Brimmell, *Communism in Southeast Asia*, pp. 295–6; 306–8; Donald P. Whitaker, *et al.*, *Area Handbook for the Khmer Republic (Cambodia)*, (Washington, D.C.: US Government Printing Office, 1973), pp. 38–9, and 175–8; 194, and Michael Leifer, *Cambodia: The Search for Security* (New York: F. A. Praeger, 1967). I have also drawn on these sources in the next few paragraphs on Cambodian developments.

115. Radio Phnom Penh, domestic service in Cambodian, 5 March 1968 (*FBIS*, 6 March 1968), and *Asian Almanac* (Johore Bahru), 18 January 1969, p. 3129.

116. 'No Holds Barred', *Far Eastern Economic Review*, 4 September 1969, p. 611; B. K. Tiwar: 'L'Etat C'est Moi', *Far Eastern Economic Review*, 28 November 1968, pp. 479–81; 'Chinese Aid for Cambodian Rebels', *The*

Australian (Sydney), 18 January 1969; W. A. C. Adie, 'Vagaries of Chinese Policy', *Mizan* (London), November–December 1967, pp. 234–5; Michael Leifer, 'Rebellion or Subversion in Cambodia', *Current History* (Norwalk, Conn.), February 1969, esp. pp. 90–93.

117. T. J. S. George, 'Charlie Khmer', *Far Eastern Economic Review*, 11 June 1970, p. 20; T. D. Allman, 'And Nowhere Else to Go', *Far Eastern Economic Review*, 5 February 1970, pp. 23–5; 'Sihanouk: Thorns Each Side', *Far Eastern Economic Review*, 15 January 1970, pp. 26–7.

118. Mark Gayn, 'Domino', *New York Times Magazine*, 22 April 1973, p. 44.

119. Douglas Pike, 'Cambodia's War', *Southeast Asian Perspectives* (New York), March 1971, p. 6.

120. J. L. S. Girling, 'Nixon's Algeria – Doctrine and Disengagement in Indo-China', *Pacific Affairs*, Winter 1971–72, p. 531.

121. B. K. Gordon and K. Young, 'Cambodia', *Asian Survey*, January 1971, pp. 30–33.

122. Donald P. Whitaker, *et al.*, *Area Handbook for the Khmer Republic (Cambodia)*, pp. 181–3.

123. *Cambodia: December, 1970.* A Staff Report Prepared for the Use of the Committee on Foreign Relations, U.S. Senate (Washington, D.C.: US Government Printing Office, 1970), p. 1.

124. See, e.g. *Réalités Cambodgiennes* (Phnom Penh), 3 December 1971, p. 8; *The Republic* (Ann Arbor, Mich.), December 1971, p. 3.

125. *Preuves* (Paris), April 1970, cited in Dennis J. Duncanson, 'Laos Emancipated', *Southeast Asian Perspectives*, March 1972, pp. 2–3.

126. 'Political Programme of National United Front of Kampuchea', *Peking Review*, 15 May 1970, pp. 7–11.

127. Peter A. Poole, 'Cambodia: The Cost of Survival', *Asian Survey*, February 1972, p. 150.

128. Radio Phnom Penh, domestic service in Cambodian, 28–9 September 1977 (*FBIS*, 29 September 1977).

129. François Ponchaud, *Cambodia: Year Zero* (New York: Holt, Rinehart, Winston, 1977); Karl D. Jackson, 'Cambodia 1977: Gone to Pot', *Asian Survey*, January 1978, pp. 76–90; John Barron and Anthony Paul, *Murder of a Gentle Land* (New York: Reader's Digest Press, 1977); *Asiaweek* (Hong Kong), 2 December 1977, pp. 32–43; *Wall Street Journal*, 22 May 1975.

130. Donald Wise, 'Cambodia: Eradicating the "Old Dandruff"', *Far Eastern Economic Review*, 23 September 1977, p. 33; also note 129 *supra*.

131. Radio Phnom Penh, domestic service in Cambodian, 26 January 1978 (*FBIS*, 27 January 1978); Radio Hanoi, international service in Thai, 24 January 1978 (*FBIS*, 27 January 1978).

132. Radio Bangkok, domestic service in Thai, 26 January 1978 (*FBIS*, 27 January 1978).

133. See, e.g., D. N. Aidit, *Sosialisme Indonesia dan Sjarat-Sjarat Pelak-*

sanaannja (Djakarta: Akademi Ilmu Sosial 'Aliarcham', 1962), esp. pp. 5–10.

134. Alex Josey, *Trade Unionism in Malaya* (Singapore: Donald Moore Publishers, second edition, 1958), p. 41.

135. Erich H. Jacoby, *Agrarian Unrest in Southeast Asia* (New York: Columbia University Press, 1949), p. 179.

136. Renze L. Hoeksema, *Communism in the Philippines*, p. 130.

137. Virginia Thompson and Richard Adloff, *The Left Wing in Southeast Asia*, p. 257.

138. Alfredo Saulo, *Communism in the Philippines*, pp. 7–9.

139. *AD-ART (Konstitusi) Partai Komunis Indonesia (PKI)* (Comité Central, Partai Komunis Indonesia, Djakarta, 1964), pp. 36–8. See also *Material for the Sixth National Congress of the Communist Party of Indonesia* (Agitation and Propaganda Department of the CC of the CPI, Djakarta, 1959), pp. 116–17.

140. 'Cambodia's Big Five', *Far Eastern Economic Review*, 21 October 1977, pp. 23–4.

141. 'Subversion in Schools', *The Sarawak Gazette* (Kuching), 31 October 1974, p. 222.

142. See in this connection esp. Douglas Hyde, *The Roots of Guerilla Warfare* (London, Sydney, Toronto: The Bodley Head, 1968), pp. 59–128.

Chapter 2

1. See, e.g., Lee Kuan Yew, *The Battle for Merger* (Singapore: Government Printing Office, 1961), p. 93 and *passim*.

2. Agence France Presse despatch, Singapore, 10 December 1976 (*Foreign Broadcast Information Service Bulletin*, hereafter *FBIS*, 14 December 1976).

3. Radio Djakarta, domestic service, 31 March 1966 (*FBIS*, 1 April 1966).

4. See, e.g., *Ketetapan – Ketctapan M.P.R.S. Hasil-Hasil Sidang Umom Ke-IV Tahun 1966* (Djakarta: C. V. Pantjuran Tudjuh, s.a.).

5. Agence France Presse despatch, Djakarta, 22 March 1978 (*FBIS*, 23 March 1978).

6. See Marcos' address to the nation on 23 September 1972, Radio Manila broadcast in English (*FBIS*, 25 September 1972).

7. *Amnesty International Report 1977* (London: Amnesty International Publications, 1977), p. 198; *ibid.*, 1975–76, p. 141; 'The Law of Preventive Detention in Malaya', *Journal of Contemporary Asia*, vol. 4, no. 3, 1974, pp. 375–80.

8. K. Das, 'Law Critics Cut Deep', *Far Eastern Economic Review*, 11 November 1977, p. 11.

9. Radio Singapore, domestic service, 16 and 18 December 1976 (*FBIS*, 20 and 22 December 1976).

10. For details see Justus M. van der Kroef, 'National Security Defense Strategy and Foreign Policy Perceptions in Indonesia', *Orbis*, Summer 1976, pp. 461–95.

11. See the articles by Catherine Lamour in *Le Soir* (Brussels), 27 and 30 December 1975 (reprinted in *Atlas World Press Review*, New York, April 1976, pp. 13–15), and Chris Mullin, 'Burma – An Enduring Struggle for Independence', *Far Eastern Economic Review*, 1 April 1974, p. 22.

12. *Economic and Political Developments in the Far East. Report by Senator Charles H. Percy to the Committee on Foreign Relations, U.S. Senate, On A Study Mission to the Far East* (Washington, D.C.: US Government Printing Office, 1973), p. 8.

13. Josef Silverstein, *Burma. Military Rule and the Politics of Stagnation* (Ithaca and London: Cornell University Press, 1977), pp. 26–30.

14. Edward Feit, *The Armed Bureaucrats. Military-Administrative Regimes and Political Development* (Boston: Houghton Mifflin, 1973), pp. 99–101.

15. Huang Ho, 'The Mystery that is Burma', *Sunday Nation* (Singapore), 6 July 1975; Feit, *The Armed Bureaucrats*, p. 102; Frank Trager, 'Burma, 1967 – A Better Ending than Beginning', *Asian Survey*, February 1968, pp. 110–11.

16. Editorial, 'Role of Intelligentsia', *The Guardian* (Rangoon), 29 June 1975.

17. On Burmese student opposition see Mya Maung, 'Burma's Surpluses of Rice and Rebels', *Pacific Community*, October 1972, pp. 130–48; William Mattern, 'Burma – Lining Up Against Ne Win', and M. C. Tun, 'Burma – Five Fiery Days of Student Unrest', both in *Far Eastern Economic Review*, 11 July 1975, pp. 27–8, and 27 June 1975, p. 20, respectively.

18. Klaus Fleischmann, 'Problems of Contemporary Burma', *Asia Quarterly*, 1973, no. 1, pp. 79–81; *Asia Research Bulletin*, 28 February 1974, pp. 2453–4.

19. *The New York Times*, 23 August 1976.

20. *The Working People's Daily* (Rangoon), 28 June 1975.

21. Frank N. Trager and William L. Scully, 'Burma in 1977: Cautious Changes and a Careful Watch', *Asian Survey*, February 1978, pp. 142–5.

22. Christian Müller in *Swiss Review of World Affairs*, November 1977, p. 12.

23. *Asiaweek* (Hong Kong), 10 June 1977, pp. 12–13, 10 February 1978, p. 33, and 17 April 1978, p. 17.

24. Editorial, *Botataung* (Rangoon), 10 May 1977, as relayed by Radio Rangoon, domestic service, 10 May 1977 (*FBIS*, 10 May 1977).

25. 'Voice of the People of Burma', clandestine in Burmese, 27 March 1977 (*FBIS*, 22 April 1977).

26. *The Communist Threat to Thailand* (SEATO Short Paper no. 44, Bangkok, August 1967), pp. 5–6.

27. The 1967 estimate is that of Peter Braestrup, 'How the Guerillas Came to Koh Noi', *New York Times Magazine*, 10 December 1967, p. 50.

28. Donald E. Weatherbee, *The United Front in Thailand. A Documentary Analysis* (University of South Carolina, Institute of International Studies, 1970), pp. 22–3.

29. On the opposition role of Thai students see esp. Ross Prizzia and Narong Sinsawasdi, 'Evolution of the Thai Student Movement 1940–1974', *Asia Quarterly*, 1975, no. 1, pp. 3–54.

30. 'Educational Development in Thailand, 1960–1970', *Education in Asia Bulletin of the UNESCO Regional Office for Education in Asia* (Bangkok), March 1972, pp. 189–98.

31. Patrice de Beer, 'Thailand's Chaotic Economy', *The Guardian*, 28 August 1977.

32. *Far Eastern Economic Review, 1972 Yearbook* (Hong Kong, 1971), pp. 322, 325.

33. Jeff Romm, *Urbanization in Thailand* (International Urbanization Survey, The Ford Foundation, s.l., 1972), p. 115.

34. *Economic Survey of Asia and the Far East, 1971* (Bangkok: United Nations, 1972), p. 60.

35. *Ibid.* Preceding data have also been cited in Justus M. van der Kroef, 'Thailand: Loosening the Linchpin', *Art International/The Lugano Review*, May 1974, pp. 66–74.

36. On Thanom's fall see Ruth-Inge Heinze, 'Ten Days in October – Students vs. the Military', *Asian Survey*, June 1974, pp. 491–508; Robert F. Zimmerman, 'Student Revolution in Thailand: the End of the Thai Bureaucratic Polity?' *Asian Survey*, June 1974, pp. 509–29; and van der Kroef, 'Thailand: Loosening the Linchpin'.

37. David Morell, 'Political Conflict in Thailand', *Asian Affairs* (New York), January–February 1976, pp. 151–84.

38. On political tensions in this period see, e.g., Kobkua Suwannathat-Pian, 'Thailand in 1976', pp. 239–63 in K. S. Sandhu (ed.), *Southeast Asian Affairs 1977* (Singapore: Institute of Southeast Asian Studies, 1977); Karl Erich Weber, 'Serendipity Missed. Report on the Parliamentary Elections in Thailand 1975', *Internationales Asienforum*, vol. 6 (1975), no. 3, pp. 302–22; Roger Kershaw, 'The Denial of Pluralist Democracy in Thailand: An Anatomy of the Crisis of August 1975', *Art International/The New Lugano Review*, January 1978, pp. 52–60.

39. On the 6 October 1976 events see, e.g., Thomas A. Marks, 'The Military and Politics in Thailand: An Analysis of Two October Coups (1976–1977)', *Issues and Studies*, January 1978, pp. 58–89; and Puey Ungphakorn, 'Violence and the Military Coup in Thailand', *Bulletin of Concerned Asian Scholars*, July-September 1977, pp. 4–12.

40. For the character and effect of the Thanin policies see Justus M. van der Kroef, 'Thailand: A New Phase in the Insurgency?' *Pacific Community* (Tokyo), July 1977, pp. 600–24.

41. *The Straits Times*, 22 October 1977.

42. *The Bangkok Post*, 10 March 1978 (*FBIS*, 10 March 1978).

43. *The Straits Times*, 25 August 1977.

44. *Keesing's Contemporary Archives*, 10 March 1978, p. 28861.

45. *Nation Review* (Bangkok), 27 January 1978, and *The Straits Times*, 20 January 1978.

46. Edward R. Kiunisala, 'Roots for Discontent', *Philippines Free Press* (Manila), 9 May 1970, p. 8, and Gracianus Ryes, 'Vision for Violence', *Solidarity* (Manila), April 1970, p. 5.

47. Frank H. Golay, 'Some Costs of Philippine Politics', *Asia* (New York), Autumn 1971, p. 46, and P. D. Hutcheon, 'Power in the Philippines: How Democratic is Asia's First Democracy?' *Journal of Asian and African Studies*, July–October 1971, pp. 207–16.

48. Justus M. van der Kroef, 'The Philippine Maoists', *Orbis*, Winter 1973, pp. 892–926. I have also drawn on this article for data in the previous and next two paragraphs.

49. Eduardo Lachica, *Huk: Philippine Agrarian Society in Revolt* (Manila: Solidaridad Publishing House, 1971), p. 180.

50. On the CPP(M-L) and NPA see esp. Southeast Asia Treaty Organisation, *The Communist Party of the Philippines*, SEATO Short Paper no. 52 (Bangkok, SEATO, 1971).

51. Cf. the PKP's 'internal bulletin', *Ang Komunista*, February 1971, p. 13.

52. *The Sunday Times* (Manila), 1 February 1970.

53. For details see Justus M. van der Kroef, 'Communism and Reform in the Philippines', *Pacific Affairs*, Spring 1973, pp. 37–8.

54. See, e.g., Report of an *Amnesty International Mission to the Republic of the Philippines, 22 November–5 December, 1975* (London: Amnesty International Publications, 1976) and Justus M. van der Kroef, 'Philippine Political Prisoners and the U.S.', *World Affairs* (Washington, D.C.), Spring 1978.

55. *The New York Times*, 26 September 1972.

56. *Asia Research Bulletin*, 31 January 1978, p. 406.

57. *Asiaweek*, 21 April 1978, pp. 22–7.

58. Brewster Grace, *The Politics of Income Distribution in the Philippines* (American Universities Field Staff Reports, Southeast Asia series, New York) vol. 25, no. 8, 1977, p. 3.

59. Cesar Vicata, 'Philippines: Rewards of Stability', *Insight* (Hong Kong), August 1975, pp. 25–42.

60. Data in this paragraph from: David Wurfel, 'Martial Law in the Philippines: the Methods of Regime Survival', *Pacific Affairs*, Spring 1977, pp. 7–8; *Far Eastern Economic Review*, 30 September 1977, pp. 15–16; *The New York Times*, 9 January 1978; and Dennis Shoesmith, 'Land Reform in the Philippines: Emancipating or Emaciating the Tenant Farmer', *Australian Outlook*, December 1974, pp. 280–1. Data in this and preceding two paragraphs are also cited in Justus M. van der Kroef, 'Philippine Communism: Recent Developments and Problems', *Issues and Studies*, March 1978, pp. 41–2.

61. *New York Times*, 14 and 15 January 1978; *Asiaweek* (Hong Kong), 3

February 1978, p. 35; 'Philippines "Rocked" by Westinghouse Scandal', *Asia Research Bulletin*, 28 February 1978, pp. 417–18.

62. *Asia Research Bulletin*, 28 February 1977, p. 297.

63. On the origins of the Moro problem see, e.g., Peter G. Gowing, *Mosque and Moro. A Study of Muslims in the Philippines* (Manila: Philippine Federation of Christian Churches, 1964); Aprodicio A. Laguian, 'The Political Integration of Muslim Filipinos', *Philippine Journal of Public Administration*, October 1969, esp. pp. 366–9; Mamintal A. Tamano, 'The Expectations of Muslims as Philippine Citizens', *Solidarity* (Manila), July–August 1975, pp. 32ff.

64. For details see van der Kroef, 'Philippine Communism: Recent Developments and Problems', pp. 47–8.

65. *Antara Daily News Bulletin*, 9 April 1978 (vol. 29, no. 202), p. 2.

66. J. Panglaykim and H. W. Arndt, *The Indonesian Economy: Facing A New Era?* (Rotterdam University Press, 1966), esp. p. 30.

67. T. K. Tan, 'Sukarnian Economics', p. 41 in T. K. Tan (ed.) *Sukarno's Guided Indonesia* (Brisbane and Melbourne: Jacaranda Press, 1967), p. 41.

68. See, e.g., Masashi Nishihaia, *Golkar and the Indonesian Elections of 1971* (Modern Indonesia Project, Cornell University, Ithaca, N.Y., 1972), and R. William Liddle, 'The 1977 Indonesian Election and New Order Legitimacy', in K. S. Sandhu (ed.), *Southeast Asian Affairs 1978* (Singapore: Institute of Southeast Asian Studies, 1978).

69. *Suara Karya* (Djakarta), 22 July 1976 (also in *Indonesian Current Affairs Translation Service Bulletin*, July 1976), and *Antara Daily News Bulletin*, 14 August 1976 (vol. 27, no. 738).

70. Justus M. van der Kroef, 'Indonesia's Political Prisoners', *Pacific Affairs*, Winter 1976–77, pp. 625–47, and *Indonesia. An Amnesty International Report* (London: Amnesty International Publications, 1977).

71. J. Stephen Hoadley, 'Indonesia's Annexation of East Timor: Political, Administrative and Development Initiatives', pp. 133–44, in K. S. Sandhu (ed.), *Southeast Asian Affairs 1977* (Singapore: Institute of Southeast Asian Studies, 1977), and *Decolonization in East Timor* (Department of Foreign Affairs, Republic of Indonesia, March 1977).

72. Ralph R. Premdas, 'Papua New Guinea in 1977: Elections and Relations with Indonesia', *Asian Survey*, January 1978, pp. 65–6.

73. Robert C. Rice and Hal Hill, 'Survey of Recent Developments', *Bulletin of Indonesian Economic Studies* (Canberra), July 1977, pp. 1–28; C. Manning, 'Survey of Recent Developments', *Bulletin of Indonesian Economic Studies*, November 1971, esp. p. 17.

74. *Quarterly Economic Review of Indonesia, Fourth Quarter, 1977* (London: The Economist Intelligence Unit), p. 5.

75. Sumitro's analysis in Antara despatch, Djakarta, 13 June 1976 (*FBIS*, 1 July 1976), and *Far Eastern Economic Review*, 3 December 1976, p. 29. See also Sumitro's analysis, published under the title 'Indonesia Toward the Year 2000' in *Ekonomi dan Kuangan Indonesia*, September 1975, and Willard Hanna,

Through A Glass Gloomily, American Universities Field Staff reports, vol. 24, 1976, no. 5, pp. 2–3.

76. 'Indonesia: In the Aftermath of Pertamina', *Insight* (Hong Kong), September 1976, p. 30.

77. For a perceptive analysis of the 15 January 1974 riots see, e.g., Peter Simms' account in *Asia Research Bulletin*, 31 January 1974, pp. 2351–6.

78. Far Eastern Economic Review, *Asia Yearbook 1978* (Hong Kong, 1978), pp. 300–05.

79. Chua Wee Meng, 'The Singapore Economy: Past Performance, Current Structure and Future Growth Prospects', pp. 220–29 in K. S. Sandhu (ed.), *Southeast Asian Affairs, 1977* (Singapore: Institute of Southeast Asian Studies, FEP International, 1977).

80. Far Eastern Economic Review, *Asia Yearbook 1978*, p. 298.

81. Editorial, 'The Threat Ebbs', *The Straits Times*, 24 September 1976.

82. See the articles on Singapore in the *Yearbook on International Communist Affairs* (Stanford, Calif.: Hoover Institution Press, 1975–76), 1975 and 1976; *Asia Research Bulletin*, Political Supplement, 31 December 1974, p. 38.

83. *Amnesty International Report 1977* (London: Amnesty International Publications, 1977), pp. 211–17.

84. John S. T. Yuah, 'Singapore: Towards a National Identity', pp. 207–19 in K. S. Sandhu (ed.), *Southeast Asian Affairs, 1977* (Singapore: Institute of Southeast Asian Studies, FEP International, 1977).

85. See in this connection Peter S. J. Chen, 'Elites and National Development in Singapore', *Southeast Asian Journal of Social Science* (Singapore), vol. 3, 1975, no. 1, pp. 17–21.

86. For the background of UMNO's policy perceptions see, e.g., James C. Scott, *Political Ideology in Malaysia: Reality and the Beliefs of an Elite* (New Haven: Yale University Press, 1968).

87. Lee Kuan Yew, *The Battle for a Malaysian Malaysia* (Singapore: Ministry of Culture, 1965).

88. For a succinct analysis of some of the dynamics of Malaysia's political parties see, e.g., Nena Vreeland, *et al.*, *Area Handbook for Malaysia* (Washington, D.C.: US Government Printing Office, 1977), pp. 229–54.

89. Justus M. van der Kroef, 'Communism and Chinese Communalism in Sarawak', *China Quarterly* (London), October–December 1964, pp. 38–66.

90. On the 1969 election and riot see Nancy L. Snider, 'Race, Leitmotiv of the Malaysian Election Drama', *Asian Survey*, December 1970, pp. 1070–80; and Felix V. Gagliano, *Communal Violence in Malaysia, 1969. The Political Aftermath* (Athens, Ohio: Ohio University, 1970).

91. For these post-riot developments also as described below in this paragraph see Vreeland, *et al.*, *Area Handbook for Malaysia*, pp. 234–6, and Marvin L. Rogers, 'Malaysia and Singapore: 1971 Developments', *Asian Survey*, February 1972, pp. 168–76.

92. See, e.g., Daniel Regan, 'Islam, Intellectuals and Civil Religion in

Malaysia', *Sociological Analysis*, Summer 1976, pp. 95–110. See also R. S. Milne, 'National Ideology and Nation Building in Malaysia', *Asian Survey*, July 1970, pp. 563–73.

93. R. S. Milne, 'The Politics of Malaysia's New Economic Policy', *Pacific Affairs*, Summer 1976, pp. 235–62; Far Eastern Economic Review, *Asia 1978 Yearbook*, p. 251.

94. Lim Yoon Lin, 'Malaysia: A Troubled Legacy', p. 152 in K. S. Sandhu (ed.), *Southeast Asian Affairs, 1977*.

95. Pran Chopra, 'The Malaysian Miracle and Dilemma', *The World Today*, May 1974, pp. 200–01.

96. Brewster Grace, 'The Politics of Income Distribution in Malaysia', *American Universities Field Staff Reports*, vol. 24 (1976), no. 9, pp. 4–5.

97. *Ibid.*, and 'Continuing Counter-Insurgency Measures in Malaysia', *Trends and Highlights* (SEATO, Bangkok), 1 January 1973, pp. 6–7.

98. J. P. Arlès, 'Ethnic and Socio-Economic Patterns in Malaysia', *International Labour Review*, December 1971, p. 544; Wolfgang Kasper, *Malaysia. A Study in Successful Economic Development* (Washington, D.C.: American Enterprise Institute for Public Policy Research, 1974), p. 37; Far Eastern Economic Review, *Asia 1978 Yearbook*, p. 249.

99. Lim Yoon Lin, 'Malaysia: A Troubled Legacy', p. 153.

100. Kasper, *Malaysia. A Study in Successful Economic Development*, p. 37.

101. Denzil Peiris, 'Angry Young Men of Southeast Asia', *The Times of India* (Bombay), 26 September 1975.

102. *Asiaweek* (Hong Kong), 28 April 1978, p. 14.

103. On the pros and cons of FELDA see, e.g., Vreeland, *Area Handbook for Malaysia*, pp. 155–6 and 309; and 'The Plight of Federal Land Development Settlers in Malaya', *Journal of Contemporary Asia*, vol. 3 (1973), no. 3, pp. 367–70.

104. Denzil Peiris, 'The Emerging Rural Revolution', *Far Eastern Economic Review*, 10 January 1975, p. 29.

105. Robert Shaplen, 'Letter from Malaysia', *The New Yorker*, 18 April 1977, p. 119.

106. Tunku Abdul Rahman Putra Al-Haj, *May 13. Before and After* (Kuala Lumpur: Utusan Melayo Press, 1969), p. 191.

107. Radio Kuala Lumpur, domestic service in English, 10 November 1977 (*FBIS*, 10 November 1977).

108. *Amnesty International Report, 1977*, pp. 198–200.

109. *The Straits Times* (Singapore), 2 September 1976.

110. Douglas Pike, 'Socialist Republic of Vietnam', pp. 387–93 in Richard F. Staar (ed.), *Yearbook on International Communist Affairs, 1977* (Stanford, Calif.: Hoover Institution Press, 1977).

111. *Ibid.*, pp. 394–6.

112. *Amnesty International Report, 1977* (London: Amnesty International Publication, 1977), p. 227.

113. William S. Turley, 'Vietnam Since Reunification', *Problems of Communism*, March–April 1977, p. 41.

114. Douglas Pike, 'Vietnam in 1977: More of the Same', *Asian Survey*, January 1978, pp. 68–75.

115. *The New York Times*, 31 May 1978.

116. VNA despatch, Hanoi, 11 May 1978 (*FBIS*, 12 May 1978).

117. Radio Hanoi, domestic service in Vietnamese, 7 April 1978 (*FBIS*, 11 April 1978).

118. Radio Ho Chi Minh City, domestic service in Vietnamese, 7 April 1978 (*FBIS*, 11 April 1978).

119. *The New York Times*, 29 and 31 May 1978.

120. *Ibid.*, 28 May 1978.

121. *The Thieu Regime Put to the Test, 1973–1975* (Hanoi: Foreign Languages Press, 1975), p. 119.

122. *The New York Times*, 10 November 1977.

123. David Rees, *Vietnam Since Liberation. Hanoi's Revolutionary Strategy* (Conflict Studies, no. 89, Institute for the Study of Conflict, London, November 1977), p. 7.

124. *The New York Times*, 29 March 1978.

125. Arthur J. Dommen, 'Laos', pp. 324–9 in Richard F. Staar (ed.), *Yearbook on International Communist Affairs, 1976* (Stanford, Calif.: Hoover Institution Press, 1976).

126. The 200 000 figure appears in David A. Andelman, 'Laos After the Takeover', *The New York Times Magazine*, 24 October 1976, p. 54.

127. John Everingham, 'Laos – A Struggle in Microcosm', *Far Eastern Economic Review*, 9 April 1976, p. 28.

128. MacAlister Brown and Joseph J. Zasloff, 'Laos 1977: The Realities of Independence', *Asian Survey*, February 1978, pp. 168–71; *Asia Yearbook 1978* (Far Eastern Economic Review, London, 1978), pp. 234–5.

129. Kaysone Phomvihan, Report to Lao SPC – Council of Ministers' Meeting, Radio Vientiane, domestic service in Lao, 6 March 1978 (*FBIS*, 17 March 1978).

130. *Asiaweek* (Hong Kong), 3 February 1978, p. 29.

131. Kaysone Phomvihan, Report to Lao SPC – Council of Ministers' Meeting (cf. note 129 *supra*), and Kaysone Phomvihan, 'The Victory of Creative Marxism-Leninism in Laos', *World Marxist Review* (North American edition), March 1977, p. 24.

132. *Philippines Daily Express* (Manila), 25 June 1977, and *The New York Times*, 11 February 1978.

133. *The Straits Times*, 5 December 1977.

134. Belgrade, Tanjug, domestic service, 19 and 24 April 1978 (*FBIS*, 21 and 26 April 1978). See also on the character of the Pol Pot regime François Ponchaud, *Cambodia: Year Zero* (New York: Holt, Rinehart, Winston, 1977).

135. For the 800 000 figure see *Asiaweek*, 5 May 1978; for more detailed

analyses of the Cambodian holocaust see John Barron and Anthony Paul, *Murder of A Gentle Land*, and François Ponchaud, *Cambodia: Year Zero.*

136. *Asiaweek*, 5 May 1978, p. 24.

137. Karl D. Jackson, 'Cambodia 1977: Gone to Pot', *Asian Survey*, January 1978, p. 81; *Asia Yearbook 1978*, p. 154.

138. Robert Keatley, 'The New Rulers of Cambodia', *The Wall Street Journal*, 22 May 1975; *Asia Yearbook 1978*, p. 155; Jackson, 'Cambodia 1977', pp. 76–90; Ponchaud, *Cambodia: Year Zero.*

139. Radio Phnom Penh, domestic service in Cambodian, 13 March 1978 (*FBIS*, 15 March 1978).

140. Belgrade, Tanjug, domestic service in Serbo-Croatian, 19, 20, 21, and 22 April 1978 (*FBIS*, 21, 24, and 27 April 1978).

141. *Far Eastern Economic Review*, 2 June 1978, p. 40.

142. On ASEAN's 'resilience' concept see Justus M. van der Kroef, 'ASEAN and U.S. Security', *Strategic Review*, Spring 1978, pp. 51–61.

143. José Veloso Abueva, 'Filipino Democracy and the American Legacy', *The Annals*, November 1976, p. 114. See also *The Asian Student* (San Francisco), Supplement, 8 April 1978, p. S–11.

144. Remigio E. Agpalo, *The Organic-Hierarchical Paradigm and Politics in the Philippines* (Quezon City: University of the Philippines Press, 1973), p. 24, also cited in Abueva, 'Filipino Democracy'.

145. Compare Roger Kershaw, 'The Denial of Pluralist Democracy in Thailand: An Anatomy of the Crisis of August, 1975', *Art International/The New Lugano Review*, January 1978, p. 58.

146. *The Straits Times*, 25 January 1978.

147. See, e.g., *The Wall Street Journal*, 17 November 1975, *The New York Times*, 25 January and 3 February 1977; 4 June 1978.

148. *Nation Review* (Bangkok), 27 May 1978 (*FBIS*, 1 June 1978).

149. *The New York Times*, 9 June 1978.

Chapter 3

1. Radio Phnom Penh, domestic service in Cambodian, 10 June 1978 (*Foreign Broadcast Information Service Bulletin*, hereafter *FBIS*, 14 June 1978).

2. Justus M. van der Kroef, 'Lenin, Mao and Aidit', *The China Quarterly*, April–June 1962, pp. 23–44.

3. D. N. Aidit, 'Masjarakat Indonesia dan Revolusi Indonesia', pp. 286–7 in Aidit's *Pilihan Tulisan* (Djakarta: Jajasen 'Pembaruan', 1960), vol. II.

4. Justus M. van der Kroef, 'The Communist Concept of National Democracy', *Studies on the Soviet Union*, vol. 4 (1964), pp. 39–63.

5. D. N. Aidit, *Pilihan Tulisan*, pp. 290–94.

6. Voice of the Malayan Revolution (clandestine) in Mandarin to Malaysia and Singapore, 8 June 1978 (*FBIS*, 22 June 1978).

7. *Ang Bayan* (English edition), 12 October 1972, pp. 10–13; 'Tasks of the Communist Party of the Philippines in the New Situation', *Bulletin of Concerned Asian Scholars*, September 1973, pp. 41–4.

8. *Ibid.*

9. Agence France Presse despatches, Manila, 23 December 1974, and 18 December 1976 (*FBIS*, 24 December 1974 and 21 December 1976).

10. 'Programme Adopted by the Fifth Congress of the Partido Komunista ng Pilipinas on February 11, 1973', *Information Bulletin* (Prague), vol. 11 (1973), no. 17–18, pp. 14–28.

11. 'Philippines: New Policy Orientation of the Martial-Law Government and the Attitude of the Communist Party', *Information Bulletin*, vol. 13 (1975), no. 3, pp. 23–6.

12. Mario Frunze, 'Marxism-Leninism and "Revolutionary" Quixotism', *Ang Komunista* (Internal Bulletin of Partido Komunista ng Pilipinas), February 1971, p. 13.

13. F. Macapagal, letter to the editor, *Asiaweek* (Hong Kong), 28 October 1977, pp. 3–4.

14. Tillman Durdin, 'Philippine Communism', *Problems of Communism*, May–June 1976, p. 47.

15. Josef Silverstein, *Burma. Military Rule and the Politics of Stagnation* (Ithaca and London: Cornell University Press, 1977), pp. 112–16.

16. *Ibid.*; and John Badgley, 'The Union of Burma: Age Twenty-Two', *Asian Survey*, February 1971, p. 151, *Asian Almanac* (Johore Bahru), 29 March 1969, vol. 7, no. 13, pp. 3245–6, and *Keesing's Contemporary Archives*, 3–10 May, 1969, p. 3332.

17. *The New York Times*, 31 January and 20 September 1973.

18. Marcus Franda, 'Northeastern India in the Wake of Vietnam', *American University Field Staff Reports*, vol. 19, 1975, no. 13, p. 5.

19. 'Voice of the People of Burma', clandestine in Burmese to Burma, 17 May 1975 (*FBIS*, 22 May 1975).

20. Citations in this paragraph from Viet Chung, 'National Minorities and National Policy in the DRV', *Vietnamese Studies* (Hanoi), 1968, no. 15, pp. 4–23.

21. Cf. e.g. 'Voice of the Malayan Revolution' broadcast, clandestine in Mandarin to Malaysia and Singapore, 17 April 1976 (*FBIS*, 19 April 1976).

22. Central Committee, Paperi, statement broadcast over the 'Voice of the Malayan Revolution', clandestine in Malay to Singapore and Malaysia, 15 September 1977 (29 September 1977). In this discussion of Paperi I have drawn on my 'Religion, Ethnicity and Communist Tactics in Southeast Asia's Plural Societies', *Plural Societies*, Winter 1976, pp. 3–26.

23. 'Voice of the Malayan Revolution', clandestine in Malay to Malaysia and Singapore, 16 March 1976 (*FBIS*, 18 March 1976).

24. 'The Plight of Federal Land Development Settlers in Malaya', *Journal of Contemporary Asia*, vol. 3 (1973), no. 3, pp. 367–70 (reprinted from *Berita Sosialis*, vol. 2, no. 4).

25. Denzil Peiris, 'Malaysia – The Emerging Rural Revolution', *Far Eastern Economic Review*, 10 January 1975, pp. 29–31.

26. 'Voice of the Malayan Revolution', in Mandarin, to Malaysia and Singapore, 27 December 1975 (*FBIS*, 31 December 1975). See also Justus M. van der Kroef, 'New Trends in Malaysian Communism', *Issues and Studies*, June 1977, pp. 59–60.

27. 'On the Question of the National Bourgeoisie and the Enlightened Gentry', in *Selected Works of Mao Tse-tung* (Peking: Foreign Languages Press, 1961), vol. 4, esp. p. 209.

28. 'The Programme of the Communist Party of Indonesia for People's Democracy in Indonesia' (November 1967), in *Build the PKI Along the Marxist-Leninist Line to Lead the People's Democratic Revolution in Indonesia* (published by the Delegation of the Central Committee of the Indonesian Communist Party, Tirana, 1971), pp. 235–80.

29. Anne Booth, 'Landownership in Klaten', *Bulletin of Indonesian Economic Studies*, November 1974, pp. 135–40.

30. *The Indonesia Times* (Djakarta), 14 January 1976.

31. Data in this paragraph from Alden Speare, 'Alternative Population Distribution Policies for Indonesia', *Bulletin of Indonesian Economic Studies*, March 1978, p. 93, citing D. H. Penny and M. Singarimbun, *Population and Poverty in Rural Java: Some Economic Arithmetic from Sriharjo* (Department of Agricultural Economics, Cornell University, Ithaca, N.Y., 1973), pp. 18–19; H. R. Redmana, H. V. J. Moir, and Daliyo, *Labour Force and Labour Utilisation in Selected Areas in Java* (Monograph Series, LEKNAS (IPI, Djakarta, 1977), vol. 1, p. 1; and R. Sinaga and W. L. Collier, 'Social and Regional Implications of Agricultural Development Policy', *Prisma* (English edition), November 1975, pp. 24–35.

32. *Indonesian Current Affairs Translation Service Bulletin* (Djakarta), February 1976, p. 138.

33. Richard William Franke, *The Green Revolution in a Javanese Village* (unpublished Ph.D. Thesis, Harvard University, Cambridge, Mass., June 1972), p. 181, also cited in W. L. Collier, *et al.*, *Tebasan HYV's and Rural Change: An Example in Java* (Agro-Economic Survey of Indonesia, s.l., November 1973, mimeo), pp. 2–3.

34. J. M. van der Kroef, 'Indonesia: Centrifugal Economies', in James W. Wiggins and Helmut Schoeck (eds.), *Foreign Aid Re-Examined* (Washington, D.C.: Public Affairs Press, 1958), p. 203.

35. *Antara Daily News Bulletin*, 6 December 1976, p. I.

36. 'Political Resolution Adopted by the Fifth Congress of the Partido Komunista ng Pilipinas (PKP) on February 10, 1973', *Information Bulletin* (Prague), vol. 11, 1973, no. 13 (245), pp. 26–31.

37. *Ibid.*

38. Cf. Lenin's 1913 essay, 'Backward Europe and Advanced Asia', in V. I. Lenin, *The National Liberation Movement in the East* (Moscow: Foreign Languages Publishing House, 1957), pp. 61–3.

39. D. N. Aidit, 'Masjarakat Indonesia dan Revolusi Indonesia', in his *Pilihan Tulisan*, vol. 2, pp. 290–91.

40. Francisco Balagtas, 'Trends of Change in the Philippines', *World Marxist Review*, July 1975, p. 45.

41. 'Voice of the Malayan Revolution', clandestine in Mandarin to Malaysia and Singapore, 22 June 1978 (*FBIS*, 29 June 1978).

42. *Ibid.*, and 'Voice of the Malayan Revolution', clandestine in Mandarin to Malaysia and Singapore, 29 April 1978 (*FBIS*, 4 May 1978).

43. Pran Chopra, 'The Malaysian Miracle and Dilemma', *The World Today*, May 1974, pp. 200–01.

44. R. S. Milne, 'The Politics of Malaysia's New Economic Policy', *Pacific Affairs*, Summer 1976, pp. 235–62.

45. Robert Shaplen, 'Letter from Malaysia', *The New Yorker*, 18 April 1977, p. 119. See also Brewster Grace, 'The Politics of Income Distribution in Malaysia', *American Universities Field Staff Reports*, vol. 24 (1976), no. 9, pp. 4–5, and pp. 8–9 for the position of 'poor Chinese' referred to below.

46. Denzil Peiris, 'Angry Young Men of Southeast Asia', *The Times of India* (Bombay), 26 September 1975.

47. *Singapore 1971* (Singapore: Ministry of Culture, Government Printing Office, 1971), p. 163.

48. Bevars D. Mabry, 'The Thai Labor Movement', *Asian Survey*, October 1977, pp. 935–6.

49. *Ibid.*, p. 940, and Andrej Amalrik, 'KGB in Asia: Thailand', *Far Eastern Economic Review*, 31 December 1976, pp. 24–7.

50. David Morell, 'Political Conflict in Thailand', *Asian Affairs* (New York), January–February 1976, p. 162.

51. 'Voice of the Malayan Revolution', in Mandarin to Malaysia and Singapore, 8 June 1978 (*FBIS*, 22 June 1978). Italics supplied.

52. *Peking Review*, 20 December 1974, p. 18.

53. J. M. van der Kroef, 'Patterns of Political Opposition in Southeast Asia', *Pacific Affairs*, Winter 1978–79.

54. Ross Prizzia and Narong Sinsawasdi, 'Evolution of the Thai Student Movement', *Asia Quarterly*, 1975, no. 1, pp. 3–54.

55. 'Educational Development in Thailand, 1960–1976', *Education in Asia. Bulletin of the UNESCO Regional Office for Education in Asia* (Bangkok), March 1972, pp. 189–98.

56. Already in 1967 authoritative sources called attention to this problem. See, e.g., *Higher Education and Development in Southeast Asia* (UNESCO, Paris, 1967), vol. II, p. 130.

57. Jeff Romm, *Urbanization in Thailand* (International Urbanization Survey, The Ford Foundation, New York, 1972), p. 115. See also chapter 3, note 33 *supra*.

58. Ruth Inge Heinze, 'Ten Days in October – Students versus the Military', *Asian Survey*, June 1974, p. 505.

59. See, e.g., 'Voice of the People of Thailand' broadcast, 6 October 1977 (*FBIS*, 7 October 1977).

60. Robert Shaplen, 'Letter From Bangkok', *The New Yorker*, 24 July 1978, p. 56.

61. *Asiaweek* (Hong Kong), 14 July 1978, esp. p. 55.

62. On the TIM and TPF see Donald E. Weatherbee, *The United Front in Thailand. A Documentary Analysis* (Institute of International Studies, University of South Carolina, Columbia, S.C., 1970).

63. *Asiaweek*, 14 July 1978, esp. pp. 46–50.

64. 'Voice of the People of Thailand', clandestine in Thai to Thailand, 1 March 1978 (*FBIS*, 3 March 1978).

65. On the Socialist Party of Thailand see *Asiaweek*, 14 July 1978, pp. 46–50, 55–6.

66. On this concept see J. M. van der Kroef, 'The Communist Concept of "National Democracy"', *Studies on the Soviet Union*, vol. 4, 1964, no. 2, pp. 39–63.

67. David Rees, *Vietnam Since 'Liberation.' Hanoi's Revolutionary Strategy* (Conflict Studies, no. 89, Institute of Conflict Studies, London, November 1977), p. 12.

68. Le Duc Tho's address, Radio Hanoi, domestic service in Vietnamese, 17 December 1976 (*FBIS*, 23 December 1976). All citations to this address in the paragraphs below are to this source.

69. William S. Turley, 'Vietnam Since Reunification', *Problems of Communism*, March–April 1977, p. 44.

70. *Vietnam Courier* (Hanoi), November 1977, p. 3.

71. Hanoi, Vietnam News Agency, in English, 16 December 1976 (*FBIS*).

72. See, e.g., Alec Gordon, 'The Role of Class Struggle in North Vietnam', *Monthly Review* (New York), January 1978, p. 26.

73. 'The Fatherland Front of Vietnam', *World Marxist Review*, January 1978, pp. 122–4.

74. Nguyen Dinh-Hoa, 'The Cultural Policy of Unified Vietnam', *Asian Thought and Society*, December 1977, p. 322.

75. Turley, 'Vietnam Since Reunification', p. 40.

76. Radio Hanoi, domestic service in Vietnamese, 7 April 1978 (*FBIS*, 11 April 1978).

77. Editorial, *Nhan Dan* (Hanoi), 10 April 1978 (*FBIS*, 19 April 1978).

78. Radio Hanoi, domestic service in Vietnamese, 24 June 1978 (*FBIS*, 28 June 1978).

79. *The New York Times*, 29 and 31 May 1978; David Rees, *Vietnam Since Liberation*, pp. 12–13.

80. LPDR premier Kaysone Phomvihan's report of 2 March to a joint session of the Lao Supreme People's Council and Council of Ministers, in *FBIS*, 17 March 1978 (Supplement).

81. Kaysone Phomvihan, 'The Victory of Creative Marxism-Leninism in

Laos', *World Marxist Review*, March 1977, pp. 15–27.

82. Martin Stuart-Fox, 'The Lao Revolution: Leadership and Policy Differences', *Australian Outlook*, vol. 31 (1977), pp. 285–6.

83. Radio Vientiane, domestic service in Lao, 4 February 1976 (9 February 1976).

84. Martin Stuart-Fox, 'The Lao Revolution', p. 287.

85. Cf. the Agence France Presse despatch of Joel Henri from Bangkok, 26 February 1976 (*FBIS*, 26 February 1976).

86. Radio Phnom Penh, domestic service in Cambodian, 28 September 1977 (*FBIS*, 4 October 1977). Citations to Pol Pot's 27 September 1977 address are to this source.

87. *Ibid.* On the general character of the Pol Pot regime see esp. François Ponchaud, *Cambodia: Year Zero* (New York: Holt, Rinehart, Winston, 1977), and Karl D. Jackson, 'Cambodia 1977: Gone to Pot', *Asian Survey,* January 1978, pp. 76–90 which have been drawn on in these paragraphs.

88. Tanjug, Belgrade, domestic service in Serbo-Croatian, 6 June 1978 (*FBIS*, 7 June 1978).

89. Pol Pot's 27 September 1977 address (see note 86 *supra*).

90. Far Eastern Economic Review, *1978 Asia Yearbook* (Far Eastern Economic Review, Hong Kong, 1977), p. 154.

91. Radio Phnom Penh, domestic service in Cambodian, 24 June 1978 (*FBIS*, 26 June 1978).

92. Far Eastern Economic Review, *1978 Asia Yearbook*, p. 154; *Far Eastern Economic Review*, 28 July 1978, p. 27.

93. *The Refugee Resettlement Problem in Thailand* (National Foreign Assessment Center, Central Intelligence Agency, Washington, D.C., May 1978), p. 7.

94. Karl D. Jackson, 'Cambodia 1977: Gone to Pot', p. 78. See also F. Ponchaud, *Cambodia: Year Zero.*

95. Tanjug, Belgrade, domestic service in Serbo-Croatian, 22 April 1978 (*FBIS*, 24 April 1978).

96. *The New York Times*, 29 July 1978.

Chapter 4

1. 'Voice of The People of Burma', clandestine, in Burmese, 28 March 1978 (*Foreign Broadcast Information Service Bulletin*, hereafter *FBIS*, 30 March 1978).

2. *Ibid.*, 14 April 1978 (*FBIS*, 19 April 1978).

3. *Ibid.*, 16 August 1978 (*FBIS*, 18 August 1978).

4. *Ibid.*, 18 August 1978 (*FBIS*, 24 August 1978).

5. *Ibid.*

6. Alfredo B. Saulo, *Communism in the Philippines. An Introduction* (Manila: Ateneo Publications, 1969), pp. 8–10.

7. Gene Z. Hanrahan, *The Communist Struggle in Malaya* (Kuala Lumpur: University of Malaya Press, 1971), pp. 35–6.

8. J. Th. Petrus Blumberger, 'Vakbeweging (Inlandsche)', *Encyclopedie van Nederlandsch-Indië* (The Hague: Nijhoff, 1917–35), vol. 7, p. 430.

9. Much of the data in this and the following paragraphs on Sarawak Communism are drawn from Sarawak Information Service, *The Danger Within. A History of the Clandestine Communist Organisation in Sarawak* (Government Printing Office, Kuching, Sarawak, 1963), unless otherwise indicated. I have also benefited from conversations with Malaysian security officials in the past decade and a half.

10. In this connection see also Douglas Hyde, *The Roots of Guerilla Warfare* (London, Sydney, Toronto: The Bodley Head, 1968), pp. 65–9.

11. Justus M. van der Kroef, 'Communist Fronts in the Philippines', *Problems of Communism*, March–April 1967, pp. 65–75.

12. *The Danger Within* (see note 9), p. 8.

13. *Ibid.*, p. 56.

14. Hyde, *The Roots of Guerilla Warfare*, p. 75.

15. *Ibid.*, p. 74.

16. See Justus M. van der Kroef, *Communism in Malaysia and Singapore. A Contemporary Survey* (The Hague: Martinus Nijhoff, 1967), pp. 154–5.

17. *The Sarawak Gazette* (Kuching), 31 October 1974.

18. R. F. Staar (ed.), *1975 Yearbook on International Communist Affairs* (Stanford, Calif.: Hoover Institution Press, 1975), pp. 379–80.

19. For the text of this constitution see *The Maoist Communist Party of the Philippines* (Southeast Asia Organisation, Bangkok, 1971), Short Paper no. 52, pp. 43–59.

20. Seventh Anniversary statement of the CPP(M-L), 26 December 1975 (*FBIS*, 5 April 1976).

21. Eighth Anniversary statement of the CPP(M-L), 26 December 1976 (*FBIS*, 5 April 1977).

22. See Guerrero's statement, entitled 'The People's Revolutionary Force is Sure to Win', 11 September 1976 (*FBIS*, 17 November 1976).

23. Eighth Anniversary statement on the NPA, made by the CPP(M-L), 29 March 1977 (*FBIS*, 1 November 1977).

24. 'Voice of the People of Burma', 24 August 1978 (*FBIS*, 29 August 1978).

25. 'Tasks of the Communist Party of the Philippines in the New Situation', *Ang Bayan*, 12 October 1972, pp. 10–13 (also in *Bulletin of Concerned Asian Scholars*, September 1973, p. 42).

26. *Prospects for Regional Stability: Asia and the Pacific. Report Submitted by a Special Study Mission to Asia and the Pacific, January 2–22, 1978*, Committee on International Relations, US House of Representatives (Washington: US Government Printing Office, 1978), p. 11.

27. See the 'Ten Point Program of the National Democratic Front' in *People's War in the Philippines* (published by Union of Democratic Filipinos, Oakland, 1974), p. 49.

28. 'Philippines: New Policy Orientation of the Martial Law Government and the Attitude of the Communist Party', *Information Bulletin* (Prague), 1975, no. 3, p. 24.

29. *To Brothers at Home and Comrades Abroad Fighting Against Imperialism, for Independence, Peace, Democracy and Socialism. For A Sound Indonesian Revolution* (Colombo: Tribune Publications, 1967), pp. 11, 12, 15.

30. *Build the PKI Along the Marxist-Leninist Line to Lead the People's Democratic Revolution in Indonesia* (published by the Delegation of the CC PKI, Tirana, 1971), esp. pp. 85–208.

31. *Ibid.*, pp. 130–49.

32. For Indonesian Communism in this period see, e.g., Donald Hindley, *The Communist Party of Indonesia, 1951–1963* (Berkeley and Los Angeles: University of California Press, 1964), and Justus M. van der Kroef, *The Communist Party of Indonesia. Its History, Program and Tactics* (Vancouver: University of British Columbia Press, 1965).

33. See, e.g., D. N. Aidit, *The Indonesian Revolution and the Immediate Tasks of the Communist Party of Indonesia* (Peking: Foreign Languages Press, 1964).

34. Southeast Asia Treaty Organisation, *The Communist Threat to Thailand* (SEATO Short Paper no. 44, August 1967), p. 50.

35. Donald E. Weatherbee, *The United Front in Thailand. A Documentary Analysis* (Columbia, S.C.: University of South Carolina Institute of International Studies, 1970), p. 33.

36. *Ibid.*, pp. 37–44. I have also relied on information supplied by Thai intelligence officials in connection with data in this and the following two paragraphs.

37. Weatherbee, *The United Front in Thailand*, pp. 50–6.

38. *Ibid.*, pp. 64, 67.

39. 'Voice of the People of Thailand', clandestine in Thai to Thailand, 9 December 1977 (*FBIS*, 15 December 1977).

40. *Ibid.*

41. *Ibid.*

42. 'Voice of the People of Thailand', clandestine in Thai to Thailand, 5 August 1978 (*FBIS*, 7 August 1978).

43. 'Voice of the People of Thailand', clandestine in Thai to Thailand, 6 August 1978 (*FBIS*, 8 August 1978).

44. 'Voice of the People of Thailand', clandestine in Thai to Thailand, 8 August 1978 (*FBIS*, 10 August 1978).

45. 'Voice of the People of Thailand', clandestine in Thai to Thailand, 20 May 1978 (*FBIS*, 23 May 1978).

46. 'Voice of the People of Thailand', clandestine in Thai to Thailand, 19 August 1978 (*FBIS*, 25 August 1978).

47. *The Bangkok Post*, 17 August 1978 (*FBIS*, 17 August 1978).

48. *Asiaweek* (Hong Kong), 14 July 1978, p. 55.

49. Haris Chandola, 'Thailand – A Report from the Northeast', *Economic and Political Weekly* (Bombay), 29 May 1976, p. 804.

50. The following citations to the 1972 CPM constitution are to the text of that document as it appears in *The Journal of Contemporary Asia*, 1973, vol. 3, no. 2, pp. 233–7.

51. This table is based on the statement of Malaysian home affairs minister Tan Sri Ghazali Shafie in the *New Straits Times* (Kuala Lumpur), 2 November 1974 (*FBIS*, 8 November 1974), and Chandran Jeshurun, 'The Security Situation in Peninsular Malaysia', pp. 98–9 in K. S. Sandhu (ed.), *Southeast Asian Affairs, 1975* (Singapore: Institute of Southeast Asian Studies, 1975).

52. 'Voice of the Malayan Revolution', clandestine in Mandarin, to Malaysia and Singapore, 31 January 1976 (*FBIS*, 5 February 1976).

53. 'Voice of the Malayan Revolution', clandestine in Mandarin to Malaysia and Singapore, 18 February 1975 (*FBIS*, 21 February 1975).

54. 'Voice of the Malayan Revolution', clandestine in Mandarin to Malaysia and Singapore, 6 December 1977 (*FBIS*, 9 December 1977).

55. 'Voice of the Malayan Revolution', clandestine in Mandarin to Malaysia and Singapore, 28 September 1976 and 15 September 1977 (*FBIS*, 6 October 1976 and 29 September 1977).

56. 'Voice of the Malayan Revolution', clandestine in Mandarin to Malaysia and Singapore, 11 December 1976 (*FBIS*, 22 December 1976).

57. William S. Turley, 'Vietnam Since Reunification', *Problems of Communism*, March–April 1977, pp. 38–41.

58. Hanoi, VNA in English, 16 December 1976 (*FBIS*).

59. *Ibid.*

60. Radio Hanoi, domestic service in Vietnamese, 17 December 1976 (*FBIS*, 23 December 1976).

61. *Ibid.*

62. *Nhan Dan* (Hanoi), 10 August 1978 (*FBIS*, 11 August 1978).

63. *World Marxist Review*, January 1978, pp. 122–4.

64. *The Military Balance, 1978–1979* (International Institute for Strategic Studies, London, 1968), p. 68.

65. Turley, 'Vietnam Since Reunification', p. 40.

66. Radio Hanoi, domestic service in Vietnamese, 13 August 1978 (*FBIS*, 15 August 1978).

67. *Ibid.*

68. Hanoi, VNA, 11 May 1978 (*FBIS*, 12 May 1978).

69. Radio Vientiane, domestic service in Lao, 1 August 1978 (*FBIS*, 8 August 1978).

70. *Ibid.*

71. *Ibid.*

72. *Ibid.*

73. Radio Vientiane, domestic service in Lao, 21 December 1976 (*FBIS*, 23 December 1976).

74. *Ibid.*

75. 'Laos: A Soft Revolution', *Newsweek* (US edition), 11 September 1978, p. 50.

76. US Central Intelligence Agency, *The Refugee Resettlement Problem in Thailand* (Washington, D.C., 1978), p. 1.

77. Pathet Lao News Agency, clandestine in English, 16 February 1976 (*FBIS*, 17 February 1976).

78. Radio Vientiane, domestic service in Lao, 7 February 1976 (*FBIS*, 10 February 1976).

79. *Ibid.*

80. Barry Kramer in *The Wall Street Journal*, 19 October 1977; John Barron and Anthony Paul, 'Cambodia: the Killing Goes On', *The Reader's Digest*, July 1978, pp. 167–74.

81. Radio Phnom Penh, domestic service in Cambodian, 28 September 1977 (*FBIS*, 4 October 1977).

Chapter 5

1. F. Macapagal, letter to the editor, *Asiaweek* (Hong Kong), 28 October 1977, pp. 3–4.

2. Frank N. Trager, 'Sino-Burmese Relations: the End of the Pauk Phaw Era', *Orbis*, Winter 1968, vol. 11, no. 4, p. 1035.

3. Herbert Feith, *The Decline of Constitutional Democracy in Indonesia* (Ithaca, N.Y.: Cornell University Press, 1962), pp. 192–3.

4. George McT. Kahin, *The Asian-African Conference. Bandung, Indonesia, April 1955* (Ithaca, N.Y.: Cornell University Press, 1956), pp. 37, 84–5.

5. Justus M. van der Kroef, 'The Sino-Indonesian Partnership', *Orbis*, Summer 1964, pp. 332–56.

6. *Peking Review*, 5 February 1965, pp. 6–8.

7. See, e.g., the *New York Times*, 11 October 1966. See also Antonia C.A. Dake, *In the Spirit of the Red Banteng. Indonesian Communists between Moscow and Peking, 1959–1965* (The Hague and Paris: Mouton publishers, 1973), pp. 326–36.

8. *Sabah Times* (Kota Kinabalu, Sabah, Malaysia), 14 September 1965.

9. On this treaty see David Mozingo, *Chinese Policy Toward Indonesia, 1949–1967* (Ithaca, N.Y.: Cornell University Press, 1976), esp. pp. 114–20.

10. *Address of the Acting President General Socharto before the Gotong Royong House of Representatives on August 16, 1967. Special Issue, Antara Daily News Bulletin* (n.d.), part III, pp. 27–8.

11. *Sunday Tribune* (Kuching), 26 November 1967; *Berita Yudha* (Djakarta), 25 November 1967.

12. *Kompas* (Djakarta), 2 August 1968; *Djakarta Times*, 5 July 1968.

13. Associated Press despatch, Djakarta, 26 April 1973.

14. *Angkatan Bersendjata* (Djakarta), 15 June 1974 (*Indonesian Current Affairs Translation Service Bulletin*, June 1974, pp. 417–18).

15. Antara despatch, Semarang, Central Java, 20 June 1974.

16. *The Indonesia Times* (Djakarta), 9 June 1978.

17. *Far Eastern Economic Review*, 16 June 1978, p. 22; *New York Times*, 24 April 1978.

18. I have expounded this thesis in greater detail in my article 'National Security, Defense Strategy, and Foreign Policy Perceptions in Indonesia', *Orbis*, Summer 1976, pp. 461–95.

19. Moscow, Radio Peace and Progress, in Mandarin to South-east Asia, 21 October 1978 (*Foreign Broadcast Information Service Bulletin*, hereafter *FBIS*, 27 October 1978).

20. Frank Trager, 'Sino-Burmese Relations: the End of the Pauk Phaw Era', pp. 1035–7; Robert Holmes, 'China–Burma Relations Since the Rift', *Asian Survey*, August 1972, pp. 686–7.

21. Anthony Polsky, 'The New Lido Road', *Far Eastern Economic Review*, 27 November 1969, p. 460, and *The Times* (London), 19 January 1968.

22. *Time*, 25 March 1974, p. 47; *The New York Times*, 21 January and 20 September 1973.

23. *The Economist* (London), 27 April 1974, p. 46.

24. Wayne Bert, 'Chinese Relations with Burma and Indonesia', *Asian Survey*, June 1975, p. 477.

25. W. A. C. Adie, 'Vagaries of Chinese Policy', *Mizan*, vol. 9, no. 6, November–December 1967, pp. 234–5.

26. Michael Leifer, 'Rebellion or Subversion in Cambodia', *Current History*, February 1969, pp. 90–91. See also *The Australian* (Sydney), 18 January 1969.

27. *The Manila Times*, 28 September 1965.

28. *Ibid.*

29. National Broadcasting System television programme, 'Meet the Press', originating in New York City, 18 September 1966.

30. Sheldon Appleton, 'Communism and the Chinese in the Philippines', *Pacific Affairs*, vol. 32, 1959, p. 378.

31. *The Sarawak Tribune* (Kuching), 17 March 1978.

32. 'China's Policy of Revolt in Southeast Asia', *Asia Pacific Record* (Singapore), January 1971, p. 12.

33. *FBIS*, 30 November 1977, and 13 March 1978.

34. *Prospects for Regional Stability: Asia and the Pacific. Report submitted by a Special Study Mission to Asia and the Pacific, January 2–22, 1978* (US Government Printing Office, Washington, 1978), p. 11.

35. Data in the preceding three sentences, including citations to the *Daily Express* from *Asiaweek*, 10 November 1978, pp. 13–14.

36. *Peking Review*, 7 June 1974, p. 8.

37. Radio Kuala Lumpur, International Service in English, 3 June 1974 (*FBIS*).

38. Data in this paragraph from V. Suryanarayan, 'Malayan Communism at the Cross Roads', *China Report* (Delhi), vol. 10, 1974, no. 4, pp. 69–70.

39. John Wong, 'The Economic Basis of the Sino-Malaysian Détente', *Asia Research Bulletin* (Background Papers), 31 August 1974, p. 2916.

40. See esp. Joseph Camilleri, *Southeast Asia in China's Foreign Policy* (Singapore: Institute of Southeast Asian Studies, 1975), p. 36.

41. Radio Peking, domestic service in Mandarin, 16 August 1977 (*FBIS*, 18 August 1977).

42. *Asia Research Bulletin*, 6 Monthly Political Supplement, 30 April 1978, p. 434.

43. For the text of this 'Declaration' see *The Indonesian Quarterly* (Djakarta: Centre for Strategic and International Studies), vol. 4, 1976, no. 2–4, p. 110.

44. Lee Lai Duo, *China's Changing Attitude Towards Singapore, 1965–1975* (Occasional Paper Series no. 22, Department of Political Science, University of Singapore, November 1975), p. 34.

45. Wu Yuan Li, *Strategic Significance of Singapore. A study in Balance of Power* (Washington, D.C.: American Enterprise Institute for Public Policy Research, 1972), p. 11.

46. As reported by Henry Kamm in *The New York Times*, 7 November 1978, and *The New York Times*, 14 November 1978.

47. Adam Malik, 'Djakarta Conference and Asia's Political Future', *Pacific Community* (Tokyo), vol. 2, October 1970, no. 1, pp. 73–4.

48. As reported by Henry Kamm in *The New York Times*, 10 November 1978.

49. *The Straits Times*, 7 July 1975.

50. Leo Goodstadt, 'Indochina: the Phoenix and the Dragon', *Insight* (Hong Kong), May 1978, p. 41.

51. For Chinese praise see *The Vietnamese People's Great Victory* (Peking: Foreign Languages Press, 1975).

52. As reported by Barry Kramer in *The Wall Street Journal*, 9 August 1978.

53. *The Straits Times*, 29 August 1978, and Barry Kramer in *The Wall Street Journal*, vol. 192, no. 4, 1978, pp. 1, 23.

54. *The New York Times*, 7 and 9 November 1978.

55. *Philippines Evening Express* (Manila), 8 July 1975.

56. On Hanoi's policies in this period see Justus M. van der Kroef, 'Hanoi and ASEAN: A New Confrontation in Southeast Asia?' *Asia Quarterly*, 1976, pp. 245–69, and the literature there cited.

57. *Nhan Dan* (Hanoi), 1 December 1971.

58. *Quan Doi Nhan Dan* (Hanoi), 22 February 1976 (*FBIS*).

59. *Nhan Dan*, 31 March 1976 (*FBIS*, 1 April 1976).

60. Radio Hanoi (VNA), in English, 9 July 1977 (*FBIS*, 19 July 1977).

61. *The Straits Times*, 7 January 1978.

62. Cf. the commentary of M. Rostarchuk in *Izvestiya* (Moscow), 20 November 1977 (*FBIS*, 23 November 1977).

63. *The Straits Times*, 17 June 1978.

64. *Asiaweek*, 4 August 1978, p. 18. For an interpretation of the SRV proposal see also Rodney Tasker in *Far Eastern Economic Review*, 4 August 1978, p. 8.

65. *The Bangkok Post*, 7 September 1978.

66. *The Straits Times*, 22 September 1978.

67. Agence France Presse despatch, Ipoh, 18 October 1978 (*FBIS*, 19 October 1978).

68. Agence France Presse despatches, Manila, 19 and 20 October 1978 (*FBIS*, 20 October 1978).

69. Radio Phnom Penh, domestic service in Cambodian, 30 October 1978 (*FBIS*, 31 October 1978).

70. David Bonavia, 'The Marxist and the Monarchy', *Far Eastern Economic Review*, 17 November 1978, p. 10.

71. Adam Malik, 'Balance of Power in Southeast Asia', *The Asian Student* (San Francisco), 27 September 1975, p. 5.

72. R. Ulyanovsky, 'The Great October Revolution and the Revolutionary Process in Asia and Africa', *Far Eastern Affairs* (Moscow), 1977, no. 3, esp. pp. 20–21.

73. M. Kapitsa, 'The War in Vietnam and Diplomatic Struggle', *Far Eastern Affairs* (Moscow) 1976, no. 4 – 1977, no. 1, pp. 18–36.

74. Y. Yuriev, 'Southeast Asia Today', *Far Eastern Affairs* (Moscow), 1976, no. 4 – 1977, no. 1, p. 41.

75. *Ibid.*, pp. 42–3; *Krasnaya Zvezda* (Moscow), 30 July 1977 (*FBIS*, 4 August 1977), and Radio Moscow in Indonesian to Indonesia, 20 October 1976 (*FBIS*, 27 October 1976). See also Justus M. van der Kroef, 'ASEAN: the View from Hanoi, Moscow and Peking', *The Contemporary Asia Review*, vol. 1, 1977, no. 1, pp. 26–7.

76. Alexander Usvatov, 'Where ASEAN is being pushed', *New Times* (Moscow), 1977, no. 3, p. 8.

77. Y. Plekhanov, 'ASEAN: Trends of Political Development', *Far Eastern Affairs* (Moscow), 1977, no. 3, esp. pp. 85–7.

78. Robert C. Horn, 'The Soviet Perspective', in Sudershan Chawla, *et al.* (eds.), *Southeast Asia Under the New Balance of Power* (New York, Washington, London: F. A. Praeger, 1974), p. 33.

79. Data in this paragraph from Robert C. Horn, 'Soviet Influence in Southeast Asia: Opportunities and Obstacles', *Asian Survey*, August 1975, p. 658.

80. *Ibid.*, p. 659. See also Justus M. van der Kroef, 'The Soviet Union and Southeast Asia', in Roger Kanet (ed.), *The Soviet Union and the Developing Nations* (Baltimore: The Johns Hopkins University Press, 1974), pp. 99–103.

81. Justus M. van der Kroef, 'Recent Trends in Indonesian-Soviet Relations', *Pacific Community* (Tokyo), July 1974, pp. 590–613.

82. A. Yuryev, 'Indonesia and her Problems', *International Affairs* (Moscow), November 1976, pp. 84–92.

83. Antara despatch, Djakarta, 20 April 1977; *Indonesia Times*, Djakarta, 19 November 1975.

84. Cited in Robert C. Horn, 'Moscow's Southeast Asian Offensive', *Asian Affairs* (New York), April 1975, p. 219.

85. See, e.g., *Selskaya zhizn*, Moscow, 16 June 1976 (*FBIS*, 18 June 1976).

86. Alexander Kakaulin and Ivan Shchedrov, 'Thailand at the Crossroads', *New Times* (Moscow), June 1975, no. 25, p. 22.

87. Alfred Biegel, 'Strategic Implications of Moscow's Concept for Collective Security in Asia', *Military Review*, February 1977, p. 7.

88. Justus M. van der Kroef, 'ASEAN's Security Needs and Policies', *Pacific Affairs*, Summer 1974, pp. 158–9.

89. Editorial, 'Soviet Proposal Comes Out as Bandung Revived', *The Nation* (Bangkok), 27 June 1975.

90. A. Sergeyev, 'Problems of Collective Security in Asia', *International Affairs* (Moscow), August 1975, no. 5, p. 51.

91. 'Peddlers of "Asian Collective Security System" Draw in their Horns', *Peking Review*, 2 April 1976, p. 20.

92. B. Ilichev in *Pravda* (Moscow), 29 October 1978 (*FBIS*, 1 November 1978).

93. 'Soviet Social Imperialists Covet Southeast Asia: the "Asian Collective Security System" is a Pretext for Expansion', *Chinese Law and Government*, Spring–Summer 1976, vol. 9, no. 1–2, p. 141; 'Moscow Changes Its Attitude Towards ASEAN', *Peking Review*, 4 August 1978, p. 16.

94. Yuri Plekhanov, 'Peking's Double Game', *New Times* (Moscow), May 1978, no. 22, pp. 23–5.

95. See, e.g., Brian Maurice, 'China's Fifth Column Worries Southeast Asia', *The Sarawak Tribune* (Kuching), 9 September 1978.

96. Editorial, 'Firyubin Visit Doesn't Erode Old Wariness', *Nation Review* (Bangkok), 1 November 1978 (*FBIS*, 1 November 1978).

97. *Antara Daily/News Bulletin*, 1 November 1978, vol. 30, no. 53, p. II, and *Far Eastern Economic Review*, 3 November 1978, p. 16.

98. Frank Mount, 'Soviet Activity in Southeast Asia', *News Weekly* (Melbourne), 26 January 1977, pp. 8–9.

99. V. Kalinin, in *Pravda* (Moscow), 4 October 1978 (*FBIS*, 10 October 1978).

100. *The Southeast Asia Record*, 7–13 December 1979.

101. *Ibid.*, 27 December 1979–3 January 1980; *Far Eastern Economic Review*, 11 January 1980, p. 18.

102. *Far Eastern Economic Review*, 2 March 1979, p. 19.

103. Cf. Truong Chin's article 'On Kampuchea', broadcast over Radio Hanoi, VNA in English, 24 November 1979 (FBIS, 28 November 1979).

104. *The Straits Times*, 3 November 1979.

105. *Far Eastern Economic Review*, 24 August 1979, p. 10.

106. *Ibid.*

107. Agence France Presse despatch by Joel Henri from Bangkok, 26 February 1976 (FBIS, 26 February 1976).

108. *The New York Times*, 4 November 1979.

109. *Far Eastern Economic Review*, 23 February 1979, pp. 8–9; *The Bangkok Post*, 25 July 1979.

110. See Henry Kamm's articles in *The New York Times*, 6 and 20 October 1979.

111. Radio Hanoi, VNA in English, 7 January 1980 (FBIS, 9 January 1980).

112. Nayan Chanda, 'Putting the Heat on ASEAN', *Far Eastern Economic Review*, 18 January 1980, p. 14.

113. Radio Singapore, domestic service in English, 20 January 1980 (FBIS, 21 January 1980).

114. Radio Phnom Penh, domestic service in Cambodian, 18 November 1979 (FBIS, 26 November 1979).

115. SPK despatch, Phnom Penh, 2 December 1979(FBIS, 5 December 1979).

116. *The New York Times*, 14 November 1979.

117. *Ibid.*

118. *The Straits Times*, 6 June 1979.

119. See, for example, 'Vietnam Cannot Afford a War', *Asia Research Bulletin*, October 1978, pp. 492–3; Leo Goodstadt, 'Vietnam's Economy: Bleeding to Death', *Insight* (Hong Kong), September 1978, pp. 72–82; Carlyle Thayer, 'Dilemmas of Development in Vietnam', *Current History*, December 1978, pp. 221–5; *Far Eastern Economic Review*, 17 November 1978, p. 13.

120. *The Southeast Asia Record*, 11–17 January 1980.

121. Douglas Pike, 'The USSR and Vietnam: Into the Swamp', *Asian Survey*, December 1979, p. 1164.

122. *Le Matin* (Paris), 20 November 1979 (despatch of Jean Leclerc du Sablon from Nong Khai (FBIS, 7 December 1979).

123. Radio Vientiane, domestic service in Lao, 27 December 1979 (FBIS, 18 January 1980).

124. *Refugees From Indochina: Current Problems and Prospects.* Committee on Foreign Affairs, US House of Representatives (Washington, D.C., US Government Printing Office, 1979), p. 17.

125. *Far Eastern Economic Review*, 1 February 1980, p. 14.

126. *Ibid.*, 14 December 1979, p. 23, and *The Southeast Asia Record*, 23–29 November 1979.

127. Radio Vientiane, domestic service in Lao, 1 December 1979 (FBIS, 3 December 1979).

128. Radio Hanoi, domestic service in Vietnamese, 15 October 1979 (FBIS, 23 October 1979).

129. *Ibid.*, 12 October 1979 (FBIS, 19 October 1979).

130. SRV Draft Constitution, as broadcast over Radio Hanoi, domestic service in Vietnamese, 15–24 August 1979 (FBIS, 21 September 1979).

Chapter 6

1. *The Straits Times* (Singapore), 7 July 1976.
2. *Ibid.*
3. Associated Press despatch, Kuala Lumpur, 24 November 1978.
4. National Foreign Assessment Center, Central Intelligence Agency, *The Refugee Resettlement Problem in Thailand* (Document Expediting Project, Library of Congress, Washington, D.C., 1978), pp. V, 7.
5. Dominica P. Garcia in *The New York Times*, 14 November 1978.
6. David D. Newsom, 'The Dominoes That Did Not Fall', *Current Policy Bulletin* (US Department of State, Bureau of Public Affairs, Washington, D.C.), October 1978, no. 36, p. 1.
7. Teodoro Benigno, 'Communist Insurgency Under Control', *The Sarawak Tribune* (Kuching), 26 August 1978.
8. *Ibid.*
9. Editorial, 'Is There a New Ballgame in Southeast Asia?' *Nation Review* (Bangkok), 7 November 1978.
10. Nayan Chanda, 'Cambodia – Waiting for the Inevitable', *Far Eastern Economic Review*, 24 November 1978, p. 10.
11. Douglas Pike, 'Vietnam Still Hopes to Form an Indochina Federation Ultimately', *The Straits Times*, 7 September 1978.
12. David Jenkins, 'Indonesia – Staying Off the Bandwagon', *Far Eastern Economic Review*, 24 November 1978, p. 33.
13. Radio Kuala Lumpur, International Service in English, 13 November 1978 (*FBIS*, 14 November 1978).
14. Radio Djakarta, domestic service in Indonesian, 14 November 1978 (*FBIS*, 14 November 1978).
15. Cited *Asiaweek* (Hong Kong), 24 November 1978, p. 13.
16. Radio Bangkok, domestic service in English, 17 November 1978 (*FBIS*, 22 November 1978).
17. *Asiaweek*, 1 December 1978, p. 21.
18. 'Voice of the People of Burma', clandestine in Burmese to Burma, 21 November 1978, and *Nation Review* (Bangkok), 22 November 1978 (both in *FBIS*, 22 November 1978).
19. See, e.g., David Wurfel, 'Martial Law in the Philippines: the Methods of Regime Survival', *Pacific Affairs*, Spring 1977, pp. 7–8; *Far Eastern Economic Review*, 30 September 1977, pp. 15–16; and Dennis Shoesmith, 'Land Reform in the Philippines', *Australian Outlook*, December 1974, pp. 280–81. The 1977 real wage estimate was supplied to the author by the Philippine Department of Labour.

20. Ho Kwon Ping, 'The Peasants in Revolt', *Far Eastern Economic Review*, 1 December 1978, pp. 40–41.

21. Citation and data in this paragraph from Ho Kwon Ping, 'Thailand's Broken Rice Bowl', *Far Eastern Economic Review*, 1 December 1978, pp. 40–43.

22. Bruce London, 'Is the Primate City Parasitic? The Regional Implications of National Decisionmaking in Thailand', *The Journal of Developing Areas*, October 1977, p. 62.

23. J. M. van der Kroef, 'Indonesia: Centrifugal Economies', in James W. Wiggins and Helmut Schoeck (eds.), *Foreign Aid Reexamined. A Critical Appraisal* (Washington, D.C.: Public Affairs Press, 1958), p. 203.

24. H. ten Dam, 'Coopereren vanuit het Gezichtspunt der Desastructuur in Desa Tjibodas', *Indonesië* (The Hague), vol. 9 (1956), pp. 89–116, and the same author's *Desa Tjibodas* (Lembaga Penjelidikan Masjarakat Desa dan Usahi Tani, Bogor, 1951).

25. Lembaga Penjelidikan Ekonomi dan Masjarakat, 'Beberapa bahan keterangan mengenai penduduk Djabres; suatu desa di Djawah Tengah', *Ekonomi dan Kevangan Indonesia* (Djakarta), vol. 9 (1956), p. 747, note 1.

26. Seth Lipsky and Raphael Pura, 'Indonesia: Testing Time for the "New Order"', *Foreign Affairs*, Autumn 1978, p. 191.

27. *Ibid.*

28. *Suara Karya* (Djakarta), July 1978 (Indonesian News Selections, hereafter INS, Collingwood, Australia, September 1978, p. 17).

29. *Kompas* (Djakarta), 3 June 1978 (INS, September 1978, p. 16).

30. *Kompas*, 10 June 1978 (INS, September 1978, p. 16).

31. 'White Book of the 1978 Students' Struggle', *Indonesia* (Cornell University, Ithaca, N.Y.), April 1978, p. 161.

32. *Ibid.*

33. *The Straits Times*, 21 August 1978.

34. Leo Goodstadt, 'Vietnam's Economy: Bleeding to Death', *Insight* (Hong Kong), September 1978, pp. 77–81. I have particularly relied on this informative article in the present paragraph.

35. Goodstadt, 'Vietnam's Economy: Bleeding to Death', p. 81.

36. Data in this paragraph were drawn from Carlyle A. Thayer, 'Dilemmas of Development in Vietnam', *Current History*, December 1978, pp. 221–5.

37. *The New York Times*, 4 December 1978.

38. *The Straits Times*, 10 December 1976.

Index

330